A GUIDE TO BIBLICAL SITES IN GREECE AND TURKEY

A Guide to Biblical Sites
in
Greece and Turkey

CLYDE E. FANT AND
MITCHELL G. REDDISH

OXFORD
UNIVERSITY PRESS
2003

R
220.91
F 216

OXFORD
UNIVERSITY PRESS

Oxford   New York
Auckland   Bangkok   Buenos Aires   Cape Town   Chennai
Dar es Salaam   Hong Kong   Istanbul   Karachi   Kolkata
Kuala Lumpur   Madrid   Melbourne   Mexico City   Mumbai   Nairobi
São Paulo   Shanghai   Taipei   Tokyo   Toronto

Copyright © 2003 by Clyde E. Fant and Mitchell G. Reddish

Published by Oxford University Press, Inc.
198 Madison Avenue, New York, New York, 10016
www.oup-usa.org

Oxford is a registered trademark of Oxford University Press

Library of Congress Cataloging-in-Publication Data
Fant, Clyde E.
   A guide to biblical sites in Greece and Turkey /
   Clyde E. Fant and Mitchell G. Reddish.
      p. cm.   Includes index.
   ISBN 978-0-19-513918-1
      1. Bible—Antiquities—Guidebooks.
      2. Greece—Antiquities—Guidebooks.
      3. Turkey—Antiquities—Guidebooks..
   I. Reddish, Mitchell Glenn, 1953– II. Title.
   220.9'1—dc21
   2003042955

Printed in the United States of America
on acid-free paper

Dedicated with gratitude to our wives,
Cheryl Hammock and Barbara Reddish,
whose loving support and patience
made this work possible.

Preface

For most people "the biblical world" suggests images of the land of Israel. Much of biblical history indeed took place within the boundaries of the modern nation of Israel, but the biblical world is not confined to that area alone. Jordan, Egypt, Syria, Lebanon, Italy, Greece, Cyprus, and Turkey also are stages upon which the biblical story was enacted. In the biblical writings, and particularly in the New Testament, the areas encompassed by the modern countries of Greece and Turkey appear prominently. Nearly two-thirds of the New Testament, including all the letters of Paul, most of Acts, and the book of Revelation, are set in either Turkey or Greece.

This book is intended to serve as a historical, biblical, and archaeological guide to biblical sites in Greece and Turkey, including sites on the Greek islands and in Cyprus. All the significant places mentioned in the Hebrew Bible and the New Testament are covered in this guide, with a few exceptions. For example, the ancient city of Haran is not included because it is in an area of Turkey that is seldom visited due to its remoteness and because virtually nothing remains today of biblical Haran. Some minor places, such as Cnidus, Adramyttium, Lasea, and Phoenix, are not included because they receive only a passing mention in the biblical text and play no role in the biblical story. Although discussed within the context of some of the site entries, the various regions and provinces of Greece or Turkey, such as Macedonia, Phrygia, Galatia, and Lycia, do not have separate entries. For example, Cappadocia, one of the most interesting areas of Turkey to visit due to its strange and intriguing landscape and its underground cities, is not covered in this volume. Although Cappadocia is mentioned in the Bible, it is not a specific site but a region.

This guide also includes no entry on one of the most impressive places in Turkey, the city of Istanbul. That is because, as important as Istanbul (or Byzantium or Constantinople) was in the history of the Christian church, it plays no role in the Bible and thus falls outside the purview of this work. Visitors to Turkey who are interested in the Bible and biblical history, however, should certainly include a visit to Istanbul. The city has much to offer anyone interested in biblical events and history, including the wealth of artifacts to be enjoyed in the archaeological museums of the city.

For each biblical site included in this volume, a description of the site's location and history is given, followed by a discussion of the biblical significance of the place. Next, a visit to the site is described, indicating the major items of archaeological interest that can be seen. The description of the site focuses on remains from the biblical period, although other structures and later additions are frequently included when they are of particular interest. In each section of the various articles, the names of historical figures related to the place appear in bold the first time they are listed. Likewise, in the "Site Visit" section, the first reference to a significant artifact or structure at the archaeological site appears in bold print. Maps are included for the larger sites. Several area maps and helpful charts are found at the end of the book.

The biblical sites are arranged alphabetically, first the sites in Greece, then the sites in Turkey. The description of Cyprus is divided into northern Cyprus and southern Cyprus. The name that is used for each place is the biblical name, following the spelling used in the New Revised Standard Version of the Bible. Where sites are known by an alternative name or alternative spelling, we have given the alternative name in the pertinent article. The modern names of each place, in addition to the biblical versions of their names, are listed in the index.

At the end of some of the entries, an additional section entitled "Other Sites of Interest" appears. This section brings to the reader's attention nearby or especially significant archaeological sites that, although they are not mentioned in the Hebrew Bible or New Testament, deserve a visit if time allows.

We have tried to provide the most current information available for each of the sites, based on our own visits to the sites and research and reports completed by other scholars. Many of the sites that are presented in this guide, however, are active archaeological sites. New discoveries and new interpretations are occurring even as we write, thus rendering some site descriptions incomplete before the book is even in print. But such problems are the welcome consequence of the fresh insights and knowledge that the archaeologist's spade unearths.

All biblical quotations are from the New Revised Standard Version. For dates, B.C.E. and C.E. are used throughout this work. C.E. (Common Era) refers to the period of time common to Judaism and Christianity and is equivalent to the period conventionally referred to as A.D. The abbreviation B.C.E. (Before the Common Era) refers to the period conventionally referred to as B.C. Dates that are preceded by an *r.* (e.g., "r. 527–565 C.E.") refer to the years in which a ruler was in office.

All photographs in the book are by the authors. The drawing of the Athenian Agora (figure 5) is used by permission of the American School of Classical Studies at Athens: Agora Excavations. The drawing of the upper acropolis of Pergamum (figure 115) is reproduced with permission from Wolfgang Radt, *Pergamon: Archaeological Guide*, 3rd ed. (Istanbul: Türkiye Turing ve Otomobil Kurumu, 1984), 37.

It is hoped that this guide will help visitors to Greece and Turkey appreciate the rich history and significance of the ancient world of the Bible. The more the reader is able to comprehend the geography, the history, the culture, and the everyday life of the biblical world, then the better equipped he or she will be to understand the biblical writings that were a product of that world.

Our experiences in visiting virtually all the sites in Greece, Turkey, and Cyprus, including the Greek islands, mentioned in Acts have given us an even deeper appreciation for the commitment and endurance of the Apostle Paul and his historic journeys throughout the Mediterranean world. While we enjoyed the convenience of (mostly) modern transportation to these far-flung sites of the ancient world, Paul and those who accompanied him traveled primarily by foot and on small sailing vessels that plied the Mediterranean, often experiencing many hardships, including shipwreck. Such travels undoubtedly required a degree of persistence and courage few people today can even imagine.

We wish to give special acknowledgment to several people who helped make this work possible. We would like to thank Necdet (Net) Özeren, a good friend and an excellent guide in his home country of Turkey. On each of our trips through Turkey, Net provided transportation, information, and a great sense of humor. In total we rode with Net more than 10,000 miles along the highways and obscure back roads of Turkey. We also extend thanks to his family, who welcomed us into their home on several occasions. Ünver Gaziz of Azim Tours in Kuşadasi, another friend, not only extended warm hospitality, but also made special arrangements for our travels through Turkey. Christiana Vaveki was a charming and well-informed guide to all the sites in Greece. Appreciation is due to James Ridgway Jr., of Educational Travel Services, Inc., for his invaluable assistance in the preparations for several trips through both Greece and Turkey.

We also express our gratitude to Stetson University, and especially to its president, Douglas Lee, and to Grady Ballenger, dean of the College of Arts and Sciences, for their encouragement of this project and their providing grants to assist with the research and production of this book. Cynthia Read, executive editor at Oxford University Press, expressed enthusiasm for the initial proposal for this project and waited patiently for its completion. Helen Mules, senior production editor at Oxford University Press, expertly guided the book through the publication process. We appreciate the skillful assistance of Lisa Guenther, senior secretary in the Department of Religious Studies at Stetson, who helped in countless ways, especially in getting the manuscript in final shape. A special word of thanks is due to Elaine York for her superb work in preparing most of the site maps, as well as all the area maps. Jack Carter used his professional skills as an architect to provide assistance also with some of the site maps in the book. Professor Sauro Gelichi of the Università Ca' Foscari di Venezia generously provided recent archaeological reports on Laodicea. Frankie Censoplano graciously helped with the translation of an Italian archaeological report. Our families continually offered encouragement and expressed interest in the production of this work. We are also grateful to countless museum personnel, informal guides, friendly passersby, and, last but by no means least, the gracious people of Turkey and Greece, who welcomed our efforts to make their beloved lands better known to others.

Finally, we especially express gratitude to our wives, Cheryl Hammock and Barbara Reddish, to whom this book is dedicated. They not only supported us during the many hours we spent on the research and writing for this work, but also patiently endured our lengthy excursions to Greece, Turkey, and Cyprus on numerous occasions to visit the sites covered in the book.

Contents

Part I: Sites in Greece

Part II: Sites in Turkey

Part III: Sites in Cyprus

Illustrations

Site Maps and Drawings

Photographs

Area Maps

Charts

Abbreviations of Biblical Books with the Apocrypha

Hebrew Bible/Old Testament

Gen	Genesis	Song	Song of Solomon
Exod	Exodus	Isa	Isaiah
Lev	Leviticus	Jer	Jeremiah
Num	Numbers	Lam	Lamentations
Deut	Deuteronomy	Ezek	Ezekiel
Josh	Joshua	Dan	Daniel
Judg	Judges	Hos	Hosea
Ruth	Ruth	Joel	Joel
1–2 Sam	1–2 Samuel	Amos	Amos
1–2 Kgs	1–2 Kings	Obad	Obadiah
1–2 Chr	1–2 Chronicles	Jonah	Jonah
Ezra	Ezra	Mic	Micah
Neh	Nehemiah	Nah	Nahum
Esth	Esther	Hab	Habakkuk
Job	Job	Zeph	Zephaniah
Ps/Pss	Psalms	Hag	Haggai
Prov	Prov	Zech	Zechariah
Eccl	Ecclesiastes	Mal	Malachi

New Testament

Matt	Matthew	1–2 Thess	1–2 Thessalonians
Mark	Mark	1–2 Tim	1–2 Timothy
Luke	Luke	Titus	Titus
John	John	Phlm	Philemon
Acts	Acts	Heb	Hebrews
Rom	Romans	Jas	James
1–2 Cor	1–2 Corinthians	1–2 Pet	1–2 Peter
Gal	Galatians	1–2–3 John	1–2–3 John
Eph	Ephesians	Jude	Jude
Phil	Philippians	Rev	Revelation
Col	Colossians		

Apocrypha

Tob	Tobit	Pr Azar	Prayer of Azariah and the Young Men
Jdt	Judith	Add Esth	Additions to Esther
Sus	Susanna	Wis	Wisdom of Solomon
Bel	Bel and the Dragon	Sir	Sirach (Ecclesiasticus)
1-2-3-4 Macc	1-2-3-4 Maccabees	Bar	Baruch
1-2 Esd	1-2 Esdras	Pr Man	Prayer of Manasseh
Let Jer	Letter of Jeremiah		

Historical Overview of Greece and Turkey

Both Greece and Turkey are fascinating countries with rich cultural and historical heritages. The people and events of the Bible play a large part in the history of these two nations, but their biblical history is only one part of the multifaceted stories of Greece and Turkey. To help the visitor to these lands place the biblical story within the larger contexts of Greek and Turkish history, the following historical overviews are provided.

▲ **Fig. 1.** Alexander the Great, the Apostle Paul, and Caesar Augustus: the three persons who most influenced biblical Greece and Turkey

History of Greece

Although evidence of culture as early as 7000 B.C.E. has been uncovered in Greece, the first kingdom of any significance developed at Mycenae around 1600 B.C.E. This powerful and warlike people conquered the earlier, more highly developed civilization upon the island of Crete and adopted much of its Minoan culture. The amazing riches accumulated by these Mycenaean rulers are on display today in the National Archaeological Museum in Athens.

Sometime after 1200 B.C.E. the Mycenaean kingdom fell to invaders, perhaps the Dorians from the Balkans. Their invasion apparently led to the earliest Greek colonies on the shores of Asia Minor. By 1000 B.C.E. previously illiterate Greece adopted the Phoenician alphabet, and in the 8th century B.C.E. **Homer** produced his great epics of Greek gods and heroes. Yet even as the culture of Greece flourished, its faltering economy placed increasing stress upon a growing population.

First-time visitors to Greece often are surprised by its rocky and mountainous landscape. Only in limited areas is there sufficient arable land to produce crops. As a result, from the earliest times its inhabitants have struggled to develop a sustainable economy. Wherever such a situation has existed for a nation, historically the inevitable result has been conflict with its more fortunate neighbors. To the east, Asia Minor was blessed with abundant, rich farmlands. As the population of the Greek city-states expanded and exceeded the limits set by their planners, the Greeks naturally sought to establish colonies there. Likewise, colonies were founded in Italy, Sicily, and even distant France and Syria. Eventually the Greeks created as many as seven hundred such daughter colonies around the edge of the Mediterranean—as Plato said, "like frogs around a pond." In carrying out this endeavor, by necessity the Greeks became a seafaring nation, and with few exceptions their early military victories were won on sea rather than on land.

With the development of the Greek fleet came also the expansion of Greek trade, not without its own problems. In Athens, particularly, trade issues became involved in social problems. Athens had escaped the Doric invasion and its threat, but its population was dominated by the wealthy landowners who declared themselves aristocracy. With the rising wealth of the merchant class, the previously exclusive decision-making rights of a few families were severely challenged, and a revolution appeared imminent. Perhaps the real hero of ancient Greece was not Hercules (Heracles) but **Solon**, chosen as archon (sole ruler) by the aristocracy to save them from an impending class war (594 B.C.E.). Refusing dictatorial powers, Solon instituted sweeping changes, including voting rights for all citizens (male only) who possessed at least two hundred bushels of wheat and all men who owned their own weapons for warfare. Furthermore, he banned all exports except olives, which were abundant, because the higher prices available abroad were causing disastrous inflation and food shortages among the poor. The revolution was averted.

This happy situation did not last long (as in all Greek tragedies), as the rule of the Thirty Tyrants followed. Nevertheless, monumental architecture and art of every sort flourished in the 6th and 5th centuries B.C.E. But the internal problems of Greece were soon overshadowed by the threat of invasion by the Persians, who had already taken the west coast of Asia Minor. **King Darius of Persia** led an assault on the mainland of Greece but was defeated at the battle of Marathon (490 B.C.E.) by the combined forces of Athens and Sparta, the legendary militaristic state on the Peloponnesian peninsula. Once more the Persians attacked with a massive army under **Xerxes**, and again, after extensive fighting, were decisively defeated on land and sea.

After the defeat of the Persians, Athens reached the zenith of its cultural and political powers under such farsighted political leaders as **Pericles**, brilliant thinkers such as **Plato** and **Socrates**, skilled artists such as **Phidias**, and the dramatists **Aeschylus**, **Euripides**, and **Sophocles**. The Acropolis of Athens became world-renowned, and the Athenian state was the envy of the world.

Yet it was none of these classical figures who altered the world to the east of Athens, at least not at first, but a man who died at the age of thirty-three years, **Alexander the Great**. Alexander was the son of **Philip II of Macedon**, the powerful military genius who conquered Greece and united it, insofar as Greece was ever united until modern times. Upon the assassination of Philip (likely engineered by the wife of Philip or by Alexander, or by both), Alexander launched an amazing eight-year military campaign to punish and conquer the Persians. That incredible effort not only succeeded militarily, but also expanded Greek culture into Egypt, Palestine, and even as far as India. When Alexander died of fever in Babylon on the return march, the triumph of Greek culture was ensured through the Hellenization of the Mediterranean world. Though Rome would conquer Greece politically in the 3rd century B.C.E., it, too, would be conquered by Greek culture.

Following the death of Alexander, his generals fought over control of his kingdom. After lengthy infighting, **Antigonus I** controlled Macedonia, **Seleucus I Nicator** controlled Syria and Asia Minor, and **Ptolemy I Soter** ruled over Egypt. The period of their rule, prior to the coming of Roman rule over the area, is known as the Hellenistic period, or the age of Greek influence across the conquered territories of Alexander the Great.

The control of Israel went back and forth between the Ptolemies and the Seleucids, but it was the Seleucids who eventually won out and ruled over Israel. **Antiochus IV**, who called himself Epiphanes, "the Revealed One," profaned the altar in Jerusalem and incurred the everlasting hatred of the Jews for his brutal attempts to force them to offer sacrifices to the gods. The result was the Maccabean Revolt and the eventual freedom of Israel from Syrian control.

Both Greece and Israel subsequently became subject to Rome politically, but neither spiritually. In Greece, Corinth was brutally destroyed and its inhabitants sold into slavery (146 B.C.E.); later, however, **Julius Caesar** would rebuild it (46 B.C.E.). Athens fell to the Roman general **Sulla** (86 B.C.E.), but **Caesar Augustus**, whose powerful reign (r. 32 B.C.E.–14 C.E.) brought in the Pax Romana (the "peace of Rome") across the Mediterranean world, made donations to the city, and created the greatest university of the world there. For centuries its philosophies and culture attracted countless Roman leaders to study in Athens. In Israel, Jerusalem was destroyed (70 C.E.) and Israel obliterated as a political entity by Roman armies under **Titus,** but the rabbis fled to Galilee to sustain the teaching of the Torah and preserve the Jewish faith, and the strange new religion called Christianity with its crucified founder, the Jewish peasant from Galilee named **Jesus of Nazareth**, eventually triumphed over the Roman eagle.

Following the death of Jesus (ca. 29 C.E.), his message was carried to Greece by the **Apostle Paul**, formerly Saul of Tarsus (in modern Turkey), a scholarly Jew and Roman citizen who had converted to the new Christian faith. Eventually the old religions of Greece would die, though slowly and not without their influence, and Christian basilicas would replace the old temples. When the Roman Empire split, Greece became part of the Eastern Roman Empire with Byzantium as its capital (395 C.E.). The Byzantine culture is still much in evidence in the Greek Orthodox churches of today.

The later history of Greece followed the sad course of the Mediterranean region in general as the country fell to one invader after another: the Slavs (6th century), the Normans (1080), and the Venetians (1204). Most decisive of all, however, the Ottoman Turks seized Athens in 1456 and the Muslim faith entered Greece. Freedom and unity were slow in coming, but in 1830 Greece finally became an independent state. The Germans occupied Greece from 1941 to 1944, and after the war the monarchy was reinstated under King George II. In 1974, following chaotic periods of political upheaval, the new republic of Greece was established.

History of Turkey

One of the most fascinating countries in the world, Turkey is a land whose history is filled with Hittites, Persians, Greeks, Romans, Seljuks, Crusaders, and Ottomans. Today Turkey is spread over two continents, Asia and Europe. The part of Turkey that is in Asia, by far the larger portion, is known as Anatolia (also known historically as Asia Minor). The European section of the country is known as Thrace. The earliest evidence of human occupation in Turkey dates to around 10,000–8000 B.C.E., during the Paleolithic Age. Cave dwellings, stone tools, and weapons have been discovered from this period. The earliest evidence of agricultural life in Anatolia is found at Hacilar, dating to around 7040 B.C.E., during the Neolithic Age. Grains (wheat and barley) and lentils, along with the bones of sheep, goats, and horned cattle, were found in the excavated houses of this ancient settlement. At Çatalhöyük, about 30 miles southeast of Konya, archaeologists discovered mud-brick houses from 6500–5500 B.C.E. that contained fascinating cultural artifacts, including tools, weapons, textiles, and plastered and mural-covered walls.

During the Early and Middle Bronze periods (3000–2000 B.C.E.), the site of Troy on the Aegean coast was first settled. In fact, four different settlements (Troy I–IV) occurred in succession at the site during this period. Also during this period an indigenous people known as the Hatti, with whom the Assyrians established a trading system, extended throughout much of central Anatolia, organized into various city-states. Around 2000 B.C.E. a group of people known as the Hittites migrated into Anatolia, likely either from north of the Black Sea or from the Caucasus region, and settled in the area. Their settlement and eventual dominance over the land seem to have been relatively peaceful. By the mid- to late 18th century B.C.E., the Hittites had established their kingdom in Anatolia, and during the following century the city of Hattusa (Bogazköy) became their capital. The Hittite kingdom, which reached its peak in the 14th century B.C.E., was a major power in the ancient Near East. A hint of its importance is seen in a letter sent to the Hittite king in the 14th century B.C.E. by the widow of the Egyptian pharaoh **Tutankhamen**. The widow requested that the Hittite king send one of his sons to her so that she might have a worthy match as a husband. (The king complied, but his son was murdered on the way.)

In the 13th century B.C.E. the expansion of the Hittite kingdom into Syria led to a military confrontation between the Hittites and the Egyptians, ruled at the time by **Ramses II** (perhaps the pharaoh at the time of the Hebrew exodus from Egypt). A major battle was fought between the two powers in 1286 B.C.E. at Kadesh on the Orontes River, which ended in a stalemate (although both sides eventually claimed victory). (The tablet containing the Kadesh peace treaty is on display in the archaeological museum in Istanbul.) The Hittite kingdom lasted until around 1180 B.C.E., when the city of Hattusa was destroyed and Anatolia was overrun, apparently by the "Sea Peoples."

From the collapse of the Hittite kingdom until approximately 800 B.C.E., little is known about the situation in Anatolia; as a result, this time has frequently been referred to as Turkey's "dark ages." This period saw the rise of a Neo-Hittite civilization, centered in southeast Anatolia and northern Syria, and of the Phrygians in central and southeast Anatolia, who became a powerful kingdom in the 8th century. The Phrygians had their capital at Gordion, and their most famous king was **Midas**, around whom many legends arose. The Phrygian kingdom collapsed in the 7th century B.C.E. At the beginning of this period, around the middle of the 13th century B.C.E., the last settlement at Troy (Troy VIIa) was destroyed by Greeks. Greek settlers had begun arriving in western Anatolia prior to the fall of Troy, but the pace of their migrations increased after the 12th century B.C.E. Chief among these Greek immigrants were Ionians, who settled and prospered in the central region of the Aegean coastal area of Anatolia. As early as the 9th or 8th century B.C.E., the Ionian cities (among them were Miletus, Priene, Samos, and Ephesus) formed the Panionion, or the Ionian League. Ionia witnessed a flourishing of human cultural achievement, including in the areas of poetry (**Sappho** and **Xenophanes**), philosophy (**Thales**, **Anaximander**, and **Heraclitus**), and architecture (the Ionic style).

Other peoples flourished in Anatolia during the first half of the 1st millennium also, including the Carians (located in southwestern Anatolia), the Lycians (along the western Mediterranean coast), and the Lydians (in western Anatolia). The Lydians, with their capital at Sardis, gained control of a large part of Anatolia during the 7th to the 6th centuries B.C.E., including the area of Ionia. **Gyges** (perhaps the "Gog" mentioned in Ezekiel 38 and 39) and **Croesus** were two of the most famous Lydian kings.

In 547 B.C.E. the Persian king **Cyrus** (who also defeated the Babylonians in 539 and subsequently allowed the exiled people of Judah to return home) defeated the Lydians and eventually gained control of almost all of Asia Minor. The Ionian Revolt erupted in 499 as several of the Ionian cities attempted to remove themselves from Persian control. The revolt failed and the Persians continued their dominance over the region. The Persians, under **Darius the Great**, attempted to conquer Athens and other areas of mainland Greece. They were defeated, however, at the famous battle of Marathon in 490. **Xerxes**, the successor of Darius, tried once more to conquer Greece. This attempt, in 480 B.C.E., also ended in failure.

In 334 B.C.E. **Alexander the Great** crossed into Asia Minor and defeated the Persians. Because of his conquests, Hellenistic culture exerted an even larger influence over the land of Anatolia. When Alexander died in 323 B.C.E., **Seleucus I** gained control of most of Anatolia (as well as Syria and Mesopotamia). The Seleucids ruled over Anatolia, at least large portions of it, until the Romans defeated the Seleucid ruler **Antiochus III**. The resulting treaty of Apamea in 188 B.C.E. ended Hellenistic rule in Asia Minor.

The Hellenistic period in Asia Minor also saw the rise of several city-states and kingdoms, among these the kingdoms of Bithynia, Pontus, and Cappadocia. One of the most significant kingdoms in Asia Minor during this period was the kingdom of Pergamum, begun in 282 B.C.E. and ruled over by a succession of Attalid kings. The Pergamene kingdom lasted until 133 B.C.E., when the last Attalid king, **Attalus III**, died. In his will Attalus III bequeathed his kingdom to the Romans.

In 129 B.C.E. the Romans established the Roman province of Asia, which included most of the territory of the former Pergamene kingdom. Eventually all of Asia Minor came under Roman control and various provinces were created by the Romans, including Asia, Bithynia and Pontus, Galatia, Lycia, Pamphylia, Cilicia, and Cappadocia. Asia Minor flourished under the Romans, who recognized the geographical and economic importance of Anatolia. The Romans enlarged and enhanced many cities throughout Asia Minor, such as Ephesus, Pergamum, Antioch, Sardis, Miletus, and Phaselis.

During the Roman imperial period, Christianity came to Asia Minor. The **Apostle Paul** traveled extensively throughout Asia Minor, establishing churches in several locations. **John of Patmos**, the author of the New Testament book of Revelation, addressed messages to seven churches located in cities in the western part of Asia Minor. In spite of persecution, this new religious movement flourished. In 330 C.E. the emperor **Constantine** chose Byzantium as the new capital of the empire and renamed the city Constantinople. His successor, **Theodosius I**, made Christianity the official religion of the empire. The eastern portion, with its capital at Constantinople, came to be known as the Byzantine Empire.

The Byzantine Empire, which lasted until the 15th century, reached its height under the rule of **Justinian I** (r. 527–565 C.E.), who reconquered Italy, the Balkans, and portions of Anatolia, all of which had been captured by various invaders from Europe, such as the Goths and the Vandals. One of the most spectacular works of Byzantine architecture, the Hagia Sophia Church, was built by Justinian. Although the Byzantine Empire continued for approximately nine hundred years after Justinian, it was greatly weakened and progressively lost territory to various invaders, including the Arabs, who made several incursions into Anatolia during the 7th and 8th centuries C.E. In 1071 a group of invaders from central Asia, called the Seljuk Turks, defeated the Byzantines at Manzikert and established the Seljuk Empire, which included most of Anatolia. The Seljuks established their capital at Nicaea (modern Iznik) and later at Konya; their kingdom came to be known as the Sultanate of Rum (that is, Rome, since the Byzantines still considered themselves to be Romans).

Greatly weakened and reduced basically to the area around the Aegean Sea, the Byzantine Empire also had to endure the Crusaders. Not only did the Crusader armies devastate the empire as they passed through Anatolia, but during the Fourth Crusade in 1201 they laid siege to the city of Constantinople. The city fell in 1204, being pillaged and ransacked by the

Crusaders, who established the Latin Empire of Constantinople. In response, the Empire of Nicaea was established, which became strong enough in 1261 to recapture Constantinople and restore the Byzantine Empire.

Meanwhile, the Seljuk Turks, whose empire experienced its greatest period during the early 13th century, were overrun by Mongols in the middle of the 13th century and gradually disintegrated. A new group of Turks, led by **Osman I**, who had established a dynasty in northern Phrygia, began to gain control over Anatolia. Osman's tribe was known as the Osmanlis, from which the name Ottoman was derived. Osman and his successors expanded their conquests throughout Anatolia and even into Europe. In 1453 the Ottoman Turks under **Mehmet II** conquered Constantinople. The city, whose name was changed to Istanbul, became the capital of the Ottoman Empire, which comprised most of Greece, the southern Balkans, and western Anatolia (and later Egypt, Palestine, and Syria, as well). The Ottomans, like the Seljuks and the Arab invaders as well, were proponents of Islam; as a result, the land that had played such a crucial role in the development of Christianity became an Islamic nation. The Ottoman Empire reached its zenith during the reign of the sultan **Süleyman the Magnificent** (r. 1520–1566), famous for the opulence of his court, the flourishing of the arts, and the fearsomeness of his army. By the 18th century the Ottoman Empire entered a period of decline, a time that saw internal weakening of the Ottoman court because of corruption and unrest, as well as a shrinking of the boundaries of the empire. (As an example of the latter, during this period Greece, with the help of European allies, was able to wrest independence away from the Turks after they defeated the Ottoman navy at the battle of Navarino in 1827.) As a result, during the 18th and 19th centuries the Ottoman Empire was regarded as the "sick man of Europe."

In 1908 a group of men called the Young Turks led a revolution in Turkey, forcing the sultan to restore constitutional and parliamentary rule (such rule had been established for a brief period during 1876–77). During World War I, Turkey served as an ally of Germany, and as a result, the war's end saw the Ottoman Empire dismantled and occupied by foreign powers. From 1919 to 1922, the Turks, led by **Mustafa Kemal** (one of the Young Turks and a Turkish general who had distinguished himself by repelling the Allied invasion at Gallipoli in 1915), successfully fought a war for independence. After the war, Turkey became a republic in 1923, with Kemal as its first president. Kemal, who adopted the surname **Atatürk** ("Father of the Turks"), became an extraordinary and much loved leader of the nation of Turkey. He instituted major reforms in the government and in the society, modernizing and Westernizing Turkey. For example, he changed the Turkish alphabet from one based on Arabic script to one using Latin script (with a few additional letters). He abolished the wearing of the fez, and he himself began wearing a Panama hat and Western suits. Even though Islam was the religion of almost the entire nation, Atatürk required that the government and its laws be secular and not religious. Few people have ever made as tremendous an impact on an entire nation as did Kemal Atatürk. He was a remarkable man and an impressive leader whose memory is highly revered throughout Turkey. Turkey continues today as a modern country, proud of its heritage and its history, including the important role that the ancient land played in the biblical story.

Part I

Sites in Greece

The political history and culture of Greece had a profound impact upon the Jewish people in the land of Israel. Although Greece was known by the earlier Israelites, few specific references to locations in Greece occur in the Hebrew Bible (the Old Testament). Like most of the surrounding countries, however, Israel came under the control of Alexander the Great during the 4th century B.C.E. From that time on, Hellenistic culture exerted its influence on Israel and the Jewish faith. Greek language, philosophy, and customs interacted with and sometimes shaped Judaism. Hellenistic rulers, including the infamous Antiochus IV Epiphanes, held political control over Israel from the end of the 4th century to the middle of the 2nd century B.C.E. Later, Greece was the location for much of the missionary activity of the Apostle Paul, evidenced both by the accounts in the book of Acts and by references in Paul's own letters. Due to the work of Paul and other early Christian workers, the Christian faith took root and prospered in the land of ancient Greece.

Amphipolis

The modern, small village of Amphipolis belies the importance of the ancient city whose name it bears. Located strategically along the Strymon River and on the Via Egnatia, Amphipolis was one of the most important cities of Macedonia in antiquity.

Location and History

The site of ancient Amphipolis is located between Thessaloniki and Kavala, about 65 miles east of Thessaloniki. From highway E90 there are signs that point the way to Amphipolis. The ancient city sits on a bend on the east bank of the Strymon River, surrounded by the river on three sides. This geographical feature gave rise to the name of the city, since Amphipolis means "around the city." The site was originally settled by Thracians, who called their settlement Ennea Hodoi, meaning "Nine Ways" or "Nine Roads," indicating the importance of the location as a crossroads for travel and trade routes. After several failed attempts the Athenians captured the area and founded the city of Amphipolis on the site of Ennea Hodoi in 437 B.C.E. under the leadership of **Hagnon**. In 424 B.C.E. the city came under Spartan control. Amphipolis was an important city both because of its strategic location on the Strymon River only 3 miles from the Aegean Sea and because of its rich natural resources of agriculture (wine, oil, and wood) and precious metals (especially gold from the mines on Mt. Pangaion). In spite of repeated attempts by the Athenians to recapture the city, Amphipolis remained a free city until its capture by **Philip II** of Macedon in 358–357 B.C.E. During the time of Macedonian rule, Amphipolis became one of the leading cities in the region. It was one of six cities chosen by **Alexander the Great** where large, costly temples were built. The city also played a significant role in Alexander's military conquests. For example, the city and the surrounding area served as the staging ground for the beginning of Alexander's conquest of Asia. After Alexander's death his wife **Roxane** and their young son, **Alexander IV**, were exiled to Amphipolis.

After the Roman victory at Pydna in 168 B.C.E., which effectively ended Macedonian rule, Amphipolis, along with the rest of Macedonia, became a Roman possession. Macedonia was divided into four administrative-economic districts, with Amphipolis being named the capital of the first of these districts. The city prospered under Roman rule, having been given the status of a free city with special privileges. A major trade center, its prosperity and strategic location were enhanced by the construction of the Via Egnatia, which went through the city. The city played a part in the Roman civil wars, when **Pompey** took refuge there in 48 B.C.E. for a brief period, and later **Mark Antony** used the city as the base for his naval fleet in his battle against **Octavian** in 31 B.C.E. During the early part of the 1st century B.C.E. the city suffered major destruction from the Thracians before they were finally brought under control by the Romans. As attested by the coinage of the city and by inscriptions and building activity, the city recovered and subsequently prospered once again.

The **Apostle Paul** traveled through the city around 49–50 C.E. Christianity eventually became a major force in Amphipolis, and the city became home to at least five impressive churches in the 5th and 6th centuries and the seat of a bishopric, evidence of the continuing importance of the city. With the invasion of the Slavs in the 8th and 9th centuries, Amphipolis was apparently destroyed. A new city, Chrysopolis, was established at the mouth of the Strymon River. The location of Amphipolis, however, was still strategically important during the late Byzantine period, as seen by the two towers, one on each side of the Strymon River, built in 1367 by two brothers, **Alexius** and **Ioannes**, who were Byzantine generals. These two brothers were also the founders of the Monastery of the Pantocrator on Mt. Athos, and the towers of Amphipolis belonged to the monastery. The towers were possibly used for storing agricultural products in the area, as well as for controlling the river crossing.

Biblical Significance

According to Acts, **Paul** left Philippi during his second missionary journey and traveled with **Silas** to Thessalonica. Acts 17:1 states: "After Paul and Silas had passed through Amphipolis and Apollonia, they came to Thessalonica." Although the extent of Paul's visit to Amphipolis is not clear, the implication from this statement is that Paul did not stay or engage in any preaching activity in the city. Rather, he simply traveled through it as he continued to Thessalonica, perhaps around 49–50 C.E. If Paul did not introduce Christianity to the inhabitants of Amphipolis, we have no information about who the responsible people were. Christianity did eventually flourish in the city, however, as evidenced by the discovery of the remains of four Christian basilicas (5th–6th centuries), a bishop's house, and a non-basilical, "central plan" church (6th century). As late as the end of the 7th century, literary sources mention that the city was the site of an episcopal see.

Site Visit

The site of ancient Amphipolis is spread over a rather large area. Some of the excavation areas are fenced off and not always open to the public.

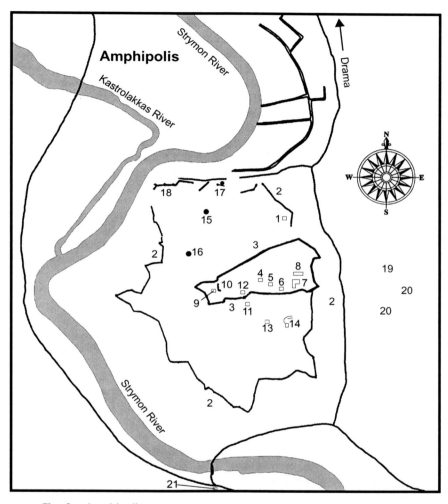

▲ **Fig. 2.** Amphipolis

1. Museum
2. Long Wall
3. Inner Wall
4. Basilica C
5. Basilica A
6. Basilica D
7. Central Plan CHurch
8. Basilica B
9. Classical House
10. Roman Wall
11. Roman Villa
12. Roman Building
13. Hellenistic House
14. Gymnasium
15. Sanctuary of Kilo
16. Sanctuary of Attis
17. Byzantine Tower
18. Ancient Bridge
19. Classical Cemetery
20. Macedonian Tombs
21. Lion Monument

The **museum**, small but with excellent displays that are well lighted and contain descriptions in Greek and English, houses a superb collection of artifacts from the archaeological finds at Amphipolis, many of them from the tombs that have been discovered, as well as informative displays on the area's history. The construction of the museum was begun in 1976 but halted a year later. It was finally completed in 1995. Among the noteworthy items in the museum are a **silver ossuary** with the **gold wreath of olive leaves** found inside it (4th century B.C.E.), a **gold stater (coin) of Alexander the Great**, a **stele** from the gymnasium with the inscribed "ephebic law," and a **bust of the god Attis** (2nd–1st century B.C.E.). The collection also contains several beautiful pieces of jewelry and gold crowns found in various graves, a silver mirror, clay figurines, pottery, weapons, coins, stelae, and architectural fragments.

Adjacent to the museum archaeologists have uncovered remains of a **building complex** from the classical period, portions of which are as early as the 5th century B.C.E. Underneath one of the ancient buildings is a **tomb**, likely of an important person in the city. The silver ossuary and gold crown from this tomb are displayed in the museum. It has been suggested that this tomb might be the burial spot of **Brasidas**, the Spartan general who died in 422 B.C.E. defending the city from capture by the Athenians.

From the museum, signs point toward the main archaeological site, which is on the acropolis of the city. The city had **two walls**: a "long wall," which enclosed the major portion of the city, and an inner wall, which encircled the acropolis. Five Christian churches were discovered on the acropolis. Built in the second half of the 5th century, **Basilica C** (or Basilica Γ, the third letter in the Greek alphabet) had a nave, two aisles, and, on the east end, a semicircular apse. The aisles were separated from the nave by a row of six columns on both sides of the nave. In the center of the nave, a smaller chapel was built during Byzantine times after the basilica had been destroyed. On the southern end of the basilica was a large vestibule. The floor of the church and portions of the vestibule were covered by an impressive multicolored mosaic with representations of animals, ivy leaves, and geometric patterns. Much of the mosaic floor still survives, but it has been covered by gravel to protect it. Southeast of Basilica C is **Basilica A**, a 6th-century church with a nave, side aisles on the north and south, an apse on the east, a narthex on the west, an exonarthex, and a vestibule further west. On the northern wall was a small room (the vestry) where the bishop changed his garments. Attached to it was a small chapel. The floor of the apse was made of marble slabs; the exonarthex and side aisles had beautiful mosaic floors with animal motifs and geometric designs. The mosaic floors of the exonarthex and the south aisle are preserved under a shelter and can be seen. East of Basilica A was a large open **cistern**.

Basilica D (second half of the 5th century) is southeast of Basilica A. This basilica had a nave, two aisles, an apse on the east, a narthex, and a vestibule. Inside the vestibule was a two-story colonnaded portico. Northeast of Basilica D is the "**central plan church**" (6th century), so called because the core of the church was a two-story colonnade in the shape of a hexagon, surrounded by a circular wall. The east side of the hexagon was not surrounded by the circular wall, since an apse jutted out on the east side. On the west side of the church was an atrium surrounded on each side by colonnaded porticoes. Portions of the floor of the church were covered with beautiful marble tiles forming various patterns, some of which can still be seen.

North of this church is **Basilica B**. Built in the 6th century, this church had a nave, side aisles, a narthex, a vestibule, and additional rooms on the north of the vestibule and the narthex. The floor of the nave was marble, while the floors of the aisles and the narthex were mosaic. In the additional room on the north of the narthex is a mosaic floor with pictures of various birds.

Several additional finds have been made within the inner wall. Adjacent to the inner wall on the west side of the acropolis a 4th-century house (the "**classical house**") was excavated, part of a neighborhood of houses in this area. Northeast of this house, a portion of a **Roman wall**, marking the western limits of the city during Roman times, was discovered. Immediately outside the southern portion of the inner wall are the remains of a **Roman villa**. Containing some mosaic floors with scenes from Greek mythology, this building has been dated to the 2nd or 3rd century C.E. Just north of this building, on the north side of the classical inner wall, another **Roman building** was discovered. This building was likely a public edifice of some sort.

A **Hellenistic house** has been uncovered further south of the inner wall. Dated to the 2nd century B.C.E., this house is still being excavated. Unfortunately, the shelter that encloses it is usually locked. With charm, you may be able to persuade one of the museum personnel or, if present, one of the excavators to allow you to have a look. Excavations so far have uncovered two rooms with a colonnaded courtyard. The walls of one of the rooms are covered with brightly decorated panels of painted plaster. The walls of the second room are covered in white plaster, incised to imitate blocks of masonry.

Southeast of the Hellenistic house is a **gymnasium**, discovered in 1982. Likely built during the latter part of the 4th century B.C.E., the gymnasium was modified several times. It was destroyed by fire, apparently in the first half of the 1st century C.E. The original entrance to the gymnasium was by means of a monumental set of steps on the east side. Part of the steps still survives. During the Roman period, this entrance was replaced on the north side by a **propylon** with two Ionic columns.

▲ **Fig. 3.** Gymnasium complex at Amphipolis

The gymnasium had a palaestra at the southwest portion of the complex, which consisted of a colonnaded courtyard for athletic contests and exercises, surrounded by several rooms. One of the rooms, in the northeast corner, served as a room for bathing and had marble washbasins. The area around the palaestra contained various statues and inscriptions. The ephebic law inscription was found on a large stele between the north propylon and the palaestra. This law code, circa 23 B.C.E., described the rules of behavior for the *ephebes* of the city. The term *ephebes* refers to males between the ages of eighteen and twenty who were training to become full citizens. North of the propylon on the north side was a **stoa**, which served as a covered running track (called a *xystos*) for use by the runners during bad weather. Parallel to the *xystos* is an open-air running track (called a *paradromis*) for use during good weather.

North of the acropolis, in different locations, two sanctuaries were discovered. One, an early-4th-century **sanctuary of Klio**, was discovered in 1958. Only portions of two walls are preserved. An inscription found here identified the site as a sanctuary to Klio, one of the nine Muses (a daughter of Zeus and Mnemosyne). The other sanctuary was a **sanctuary of the god Attis**, originally a Phrygian god. The sanctuary contained a building with an inner courtyard paved with stones and a circular hearth in the center.

⚜ **Fig. 4.**   Remains of the ancient bridge at Amphipolis

Several sections of the city's **long wall** and accompanying towers and gates have been uncovered, some of which date to the classical period. One of the most interesting sections to visit is a part of the north wall that contains **gate B** and **gate C** (or Γ). To visit this portion of the wall, travel by car from the museum to the Drama road and turn left. Then take the first left turn. This road leads soon past a **Byzantine tower** on the left, one of the two towers built by Alexius and Ioannes (see above). The second tower is across the Strymon River. A short way along this road is a large section of the wall. At the east end of this section of the wall is the foundation of a **5th-century house** with a well. Just west of this is gate B. West of gate B there are conduits in the wall for draining excess water after heavy rains. Farther west is the base of a **round tower**, later enclosed by a square tower. In the wall near the tower is a series of trapezoid-shaped drainage conduits.

Farther west is gate C, or the bridge gate, so called because this gate stood at the end of the **bridge** that crossed the Strymon River. The remains of the bridge, with its fossilized timbers and wooden stakes that served as supports, can be seen behind the fenced shelter. The bridge has been dated to the 5th century B.C.E. Some of the stakes (the lower ones) come from this early period. Others were added during Roman and Byzantine times. This is thought to be the same bridge mentioned by the

Athenian general and historian **Thucydides** when he discussed the battle between the Spartans (led by Brasidas) and the Athenians (led by Kleon) for control of Amphipolis in 422 B.C.E.

Return to the Drama road and head south. On the left, shortly past the turn on the right to the main archaeological site, are the locations of the **classical cemetery** and two **Macedonian-style tombs** that were discovered. Farther south, take the road to the right that leads to Nigrita. After crossing the old Strymon bridge, turn left. On the right is the **Lion of Amphipolis**, an imposing monument from the last quarter of the 4th century B.C.E. This large, impressive sculpture of a seated lion was erected in this spot in 1936–37 near the spot where it was discovered. Pieces of the lion sculpture were found at various times from 1912 to 1931. The lion was reassembled and placed on the base on which it now stands. The base is not the original one but is composed of blocks found in the river. The original base consisted of a Doric colonnade supporting a platform on which was a stepped pyramid base that served as the base for the lion sculpture. Opinions differ concerning whether the sculpture was a funerary monument or a monument erected in honor of a distinguished citizen of the city. A widely held speculation is that the statue was a monument erected in honor of **Laomedon**, one of Alexander the Great's most important admirals and a devoted companion, who later became for a brief period the satrap (governor) of Syria (which included Palestine).

Apollonia

Apollonia of Macedonia, a city scarcely known even in Greek history, is on the verge of new prominence as a recent discovery brings its past to light.

History and Location

In the summer of 2000 a farmer digging in his fields near Nea ("new") Apollonia, 30 miles east of Thessalonica, made an amazing discovery. In the bottom of a trench he found a wreath of thirty solid-gold ivy leaves, decorated with two bunches of grapes, that weighed more than a pound. Only three other wreaths of this type and quality have ever been discovered in all of Greece. Archaeologists from Thessaloniki dated the find at approximately 350 B.C.E., or more than 2,350 years old. (This remarkable wreath is currently on display in the Archaeological Museum in

Thessaloniki.) The following day their probings uncovered a statue believed to be an image of the goddess known as the Nike of Samothraki, or the Winged Victory of Samothrace.

Subsequently, massive fortifying walls and five towers from the 5th century B.C.E. were uncovered. Likewise, two pottery kilns and sixteen cist (stone slab) graves have been unearthed. Archaeologists now believe that this finding marks the location of ancient Apollonia of Macedonia. More surprising, they estimate its population at 10,000, roughly the same as that of Athens during the same period. The city is believed to have existed from approximately 400 B.C.E. to the 8th century C.E. and to have reached its zenith under **Philip II of Macedon**, the father of **Alexander the Great**.

The first inhabitants of Apollonia were refugees from the nearby Chalkidiki peninsula who fled that location when it was threatened by Athenian warships during the Peloponnesian War. Prior to the recent discoveries, Apollonia was known only as a station on the ancient trade route between the east and west. **King Xerxes of Persia** passed through the area in 480 B.C.E. (Herodotus 7.112–115), as did Alexander the Great in his epic journey to the east some 150 years later (Arrian, *Anabasis* 1.11.4). Later, under the Romans (146–120 B.C.E.), this same route was paved for military use and became famous as the Via Egnatia (named for **Gnaeus Egnatius**, proconsul of Macedonia at that time). This historic road was approximately 450 miles long and ranged from 10 to 30 feet wide, depending on the terrain. Stations, known as *mutatia,* were established at regular intervals along the road to change pack animals; other stations were created for provisions and overnight accommodations (*mansiones*). During the Roman period, popular use of the road made its traffic so heavy that **Cicero** once delayed his departure from Thessalonica (July 57 B.C.E.) because of "the constant traffic" on it, waiting for a less-traveled season. Originally Apollonia functioned merely as a stopover on this busy road, but later it expanded into a city of some prominence.

Biblical Significance

Were it not for a single reference in the New Testament, Apollonia would be unknown in the biblical record. Acts 17:1 mentions in passing that after leaving Philippi, **Paul** and his companions passed through Amphipolis and Apollonia on their way to Thessalonica, "where there was a synagogue of the Jews." Some authorities have argued that this reference means there was no synagogue in Apollonia; others insist it has no such meaning and indicates only the intention of the missionaries to proceed to such a location in Thessalonica. When Apollonia historically seemed to be no more than an insignificant station on the Via Egnatia, it was easy to imagine that it contained no sizable Jewish population. After the recent discoveries, the matter is not so certain. A city of such size likely would have had at least one synagogue, and possibly several. Additional exploration may eventually provide a definitive answer.

Site Visit

At this writing, the work at Apollonia is so recent that no official archaeological site has been established. Prior to a visit in this area (to Amphipolis or Philippi, for example), contact the Archaeological Museum at Thessaloniki to obtain specific information regarding what is available to be seen of ancient Apollonia and the best route for getting there.

Athens

In the Mediterranean world, only Rome rivals Athens as a city famed for its antiquities. Ancient travelers came to marvel at its grand temples and civic buildings, just as tourists do today. Wealthy Romans sent their children to Athens to be educated by its philosophers and gain sophistication in the presence of its culture. Democracy, however faltering its first steps, began in this city, and education and the arts flourished in its environment. Even at the height of the Roman Empire, the Western world's government may have been Roman but its dominant cultural influence was Greek. Latin never spread abroad as a universal language, but Greek did, in its Koine (common) form. By the 4th century B.C.E. this Attic dialect of Plato and the Athenian orators was already in use in countries around the Mediterranean. The monuments of Athens and the treasures of its National Museum still amaze and delight millions of visitors from every nation who come to see this historic cradle of Western culture.

Location and History

A settlement of some significance already existed at Athens in Mycenaean times (1600–1200 B.C.E.). Toward the end of the Dark Ages (1200–750 B.C.E.) the unification of Attica, a territory surrounding Athens of some 1,000 square miles, was accomplished under the Athenians. The resulting city-state was governed by aristocrats constituted as the Council of the Areopagus, named for the hill below the Athenian Acropolis where they commonly met. But only the nobility—defined as the wealthy male landowners—had any vote in the decisions that influenced affairs in the city, a situation increasingly opposed by the rising merchant class and the peasant farmers. The nobles seemed paralyzed by the mounting social tensions, and a class revolution appeared imminent. In 594 B.C.E. the nobles in desperation turned to **Solon**, also an aristocrat, whom they named as archon (ruler) of the city with virtual dictatorial powers. Solon, however, refused to rule as dictator of the city, instituting instead a series of sweeping reforms that mollified the lower classes without destroying the aristocracy. (For example, he banned the export of all food goods except olives, which were abundant, to lower food prices for the common people.) Nevertheless, the acute tensions of social stratification were never overcome until the further reforms of the lawgiver **Kleisthenes** (508 B.C.E.).

To the east, the Persians, who had overcome the Babylonian Empire, began to move westward, first capturing the Greek colonies of Ionia (the west coast of modern Turkey), then moving against Athens itself. The Persian king **Darius** ordered an assault on the city, but his army was defeated by the Athenians on the plains of Marathon, northeast of Athens (490 B.C.E.). Ten years later the Persians returned under **Xerxes**, the son of Darius, with an enormous army and powerful fleet. This time their defeat by the Athenians and their allies was decisive.

Athens' troubles were not limited to foreign invaders. Tensions between Athens and its chief rivals, Corinth and Sparta, were always high. Athenians derided Spartans as militaristic barbarians and Corinthians as immoral drunkards (whenever a playwright wished to depict a drunk on stage, he was always shown wearing the Corinthian hat). Both of these city-states despised Athens as an arrogant city living in the past. The subsequent Peloponnesian War with Sparta (431–404 B.C.E.) forced Athens to relinquish its empire and reduce its military strength, particularly its once powerful fleet. (The outbreak of the war terminated the building of the new Propylaea—the monumental entrance gate that still stands as the access to the Acropolis today—commissioned by the great statesman and builder of the Acropolis, **Pericles**, and begun in 437 B.C.E.) It would be fifty years before Athens was able to regain a semblance of its former maritime dominance.

Surprisingly, perhaps, the final blow to Athenian preeminence came from neither of these great rivals but from a new force from the north. The Macedonian empire built by **Philip II** had already encompassed northern and central Greece, and in 338 B.C.E. it challenged Attica in the battle of Chaeronea. Athens and its allies proved no match against the armies and strategies of Philip. Like numerous invaders before and after, however, Philip treated Athens with unusual leniency, especially considering the merciless treatment Athens had given many of its conquered foes. Nations victorious over Athens always seemed torn between wreaking vengeance upon an enemy and extending mercy to a classical city of ancient culture. (The treatment accorded to Paris and Rome in World War II is a modern example of the same feelings.)

Alexander the Great, the son of Philip, even exceeded his father in amazing military exploits, particularly his eight-year campaign of vengeance upon the Persians that took him as far as India. Nevertheless, his daring finally proved his undoing, as most of his army died on the return march and he himself died of fever in Babylon. Following Alexander's death (323 B.C.E.), Athens attempted an unsuccessful revolt from Macedonia, with the result that the Athenian democracy was abolished and only sporadic attempts were made later to revive it.

All of these struggles proved academic when the world's next great superpower, Rome, invaded the Greek peninsula (168 B.C.E.). Athens again enjoyed special favors when it sided with Rome against Macedonia, only to lose them when it sided with **Mithradates VI of Pontus** in an ill-advised rebellion against Rome (88 B.C.E.) that was put down by the Roman general **Sulla**. Thereafter Athens increasingly became a university town and a center of culture, philosophy, and education but no longer a player on the world's political stage.

In some ways this loss of military and political power may have worked to the advantage of Athens. No longer a threat to the world's powers, the city was gifted by its Roman rulers with public works projects and cultural improvements. The emperor **Hadrian** (r. 117–138 C.E.), in particular, lavished monuments and other building projects upon Athens, and **Marcus Aurelius** (r. 161–180 C.E.) endowed the city with four chairs of philosophy, thereby creating the world's first great university. Perhaps even more important, Athens was never forced to become part of the Roman provincial system but was exempted from Roman taxes and allowed to exercise judicial authority over its own citizens. **Constantine** (312 C.E.) likewise favored Athens by not taking statues and other treasures from its temples, as he did elsewhere, when he was establishing his capital at the new Constantinople (modern Istanbul). Although the Herulian Goths (a tribe from the steppes of Russia) caused extensive damage to Athens in 267 C.E., the Visigoths under **Alaric** left the city untouched in 396 C.E., though they sacked nearby Eleusis.

The increasing dominance of Christianity, however, permanently altered the nature of Athens. The emperor **Justinian** ordered the philosophical schools of Athens closed, and sometime in the 6th century the Parthenon was converted into the Church of the Virgin Mother of God. The invasion of the Slavs in 584 C.E. left the city extensively damaged and further reduced in importance, a condition that persisted until modern times. But perhaps the worst disaster ever to befall Athens occurred in 1687 during the war between the Turks, who held Athens, and the Venetians, who were laying siege to it. During five days of constant bombardment of the city, a Venetian cannonball struck the Parthenon, which was being used as a powder magazine by the Turks, and the most magnificent of all classical buildings was blown apart.

Biblical Significance

From our modern perspective on Athens, it may seem strange to us that the city played a lesser role in the journeys of **Paul** than places such as Corinth and Ephesus. Athens was still a renowned center of philosophy in the 1st century, but Corinth and Ephesus, along with Antioch, Alexandria, and of course Rome, had far surpassed it as crossroads of activity. In comparison to these cities, in the 1st century Athens was a relatively small city of perhaps 20,000 to 25,000 inhabitants. The Roman poet **Horace** (66–8 B.C.E.), who studied in Athens at the age of nineteen (in 46 B.C.E.), referred to it as an "empty" (*vacuae*) or quiet city. Athens could not be overlooked by the early Christian missionaries, but it never became a base of operations for Paul as did Corinth and Ephesus. So far as we know, no letters were written to Athens by Paul; we hear nothing of the church at Athens until much later in Christian history, and then it does not seem to have had the prominence of others.

Some authorities believe this situation is due to Paul's "philosophical" sermon to the Athenians on Mars Hill, and that Paul himself later repudiated such an approach. They base this belief on his famous words to the Corinthians, "I have decided to know nothing among you except Jesus Christ, and him crucified"(1 Cor 2:2). In fact, nothing but conjecture links this remark to his sermon on Mars Hill (50 C.E.), and there is no evidence that Paul regarded his approach to the Athenians as misguided. In fact, the Acts account is careful to point out that several people responded favorably to Paul's sermon, including a member of the Council of the Areopagus, **Dionysius**, and a prominent woman named **Damaris**.

What was the setting for this sermon? Paul likely came to Athens by sea, docking at the port of Athens (Piraeus), though it is possible he traveled overland from Beroea, or Veria, where he had been forced to leave because of instigators from Thessalonica. The text of Acts 17:14, however, implies a sea journey. He had left his traveling companions, **Timothy** and **Silas**, at Beroea and was accompanied to Athens by unnamed Christians. Paul subsequently sent them back to Beroea with a message requesting Timothy and Silas to join him as soon as possible. While he was waiting for them, Paul initiated contact with the Athenians by arguing for his faith in the local synagogue, as was his custom. According to Acts, he also spoke "daily" in the Athenian agora, the civic and cultural center of Athens. Athens had lost its preeminence in commerce, but it was still the world's center for philosophy and dialogue. No one liked "telling or hearing something new" (Acts 17:21) more than the Athenians.

In the course of his dialogues in the agora, some Epicurean and Stoic philosophers debated with him. Although Paul was a Jew, their philosophies were not unknown to him. Tarsus, his home city in Cilicia (Asia Minor, modern Turkey), was itself a major center of philosophical learning in the 1st century. Three well-known Stoic philosophers—**Zeno of Tarsus**, **Antipater of Tarsus**, and **Chrysippus**, among others—were natives of the city. The Epicureans were bitter rivals of the Stoics, and both philosophies were current in Athens at the time of Paul's visit. What were their beliefs?

Zeno, the founder of Stoicism, and **Epicurus**, the founder of Epicureanism, were contemporaries (ca. 341–264 B.C.E.) but could scarcely have been more different. Epicurus was a native of Athens, though born on Samos (341 B.C.E.); Zeno was a foreigner, a resident alien in Athens, born in Kition on Cyprus, the son of a Phoenician merchant. Epicurus was wealthy and taught his chosen friends in a garden outside the city walls; Zeno was an ascetic who taught any and all who chose to listen to his public lectures in the Stoa Poikile, the "Painted Stoa," in the Athenian agora. The Epicureans established a religious association, often referred to as "the Garden" because of their original meeting place, that taught a radical individualism and materialism in which only the happiness and imperturbability of the individual were ultimate values; even society and community existed only for the good of the individual. The gods existed but took no part in human affairs. As for an afterlife, there was nothing after death. The Stoics, on the other hand, saw logos, or reason, as the living, intelligent, controlling principle of the universe. They believed that the gods of the nations were simply various names for this divine reason. The duty of the individual was to find for themselves this controlling, individual reason in order to live in harmony with their true natures. The goal of life for the Stoics, therefore, was not pleasure but rationality. All emotions, whether positive or negative, were viewed as diseases of the soul to be purged.

Naturally, the teachings of Paul would readily call for debate from both philosophies. Some—perhaps the materialistic Epicureans—scoffed at his teachings, saying, "What does this babbler wish to say?" (The Greek word translated as "babbler"—literally, "seed-picker"—originally referred to birds picking up seeds, later to scrap collectors in the market, and then, metaphorically, to anyone who picked up scattered ideas without understanding.) But according to Acts, others—perhaps the Stoics—believed Paul was teaching about foreign deities, possibly **Jesus** and **Anastasis**, since he was preaching about Jesus and the resurrection (in Greek, *anastasis;* Acts 17:18).

Paul then was invited to go up on Mars Hill, just above the agora, apparently to present his views in a more comprehensive fashion for both Stoics and Epicureans and anyone else who cared to attend. (Some interpreters believe that he was actually taken before the Council of the Areopagus, but that does not fit the meaning of the text.) The book of Acts records Paul's sermon on Mars Hill, sometimes referred to as his "Unknown God" sermon:

> Then Paul stood in front of the Areopagus and said, "Athenians, I see how extremely religious you are in every way. For as I went through the city and looked carefully at the objects of your worship, I found among them an altar with the inscription, "To an unknown God." What therefore you worship as unknown, this I proclaim to you. The God who made the world and everything in it, he who is Lord of heaven and earth, does not live in shrines made by human hands, nor is he served by human hands, as though he needed anything, since he himself gives to all mortals life and breath and all things. From one ancestor he made all nations to inhabit the whole earth, and he allotted the times of their existence and the boundaries of the places where they would live, so that they would search for God and perhaps grope for him and find him—though indeed he is not far from each one of us. For "In him we live and move and have our being"; as even some of your own poets have said, "For we too are his offspring." Since we are God's offspring, we ought not to think that the deity is like gold, or silver, or stone, an image formed by the art and imagination of mortals. While God has overlooked the times of human ignorance, now he commands all people everywhere to repent, because he has fixed a day on which he will have the world judged in righteousness by a man whom he has appointed, and of this he has given assurance to all by raising him from the dead. (Acts 17:22–31)

Thus far no altar with the inscription "To an unknown God" has been found in Athens. In any event, Paul used the saying to establish a point of commonality with his audience. Similarly, he used two poetic quotations (Acts 17:28). Identification of the first is uncertain; the second is a quotation from **Aratus**, a Stoic from Paul's native region of Cilicia.

The results of the sermon were mixed. Some said they would hear Paul again, but others scoffed at the notion of the resurrection of the dead, a very un-Greek idea. In Greek philosophy, the body typically was regarded as a hindrance to the spiritual nature of the soul and therefore not something to be carried into an afterlife. Several persons, however, did attach themselves to the Christian movement "and became believers" (Acts 17:34). Paul then left Mars Hill. Nothing further is said concerning any events in Athens, except that Paul next left there and went to Corinth (Acts 18:1).

Site Visit

The ancient travel writer **Pausanius** visited Athens in 150 C.E. and left an account of what he saw as he traveled through the city. Since he, too,

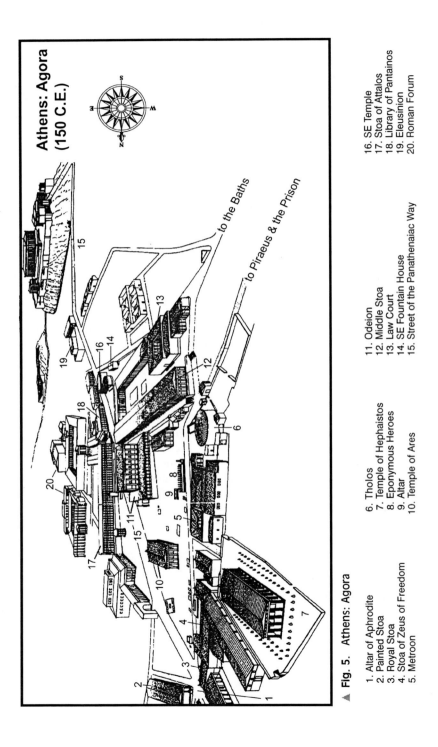

Athens: Agora (150 C.E.)

Fig. 5. Athens: Agora

1. Altar of Aphrodite
2. Painted Stoa
3. Royal Stoa
4. Stoa of Zeus of Freedom
5. Metroon

6. Tholos
7. Temple of Hephaistos
8. Eponymous Heroes
9. Altar
10. Temple of Ares

11. Odeion
12. Middle Stoa
13. Law Court
14. SE Fountain House
15. Street of the Panathenaiac Way

16. SE Temple
17. Stoa of Attalos
18. Library of Pantainos
19. Eleusinion
20. Roman Forum

to the Baths

to Piraeus & the Prison

landed at Piraeus and walked up to the Acropolis, much of what he described also would have been what Paul observed when he was in the city a century earlier. If Paul walked north from the harbor, as Pausanius did, he would have entered Athens through the **Dipylon**, or Double Gate, to the **agora**, on its northwest side. Our tour therefore will begin at that point and proceed to the **Areopagus**, then to the **Acropolis**, followed by the **Roman Forum**, **Hadrian's Library**, the **Olympieion**, and finally, the **National Museum**.

The Agora

Before going in the main entrance to the **agora** on Adrianou Street, notice the excavations on the side of the street opposite the site. Amid the ruins it is possible to pick out a portion of the Stoa Poikile, or **Painted Stoa** (450 B.C.E.), where **Zeno**, the founder of Stoic philosophy, gave his public lectures, and the remains of the **Altar of Aphrodite** (500 B.C.E.). The Painted Stoa was so named because of the famous paintings within, including those of the Fall of Troy and the Battle of Marathon. By the 1st century, however, these paintings had been removed.

Across from these ruins, on the site side of Adrianou Street and between the street and the Piraeus railroad line, lie the remains of the Stoa Basileios, or **Royal Stoa**. The building was not large—some 60 feet long with eight Doric columns on the east side, the porch side; the other three walls were of solid masonry—but it was famous as the seat of the *archon basileios*, the "royal magistrate" who assumed the cultic duties of the previous monarchs. One of these responsibilities was to try offenders guilty of impiety, and thus this stoa may have been the site of the trial of **Socrates** in 399 B.C.E., when he was condemned to death and forced to drink the fatal hemlock. According to **Demosthenes** (325 B.C.E.), the Council of the Areopagus also sometimes met here. Upon the massive, rough-cut rectangular stone, still in its original place, elected officials of Athens stood to pledge to uphold the laws of the city.

Before entering the site, notice two landmarks that are valuable in gaining orientation to the agora. Above, on the hill to the right, is the **Temple of Hephaestus**, the finest extant example of a Greek temple in all of Greece. Ahead, and to the left, bordering the eastern side of the agora, the largest and most prominent building on the site is the **Stoa of Attalus**, magnificently restored between 1953 and 1956 by the American School of Classical Studies. The other remains mostly consist of foundations not always easy to identify, but those of greatest significance will be described.

First, go up the hill to the Temple of Hephaestus. From this location it is possible to see most of the agora, and thus it is an excellent vantage point for orientation to the site. The Stoa of Attalus, directly across on the east, runs due north and south (the north is on the left). The main part of the square between these buildings was cut by a broad diagonal street, the **Panathenaic Way**, which still leads the way to the Stoa of Attalus. The street got its name from a processional held there every four years during the national festival called the Panathenaia, which began in the agora and ascended to the Acropolis. This celebration occurred on the 28th of the Greek month Hekatombaion (July/August), the birthday of Athena. The Parthenon frieze depicts this procession as it assembled in the agora. Before the Romans built the **odeion** and the **Temple of Ares** in the 1st century, the center of the square was mostly open, and it was framed by magnificent buildings on all sides. According to the work of the American School of Classical Studies and the account of Pausanius, the **Athenian law courts** bordered the south of the agora (on the right); the Stoa of Attalus enclosed it on the east; the Painted Stoa and other public buildings stood on the north; and directly below the Temple of Hephaestus, on the west, were located the administrative buildings of Athens.

The Temple of Hephaestus was built at approximately the same time as the Parthenon. Dedicated to the patron divinities of the smiths and the arts, Hephaestus and Athena, statues of these gods were placed in the temple around 420 B.C.E. (Evidence of numerous metalworking and potters' shops have been found in the area around the temple.) Because it was converted into a Christian church in the 5th century C.E., it has been preserved in remarkable condition. During its renovation into a church, the original timber roof, typical of Greek temples, was replaced by the barrel-vaulted roof of today. Likewise, a new entrance was made in the west wall. The east end of the building, which was its main entrance, still retains the original coffered ceiling. The frieze above this entrance, as well as that above the west entrance, depicts mythical battle scenes. The metopes (square panels) on the east portray the labors of Hercules and Theseus. As today, the building was encircled by plants placed in flowerpots, evidence of which was found during excavation.

Return down the hill toward the east, where the steps leading down go past a circular foundation and floor, the remains of the **Tholos**. Originally built in 465 B.C.E., it was rebuilt after its destruction by the Roman general **Sulla** in 86 B.C.E. The Tholos was the meeting place for the fifty senators of Athens, one-third of whom were required to be on duty there twenty-four hours a day to handle any situation that might call for their decision. Meals were prepared in an adjacent annex on the northeast. The building also housed the set of official weights and measures for Athens.

Turn to the right and proceed south for approximately 100 yards. Virtually at the end of the site and outside the agora proper, on the left side of the **Great Drain,** are the remains of the **State Prison** of Athens, believed to be the place where **Socrates** was forced to drink the poisonous hemlock, a common form of execution in ancient Athens.

Return to the Tholos. Two buildings originally stood on its left, the **Bouleuterion**, closest to the hill, and the **Metroon**, facing the square. The Council of Five Hundred held their meetings in the Bouleuterion (from *boule*, to "cast" votes, referring to the means of making council decisions). Fifty members (men only) were chosen by lot from each of the ten "tribes" (leading families) of Athens. The Metroon (2nd century C.E.), which was a shrine to Meter, mother of the gods, held the official records of Athens.

In front of the Metroon there is a headless statue of **Hadrian**; directly across is the platform upon which stood the **bronze statues of the Eponymous Heroes** (4th century B.C.E.), the mythical founders of the ten political divisions of Athens. It was later enlarged to the south to add the statue of Hadrian as a benefactor of Athens. On the front of the pedestal, public notices, including lists of draft-eligible young men, were displayed on whitewashed wooden tablets. Next to it, on the east, the large **marble altar** (4th century B.C.E.) likely was dedicated to Zeus of the Agora (Zeus Agoraios). The next building to the north, on the west side of the road, was a large stoa known as the **Stoa of Zeus of Freedom** (Zeus Eleutherios; 430–420 B.C.E.), often frequented by Socrates.

Proceed next down the Panathenaic Way in the direction of the Stoa of Attalus. On the right is the foundation of the **Temple of Ares**, followed by the **odeion** in the center of the agora. The Temple of Ares (the god of war) originally stood elsewhere and was moved to the agora in 15 B.C.E. The odeion, built in 20 B.C.E. by the Roman general **Marcus Agrippa**, son-in-law of Augustus, seated 1,000 and was famed for its absence of interior columns. Apparently the span of the roof was more than the structure could support, and the roof collapsed, probably shortly after the visit of Pausanius (150 C.E.). It was rebuilt in 170 C.E. with a dividing wall for support, which reduced the seating to 500 and caused it to be used only as a lecture hall. A **colonnade**, adorned with colossal marble statues of giants and Tritons, was added on the north. The building was burned to the ground in 267 C.E. by the Herulians and later rebuilt (ca. 400 C.E.), probably as an administrative palace and/or residence for **Eudocia**, Athenian empress of Byzantium (not a gymnasium, as archaeologists originally believed).

The remaining ruins to the east comprise the **South Square** (2nd century B.C.E.), consisting of the **Middle Stoa** on the north, joined by the **East Stoa** and the **South Stoa** and enclosed on the west by the **Law Court building**. At the southern corners of the square are the remains of two fountain houses, the **Southeast Fountain House** and the **Southwest Fountain House**. On the north side of the Law Court, the **stone-lined pit** marks the location of an ancient **water clock** (4th century B.C.E.).

The **Stoa of Attalus** was given to Athens (150 B.C.E.) by **Attalus II**, king of Pergamum, who had studied in Athens. Faithfully reconstructed

▲ **Fig. 6.** The Stoa of Attalus in the agora of Athens as seen from Mars Hill

by the American School of Classical Studies, it gives a magnificent sense of the impressiveness of ancient Athens when all of its classical buildings stood in the agora. The ancient writer Pausanius does not mention the building, perhaps because of its pedestrian use as a shopping mall with twenty-one shops on each of its two floors, but also perhaps indicating that this splendid building was not regarded as special amid the other architectural wonders of the agora. Today it houses the **Agora Museum**. Among many items in the museum not to be missed: under the porch of the stoa, several notable sculptures, including the large **statue of Apollo**; a **marble stele** showing Democracy crowning a figure representing the deme (the populace) and inscribed with a law against tyranny (336 B.C.E.); and sculpture from the Temple of Hephaestus. Inside are objects from each of the historic periods in the life of Athens, including **a voting device** for choosing public officials by lots; a **terra-cotta figure of a kneeling boy** (6th century B.C.E.); **clay bowls** from the prison, believed to have held the poisonous hemlock, such as used to kill Socrates; and **ostraca** (pieces of broken pottery with writing on them) used by the citizens each year to vote to banish the political figure they deemed most harmful to the city of Athens. (These "ostracized" persons were banished from Athens for ten years, but without loss of property.) The English word *ostracism* comes from this practice.

On the south side of the Stoa of Attalus, a marble roadway called the **Broad Street** (30 feet wide) was constructed in the 2nd century C.E. Strictly for pedestrian use and bordered by colonnaded shops, it led to the **Roman Forum**. On the other side of the road, toward the Acropolis, lay the **Library of Pantainos** (100 C.E.). A **plaque** from the library, now in the Agora Museum, states the **library's rules**: "No one shall remove a book for we have taken an oath. Open from the first hour to the sixth." Farther up the hill, on the left, is visible the partly excavated **Eleusinion**, sanctuary of Demeter, goddess of grain, and Persephone, her daughter. In this temple were kept the sacred objects from Eleusis, the central shrine of the Eleusinian mysteries, until they were returned in procession during the celebration of the mysteries in August. (See "Other Sites of Interest," below.)

The Areopagus

As you begin the ascent to the Acropolis, on the left is a limestone outcropping of rock known as the **Hill of the Areopagus**. Sixteen steps lead from the main path up to its top. (A word of warning: These well-worn steps are as slippery as polished glass! Use extreme caution in climbing.) To the right of the steps is a large **bronze tablet** inscribed with the words of Paul's sermon on Mars Hill. The Areopagus takes its name

▲ **Fig. 7.**　Mars Hill as seen from the Acropolis of Athens

from the root word *pagos,* meaning "rock," and from either Ares, the god of vengeance and war, whom legend says once was tried there for the murder of one of the sons of Poseidon, or the Arae, the mythical Furies. Apparently its meaning was debated even in antiquity, as Pausanius lists various interpretations of the name.

Originally some sort of structure must have stood on the hill. In the 1st century B.C.E. the Roman architect **Vitruvius** refers to "an ancient type of building, to this day covered in mud" (*On Architecture* 2.1.5). We know the hill was the meeting place for the Council of the Areopagus, at first the supreme court and chief legislative body of Athens. But following later reforms in the 5th century B.C.E., the council was stripped of much of its power. Subsequently it had jurisdiction only over impiety and "blood crimes," i.e., murder. The council was said to meet in the open air because its judges did not wish to be tainted by the bloody crimes of those it judged. By the 1st century the Romans seemed to have broadened the scope of its authority again, but the council obviously was limited to making whatever judgments the Romans would allow. For the first time also, Romans were sometimes numbered among the council members. At the top of the hill were two large stones used in trials: the Stone of Wrath, upon which the prosecutor stood, and the Stone of Shame, where the accused stood.

Where Paul delivered his sermon is not known, but probably it was on the lower, gentler slopes of the hill where a crowd could gather. In any case, the hill today likely has a somewhat different appearance from that of the 1st century, since it was badly damaged in 1651 by a major earthquake that destroyed the **Church of St. Dionysius** on its lower slope.

The Acropolis

The **Acropolis of Athens** was initially used for defensive purposes. Typically in ancient cities, women and children were placed in the acropolis (the word means "upper city") in times of war for protection. Rising more than 500 feet at its highest point, with steep slopes on all sides except the west, the Acropolis of Athens was ideal for this purpose. Apparently, however, this Acropolis also had a sacred use from the earliest times. By 750 B.C.E. the Acropolis was sacred to Athena, patron goddess of the city, and the religious function eventually became the exclusive purpose of the site. But since the primary role of religion in ancient times was civic and corporate rather than private, many of the monuments erected on the Acropolis celebrated the victories of Athens over its enemies. These included various structures to honor the heroes of such victories and others that remembered various donors to this site of civic celebration. Other splendid buildings were erected by **Peisistratos,** tyrant (sole ruler) of Athens (r. 560–546 B.C.E.), who also reinstituted the Panathenaic festival and introduced the cult of Dionysus with its perfor-

Athens: Acropolis

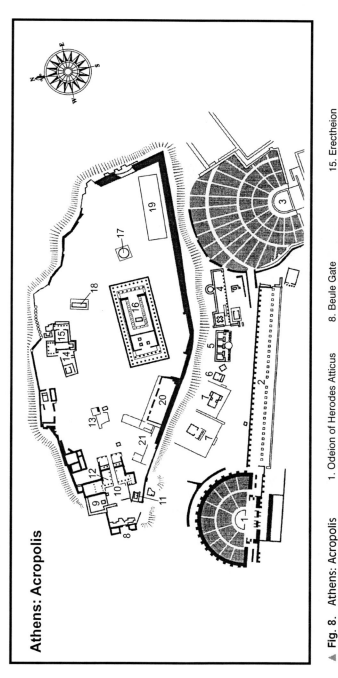

▲ **Fig. 8.** Athens: Acropolis

1. Odeion of Herodes Atticus
2. Stoa of Eumenes
3. Theater of Dionysus
4. Asclepeion
5. Ionic Stoa
6. Sacred Spring of Pan
7. Temples of Isis and Themis

8. Beule Gate
9. Pedestal of Agrippa
10. Propylaea
11. Temple of Athena Nike
12. Pinakotheke
13. Athena Promachos (base)
14. Pandroseion

15. Erectheion
16. Parthenon
17. Temple of Augustus and Roma
18. Altar of Athena
19. Acropolis Museum
20. Chalcotheke
21. Brauronion

mance of tragedy. These cult dramas eventually led to the development of the Greek theater.

All the buildings of the Archaic period (7th–6th century B.C.E.) were destroyed by the Persians in 480 B.C.E. In the Classical period the Acropolis reached the height of its glory under the leadership of **Pericles**. The **Parthenon** (447–432 B.C.E.), the **Propylaea** (437–432 B.C.E.), the **Temple of Athena Nike** (432–421 B.C.E.), and the **Erechtheion** (421–406 B.C.E.) were the result of his leadership. Later the Romans added only one building, the **Temple of Roma and Augustus** behind the Parthenon. When the Herulian Goths attacked Athens (267 C.E.), the **Beule Gate** (named for the French archaeologist who discovered it) was constructed for defense.

Before ascending to the buildings on the Acropolis proper, turn to the right to view the structures on its **southern slope**. The first is the **Odeion of Herodes Atticus of Marathon** (161 B.C.E.), the incredibly wealthy benefactor of Athens who built it in memory of his wife, **Regilla**. The odeion was used for oratorical and musical performances. This beautiful building, which could seat 5,000 spectators, had an elaborate stage wall that rose 85 feet to the height of the roof and was decorated with many statues and columns. The roof was constructed of cedar, and the floor of the orchestra and the rows of seats were covered with marble. The odeion was destroyed when the Herulians set fire to it in 267 C.E. and the roof collapsed.

Beyond the odeion, on the lower terrace, are the ruins of the vast **Stoa of Eumenes**, some 490 feet long, built by **King Eumenes II of Pergamum** (r. 197–159 B.C.E.), brother to Attalus II, who built the Stoa of Attalus in the agora. This two-story structure, however, was designed not to accommodate shops but as an elaborate promenade between the **Odeion of Herodes Atticus** and the **Theater of Dionysus** to provide protection from sun and rain. It also was destroyed in the 3rd century C.E., and all that remains are the series of **buttresses** that supported the terrace behind it.

Above the Stoa of Eumenes, and to the left (west) of the Theater of Dionysus, can be seen the scant remains of the **Asclepeion**, a center for healing run by the priests of Asclepius. The **sacrificial altar** remains, but it is difficult to discern amid the various stones currently being stored there. Farther west, next to the Asclepeion, are the ruins of the **Ionic Stoa**, used as banquet rooms; the **Sacred Spring of Pan** (its **marble basin** still remains); and the adjoining **temples of Isis and Themis** (goddess of order).

The **Theater of Dionysus** (333 B.C.E.), whose construction was initiated by the orator **Lycurgus**, was a successor to even earlier theaters of the 6th and 5th centuries B.C.E. This famous theater—in which premiered the works of the three great Greek tragedians, Euripides, Sophocles, and Aeschylus—was the home of Greek drama and the birthplace of the tragedy. Today only twenty-five tiers of seats remain of the original sixty-four rows. Later another fourteen rows were added above them, bringing the seating capacity to approximately 17,000 spectators. The **marble thrones** in the front row were for prominent officials. The one in the center was for the priest of Dionysus Eleutherios; the one above it was for the **Emperor Hadrian**. The standing marble slabs between the orchestra and seats were erected as a barrier in the Roman period when gladiatorial fights with wild animals were held in the theater. (Gladiatorial games were strictly a Roman invention; the Greeks had no such contests.) Originally a **sanctuary of Dionysus** adjoined the theater. (The best view of the Stoa of Eumenes and the Theater of Dionysus is from above, from the south wall around the Acropolis.)

The **Propylaea** ("before the gate") visible today is the fourth of such structures to be built at this site; earlier ones were destroyed in various wars. The road from the agora below, the **Panathenaic Way**, led up to this point. A flight of marble steps ascends to the hall of the Propylaea. One step is of gray Eleusinian marble; the others are of white Pentelic marble. The **monumental pedestal** (25 feet tall) on the left of the steps originally was designed for a statue with a chariot and four horses to honor King Eumenes II of Pergamum for his contribution of the Stoa of Eumenes. Later it was reinscribed with a dedication to **Marcus Agrippa** in honor of the odeion he contributed to the agora. Designed by the architect **Mnesicles** and begun upon the completion of the Parthenon (437 B.C.E.), the Propylaea consisted of a central section with five doorways, originally fitted with wooden doors, and projecting wings on either side. The wing on the left side, the north wing, was known as the **Pinakotheke**, or art gallery, because of the magnificent collection of paintings inside. In 150 C.E. Pausanius named a number of the paintings he could recognize, including some by **Polygnatus of Homer** (5th century B.C.E.). The room was used for official banquets by dignitaries who reclined on couches in the Greek fashion. The wing on the right side, the south wing, could not match the other in design because of the Temple of Athena Nike and other buildings that impinged upon it. This wing was never completed due to the start of the Peloponnesian War (431 B.C.E.).

The small temple on the right (south) of the Propylaea housed the wooden statue of Athena Nike (Athena of Victory) and was known as the **Temple of Athena Nike**. The temple was begun in 430 B.C.E. following the construction of the Parthenon and the Propylaea. Its simple design and use of Ionic columns contribute to its elegant appearance, especially in contrast to the massive structure of the Propylaea with its Doric columns. Since the goddess Athena, in contrast to the winged goddess Nike, had no wings, Pausanius said that the Athenians erected it so that victory could not fly away from Athens. It was called the Temple of Apteros Nike (Wingless Victory). The **frieze** about the building shows various gods of Olympus, including Zeus, Poseidon, and Athena, as well as scenes from the Persian Wars. Some of the finest sections of the frieze were carried off by **Lord Elgin** and are now in the British Museum.

Inside the Propylaea, the first sight to greet the eyes of the ancient visitor was the towering **bronze statue of Athena Promachos** (Athena the Champion), nearly 30 feet tall, created by the famous sculptor **Phidias** and dedicated after the famous Greek victory at Marathon (490 B.C.E.). The statute was said to have taken nine years to complete. Athena was portrayed holding a spear and shield, the shield decorated with a scene from the battle of the Centaurs by the painter **Parrhasius**. Parts of the **marble base** of the statute, with a large egg-and-dart pattern, are still in place. Pausanius said that the crest of Athena's helmet and the tip of her spear were visible when ships rounded Cape Sounion. Eventually the statue was carried to Constantinople. In one of the great cultural losses of antiquity, this statue was wantonly destroyed during the siege of Constantinople (Fourth Crusade, 1204) because the enraged citizens perceived the extended hand of Athena as beckoning, as if in welcome, toward the invaders.

Behind the statue, to the left, on the north side of the Acropolis, was the **Erechtheion**, begun in 421 B.C.E. and not completed until 406 B.C.E. In many ways this temple was the most complex structure on the Acropolis. The building took its name from **Erechtheus**, legendary first king of Athens, sometimes identified with Poseidon. This shrine consisted of a central hall with lateral structures on either side. Furthermore, it was built on four different levels, had three different roofs, and was furnished with Ionic columns of three different dimensions. A **temple** dedicated to **Athena Polias** (Athena of the City) occupied the eastern end of the Erechtheion. It contained an ancient wooden cult figure the Athenians believed had fallen from heaven. The western part of the building held the tomb of King Erechtheus, who was said to be the foster child of Athena. The dividing wall between these sanctuaries was removed during later alterations.

On the south side of the Erechtheion, the side nearest to the Parthenon, stands the most famous feature of the building. Instead of columns, **female statues** called **caryatids** were used to support the **south porch**. The statues took their name from the maidens of Caryae in Laconia, who carried vessels on their heads during an annual festival there. One of the statues was carried to London by Lord Elgin, along with other antiquities known as the Elgin Marbles. The south porch sheltered the **Tomb of Kekrops**, mythical founder of the Athenian royal family line. The **north porch** of the Erechtheion is surrounded by six columns with elaborate bases and capitals, and above the elegant doorway leading into the temple was a frieze of gray Eleusinian marble with white marble figures, now in the Acropolis Museum.

▲ **Fig. 9.**   The caryatids of the Erechtheion, Athens Acropolis

The remains of a rectangular enclosure beyond the west end of the Erechtheion marks the location of the **Pandroseion**, a shrine dedicated to Pandros, daughter of the mythical king Kekrops. The **olive tree** that now grows in this location commemorates the ancient tree given to the city of Athens by Athena following her victory over Poseidon in their contest to be patron of Attica.

The crown jewel of the Acropolis, the **Parthenon** (House of the Maiden/Virgin), was commissioned by Pericles following the defeat of the Persians in 447 B.C.E. as part of his grand scheme to make the Acropolis once again the envy of the world. According to Plutarch, the great sculptor Phidias was given the general direction of construction ("director and supervisor of the whole enterprise," *Lives* 13:4) and **Iktinos** was appointed as architect. The foundations had been laid in 490 B.C.E., prior to the Persian attack (480 B.C.E.), and other work had been done before 450 B.C.E., but the entire plan was revised and expanded by Iktinos.

The Parthenon was erected upon three vast **platforms**, each of them 20 inches tall, with seventeen Doric columns on each side and eight at

▲ **Fig. 10.**   The Parthenon on the Acropolis of Athens

each end. The fluted columns are 34 feet high and 6 feet 3 inches in diameter at the bottom, tapering to a diameter of 4 feet 10 inches at the top. Furthermore, the columns have a slight bulge approximately two-fifths of the way up from the platform, and they lean slightly inward. It has been estimated that if the columns were continued indefinitely upward, they would meet one mile up in the air to form a gigantic pyramid. The purpose of this sophisticated engineering was to ensure that the vertical lines of the temple appeared straight, so that the entire impression of the building would be lively and light in spite of its mass. The roof of the building was originally covered with marble tiles, and the entire structure was unique in its almost exclusive use of marble as a construction material. When completed, the Parthenon was the largest temple of the classical world.

The interior of the Parthenon was divided into two parts. The **cult statue of Athena** stood in the **east cella**, surrounded by a colonnade of twenty-three columns and an entrance portico with six columns. The **west cella**, which probably contained the **treasury** of the temple, also was entered through a portico with six columns and had four Ionic columns to support the roof. Completed in 438 B.C.E., the statue of Athena was designed and constructed by Phidias himself. On its base it stood nearly 40 feet tall, supported by a massive post. The face and hands were of ivory. According to Thucydides, more than 40 talents of gold (approximately 250 lbs.) were used to plate the remainder of the enormous statue. These plates were removable so that the weight of the gold could be checked periodically. The goddess stood upon a large platform upon which the Pandora myth was depicted. Her left hand rested upon her shield, her spear leaned against her left shoulder, and in her right hand she held a small image of Nike. The statue eventually was carried off to Constantinople and destroyed there in 1203 C.E. The great **Ionic frieze** around the outer wall of the cella, 525 feet long, depicts the lively movement and excitement of the great Panathenaic procession.

The exterior of the temple was once colorful. The various decorations of the building as they exist today, such as the metopes, are simply white marble, but it should be remembered that in ancient times both buildings and statues were brightly colored. Each of the pediments at either end of the temple featured Athena. Her birth from the head of Zeus was portrayed on the east, and her contest with Poseidon, one of the most sophisticated sculptures of the Parthenon, was depicted on the west. The **Doric metopes** around the building show a **fight with centaurs** (south side), a **fight with giants** (east side), a **fight with Amazons** (west side), and the **fall of Troy** on the north side. The east architrave still shows the holes that held 345 bronze letters of an inscription in honor of **Nero** (62 C.E.), as well as the marks left by fourteen shields placed there by **Alexander the Great** as trophies of his victory over the Persians in 334 B.C.E.

The Parthenon is the object of an extensive conservation project today to protect it from the elements, particularly the devastating effects of pollution and acid rain, as well as from the millions of tourists who have viewed (and handled) it over the centuries.

The Acropolis has a splendid **museum** located to the rear of the Parthenon. The various treasures of the Acropolis are displayed in nine galleries. Among the most outstanding objects to be seen include a large **figure of an owl**, the symbolic representation of Athena; a **head of the youthful Alexander the Great; four of the original six caryatids** (another is in the British Museum, and one has been destroyed); the famous **statue of the Moschophoros** (the "calf bearer"); a colorful and strange **serpentine creature** with three heads, believed to be a representation of **Nereus**, the sea monster with the ability to change its shape; the **Kritias Boy** (named for its sculptor) and the **Blond Youth**, both masterpieces of the Severe style; sections of the **Parthenon** and **Erechtheion friezes**; and various **korai**, the votive images of maidens given to Athena by various donors, which were erected in the open air all over the Acropolis.

Return to the Propylaea along the **southeast wall** (to the left at the exit to the museum) to obtain a magnificent view of the lower slope of the Acropolis and its structures. Just past the steps of the Parthenon, on the left, lie the ruins of the **Chalkotheke,** which once housed bronze vessels and armor. Note also, before the Propylaea, the remains of the **Brauronion,** cult temple of Artemis of Brauron. It was transferred from Brauron to the Acropolis in the 6th century by **Peisistratos the Tyrant,** a native of Brauron.

The Roman Forum

The site of the Roman Forum is below the north side of the Acropolis, adjacent to Polygnatou Street. Late in the 1st century B.C.E. Athens used donations from the **Emperor Augustus** and **Julius Caesar** to construct this forum on the east of the ancient Athenian agora. The two areas were connected by the **Broad Street,** a 30-foot-wide, pedestrian-only marble street that began at the **Library of Pantainos** in the agora and ended at the **Gate of Athena Archegetes** on the west side of the forum.

The Roman Forum measured 320 feet by 370 feet and had gates on the east and west. The most notable structure in the forum today is the **Tower of the Winds** on the east side of the forum, named for the **reliefs of the Eight Winds** on the frieze about the top of the tower. Originally the tower was a complete ancient weather station, designed by a famous Macedonian astronomer, **Andronikos of Kyrrhos.** Sundials were mounted on the exterior sides of the building, a water clock operated inside the tower, and the **bronze weather vane** on top indicated the wind direction over the applicable image of one of the Eight Winds. Also on the east side is the spacious **public latrine** (like all such ancient facilities, short on modesty but long on accommodations; this one seated sixty-eight). The forum was surrounded by Ionic columns and paved with marble. A **fountain** also stood on its south side.

The Library of Hadrian

A mere 50 feet away and adjacent to the Roman Forum, the **Library of Hadrian** (132 C.E.) parallels the forum area on the north side. (At the time of this writing, the area is completely enclosed by a fence and is not accessible.) The library can be viewed from Adrianou Street at Odos Areos or from Aiolou Street on the east side. It was designed with a **colonnaded courtyard** that held a **reflecting pool** and **niches** (which still can be seen) where books were stored in the wall of the library building proper. Corinthian columns decorated its west façade. Lecture rooms also were a part of the library. The **sloping floors** that can be seen in the library area were in such rooms. Pausanius said that this elaborate building was built of Phrygian marble and contained rooms with gilded ceilings, fine paintings, and numerous statues. He was most impressed, however, with the hundred columns of purple and white marble from Dokimion in Turkey. These have long since been carried off.

The Olympieion

The grounds of the **Olympieion** are bordered on the west by Leoforos Amalias and on the north by Leoforos Olgas, where the entrance is located.

When completed in 130 C.E., the **Temple of Olympian Zeus** was one of the largest temples in the ancient world, 135 feet wide and 340 feet long with 104 Corinthian columns, 55 feet tall, constructed from 15,500 tons of Pentelic marble. Today only sixteen of those columns remain, fifteen standing and one collapsed. The inner cella of the temple held an enormous ivory and gold statue of Zeus and an imposing portrait statue of Hadrian, who had his own altar in the temple and was worshiped alongside Zeus. In fact, Pausanius said the entire area was "full" of statues and images of **Hadrian,** who completed the temple.

For centuries the temple remained unfinished after it was begun in 517 B.C.E. by **Peisistratos the Younger,** grandson of the tyrant **Peisistratos**. After the collapse of the reign of the Thirty Tyrants, the project was abandoned. Finally, **Antiochus IV Epiphanes,** king of Syria, who had spent part of his youth in Athens and is best known for his hatred of the Jews and desecration of the temple in Jerusalem, commissioned a Roman architect to complete the great temple (ca.175 B.C.E.). The remaining columns date from this period.

Upon the death of Antiochus (164 B.C.E.), construction once again was halted. Some additional work was done during the time of **Augustus,** but it remained for Hadrian to complete the temple precinct wall and place the statues inside. The imposing **Arch of Hadrian** was constructed in honor of the emperor following the completion of the temple, and Hadrian himself walked through it to attend the dedication of the temple in 131 C.E. The western side of the arch (toward the old city) carries the **inscription** "This is Athens, the city of **Theseus.**" The inscription on the eastern side of the arch facing the temple (and toward a section of Athens that had been newly renovated by Hadrian) states, "This is the city of Hadrian and not of Theseus."

Also in the vicinity of the Olympieion, on its northern side, are the remains of a **Roman bathhouse** (2nd century C.E.). In the area to the south below the temple platform can be seen three ruins of significance: the remains of a **temple to Apollo** (450 B.C.E.); ancient **law courts** that dealt with accidental killings; and the smaller ruins of a **sanctuary to Kronos and Rhea** (150 C.E.).

Anyone interested in viewing the site of the ancient **Panathenaic Stadium** should go east down Leoforos Olgas to the modern **Olympic Stadium** that was constructed in the same location. This stadium was the site of the first **modern Olympic Games** in 1896. The original stadium was built by **Lycurgus** in 335 B.C.E. It had a playing field 610 feet long and 100 feet wide and contained a track approximately 600 feet long (185 meters, which is a *stadion*, a Greek unit of measure), with four **double herms** standing at the finish line. When the "double stadion" race was held, the runners made a complete circuit around the herms. (These strange figures were slender, square pillars with a portrait head on the top and a phallus on one side.)

Sometime prior to the **Great Panathenaia** of 143 c.e., **Herodes Atticus** donated new marble seating for the stadium and renovated the facilities. All that remains of the original structure are some fragments and blocks of stone from the **parapet**, and the **herm** on the west, at the far end of the stadium.

The National Archaeological Museum

Do not miss this museum—even certified non-museum-goers find it fascinating. The **National Archaeological Museum** certainly ranks among the top five museums in the world. No matter where in the Greek world any traveler might go subsequently, including the Greek islands, the best of the ancient treasures of Greece are located here. During World War II these irreplaceable objects were buried in the basement under thick layers of sand. The displays in the museum are generally well labeled, but anyone wishing more than the names of the thousands of exhibits in these galleries is strongly encouraged to purchase a complete **museum guide** in the foyer before entering. It is beautifully done and worth the money.

Even a cursory description of the most renowned objects in the museum gives an indication of the quality of this outstanding collection:

On the first floor: magnificent **golden artifacts** from **Mycenae** discovered by **Heinrich Schliemann**, including the so-called **death mask of Agamemnon** (actually it predates Agamemnon); **gold rings** with such tiny, detailed engraving as to be incredible for such an ancient period (1500–1400 b.c.e.); **inlaid gold and silver daggers**; **Early Cycladic figures** (2700 b.c.e.) of a **harpist** and a **flute player** that appear to be modern art; enormous **bronze statues** recovered from the sea, such as the famous **statue of the Boy Jockey** on a galloping horse, the famous **statue of Poseidon**, and one of the "**Marathon Ephebe**"; an extensive collection of funeral monuments and tombstones, some still preserving traces of paint; Egyptian mummies; Hellenistic gold jewelry; busts of most of the famous Roman emperors, along with a famous **equestrian statue of Augustus**; and a **bronze helmet** of the Illyrian type with a **gold funerary mask**.

On the second floor: the **Thera Gallery**, which contains not-to-bemissed artifacts from the island of Thera (modern **Santorini**), whose partial disappearance due to the cataclysmic explosion of the island's volcano possibly gave rise to the myth of the city of **Atlantis**. The unique and colorful objects in this gallery include life-size **wall paintings**, including those of **exotic animals and fish**, the often-reproduced **Boxing Boys**, and the **Fish Seller** displaying his catch.

▲ **Fig. 11.** The Boy Jockey in the National Archaeological Museum, Athens

Other Sites of Interest

Several other sites of interest are in easy reach of Athens. Only 22 miles to the west, directly on the route to Corinth, the site of the **Eleusinian mysteries at Eleusis** (Elefsina) is well worth a visit. Located in an unappealing industrial area, the remains of the **precinct and sanctuary of Demeter** are imposing. The Eleusinian cult celebrated the myth of Demeter, the goddess of grain and fertility, and her daughter, Persephone (also known as Kore), who was carried away to the underworld by Hades. Zeus, however, ordered that she must be returned to earth every spring so that grain would grow again. The cult became one of the most prominent mystery religions in all of Greece, if not the most prominent.

A **temple to Artemis** stands at the entrance to the site. Next are the dual entrance gates, the **Lesser** and the **Greater Propylaea**. To the right of them is the **Plutonion**, a cave sacred to Pluton, god of the underworld. The Eleusinian mysteries were celebrated in an enormous hall known as the **Telesterion**, which measured 170 feet by 160 feet and held seven rows of six columns. The initiates came to Eleusis in a great processional that began in Athens and made its way to the sanctuary, where they were initiated into the mysteries. They were led on their journey by priests with torches, and at Eleusis the rites were celebrated at

▲ **Fig. 12.** The Ninnion Tablet, depicting the presentation to Demeter of initiates into the Eleusinian mysteries, in the Eleusis Museum (copy of the original in the National Archaeological Museum)

night. Typically, such mysteries granted the assurance of eternal life to the initiates. Two degrees, or stages, of membership were possible, known as the **Lesser** and the **Greater Eleusinia**. Little else is known of the initiation, though it might have involved the display of a sheaf of grain.

A **rock-cut terrace** with its original seating still exists on the slope adjacent to the Telesterion. Above it, a small **museum** houses reliefs and sculptures pertinent to the mysteries. One rare plaque, the **Ninnion Tablet** (copy; original in the National Archaeological Museum, Athens), portrays a scene from the initiation rituals. The structures at Eleusis principally date to the 6th and 5th centuries B.C.E., though additions still were being made into the Christian period.

Another site of great interest to visitors to Greece is **Delphi**, home of the famous oracle of Delphi, known as the Pythia, and the **Temple of Apollo,** where the oracle presided. It may be easily reached from Athens by bus (bus station B) or by rental automobile on modern highways. Day trips also may be arranged from area hotels.

Delphi is located high in the mountainous region to the north of Athens, yet it surprises visitors with a view to the Gulf of Corinth below. When it is surrounded by blooming almond trees in the spring, Delphi is surely one of the most beautiful places in the world. The ancient Greeks agreed and described it as the center (literally, the navel, *omphalos*) of the world.

The **Sacred Precinct of Delphi** comprises, in addition to the Temple of Apollo, an impressive **theater**, the **bouleuterion** (council chamber) of the city, numerous **treasuries** of Greek cities that held valuable offerings to Apollo, and many monuments and altars. From the entrance, the **Sacred Way** leads uphill between the bases of monuments that celebrated military victories and more than twenty treasuries that held votive offerings. **The Treasury of the Athenians** (510 B.C.E.) has been reerected in the form of a Doric temple.

The Temple of Apollo itself was originally built in the 7th century B.C.E.; it burned to the ground in 548 B.C.E. and was rebuilt in 531 B.C.E. This later temple collapsed from an earthquake in 373 B.C.E. Only the foundations of the third temple (346–320 B.C.E.) remain today. The **pronaos** of this temple held sayings of the Seven Sages of Greece, including "Know thyself," which had no reference to psychological self-knowledge, as widely understood today, but to the understanding that the viewer was a mortal and not a god. The oracle, or Pythia, was always a middle-aged peasant woman who gave garbled answers to the questions of inquirers, which had been previously submitted on a tablet and were returned by the priests with the answer (moderated by them) on a sealed tablet the following day.

The **theater** (4th century B.C.E.), above the Temple of Apollo, could seat 5,000 spectators. Higher yet above the theater, the **stadium** was the location of the Pythian Games, one of the four Panhellenic contests of the Olympic Games. The games were named in honor of the slaying of Python, a mythical serpent, by Apollo (as was the Pythia).

To the east of the Sacred Precinct lie the remains of several structures of interest: the ancient **gymnasium**, the **Sanctuary of Athena Pronaia** (Athena Before the Temple), the circular **Tholos**, and various treasuries.

The outstanding **Museum of Delphi** should not be missed. Among its large collection of objects from the site: an **omphalos stone** (Roman period); a **life-size silver and gold bull** found in the area of the **Treasury of the Corinthians**; the **Sphinx of the Naxians**; and the famous **bronze statue of the Charioteer** (ca. 474 B.C.E.) by Sotades of Thespiai.

In some ways a similar site, the **sacred island of Delos** may be reached from Athens by way of Mykonos. Regular flights are available from Athens to Mykonos. There are no accommodations on the tiny island, and all visitors must come by ferry from Mykonos and return in the same day. Approximately four hours should be allowed to view the site.

Delos achieved honor as the birthplace of Apollo and the home of a famous shrine to the god. During the Hellenistic period the island became a notable center for trade throughout the Mediterranean, but following its destruction by **Mithradates** (88 B.C.E.) and pirates (69 B.C.E.) Delos remained virtually deserted except for a few attendants at the **Temple of Apollo**. Today the island attracts thousands of visitors a year.

Though the island is small, the ruins of its various antiquities extend over a large area. For the most part the various remains are fairly well labeled, but the site is nevertheless complex and confusing. Visitors would be well advised to purchase a separate guidebook for the island. At least twenty major structures are scattered about the area, and extensive ruins are to be found in the **Theater Quarter**, the **Harbor Quarter**, and the **Commercial Quarter**, in addition to the **Sacred Precinct** itself and various **residential districts**. Outstanding objects to be viewed include the famous **marble lions** (now in the museum; replicas stand in the original location), the **Hall of the Bulls**, the **Agora of the Italians**, and the **House of the Trident** with its beautiful **mosaic floor**. The remains of a large **synagogue** have been discovered on the island, including a "**seat of Moses**" and a **cistern** (possibly a *mikveh*, or pool for ritual cleansing). Two inscriptions discovered nearby suggest that the synagogue, built in the mid-second century B.C.E., was established by Samaritans for their cult.

The **museum** contains a large number of architectural fragments and remains from the island, as well as the original marble lions, **three seated women** (7th century B.C.E.), and various other sculptures, stelae, pottery, and votive offerings.

Beroea

Virtually nothing remains from the ancient city of Beroea, once the second city of the Macedonian Empire. In the 1st century the Apostle Paul found Beroea hospitable to his message, and today the city contains the most notable individual monument in Greece to the Christian missionary.

Location and History

The ancient city of Beroea today is known as Veria, located 42 miles west of Thessaloniki and 9 miles northwest of Vergina. Public buses are available from Thessaloniki's KTEL stations (be sure to use the west side stations). Check carefully for departing and returning times, as the frequency of connections varies. Fares are inexpensive, less than $10 round trip. It is possible, if desired or time is limited, to make a day trip from Thessaloniki to nearby Vergina, go on to Veria, and return.

Beroea was first mentioned by Thucydides in his histories when he records that the Athenians failed to take the city by siege in 432 B.C.E., during the Peloponnesian War. Plutarch later tells of a successful siege of Beroea in 288 B.C.E., after which the city was occupied by **Pyrrhus**. The Gauls who later robbed the royal tombs at Vergina were unsuccessful in taking Beroea. The city became part of the Roman Empire in 148 B.C.E. and was the site of training for the armies of **Pompey**, who spent the winter of 49–48 B.C.E. in Beroea prior to the battle of Pharsalos (48 B.C.E.). In the 1st century C.E. Beroea found favor with several of the Roman emperors and became an international city of varied races and religions. The **Apostle Paul** visited the city in 50 C.E. Later **Diocletian** made Beroea one of the two capitals of Macedonia.

Biblical Significance

The biblical account of **Paul's** visit to Beroea, following his escape from the hostility at Thessalonica, is found in Acts 17:10–15:

> That very night the believers sent Paul and Silas off to Beroea; and when they arrived, they went to the Jewish synagogue. These Jews were more receptive than those at Thessalonica, for they welcomed the message very eagerly and examined the scriptures every day to see whether these things were so. Many of them therefore believed, including not a few Greek women and men of high standing. But when the Jews of Thessalonica learned that the word of God had been proclaimed by Paul in Beroea as well, they came there too, to stir up and incite the crowds. Then the believers immediately sent Paul away to the coast, but Silas and Timothy remained behind. Those who conducted Paul brought him as far as Athens; and after receiving instructions to have Silas and Timothy join him as soon as possible, they left him.

Because of the conflict that had erupted in Thessalonica, the disciples there spirited Paul and **Silas** away by night to Beroea. The route taken is not described, but probably the group traveled by way of Pella, 12 miles north of Beroea. Again, as was Paul's custom, he began his mission work in the city by speaking in a synagogue. The reception in the synagogue of Beroea, unlike in Thessalonica, was open and largely responsive. The text of Acts even describes the response as "eager." The people were said to examine the scriptures daily (the Hebrew scriptures, i.e., the Old Testament) to see whether Paul's statements concerning Jesus as Messiah were borne out by the words of the prophets. As a result, many in the city, both Jews and Greeks, became converts. How long Paul remained in Beroea is not indicated, but his visit was probably longer than suggested by the condensed narrative of Acts.

This positive reception came to an end when those in Thessalonica who had become upset by Paul's teachings learned that he was in Beroea and came there to incite the crowds also. Subsequently Paul was escorted by "the believers" toward the coast. Whether he next traveled to Athens by land or sea is unclear, but most scholars believe the journey would have been made by sea.

Site Visit

Unfortunately, little remains of the city that Paul knew. Only along Elia Street is there evidence of once fine **streets** with **curbs** and a **drainage system**. Likewise, the remnants of **shops** in Parodos Edessis Street and evidence of **public baths** in Pindou Street, not far from Agiou Antoniou Square in the center of the city, suggest the nature of the ancient city. At

▲ **Fig. 13.** Mosaic depicting the Apostle Paul preaching at Beroea

the north entrance to the city (the highway from Thessaloniki) can be seen portions of a **wall** dating from the 3rd century C.E., known as the **"marble tower."** During this century, in which Beroea was invaded by various "barbarian" tribes from the north, the walls about the city were hastily repaired and reinforced with architectural fragments and stones of various sorts.

Those interested in biblical history should be sure to visit the impressive **monument to the Apostle Paul** in the southern part of the city, which is also referred to as the **Bema** (take Mitropoleos Street to Orologiou Square, then left on Kolokotroni Street to Mavromihali Street). It is said to incorporate the steps from the original synagogue from which Paul delivered his sermons, although actually the entire structure was erected in 1961.

The **Archaeological Museum** (at Leoforos Anixeos 47) is also of interest. Among the finest offerings of this small museum are an **iron sword** with an **ivory handle** (4th century B.C.E.); a unique **stele** with **rules for the gymnasium** and its administrator, very rare (2nd century B.C.E.); and various fine bronzes, sculptures, and grave stelae.

Cenchreae

Today it is hard to imagine the busy harbor of ancient Cenchreae, one of the most important ports in the Roman world, at the desolate spot on a small bay that marks its former location. Yet the underwater ruins there still suggest the history of famous travelers, such as the Apostle Paul, whose feet once walked on the sunken stones.

Location and History

To reach Cenchreae, follow the signs from Corinth to Isthmia and continue toward the village of Keries, some 3 miles past Isthmia. The site is not well marked but is easily discernible from the road.

Cenchreae, the eastern port of Corinth on the Saronic Gulf, enabled maritime travel and commercial activity between Asia Minor and Corinth. The harbor was certainly in existence by the time of the Peloponnesian War and likely was constructed considerably earlier. It was first mentioned by Thucydides in his description of the attack by the Athenians upon Corinth in 425 B.C.E. The site was abandoned following the destruction of Corinth in 146 B.C.E., but new harbor facilities were built when **Julius Caesar** revived Corinth in 44 C.E. Two new moles (break-waters) were added at that time to provide a deep-water port. Strabo later described Cenchreae as the naval station of Corinth, 70 stadia (7 miles) to the east, and the port used for its trade with Asia (the western coast of Asia Minor, modern Turkey). Pausanius said that the harbor got its name from **Cenchreas**, the son of **Poseidon** and **Peirene**. He described Cenchreae as having a bronze statue of Poseidon on a mole that extended into the sea at the southern end of the harbor, with temples of **Isis** and **Asclepius** at the same end of the harbor. A temple of **Aphrodite** stood at the north side of the harbor. Cenchreae also was the port used by the **Apostle Paul** in the 1st century in his travels to Asia Minor and Syria. The harbor was badly damaged by earthquakes and tidal waves in 365 and 375 C.E., but it was later restored and continued to be a significant port until its final destruction by the Slavs around 580 C.E.

Biblical Significance

Cenchreae is mentioned twice in the New Testament, in Acts 18:18 and Romans 16:1. After his stay at Corinth, **Paul** sailed for Syria from Cenchreae. He also cut his hair there, "for he had a vow." Apparently this was a Nazarite vow of consecration (Num 6:5) in which the hair would not be cut until the vow had been fulfilled. We are not told what the vow concerned. In Romans 16:18 a woman named **Phoebe**, whom Paul called a deacon and benefactor of the church at Cenchreae, seems to have been given the important task of carrying Paul's letter to the Romans. The term *benefactor,* or *patron,* was used of wealthy individuals in the Greek and Roman world who made generous donations for the support of temples. In addition to the fact that Phoebe had the resources and the freedom to travel to distant Rome, this term indicates that she was a woman of means. Leadership roles such as this for women were not un-usual in the Roman world of the 1st century, or in Asia Minor, as they would have been in Israel. Inscriptions have established that women even served as "rulers" (principal lay officials) of synagogues in Asia Minor, something unthinkable in Israel. (Some authorities argue that the term translated as "rulers" was only honorific; the evidence is mixed.)

Site Visit

Little remains of the harbor or structures of Cenchreae, but it is still fas-cinating to see the remnants of the **breakwater** and the **warehouses** on the southern end of the harbor. The outline of the **south pier** and its breakwater can be clearly seen, even though now submerged by nearly 6

▲ **Fig. 14.** Harbor installations at the south jetty at Cenchreae

feet of water due to the increase of the tidal level over two millennia. On the right-hand side of the breakwater, several feet out into the water, the remnants of **commercial fish tanks** used for the storage of the fishermen's catch are still visible. Portions of the **foundation of the Temple of Isis**, some on the edge of the land and some in the water, also remain.

Through an underwater excavation project at Cenchreae, fifty **ancient wooden crates** were found sunken at the edge of the harbor. They contained opus sectile panels (colored glass) portraying the harbor of Cenchreae in a panoramic view as it would have been seen by ships approaching the port. This is a magnificent **mosaic work**, now restored in the **museum at Isthmia**, which was apparently intended to be erected in the sanctuary of Isis or nearby. These panels had arrived at Cenchreae by sea and were being kept in the Temple of Isis when an earthquake struck (375 C.E.), destroying the harbor under a tidal wave and damaging the panels beyond use. Be sure to look for this fascinating mosaic in the small museum. It provides an unmatched opportunity to view the harbor much as it must have appeared in the time of Paul.

At the other end of the bay, the **northern breakwater** mentioned by Pausanius is visible, though submerged. Additional structures there include the **walls of a lighthouse** or **tower**, a **brick complex** of uncertain use, and the **limestone base of a large tomb** that may have belonged to a man named **Regulus**, according to a Latin inscription found with it.

Other Sites of Interest

To visit the site of **ancient Isthmia**, return on the highway to Corinth and turn at the sign for the **Archaeological Museum**, which is in the village of Kyra Vrysi. The site is not well cared for or labeled, but there is enough of interest to be well worth seeing. The museum alone is worth the visit to Isthmia.

Isthmia was the site of one of the famous **Panhellenic festivals** or games, and its proximity to Corinth has caused many commentators to believe that it was the place where the Apostle Paul got his knowledge of sporting events. In any case, he certainly shows an acquaintance with the vocabulary of such contests as boxing, wrestling, and running, which were held in Isthmia. He also refers to Christians striving for something more than "a perishable crown," which may refer to the curious custom at Isthmia of awarding a wreath of wilted celery to victorious athletes. A wreath of wild celery, not wilted, formed the victor's crown at Nemea, while the better-known laurel wreath was used at Delphi (the Pythian Games), and one of wild olive at Olympia. From a rare mosaic at Corinth, the wilted celery wreath is shown around a victorious athlete's brow and tied with a knot (perhaps of ribbon) behind the neck.

The games were used in 196 B.C.E. by the Roman general **Flamininus** to announce the freeing of Greece by the Romans. In 66 C.E. the emperor **Nero** also visited the games (and sang); extensive renovations to the stadium and facilities were conducted prior to his visit. In addition to competing in the contest of singing to the lyre, which he won, as usual, in spite of a voice said to be "weak and husky," Nero also took first place in the herald's competition. He delighted the assembly, if not by his singing (which was reported by several ancient commentators as causing some Romans obliged to listen to it to leap from the second-floor windows of theaters), by declaring that their province once again was free.

The site contains the remains of the **sanctuary of Poseidon**, a **theater**, **baths**, and a **shrine to Palaimon**, a local deified boy-hero who drowned and whose body was brought to shore by a dolphin. Perhaps most interesting at the site is the **starting line** for the stadium, still visible. The starter for the races stood in a pit and controlled, by lines attached to them, sixteen horizontal bars hinged to posts, behind which the runners stood. When the starter pulled all the lines simultaneously, the bars dropped and the runners began the race.

The **museum** contains the fascinating **panoramic mosaic of the harbor scene**, not to be missed, as well as inscriptions and monuments from the Greek games and numerous other objects from the site.

Corinth

No city in the ancient world both benefited and suffered from its location more than Corinth. Situated on the main north-south route between northern and southern Greece, and with two good ports that linked it to Italy on the west and Asia Minor on the east, Corinth quickly became a center for commerce. But the location of Corinth also had its downside. The city often found itself caught in the middle between hostile neighbors, Athens to the north and Sparta to the south. Armies crisscrossed its streets as often as merchants, and more than once the city had to arise from ashes and rubble. Today only Athens attracts more interest in Greece for its historic antiquities than Corinth. It ranks as a must-see location for every traveler to Greece.

Location and History

Ancient Corinth is located less than two hours south of Athens. Tours run often from local hotels. Likewise, a rental automobile gives easy access and makes it possible to see nearby sites of interest not on the usual tours.

The great city of Corinth prospered for many reasons. In addition to its prominence as a center for trade and commerce, agriculture also flourished in the area. The soil around the city was thin and rocky, but just to the west, along the Nemean River, a rich plain produced heavy harvests of grain and other crops. Raisins were first developed there, and the word *currant* is a medieval corruption of *Corinth*. Tourism was another important source of income. The famous Isthmian Games, second only to the Olympic Games and more prestigious than those held in Delphi and Nemea, brought thousands of tourists to Corinth every two years and further added to its fame and fortune. During its early period Corinth also attracted many travelers to its famous (or notorious) Temple of Aphrodite atop the Acrocorinth ("high Corinth," or upper Corinth, the portion of the city atop the 1,900-foot mountain to the southeast of the city). Additionally, according to Plutarch, these multiple sources of wealth caused Corinth to become one of the three great banking centers of Greece, along with Athens and Patrae.

The site of Corinth was occupied at least as early as 4000 B.C.E., and the original settlement seems to have been in the area of the Temple of Apollo. The city likely was named for **Corinthus**, whom the Corinthians believed to be a son of Zeus. Corinth was wealthy as early as the Mycenaean period, and this wealth, along with its favorable location, naturally attracted invaders. At various periods in its early history, the site of Corinth was virtually abandoned due to wars and frequent earth-quakes in the area. In 1000 B.C.E. Dorians from Argos in northern Greece located in the region and resettled Corinth. Ports were developed on both sides of the narrow isthmus, Lechaion on the Gulf of Corinth (west) and Cenchreae on the Saronic Gulf (east). The names of these ports were taken from children of Poseidon (the Roman Neptune), god of the sea, for whom a temple was erected near Cenchreae. Strabo would later refer to Corinth as "master of two ports" (*Geography* 8.6.20a).

Trade expanded when Corinth founded colonies to the west, called "daughter cities," at Syracuse and Leukas, among others. These new cities provided markets for Corinthian exports. A variety of goods were exported, including terra-cotta objects and Corinthian bronzes, which became legendary and enormously valuable. Corinthian bronze had a distinctive coloration, apparently similar to pink gold. (How it was made is still unknown, as it was even in antiquity. Probably it was made of an amalgam of copper, tin, and perhaps gold, which was then surface-treated as well.) By the 1st century C.E. the collection of art pieces made from the metal rivaled the later "tulipmania" in Europe, when tulip bulbs sold at incredible prices. In 49 C.E. Seneca ridiculed the fanaticism of the collectors of Corinthian bronzes and called it "a mania," as did his uncle, Pliny the Younger, who principally was complaining that collectors had driven prices so high he could not afford any more pieces for his own collection. Additionally, the Jewish historian Josephus said that one of the gates of the Second Temple in Jerusalem, legendary for its beauty, was made of Corinthian bronze: "Of the gates nine were completely overlaid with gold and silver as were also their door posts and lintels; but one, that outside the sanctuary, was of Corinthian bronze, and far exceeded in value those plated with silver and set in gold" (*Jewish War* 5:201–205).

As Corinth's products traveled across the seas, its naval power increased, and it was the Corinthians who perfected the warship known as the trireme. In the late 8th century B.C.E., when the Bacchiad clan of Dorians came to power in Corinth and adopted "modern" tactics of warfare, including the phalanx formation and the hoplite warrior (heavily armed infantry), the city soon became a military presence in the region. The Bacchiadae held power until the 7th century, when they were overthrown by **Cypselus**, a native prince, who used these same tactics against them. It was he who constructed the walls about the city, over 6 miles in length. Cypselus ruled as tyrant (dictator) for thirty years until succeeded by his son, **Periander** (r. 627–587 B.C.E.).

The reign of Periander has been described as the golden years of ancient Corinth. The prosperity of the city during his rule permitted him to undertake extensive construction projects. The fountain around the springs of Peirene was built, as was the stone roadway toward the port of Lechaion.

(The "long walls" that stretched on either side of this road for protection, connected to the existing city walls, were not erected until 450 B.C.E.) Periander dreamed of opening a canal across the isthmus, as had his father, but was unable to accomplish the difficult project. Instead he constructed the *diolkos,* a stone roadway that permitted small ships to be skidded in grooves on a wheeled platform from one side of the isthmus to the other. This development enabled vessels to go to either gulf without having to sail around the tip of the Peloponnese, a particularly treacherous stretch of water. Sailors in the early centuries had a saying: "When you circle Cape Maleae, say goodbye to home!" (Strabo, *Geography* 8.6.21). Not coincidentally, the *diolkos* also enabled Corinth to become rich from its charges for such convenience.

The 6th century B.C.E., however, marked the pinnacle of Corinth's glory in the Greek period. As its rival, Athens, continued to develop, Corinth was eclipsed and fell into a slow decline. Continuous warring with Sparta and Athens only weakened Corinth further, and Sparta came to ascendancy in the region after the Peloponnesian War (431–404 B.C.E.). But in 338 B.C.E. **Philip of Macedon**, the father of Alexander the Great, conquered the area and made Corinth the center of the Hellenic League, after which the city enjoyed renewed prosperity. (The meetings of the Hellenic League were held in the Sanctuary of Poseidon at nearby Isthmia.) **Alexander** himself visited the city to meet the famous Cynic philosopher **Diogenes** (400–325 B.C.E.), who, according to tradition, lived in a barrel on the lower slopes of the Acrocorinth, a pleasant residential area known as Craneum. It was there, according to a well-known story, that Diogenes asked Alexander to move to one side because Alexander was blocking the sun from his barrel: "When Diogenes was sunning himself in Craneum, Alexander came and stood over him and said, 'Ask of me anything you desire.' To which he replied, 'Stand out of my light!'" (Diogenes Laertius, *Lives of Eminent Philosophers* 6.2.77).

Pressures from Corinth's neighbors increased throughout the following century, and in 338 B.C.E. Corinth came under a century of Macedonian rule. Yet their problems with traditional rivals soon appeared insignificant in the face of the threat from a new superpower, Rome. Following the Macedonian Wars the Romans controlled all of Greece. At first their presence had a stabilizing effect on the region. In 196 B.C.E. Rome gave the cities of Greece virtual independence and permitted them to form alliances with one another. Corinth became a member of the Achaean League (*Achaea* refers to southern Greece), and for half a century the city enjoyed peace.

Rome soon became convinced that these alliances posed a threat and in 147 B.C.E. ordered Corinth to dissolve the league. Corinth refused. (Strabo writes in *Geography* 8.6.23a that when the Roman ambassadors came to Corinth to discuss the matter, buckets of filth were poured down on their heads from the second story of a house—an act of dubious diplomacy.) When Sparta withdrew from the league, Corinth and the remaining members of the league attacked Sparta. In retaliation Rome invaded southern Greece with an army of 23,000 infantry and 3,500 cavalry, plus servants and auxiliaries. After three armies of the league were defeated north of the isthmus, Corinth could only defend itself with an army of 14,000 infantry and 600 cavalry, largely composed of untrained slaves.

In 146 B.C.E. **Lucius Mummius**, the Roman general, entered the city and destroyed it, pulling down its buildings and burning everything that would burn. First, however, he looted it of its treasures and precious art objects, the best of which he sent to Rome. The lesser spoils he gave to a general from Pergamum, **Philopoemen**, who had been sent by **Attalus II**, the Pergamene king, in support of the Roman attack. (According to Pausanius in *Description of Greece* 7.16.8, some of these objects were still in Pergamum in his day.) Most of the inhabitants of Corinth had fled; of those who remained, he executed most of the men and sold the women, children, and freedmen into slavery.

Plutarch tells of an incident immediately following the destruction of the city concerning a young Corinthian prisoner of war who was in a group being reviewed by Mummius to learn which of them could read and write. The young man wrote a verse from Homer's *Odyssey:* "O thrice and four times happy the Greeks who died then!" Mummius was said to be moved to tears by his patriotism and freed him and all his relations (*Moralia* 737a).

For the next one hundred years the site of Corinth was largely desolate, though never completely abandoned. It is likely that some survivors straggled back to make their homes among the ruins, and probably some priests still served at the Temple of Apollo, which had been spared, as had the South Stoa, but otherwise the city became little more than a village.

Julius Caesar began the rebuilding of Corinth in 46 B.C.E., the same year as his death; the **Emperor Augustus** continued his work. Caesar established the city as a Roman colony and populated it with freemen (both Italian and Greek), slaves, freedmen (ex-slaves), and some veterans from the legions. One estimate places the population of Corinth as one-third freemen, one-third slaves, and one-third freedmen. Freedmen were emancipated slaves, but they still owed certain duties to their former masters (presumably in gratitude for their release). Most freedmen were glad to have the opportunity to create a new life for themselves in a frontier city, where the distance from their former masters made further duties impossible and where their children would enjoy full citizenship. The majority of them took up lives as workmen, small merchants, or artisans. But since many freedmen had had extensive experience doing business for their former masters (it was considered unseemly for nobility to engage directly in business), some of them amassed fortunes and enjoyed newfound status in their new home.

Corinth soon became a fully Romanized city. Its language even became Latin, at least in official matters, until the end of the 1st century C.E., although the Greek language must have persisted among the common people. (Paul wrote to the Corinthians in Greek.) The Romans established it as the capital of Achaea, the Roman province of southern Greece, and Corinth once again became a thriving center for commerce and trade, the preeminent city in Greece. Construction activity was intense, especially under the emperors **Tiberius** (r. 14–37 C.E.) and **Claudius** (r. 41–54). At the height of its Roman period, Corinth overshadowed Athens. Some estimates place its population as high as 300,000 (Athenaeus, 2nd century C.E.; other estimates are lower). Within its walls it covered an area twice as large as Athens. But because fully a quarter of the city was covered with public buildings, its population density may have been as high as 200 persons per acre. If that is true, only modern industrial slums are so crowded. (Other estimates disagree and place the population at no more than 60,000. Thus far no definitive agreement has been reached.)

According to Dio Chrysostom (40–120 C.E.), **Diogenes** chose Corinth to propagate his philosophy because the city was situated at the crossroads of Greece, where "large numbers gathered" (*Discourses* 8.5). In those years its forum was crowded with merchants, philosophers, sailors, and travelers from every nation; many seeking cures, both physical and spiritual, visited its Asclepeion or one of its numerous temples on the slopes of the Acrocorinth. Later in the Roman period, gladiators fought in the odeion and theater, which had been converted for that spectacle, and even mock sea battles were conducted there. The Jewish philosopher Philo said that Corinth also had a significant Jewish population, although surprisingly few traces of that community remain. One lintel of a synagogue from the 4th century or later may be seen in the courtyard of the museum.

In the second century Corinth experienced renewed prosperity for a short time under the emperor **Hadrian**, but by 267 C.E. barbarians had overrun the city. Nevertheless, it survived that assault and subsequent destruction by the Goths under **Alaric** in 395 C.E. Corinth enjoyed a brief revival under **Justinian** in the 6th century, in spite of earthquakes that caused great damage in 522 and 551 C.E. The days of its glory, however, had passed, and a long decline ensued. Later centuries saw it ruled by the Franks (1212), Byzantines (1395), and others. The ruins visible today stem largely from the Roman period.

Biblical Significance

From the evidence in Acts, his two letters to the Corinthians, and the letter to the Romans, **Paul** made three visits to Corinth. The first resulted in the establishment of the church in Corinth (Acts 18:1–18; 1 Cor.15:1–2). He was accompanied on this initial visit by **Timothy** and **Silvanus** (**Silas**). Paul remained in Corinth for eighteen months and made his living as a leatherworker. Thanks to an inscription that was found at Delphi concerning **Gallio**, the Roman governor (proconsul) in Corinth, the dates for this visit can be established. Gallio seems to have taken office in July of 51 C.E. and served only one year. Since Paul was forced to appear before Gallio due to a complaint lodged against him by the Jewish synagogue in Corinth, he likely arrived there in early 50 C.E. and departed in late 51 or in 52 C.E.

His second visit was occasioned by conflict in the church and challenges to his leadership, as reported to him in Ephesus by "**Chloe's** people" (the household of a member of the church in Corinth). Their information caused Paul to make a brief visit that he later described as unpleasant and "painful" (2 Cor 2:1).

A promised third visit had to be postponed until the crisis with his critics had been resolved. This last visit finally occurred after reconciliation with the Corinthian church had been accomplished and the church had prepared an offering for the impoverished Christians in Jerusalem. Paul then went to Corinth, received the offering, and headed a delegation to take the contribution to Jerusalem (Rom 15:25–31). The dating of this third visit is uncertain but possibly took place in 55–56 C.E. After Paul left Corinth, he never again returned to Greece.

Archaeology has illuminated numerous references to the Corinthians in both Acts and the letters of Paul, as discussed below.

The Synagogue

When Paul first came to Corinth, he naturally sought out a **synagogue**, as was his custom, to begin his Christian evangelizing. Not far from the entrance structure (**propylaea**) to the forum/agora on the Lechaion Road, a **lintel stone** was found with crude lettering: "Synagogue of the Hebrews." Since stones were often scattered from their original location by later destruction and some were moved elsewhere to be used in new construction, it is by no means certain that the original synagogue was in this area. Furthermore, this lintel stone dates from three or more centuries after the time of Paul. However, the size of the stone suggests that it may not have been moved far from its original location, and new synagogues frequently were erected on the site of previous ones. Since we know Paul lived for a time in a house owned by a Gentile "worshiper of God," **Titius Justus**, which was adjacent to a synagogue, it is tempting to think of his residing somewhere in that vicinity. Corinth may have had more than one synagogue; **Crispus** and **Sosthenes** are both named in Acts as the "official" (*archisynagogos*) of a synagogue, but the relation between the two and the synagogue mentioned is unclear (Acts 18:8, 17).

Paul's Trade

All Jewish teachers of the Law (Torah) in the 1st century had a trade, and Paul was no exception (rabbis as such seem to have developed first in the late 1st or early 2nd century). He supported himself by the leatherworker's trade (1 Cor 4:12). Tents were made of leather, and even in the urban center of Corinth tents were in demand. Sailors in port frequently camped in tents rather than paying for accommodations on shore, and the thousands of visitors to the Isthmian Games often preferred tents to the limited and sometimes dubious inns of the day. Paul worked in a shop with a fellow Jew, **Aquila**, and lived with him and his wife, **Priscilla**, who had come from Italy after the edict of Claudius banishing some Jews from the city of Rome: "Paul went to see them, and, because he was of the same trade, he stayed with them, and they worked together—by trade they were tentmakers" (Acts 18:2–3).

The family that owned such a shop would have slept in a loft above the workshop, accessible from a wooden ladder at the rear of the shop, with a shuttered window above the front door. A hired worker, such as Paul, would have made his bed in the workroom. The work was hard. Ancient authorities agree that such artisans were forced to work seven days a week without holidays just to eke out a meager existence. Paul himself says, "We grow weary from the work of our own hands" (1 Cor 4:12). Furthermore, their status in society was extremely low. Writers such as Lucian (120 C.E.) called such workers "an abominable class of men, toiling from morning till night, doubled over their tasks" (*Fugitives* 227), and Cicero wrote, "Unbecoming to a gentleman, too, and vulgar are the means of livelihood of all hired workmen whom we pay for mere manual labor. And all artisans are engaged in vulgar trades, for no workshop can have anything liberal about it" (*On Duties* 1.150). Paul writes, "We have become like the rubbish of the world, the dregs of all things, to this very day" (1 Cor 4:13).

The forty-four shops in the North Market had been recently completed at that time, each of them approximately 9 to 12 feet wide, 12 feet deep, and 13 feet high. Their doorways (7.5 feet wide) provided the only source of light, so the sliding doors in front of the shops remained open during working hours. In the winter a brazier with hot coals had to be placed in the doorway to ward off the cold. It is easy to imagine Paul using such a shop to acquaint visitors and curious passersby with his message.

The Corinthian Congregation

A surprising amount of detail regarding the makeup of the Corinthian congregation may be gained from an understanding of the situation in Corinth. Paul said that not many of the new Christian church "were of noble birth" (1 Cor 1:26), but the new Roman city provided opportunities for those who were not of the nobility to acquire respectability and even wealth. It is apparent from 1 Corinthians that several members of the congregation had significant social status. **Erastus**, likely a Corinthian freedman who had made money in business, was the city treasurer, and he may also have been an aedile (an officer in charge of public works), one of the two highest city officials (Rom 16:23). **Crispus** and **Sosthenes** were rulers of the synagogue (Acts 18:8, 17), though it is not clear that Sosthenes was in fact a member of the congregation. **Crispus** and **Stephanas** owned homes (1 Cor 1:14, 16), and the house of **Gaius** was large enough for the whole congregation to meet there (1 Cor 1:14). **Phoebe**, a deacon of the nearby church at Cenchreae, is called a "benefactor" or "patron" of Paul and of the church as a whole (Rom 16:1–2). The same term was used for women who were significant and generous donors to the Greek and Roman temples. It was not uncommon for women to serve as officers in organizations in the Greco-Roman world. Jewish women frequently even served as "rulers of the synagogue." (However, it is a matter of debate whether the title actually represented the holding of an office or was merely honorific, or perhaps was first used to describe an officeholder and was later expanded to include any significant patron of the synagogue.)

No doubt the percentage of the congregation who were members of the upper class was low (1 Cor 1:26), and not many were wealthy. But they were not impoverished, either; all were expected to contribute to an offering for the poor in Jerusalem (1 Cor 16:2; 2 Cor 8:1–6). Nonetheless, the new church seems to have been guilty of the same social discrimination in their observance of the Lord's Supper as the Romans at banquets referred to by the Roman writers Pliny the Younger and Juvenal, where the wealthier guests were said to eat better food than the poorer guests and at different sittings. Paul wrote to the Corinthian church: "When you come together, it is not really to eat the Lord's supper. For when the time comes to eat, each of you goes ahead with your own supper, and one goes hungry and another becomes drunk. What! Do you not have homes to eat and drink in? Or do you show contempt for the church of God and humiliate those who have nothing?" (1 Cor 11:20–22).

Furthermore, the Romans customarily segregated their guests at banquets so that the more esteemed dined in the triclinium, where they could recline and dine on the finer foods and wines. The lesser guests ate poorer food (and often less of it) and drank cheap wine in the open atrium area. Pliny the Younger, on dining with a rich acquaintance:

> The best dishes were set in front of himself and a select few, and cheap scraps of food before the rest of the company. He had even put the wine into tiny little flasks, divided into three categories. . . . One lot was intended for himself and for us, another for his lesser friends (all his friends are graded) and the third for his and our freedmen. (*Letters* 2.6)

The Corinthian congregation usually met in small groups in private homes ("house churches"; "the church in the house of," 1 Cor 16:9), but occasionally they all met together ("the whole church," 1 Cor 14:23). Perhaps these individual meetings of smaller "cells" of the church may partly account for the partisan divisions so notorious in the Corinthian church: "Each one of you says, 'I belong to Paul,' or 'I belong to Apollos,' or 'I belong to Cephas' [Peter], or 'I belong to Christ'"(1 Cor 1:12).

Based on the size of the larger villas excavated in the vicinity of Corinth, no more than fifty persons could have gathered inside any one home, including the open atrium area. This would suggest that the total membership of the congregation at Corinth may have been little, if any, larger than fifty people, if indeed the "whole church" met sometimes at one house, such as that of **Gaius** (Rom 16:23).

The Body of Christ

Paul reminded the Corinthians that the church was the "body of Christ" and they were "members" of that body, each with valuable gifts, just as the several members of the human body have their own specialized functions and worth (1 Cor 12:12–27). In the museum at Corinth a curious collection of terra-cotta body parts can be seen, votive offerings dedicated at the Asclepeion in thanks for healing by Asclepius, Greek god of healing. Perhaps when Paul used the metaphor of the body he was thinking of the gratitude of those healed for each of the various parts of their bodies and the importance of each "member" to the functioning of the body as a whole.

Meat Offered to Idols

One particularly vexing problem for the young congregation was the question of meat offered to idols (1 Cor 8). During the great feast days so much meat was offered to the gods that the priests and the wealthy could not eat it all. The surplus therefore drove down the price of meat in the *macellum,* or meat market, providing the ordinary people a rare opportunity to obtain meat. Banquets were also given at such times in the dining rooms of the Asclepeion by guilds and social clubs, and also by the well-to-do: "Herais invites you to dine in the room of the Asclepeion at a banquet of the Lord Serapis tomorrow the 11th from the 9th hour" (*New Documents 1981* n. 52). For some in the church, termed by Paul "the strong," the matter was not a problem, as it was not to Paul himself. But to others, called "weak believers," to eat that meat was to engage in spiritual pollution. Paul says Christians may partake freely of the food without asking any questions. But if the host makes a point of saying it was meat from pagan sacrifice, the Christian should refuse it to avoid giving the wrong impression. Furthermore, if the faith of a weaker Christian would be harmed, the strong should not cause the destruction of that person's insecure faith by exercising their freedom to eat such meat. Love must be the controlling principle in the family of faith, the Body of Christ (1 Cor 8–11).

Athletic Metaphors

It was in his writings to the Corinthians that Paul first used athletic metaphors. In the years 49 and 51 C.E. the Isthmian Games were celebrated at Corinth, and it is possible that Paul attended them. (Jews in Palestine generally avoided such pagan events, but in Asia Minor that does not seem to have been the case. At Miletus, for example, Jews had their own reserved seats in the theater.) Certainly Paul was in a sports-mad environment. In 1 Corinthians he uses metaphors from boxing, wrestling, and running (1 Cor 9:24–28), and he refers to the "perishable crown" awarded to the winning athletes. At various times in the Isthmian Games the victor's wreaths were made of pine or wilted celery (certainly a "perishable" crown), in contrast to the fresh celery used at the Nemean Games.

This curious custom began in Nemea at funerary games in remembrance of the legend of Opheltes, son of Lycurgus, king of Nemea. An oracle had said that the infant would not grow up to be strong and healthy if he touched the ground before he learned to walk (the oracle never explained how this might be possible, of course). By accident, his nurse one day laid him on a clump of wild celery, whereupon he was fatally bitten by a giant snake. At Nemea the judges of the games wore black, and for a time at Isthmia the victor's crown was made of withered celery.

From an inscription found at Delphi it is evident that women also participated in these games in the Roman period. On the inscription from Delphi, a father celebrates the victories of his three daughters in the 200-meter races; one daughter even won the war chariot races. (No doubt such liberated conduct was part of the background of the controversy concerning appropriate behavior by women in this new age, as seen in 1 Cor 11:2–16.) The length of the 200-meter race, or the 1-stadium race, varied among the four sites for the Greek games: 178 meters at Delphi, 181.5 meters at Isthmia, 184.96 meters at the Panathenaic Games, and 192 meters at the Olympic Games.

Immorality at Corinth

Paul writes to counter problems in the church concerning immorality within the membership (1 Cor 5:1–6:20). This certainly was not the first time in ancient history that Corinth had been linked to immoral conduct. Beginning with the rivalry between Athens and Corinth in the 4th century B.C.E., Athenian writers enjoyed lampooning Corinthians as especially degraded. Plato and Aristophanes even coined words to designate acts of immorality using its name, and a stock figure in Greek theater was the drunk wearing the Corinthian hat.

In antiquity a temple to Aphrodite stood on the higher east peak of the Acrocorinth, and Strabo claimed that a thousand sacred prostitutes served there (*Geography* 8.6.20c). However, he had misunderstood an earlier reference to the women—mostly Corinthian matrons, but including prostitutes—who had entered the temple to pray during the wars with the Persians. Furthermore, no evidence of any structure large enough to accommodate so many people has ever been found on the Acrocorinth. Archaeological evidence found by the American School of Archaeology at Athens indicates that the Temple of Aphrodite was approximately 33 feet wide by 52 feet long, insufficient for such a number. Of course, Corinth was a port town and prostitutes were numerous. But sacred prostitution was not a practice among the Greeks, as it was in certain religions of the Near East, and Corinth was likely no more and no less immoral than other Greco-Roman cities—including Athens.

Site Visit

Ancient Corinth comprises three sites: the canal across the isthmus, the main site with its museum and Roman forum, and the fortifications and ruins atop the Acrocorinth.

The Canal

The first sight of interest for any visitor to ancient Corinth is the canal across the isthmus. The modern canal, completed in 1893, connects the Aegean Sea on the east with the Adriatic Sea on the west. The completed canal was about 3.5 miles long, 75 feet wide at the top, and 65 feet wide at the bottom. A portion of the **diolkos** (the roadway built to move cargo and small boats across the isthmus) near the Adriatic side has been uncovered and can be seen. The advantages of a canal were not lost on the ancient Greeks. Lacking the technology to accomplish such a feat, Periander built the *diolkos* in the 6th century B.C.E. A movable wooden platform ran along the roadway in grooves approximately four feet apart. Smaller vessels—generally

▲ **Fig. 15.** The canal at Corinth

military—could be loaded directly onto the platform, but heavily laden commercial ships had to be unloaded first and their cargo transported across the isthmus while the ships and their crews made the hazardous voyage around the Peloponnesus.

Later **Julius Caesar** intended to dig a canal, but his plans were cut short by his death. In 40 C.E. the emperor **Gaius** (**Caligula**) had similar intentions and sent his chief centurion to survey the site. He sought the opinion of Egyptian engineers, who declared that the level of the Corinthian gulf was higher than that of the Saronic and therefore cutting through the isthmus would result in flooding the whole of Greece.

In 67 C.E. **Nero** himself broke ground for a canal with a golden mattock handed to him by the governor of Greece, and the emperor insisted on carrying off the first basketload of earth on his own shoulders. (First, of course, he opened the proceedings by singing a pair of hymns to the gods, which was probably as painful to the laborers as the digging.) Josephus, the Jewish historian, says that after the revolt in Galilee **Vespasian** sent 6,000 of the strongest Jewish prisoners to Corinth "to dig through the isthmus." (No doubt many of these later settled in Corinth, expanding its Jewish population.) The work began on both sides and continued for three months. Digging, however, only proceeded through alluvial soil and could go no further when it hit granite bedrock. The work was halted when Nero encountered a revolt in the west and budget problems at home. The project was abandoned following his death. The *diolkos* would have been in use in Paul's day.

▲ **Fig. 16.** The Temple of Apollo (Archaic Temple) at Corinth

Main Site

Perhaps the best place to begin a visit of the city itself is at the interesting **museum of Corinth**, located at the northwest corner of the archaeological site. The museum consists of long galleries arranged around a central courtyard. The **Greek Gallery** to the right of the entrance hall contains finds from the Neolithic through Mycenaean periods. Note particularly a case of objects from the **Sanctuary of Demeter** and **Kore**; a **sphinx** (6th century B.C.E.), still showing traces of paint; tall **Mycenaean kylites** (slender, single-footed vessels; early 13th century B.C.E.); an **inscribed stone** (archaic Corinthian writing) that guarded the Sacred Spring in the agora: "Sanctuary boundary; do not come down. Fine, 8 drachmas"; and a **sarcophagus** containing the bones of a youth (5th century B.C.E.).

The **Roman and Post-Classical Gallery**, to the left of the entrance, principally displays sculptures and mosaics from the Roman period: a **statue of Augustus** as Pontifex Maximus, **mosaics** (2nd century C.E.) from a villa outside the northwest wall, and a Roman copy of a **statue of an athlete**. Other interesting objects include Attic vases, small altars, and a **copper mirror** with a representation of a woman with her hairdresser and slave. Note particularly the **head of Nero** (1st century C.E.). It is unusual in that his face shows a light beard, as if unshaven, a sign of mourning. Also a **head of Tyche** wearing the *polos,* a crown in the form of a city wall, is a fine example of the goddess of success and patron of cities. Perhaps the most spectacular finds from ancient Corinth are the two **monumental statues of barbarian slaves** that once adorned the Captives Façade facing the agora, just before the propylaea/entrance gate to the **Lechaion road**.

The **Asclepeion Room** (open on request) displays a curious collection of **body parts**, votive offerings to the god of healing, Asclepius. Whenever a sick person found healing for some part of the body, it was customary to dedicate a terra-cotta representation of the healed organ to Asclepius. The uniformity of these clay figures establishes that they were not made by the donors but purchased ready-made from local artisans. (The pairs of breasts likely do not signify healing from cancer or other ailments, but rather the answer to prayers for a successful pregnancy. The male organs likewise probably represent cures for impotence.) Cases about the wall contain jewelry and weapons from the Turkish period.

The enclosed **courtyard area** holds larger finds from the site: **friezes** from the theater (Hadrian's rebuilding) depicting scenes of Amazonomachy (legendary battles with the Amazons) and the labors of Hercules, a white **marble lintel** with the inscription "Synagogue of the Hebrews" (likely 4th century or later), and the **goddess Roma** and other statues from Temple E.

Corinth

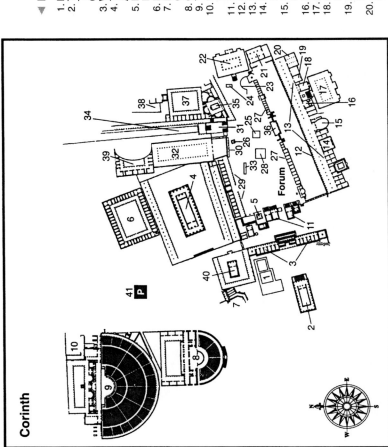

▼ **Fig. 17.** Corinth

1. Museum
2. Temple E/ Temple of Octavia
3. West Shops
4. Temple of Apollo
5. Babbius Monument
6. North Market
7. Fountain of Glauke
8. Odeion
9. Theater
10. Erastus Inscription
11. Roman Temples
12. South Stoa
13. South Shops
14. Duovir's Office (?)
15. Council Chamber
16. Fountain House
17. South Basilica
18. Governor's Office (?)
19. Director of the Games
20. Judges of the Games
21. Southeast Building
22. Julian Basilica
23. Curved Wall
24. Starting Line
25. Stone Platform
26. Statue of Athena
27. Central Shops
28. Altar
29. Northwest Shops
30. Captives Façade
31. Entrance Gate
32. North Basilica
33. Terrace Wall/ Sacred Spring
34. Lechaion Road
35. Fountain of Peirene
36. Bema
37. Precinct of Apollo/ Macellum
38. Baths
39. Semi-circular Building
40. Temple of Hera
41. Parking

Outside the museum and immediately to the right are the **foundations of Temple E**, also known as the **Temple of Octavia** (sister of Augustus). The temple was built on a podium with Corinthian columns. This may be the temple referred to by Pausanias that once held a statue of Octavia seated upon a throne.

Proceed directly on the path from Temple E to the **excavation site**. (En route, note the examples of the **three types of Greek columns**, Ionic, Doric, and Corinthian.)

Prominent on the elevated ground to the left is the 6th-century **Archaic Temple**, known also as the **Temple of Apollo**, which overlooks the forum to the south. Seven columns, approximately 24 feet high and 6 feet in diameter, remain standing of the thirty-eight Doric columns that surrounded the two rooms of the shrine. Originally an additional two rows of internal columns supported the roof. The temple was restored by the Romans in 44 B.C.E. Visible also to the north from this location are the ruins of the **North Market**, a series of shops built around a central peristyle courtyard. Earlier, a **Greek bathhouse** stood on this site.

To the west of the temple and on a lower level lies the **Fountain of Glauke,** supplied with water by a conduit from the Acrocorinth, virtually nothing of which remains except four reservoirs cut in the rock. It was named for the legendary daughter of a king of Corinth who threw herself into its waters to escape the flames of the magical robe sent her by Medea. Originally the fountain was covered by a building approximately 45 feet long and 40 feet wide. In the same direction, but across the road, lie the **odeion** and **theater**. The odeion (a small theater used for musical events), which held 3,000 spectators, was built by the Romans toward the end of the 1st century C.E. The theater dates from the 5th century B.C.E. and later was rebuilt by the Romans, who added a multistory stage building. In Paul's time it seated approximately 14,000 spectators. Both of these facilities were later used for gladiatorial spectacles; the theater was even fitted for mock sea battles.

In the **paved area** between the theater and the North Market area there is a feature of particular biblical interest. An **inscription**, formerly in bronze letters (all removed by looters except for two small punctuation marks), was set in gray Acrocorinthian limestone in the 1st century C.E. Only the outline remains: "**Erastus** in return for his aedileship [the post of a chief city official] laid [this pavement] at his own expense." In Romans 16:23 Paul mentions a city treasurer named Erastus. The name was not a common one, and it is quite possible that this inscription was made by the same person. If so, this is an important discovery, as it is only the second name of a person in the New Testament connected to the Christian movement yet found by archaeology; Sergius Paulus, governor of Cyprus and Paul's first convert on Cyprus, is the other. (Three more will be added to this list if the recently discovered inscription on

▲ **Fig. 18.** The Erastus inscription at Corinth

the "James ossuary"—"James, son of Joseph, brother of Jesus"—proves to refer to Jesus of Nazareth and his father and brother, which, however, seems unlikely at this time.)

Approximately 400 yards north of the theater lie the ruins of the **Asclepeion,** a shrine devoted to healing; here, typically, it is in a quieter area than the city itself. The location has splendid views of water and mountains with a good water source nearby (the **Spring of Lerna**), all regarded as important to healing. A small **Doric temple** stood in the center of a colonnaded court, over the site of an earlier temple to Apollo. Visitors entered the complex through a door in the east wall. Immediately to the left stood a small **water basin,** perhaps to hold some type of holy water. A long **altar** stood on the right, in front of the entrance to the temple; at its far end a **stone offering box** was discovered in which were copper coins. The **square holes** in the pavement on either side of the temple may have retained sacred serpents. (The serpent was regarded as a sign of healing because it shed its skin in renewal.)

At the west end of the temple square stood the **abaton building,** sleeping quarters and "hospital" for those who sought healing from the god Asclepius. To its left, steps descend into a small **pool** that served for ritual cleansing. This building had two levels, one at the level of the temple court and another below at the level of the **Lerna complex** that stood on lower ground than the temple. This lower story contained **dining rooms** with couches and tables. Apparently food was cooked on the blackened stones in the center of the rooms. Outside these rooms lay a colonnaded court that provided a shaded place for guests to stroll and get exercise. On the south side of the colonnade, in the face of the rock bluff it adjoins, were **draw basins** for water and steps that led down to the spring.

As early as the time of Augustus the Asclepeion also boasted a 6-foot-deep swimming pool, a short distance to the west, and banquets could be held in the facility by well-to-do citizens of Corinth, who must have used the place as a kind of local country club. The entire arrangement of the complex was designed as a place of rest and refreshment.

Once patients entered the abaton, they lay down on pallets in the darkened room and slept in a drugged state while waiting for healing from Asclepius. Those who were healed were expected to bring a votive offering to the temple. Apparently many regarded their treatment as successful. Excavators uncovered 10 cubic meters of life-size terra-cotta limbs and organs in the Asclepeion precinct.

The **Corinthian forum**, one of the largest in the ancient world (approximately 600 feet by 300 feet), does not seem to be the site of the earlier Greek agora. Only a racecourse, a possible viewing area, and various cult places have been identified from that period. An initial orientation to the forum is helpful before beginning to tour it.

The **west end** of the forum (in front of Temple E) was bounded by a monument and six small temples in front of shops. Pausanius refers to a fountain dedicated to Poseidon there also. The **east end** was dominated by the Julian Basilica. The **south side** was bounded by the South Stoa; the **north side** included the northwest shops, the Captives Façade, the entrance gates (propylaea), and a low terrace wall behind the Fountain of Peirene. In front of the South Stoa, and parallel with it, were the central shops, on either side of the bema (rostrum/tribunal platform). In the Roman period a large statue of Athena stood in the middle of the forum.

Little remains of the six original temples in the west end of the forum. The **Babbius Monument**, a circular structure of eight Corinthian columns supporting a conical roof, was erected by a self-congratulatory individual, Babbius Philinus, and dedicated to himself. Like Erastus, this man, also an aedile, probably was wealthy but not of noble birth (lack of a family name on the inscription, in the Roman custom, so indicates), a self-made freedman who had gained wealth in the new Roman colony. Paul may have had in mind such inscriptions as this when he wrote: "You yourselves are our letter, written on our hearts, to be known and read by all" (2 Cor 3:2).

The **South Stoa** was 500 feet long, the largest classical building in Greece and the longest stoa in the Roman Empire. The original Greek structure was built in the 4th century B.C.E. and contained a colonnaded row of thirty-three **shops**. Seventy-one Doric columns faced the agora, and another thirty-four Ionic columns stood in the center of the double colonnade. Each shop contained two rooms, and the front room of all but three of these had a well that was supplied from the Peirene system. These shops likely served as places of refreshment for visitors to the agora. **Stairs** at either end of the stoa led up to second-story rooms. At the west end of the stoa, **eight-foot walls** from the Greek period still remain, and a section of **roof** has been rebuilt using tiles found in the wells.

In the Roman period the rear of the stoa was remodeled to add **administrative offices**. Several of these rooms have been tentatively identified. Beginning at the west end are a square room, perhaps the **office of the duovir** (a chief city official); the **bouleuterion** (council chamber), with its curved stone benches; a **marble fountain**; then, behind the line of offices, the **South Basilica** (law courts); next in the line of offices, the **office of the Roman governor** (?), with marble floors and the base of a statue inscribed to another procurator; in the third room from the east end of the stoa, the **office of the agonothetes**, director of the Isthmian Games; a **mosaic of a victorious athlete** before the goddess of fortune, Eutychia (interestingly, wearing the wreath of wilted wild celery of a victor in the Isthmian Games, likely the "perishable crown" mentioned by Paul; the mosaic is under a shed but unfortunately not visible due to its protective covering of silt); then the **office of the judges of the games**. At the end of the stoa stood the **Southeast Building**, which possibly held the archives of the Roman colony.

The east end of the forum was enclosed by the **Julian Basilica**, dedicated to the Julia family of Caesars, and in which four imperial statues were found. In front of this building is the original **starting line of a Greek racecourse** with places for sixteen runners; in this vicinity also, a **curved wall**, possibly a viewing stand for judges. At the juncture of the Julian Basilica and the Southeast Building, a line of shops, known as the **Central Shops**, crossed the forum from east to west. In the center of this line stands the base of the **bema**, an elaborate ceremonial rostrum (none of the spectacular upper portions of the structure remain) used by Roman officials to address the public. Across from the bema is a **rectangular stone** where those stood who were brought before the tribunal. In the Middle Ages a small **Christian church** with three apses was built over this location, probably indicating the belief that Paul stood before the Roman governor **Gallio** at this location. (But see the notes on the North Basilica, below.) In the center of the forum area stood also an **altar** for public sacrifices.

A series of fifteen shops, the **Northwest Shops**, adjoined the temple area on the west end of the forum and the **Captives Façade** below them on the east (opposite the bema). The **vaulted structure** remaining today was used in later Christian times as a church. The Captives Façade was a two-story screen in front of a forecourt to the North Basilica; it also adjoined the **entrance gate** (propylaea) to the forum. This façade consisted of Corinthian columns that supported a second story of **monumental figures** of barbarian captives, two of which are in the museum. Next is the **propylaea**, a Roman triumphal arch that replaced an earlier Greek gate and bore two gilded bronze chariots in the time of Pausanius.

Beyond the propylaea, a low **terrace wall** with two openings, one of which leads down a stairway to the **Sacred Spring** (locked; opened with permission of the custodian). In the 5th century B.C.E. the spring was above ground and served by two lion's head spouts (one now in the museum). Later renovations to the area elevated the surrounding ground level. On the elevated ground beyond the terrace wall once stood a small **shrine** that was connected to the wall by a tunnel. The tunnel was entered through a secret door in the wall, apparently so a priest could deliver oracles through a hole in the floor of the shrine.

The road from the port of Lechaion entered the forum at the propylaea. Since steps led from the road to the propylaea, vehicles such as chariots and wagons were prevented from entering the forum. The 35-foot-wide **Lechaion Road** itself was paved in the 1st century C.E., as were its elevated **sidewalks**; **gutters** carried away rainwater. Immediately to the right is the **Fountain of Peirene**, perhaps the most impressive structure on the site. Rebuilt numerous times, this facility was erected over a natural spring. The Romans added the **open-air fountain** in the

▲ **Fig. 19.** Lechaion Road at Corinth, with the Acrocorinth in the background

▲ **Fig. 20.** The Fountain of Peirene at Corinth

45-foot-square courtyard and covered the walls of the courtyard with marble. In the 2nd century the **side walls** on the inside of the arched water chambers were painted dark blue and decorated with paintings of fish (see chamber 4).

Just beyond the fountain, on the same side of the road, is the **Peribolos of Apollo** (the precinct of Apollo), a large court once surrounded by a marble colonnade. The bronze statue of Apollo mentioned by Pausanias may have stood in the center. In Paul's day this precinct did not exist. At that time the space was occupied by the **macellum**, the meat and fish market mentioned by Paul in 1 Corinthians 10:25–26: "Eat whatever is sold in the meat market without raising any question on the grounds of conscience, for 'the earth and its fullness are the Lord's.'"

Remains of a large bath complex adjoin this area, perhaps the **Baths of Eurycles** described by Pausanias as the finest in Corinth; also nearby is a **public latrine**. Across the road, near the propylaea, are the foundations of the rectangular **North Basilica** (190 feet by 70 feet; 1st century C.E.). If Paul was called before Gallio in a formal hearing, likely he appeared in this building rather than at the bema. However, it is quite possible that the governor was hearing complaints at the public bema at the time of the incident reported in Acts 18:12–17:

> But when Gallio was proconsul of Achaia, the Jews made a united attack on Paul and brought him before the tribunal. They said, "This man is

persuading people to worship God in ways that are contrary to the law." Just as Paul was about to speak, Gallio said to the Jews, "If it were a matter of crime or serious villainy, I would be justified in accepting the complaint of you Jews, but since it is a matter of questions about words and names and your own law, see to it yourselves; I do not wish to be a judge of these matters." And he drove them all from the tribunal. And they all seized Sosthenes, the ruler of the synagogue, and beat him in front of the tribunal. But Gallio paid no attention to these things.

Beyond the North Basilica stood a **semicircular building** that replaced an earlier Roman market. At this point the Lechaion Road exits the site.

Acrocorinth

(A difficult two-hour walk from the archaeological site up a road that becomes steeper as it climbs; allow at least another hour and a half to visit. Fine view.) The most highly visible part of Corinth, if not the most

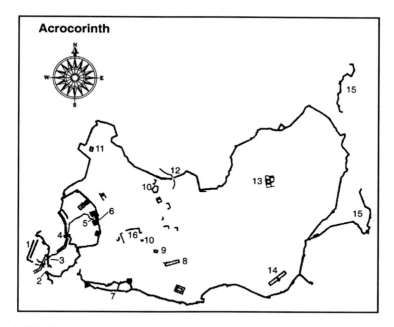

▲ **Fig. 21.** Acrocorinth

1. Venetian Moat
2. Graves
3. Gate 1
4. Gate 2
5. Gate 3
6. Hellenistic Tower
7. Frankish Castle
8. Store Room
9. Well
10. Mosque
11. Houses
12. Gate
13. Temple of Aphrodite
14. Spring of Peirene
15. Outer Fortifications
16. Byzantine Cistern

▲ **Fig. 22.** Defensive walls on the Acrocorinth

important, is the **Acrocorinth**. Typical of ancient cities, Corinth was located at the base of a mountain that could serve as a defensive stronghold in times of war. In Paul's day the road from Corinth to the summit passed temples to various Greek gods, as well as mystery cult sanctuaries to Isis, Demeter, Serapis, the Magna Mater, and others. The remains of the **Sanctuary to Demeter** can be seen on the lower slopes of the mountain, just below the road to the Acrocorinth.

Little from antiquity remains to be seen at the summit. Those interested in defensive fortifications will be interested in the Venetian-era **moat** and three successive **medieval walls** on the western slope with their **monumental gates**. To the right of the third gate is a **Hellenistic tower** over 35 feet tall that dates to the 4th–3rd century B.C.E. The most famous structure on the Acrocorinth in antiquity was the world-renowned **Temple of Aphrodite**, which stood at the summit of the mountain. Nothing of the temple remains except for some cuttings in the rock that were the footings for the foundation of the temple, and a few large stones that were used in later construction projects but are believed by some authorities to date to the original sanctuary.

Just below the temple, on the south side of the hill, flowed the **Upper Peirene Spring**. A pool can still be seen there within a **well house**; its concrete roof is modern but the barrel-vaulted inner ceiling dates to the Hellenistic period (3rd century B.C.E.). The cold (but undrinkable) water is never less than 10–12 feet deep. The ancient graffiti on the walls were left by marble workers in memory of relatives and friends.

Later invaders built a variety of buildings on the summit, the ruins of which remain, including a **Frankish stronghold** with its walls and tower, a **Byzantine cistern**, two **mosques**, and a few dwellings and storage buildings.

Cos

Cos, home of Hippocrates, the father of modern medicine, is the third largest island of the Dodecanese (Twelve Islands). In antiquity its population was 120,000, eight times that of today. Its fame derived from the renowned Asclepeion of Cos, a healing center and religious shrine devoted to Asclepius, the god of healing. Tourists still come to marvel at this spectacular architectural structure, and international medical conferences are conducted on the island in memory of Hippocrates.

Location and History

Cos (also spelled Kos) lies only 3 miles off the coast of Turkey, near the Bodrum peninsula. Connections are available to the Turkish mainland by ferry, and a fascinating circuit of biblical sites can be made from Athens through the Greek islands to Cos and then up the western coast of Turkey for a departure from Istanbul. Access to Cos by air is available from Athens (three flights daily), or by ferry from Piraeus, Rhodes, or Thessaloniki through Samos. Hydrofoils are available from Rhodes and Samos for faster trips. (Always check ferry and hydrofoil schedules closely; frequent and erratic changes occur, particularly with hydrofoils in the event of high winds.)

Cos was settled by the Mycenaeans in 1425 B.C.E., and Homer described it

▲ **Fig. 23.** Asclepius in the National Archaeological Museum, Athens

as heavily populated (*Iliad* 14:225). Pliny referred to it as a major shipping port (*Natural History* 15:18). Among its exports were wine, purple dye, and elegant, diaphanous fabrics of silk (raw silk; pure silk from the Orient did not reach the west until the 3rd century C.E.). Aristotle wrote that silk fabric was invented on the island of Cos: "A class of women unwind and reel off the cocoons of these creatures [caterpillars] and afterward weave a fabric with the thread thus unwound; a Koan woman by the name of Pamphila, daughter of Plateus, being credited with the first invention of the fabric" (*The History of Animals* 5.19).

Cos reached the pinnacle of its prosperity and power in the 7th and 6th centuries B.C.E., but by the end of the 6th century B.C.E. it had come under the control of Persia. When the Persians were defeated by the Greeks in 480 B.C.E., Cos entered a series of alliances with the Athenians and the Spartans. By alternating its allegiance between these powerful enemies, Cos was able to survive, but not without frequent wars and subjugation. In 309 B.C.E. **Ptolemy Soter I**, ruler of Egypt and one of the successors to Alexander the Great, spent the winter at Cos. His wife, **Veronica**, gave birth there to a son, **Ptolemy II Philadelphus**, and subsequently Cos enjoyed close relations with Egypt through many centuries.

The Romans later took control of Cos, and it became part of the eastern province of the Roman Empire. **Herod the Great** of Judea spent considerable time at Cos and made gifts to the Asclepeion. In 32 B.C.E. the emperor **Tiberius** granted the right of asylum to the Asclepeion of Cos. Later Cos, along with all of the Roman Empire, was forced by the powerful cult of emperor worship to make sacrifices to the emperors as gods and erect temples in their honor.

During the Christian era Cos developed one of the strongest Christian communities in the Greek islands. After the time of Constantine the Great, it became part of the Byzantine Empire, but over the next nine hundred years Cos passed through the hands of the Goths, the Slavs, the Saracens, the Normans, the Venetians, and the Genoans. In 1315 C.E. the island came under the control of the Knights of the Order of St. John of Jerusalem. **Sulëyman the Magnificent** seized Cos after months of intense siege and for the next four hundred years the Turks ruled the island. In modern times the Italians "liberated" Cos from Turkey, and after World War I it remained under the control of the Italian fascist regime. In World War II the Germans occupied the island until the end of the war, but in 1948 Cos was reunited with Greece.

Biblical Significance

The island of Cos is mentioned only once in the Bible. As **Paul** was returning to Jerusalem from his third and final missionary journey, he sailed from Miletus in Asia Minor to Cos, and from there to Rhodes. According to Acts 2:11, Paul spent one night at Cos: "When we had parted from them and set sail, we came by a straight course to Cos, and the next day to Rhodes, and from there to Patara."

In the case of Rhodes, it is uncertain whether Paul spent any time at the island, but the text is clear that Paul's ship overnighted at Cos. Nothing is said about Paul visiting the island but, depending on the time of arriving and departing, he might well have done so. Undoubtedly he would have known of the famous Asclepeion of Cos and its most renowned student and teacher, **Hippocrates**, and might have wished to view it. At the very least, certainly he would have taken opportunity to leave the cramped quarters of the ship for the pleasant harbor and small city of Cos, if only for a brief time.

It is not unreasonable, either, that he may have spent the night on shore. The tentmaking trade, at least in the Greco-Roman world, depended upon sailors for a significant portion of its business. Tired of the confines of their ship and often unwilling to spend time in the dirty and notoriously dangerous inns of the port towns, sailors generally owned tents and used them for camping on shore when they were in port. As someone who earned his living by leatherwork and tentmaking, it is quite possible that Paul owned a tent and used it for sleeping accommodations on shore, when necessary, on his lengthy sea voyages. Nothing further is said in the text, however, about other events or visits on Cos. Typically, local traditions say that Paul won converts on the island and founded the Christian movement there.

Site Visit

The antiquities of Cos are located in two areas. Various Greco-Roman ruins are located in the vicinity of the city of Cos, and its famous Asclepeion is at the top of a hill approximately 2 miles outside of town. The city also has a fine archaeological museum.

City Archaeological Sites

South of the castle in the **Plateia Platanou** (Plane Tree Square) stands the famous **Hippocrates Plane Tree**, reputed to be the very tree under which the great physician Hippocrates (460–370 B.C.E.) taught his pupils. The tree may be the oldest in Europe (perhaps over two hundred years old), but at best it is only a recent descendant of the original.

South of the tree is the ancient **agora** of Cos. It is pleasant to stroll through the extensive site (500 feet by 250 feet), but the ruins are confusing and poorly marked. This agora was constructed during the Hellenistic period (366 B.C.E.), and its principal monuments include, on the north side, the remains of the large **Temple of Hercules**, the **sanctuary of Venus**, and the **Great Basilica** (5th century C.E.).

To make a circuit of the antiquities of Cos town, exit the agora on the west side, turn left, and walk south on Vasileos Pavlou to Grigoriou. To the left are the scant ruins of the **Temple and Altar of Dionysus** (3rd century B.C.E.), and diagonally across from this site is the **Casa Romana**. This villa, discovered in 1933 by Italian archaeologists, dates from the 3rd century C.E. and was built on the ruins of an earlier Hellenistic house. The house comprises three large courtyards surrounded by adjacent rooms. Each of the courtyards, or atria, contains **mosaics**: the first atrium has a floor mosaic depicting a lion attacking a wild goat and a leopard attacking a deer, and an adjacent room has a mosaic of aquatic creatures. The second atrium contains a **pool** in its center, surrounded by a mosaic of dolphins and a water spirit. The third atrium is the largest and is surrounded by a double row of columns supporting a balcony. Other rooms in this large and impressive house contain **wall murals** and floor mosaics.

Proceed west down Grigoriou to the next area of extensive ruins. On the right are wooden shelters that cover **mosaics** from the ruins of the **Europa House**, named for its mosaic depicting the abduction of Europa by Zeus in the guise of a bull (3rd century C.E.). It was here that the **statues of Asclepius, Hygieia**, and others now in the Cos Archaeological Museum were discovered.

In this location a section of the principal Roman road of the city, the **decumanus maximus**, is clearly visible and runs parallel to the modern street. This paved road leads past the ruins of a **Christian basilica** and the **western baths**, distinguished by portions of a domed chamber that covered an enormous **mosaic**. Across Grigoriou to the south is the largely reconstructed **odeion**, or music theater, small but beautiful. In the basilica on the north is the so-called **nymphaeum**. The structure is elaborate enough to have been a decorative fountain, as it was long believed, but in fact it was the **public latrine** of Roman times. Its eleven columns and walls to the height of 5 feet show something of its former elegance. The last of the notable antiquities in this area are the spectacular remains of the **Hellenistic Gymnasium Xysto**, distinguished by the seventeen columns remaining from the original eighty of the structure. (The gymnasium derived its name from the tool, the *xystos*, used by athletes to scrape off the oil used to anoint their bodies prior to exercise or competition; later, *xystos* referred to a gymnasium for adult men.)

Go north on Tsaldari toward the harbor to complete this circuit of the antiquities of Cos. Turn right on Martiou; on the right is a complex of **Greco-Roman baths**, some as early as the 4th century B.C.E. Two blocks farther ahead on the left is the **Cos Archaeological Museum.**

The museum is located in Eleftheria Plaza and contains three large galleries. Among the outstanding items in this well-designed museum

▲ **Fig. 24.** Mosaic of Hippocrates and a citizen of Cos welcoming Asclepius to the island, 2nd–3rd century C.E. (Archaeological Museum, Cos)

are a superb **floor mosaic** of Hippocrates and a citizen of Cos welcoming the god Asclepius, who is descending from a boat (2nd–3rd century C.E.); statues from the Europa House; a **statue of Hermes**, seated; a **head of the emperor Trajan**; a fine **statue of Hippocrates**; a colossal **head of Hercules**; and a **relief of a banquet scene** from the 6th century B.C.E.

Asclepeion of Cos

By far the most striking and notable antiquity on the island is the Asclepeion of Cos, dramatically located on a hill southwest of the town. City buses run frequently to the site. (To reach the bus station, walk south on Vasileos Pavlou; turn right at the Olympic Airways office.) This location affords a spectacular view of the city and the southern shoreline of Turkey.

Unlike the other healing shrines to the god Asclepius in Greece and Asia Minor, which were numerous—at least three hundred such shrines existed in antiquity, all of which employed drugs and suggestion to effect psychosomatic cures—the Asclepeion at Cos used the scientific methodology of its time. The greatest of the physicians of Cos was the renowned **Hippocrates**, who both studied and taught at the institution. Some of the techniques of Hippocrates predated their later "discovery" by modern medicine. His fame continues worldwide through his oath of fidelity to the practice of medicine, the "Hippocratic oath," still used today by modern physicians.

The construction of the sanctuary spanned four centuries and occurred in three phases, beginning in the 3rd century B.C.E. The design of the structure, featuring **three ascending terraces**, seems to have been influenced by the Oriental styles popularized by the eastern campaign of Alexander the Great. A monumental **marble stairway**, more than 40 feet wide in some sections, links the three terraces. Much of the stairway has been restored, but portions of the original are still in place.

The first ruins at the ground level on the approach to the Asclepeion are remnants of **Roman baths** from the 1st century C.E. Above this level the first terrace is reached by twenty-four steps. Here were located the **healing center** and **school of medicine**. Patients likely were treated within the rooms around the circumference of the walls. At the southern end of the terrace, the massive **retaining wall** for the second level contains a **fountain** and **water troughs** fed from springs. A **statue of Pan** stands in a niche to the left of the steps; to the right, an **inscription** on a statue base refers to one of the famous physicians of the Asclepeion, **Xenophon**. (Actually, he was remembered primarily for his financial help in restoring the sanctuary after an earthquake, decorating it with statues he brought from Rome, and establishing a medical library on the site. As a physician, his principal claim to fame was assisting the **wife of the emperor Claudius** in poisoning him. So much for the Hippocratic oath.) On the east side of the terrace are remains of **baths** from the 3rd century C.E. (known as the **Thermes**). To the left of the entrance to this terrace and about the walls are five **underground, windowless rooms**, the use of which is uncertain.

▲ **Fig. 25.** Remaining columns of the Temple to Apollo, second level of the Asclepeion at Cos

▲ **Fig. 26.** Overview of the Asclepeion at Cos from the third level

Above the retaining wall on the second terrace is the **Sacred Area**, reached by thirty steps, originally dominated by the large **Altar of Asclepius**. This structure had various incarnations, the most famous of which was the altar built in the 2nd century B.C.E. that copied the Great Altar of Zeus in Pergamum. Behind the altar area are the ruins of a **Roman temple**; a curved **stone seat** is still in place. On the western side of the terrace are the remains of the oldest **Temple of Asclepius** (4th century B.C.E.), with a few remaining columns. It once contained a painting of Aphrodite rising from the sea by **Apelles**, a famous painter of the 4th century B.C.E. This painting was among the art treasures taken to Rome by the emperor **Augustus**. Also on the west was a **small temple** to the emperor **Nero**. To the east stand the remains of the 2nd-century-B.C.E. **temple to Apollo**, marked by seven columns that have been restored. Other structures at this level included a few **houses for priests** and the **Treasury** of the temple.

The third terrace is reached by the **longest of the staircases** (sixty steps); it once held the greatest of the temples to Asclepius (2nd century B.C.E.). Originally surrounded by 104 columns, this **Doric-style temple** was more than 100 feet long and 50 feet wide and held the **cult statue of Asclepius** and his daughter, **Hygieia**. Little remains of this great temple today except the foundation and marble floor. A stone **portico** surrounded the terrace on three sides (2nd century C.E.), which replaced a former wooden structure.

The Asclepeion of Cos remained a center for healing until 554 C.E. Typical of most ancient sites, over the centuries the Asclepeion was stripped of most of its stones and monuments, and the Knights of St. John even used the area as a quarry.

Crete

Crete is the largest and most southerly of all the Greek islands. It is also one of the most visited, due to both its beauty and its famous ancient sites. By far the best-known of these attractions is the spectacular Palace of Knossos, reconstructed over a period of thirty-five years by its discoverer, Sir Arthur Evans, who put more than a million dollars of his own money into the work. Scholars have criticized his reconstruction as a fanciful and not altogether accurate representation of the original, but millions of tourists delight in being able to see more at an ancient site than foundations, scattered stones, and a few columns.

But Knossos is not the only dramatic ruin of antiquity on the island. Gortyna and Phaistos should not be missed, and for Christians the harbor of Kaloi Limenes (called Fair Havens in the New Testament) is a place of importance in the life of the Apostle Paul. Likewise, the Basilica of St. Titus at Gortyna commemorates the ministry of Titus, a Greek convert who was a disciple of Paul (Gal 2:3), as described in the New Testament book of Titus. Furthermore, Iraklion possesses an archaeological museum second only to the National Museum in Athens.

Location and History

The only site on Crete mentioned in the Bible, though Crete itself was said to be the place of the ministry of **Titus** (Titus 1:5), is the harbor of **Kaloi Limenes** (Good Harbor), referred to in the Book of Acts as Fair Havens (Acts 27: 8). After two thousand years, the site is known by the same name today. Even in New Testament times the place was distinguished only as the harbor for the nearby city of Lasea, a flourishing commercial city in the Roman period. Today the tranquil bay in its remote location harbors nothing more than sunbathers who visit its beaches to enjoy the beautiful waters of the Mediterranean. The site can be reached best by automobile, or by taking a bus from Iraklion to Moires/Mires. (Bus station B, approximately two hours, eight buses daily; take the same bus that goes to Gortyna and Phaistos.) Beyond Mires, unless a new bus schedule has been implemented, it will be necessary to travel south by taxi to Kaloi Limenes (inquire at bus station B). Ask the driver before he is hired if he will wait for you there; a half hour is ample time. (Request a driver who speaks at least a few words of English, if possible, and always get the fare negotiated and written on a slip of paper before you go.) A day trip by bus and taxi can easily make the loop from Iraklion to Gortyna to Phaistos.

▲ **Fig. 27.** Fair Havens (Kaloi Limenes) on Crete

Biblical Significance

Paul's visit to Kaloi Limenes was entirely accidental. As he was being transported as a Roman prisoner from Caesarea to Rome, the ship encountered strong headwinds, and it was only with great difficulty that they were able to put in at Kaloi Limenes (probably 59 or 60 C.E.). How long they remained at Kaloi Limenes is uncertain, but the text implies that it must have been several days. Paul advised them to remain there for safety, as they were already entering the time when all sailing on the Mediterranean virtually ceased for the winter. The owner of the ship and its captain, however, decided it would be safer to winter at the port of Phoenix, farther along the coast to the northwest, because it offered more shelter from the prevailing winds of winter. (The location of Phoenix has been much debated by scholars. Both Lutro and Phineka, which retains something of the ancient name, have been identified.)

This proved to be a disastrous experience. As soon as they rounded the sheltering cape to the west, a fierce wind from the north drove them away from Crete toward Cauda, a small, virtually uninhabited island (even today only a few fisherman live there), the southernmost part of Greece and indeed, of Europe itself (Acts 27:1–16). They were not able to make port there, either, and eventually were driven aimlessly by the winds until their ship ran aground and wrecked upon Malta. No lives, however, were lost (Acts 27:43).

▲ **Fig. 28.** Palace at Knossos on Crete

Site Visit

Other than the beautiful **harbor** itself, there is little to see at Kaloi Limenes. On the hill above the bay, there is a small white **chapel** dedicated to Paul that is built on top of the ruins of an older church. This vantage point affords a magnificent view of the entire bay and coastline to the east (marred, unfortunately, by a row of modern storage tanks built on the largest island of the bay). A short distance below the chapel to the west is a **cave** where local legend has it the apostle stayed while at Kaloi Limenes.

Other Sites of Interest

Since **Knossos** is not a biblical site, it is included only as a nearby place of interest. (It does, however, have an indirect connection because of the possible relation between the Mycenaean invaders who once lived there and the biblical Philistines.) Nonetheless, it is placed first both because it is the site nearest to Iraklion and therefore most likely to be visited first and because the Minoan culture it represents was the predecessor of all the later cultures that developed. Knossos is only 3 miles south of Iraklion and is easily reached by either automobile or bus. Buses run every 10 minutes from either bus station A or two bus stops on Avgoustou Street (take bus no. 2).

The site at Knossos was first occupied in the Neolithic Age (6000 B.C.E.). But it was during the Bronze Age (2800–1100 B.C.E.) that Knossos and the Minoan civilization reached their pinnacle of cultural brilliance. The original palace, built around 1900 B.C.E., was destroyed by an earthquake in 1700 B.C.E. A new palace was built shortly thereafter that occupied approximately 5.5 acres. The Minoan culture has become renowned in modern times for its colorful and elaborate frescoes portraying, among other things, "bull leaping" (believed to have been either a sport or a religious ritual in which both young men and women vaulted over the back of bulls, although in recent times some scholars have argued that such portrayals were only fanciful rather than literal representations). Famous legends from Knossos also caught the imagination of people worldwide, such as the adventures of King Minos and the Minotaur (the mythical beast imprisoned in the labyrinth to whom victims must be sacrificed), and the flight of Daedalus and his son, Icarus, with the subsequent death of Icarus when the wax on his wings melted because he flew too near the sun.

The indigenous Minoan civilization was supplanted by Mycenaean invaders from mainland Greece sometime after 1450 B.C.E., though they continued to use the palace and to make additions to it. It is believed that this warlike culture formed part of the subsequent group known as the "Sea Peoples" that attempted to invade Egypt, were repulsed by Ramses III, and settled instead along the southern coast of Israel. These people became famous in the Bible as the Philistines, against whom both kings **Saul** and **David** fought. Around 1300 B.C.E. a devastating fire completely destroyed the palace, bringing to an end the era of the magnificent Palace of Knossos. For approximately a thousand years thereafter, the city-state of Knossos continued to the north and west of the area of the palace. It remained as the largest and most powerful of the Cretan cities until the Roman period, when its opposition to the Romans caused it to be replaced by Gortyna as the leading city and the seat of government in 67 B.C.E. In later centuries, along with mainland Greece, the area endured the occupation of a series of invaders including, in the 20th century, the Germans (1941), who made their headquarters in the nearby Villa Ariadne, originally built to serve as the central office of the Archaeological Mission of Knossos.

The restored **Palace of Knossos** today is too complex to summarize briefly. However, the area is readily navigated and most of the major attractions are easily identifiable. In addition to the colorful buildings and frescoes (the originals of which are in the **Archaeological Museum of Iraklion**), be sure to notice the **throne room** with its guarding **griffins**, which may have been a shrine for the **high priestess**; the **Queen's**

Chamber with its own bathroom, complete with terra-cotta bathtub and what is said to be the first flush toilet; the enormous pithoi, jars that held stores of grain, wine, and olive oil; and, throughout the buildings, the sophisticated system of windows and light wells for ventilation and light.

The archaeological site of Gortyna (also known as Gortyn and Gortys) is approximately 30 miles southwest of Iraklion. It can be reached by bus from bus station B on the same bus route that goes to Phaistos (approximately two hours, with eight buses daily; Phaistos is approximately 9 miles farther to the west, past Mires). Allow approximately one hour for viewing.

Gortyna is the largest archaeological site in Crete. Homer (*Iliad* 645) said it was famous for its walls, and Strabo (*Geography* 10.4.11) called it second only to Knossos in power. In the 2nd century C.E. the perimeter of the city was approximately 6 miles long, and its population at that time has been estimated at between 75,000 and 100,000 inhabitants. Throughout Roman imperial times Gortyna was the political center and chief city of Crete. Although the New Testament does not refer to the city, it is mentioned in the Apocrypha (1 Macc 15:23), where Gortyna is listed as one of the recipients of a letter from the Roman consul Lucius requesting Jews to support the high priest Simon and demanding extradition for any Jew who has taken refuge from him in any of those cities. The letter suggests that a Jewish community with frequent commerce between Crete and Judea must have existed at that time in Gortyna. This may explain the tradition, preserved in the Basilica of St. Titus, that Gortyna was the center of the ministry of Paul's disciple, Titus.

The site lies on both sides of the highway to Mires, though the most-visited remains are on the north side. These include the Hellenistic-Roman odeion, the Great Inscription, the Basilica of St. Titus, the amphitheater, and the acropolis. Of these, the Basilica of St. Titus and the Great Inscription in the odeion are by far the most significant and deserve further description.

▲ Fig. 29. Painting of St. Titus in the Basilica of St. Titus, Gortyna, Crete

The church known as the Basilica of St. Titus dates from the 6th century C.E., although local tradition says that it stands upon the spot where Titus was martyred. (No historical reference exists, however, concerning the death of Titus). The church was once covered with a vaulted roof and entirely constructed of ashlar stones. One remaining wall holds a modern **painting** of the **Apostle Titus**.

The odeion with the Great Inscription upon its north wall dates from the 1st century C.E., but it is built over the site of an earlier **Hellenistic building** whose walls originally held the ancient inscription (500 B.C.E.). The odeion itself is unremarkable, but the law code of the Great Inscription is world-renowned. Although only 108 lines remain from the original 624 lines in the inscription, they are enough to reveal a complete system of laws dating from the Minoan era. The inscription is written in the ancient Doric dialect, each line of which alternates left to right, then right to left; this is known as "boustrophedon" style, or as the ox plows each row in the fields, back and forth. Later Greek cities based much of their own law systems upon this comprehensive code that included regulations for trade, family law, and personal rights.

The ruins on the **south side** of the highway cover an enormous area, and those parallel to the road can be readily explored; if the visitor has ample time, wandering farther south across the Mesara plains and through the pleasant groves will give a good idea of the great size of Gortyna in the Roman Age. The most notable of these ruins include the **Praetorium**, the **Sanctuary of the Egyptian Gods**, the **Temple of Apollo**, and, farther south, the **amphitheater**, the **large Roman baths**, and the **hippodrome** (farthest south, and poorly preserved). All of these are interesting, but if time is limited, a brief visit to the **Praetorium** will give an impression of this powerful seat of government and location of the residence of the Roman governor of Crete. The present ruins date mostly to the 4th century C.E., though some are as early as the 2nd century C.E. Just east of the Praetorium is a **small bath complex**, probably used by the Roman proconsul.

The spectacular ruins at **Phaistos** are second only to Knossos as an ancient archaeological site on Crete. From the pleasant restaurant terrace on the hill above, the remains of the great **Minoan palace** sprawl across an extensive area. Phaistos dominated the plains of Mesara, the most fertile area of Crete. The first palace at Phaistos was built around 2000 B.C.E. and rebuilt in 1700 B.C.E. after it was destroyed by a series of devastating earthquakes. Initially Phaistos seems to have existed as an independent city-state, but following 1700 B.C.E. it came under the rule of Knossos. All of the Minoan palaces were destroyed around 1450 B.C.E. by earthquakes that shook the whole island. Phaistos continued as an important center until approximately 200 B.C.E., when it was invaded and destroyed by neighboring Gortyna, the new power in the region.

The palace area is dominated by a **monumental staircase** and a series of three **courtyards**, arranged on varying levels. **Storerooms,**

silos, large storage jars decorated with ropes and medallions, various **sitting rooms** with benches, and the **Royal Quarters** make this one of the most fascinating archaeological sites in all of Greece. Perhaps the most intriguing object discovered at Phaistos is the mysterious **Phaistos disk,** replicas of which are on sale in every tourist shop in Crete. Hieroglyphic symbols, which some scholars have surmised are perhaps a hymn or prayer, are arranged in a spiral pattern on the face of the clay disk. Despite repeated efforts, however, the symbols have never been translated.

Although it bears no direct connection, so far as we know, to any biblical reference, Phaistos should be on every traveler's itinerary in Crete.

The **Archaeological Museum of Iraklion**, regarded as the second finest in all of Greece, should not be missed. Twenty galleries contain countless treasures from the Neolithic Age to the Roman period and feature magnificent finds from the Minoan palaces. Among the most notable objects: Neolithic figurines and models of boats and carts, the **"Town Mosaic"** from the Palace of Knossos depicting the façades of houses, the famous **Phaistos disk**, cult vessels and artifacts, the **"Snake Goddess"** (since snakes came from beneath the ground, they were believed to be connected with the underworld, perhaps as messengers), elaborate gold jewelry, a unique **clay model of a Minoan house,** ivory objects, a colorful **fresco** found at the Palace of Knossos depicting **acrobats performing bull leaping,** a spectacular **bull's head with golden horns,** a **rock-crystal rhyton** (libation vessel) carved from a single block of rock crystal with a handle of crystal beads strung on a bronze wire, a **clay fruitstand** colorfully decorated with spiral patterns, a **gold signet ring** depicting women in an ecstatic dance, and magnificent frescoes and carved objects.

Mitylene

The beautiful island of Mitylene, known also as Lesvos or Lesbos, serves only as a footnote in the biblical account of the journeys of the Apostle Paul, but its fine museums and splendid scenery make it well worth including in visits to the Greek islands. Noted since antiquity as a place of unusual warmth and sunshine, even in winter, this third largest of the Greek islands produces the finest olive oil in all of Greece. The interior of the island is mountainous and forested, and the northern side of the island, around picturesque Methymna, provides excellent beaches.

Location and History

Mitylene (also the name of the capital city) lies less than 10 miles off the Turkish coast. It can be reached by flights from Athens and Thessaloniki (approximately one hour); ferries also run from these ports, but the crossing time is 9–12 hours. There is a ferry that connects the island to Ayvalik, Turkey; Pergamum is only 35 miles inland.

   Until the 6th century B.C.E., when **Pitticus**, one of the Seven Sages of Greece, served as sole ruler of the island (r. 589–579 B.C.E.), the towns of Mitylene and Methymna struggled for dominance of the island. During this time Mitylene developed a strong maritime fleet, extended its commerce as far as Egypt, and achieved fame for its notable poets, **Alcaeus** and **Sappho** (6th century B.C.E.). The poetry of Sappho was greatly admired by both Solon and Plato, who called her the tenth Muse. An aristocrat who established a school for women at Mitylene, Sappho became world-famous, or infamous, because of her love poetry concerning women. Much of the ridicule directed toward her came from the Athenian comic poets, who lampooned the greater freedom given to women on Mitylene. In the 4th century B.C.E., the famous philosophers **Aristotle** and **Epicurus** both taught on Mitylene. **Julius Caesar** first won distinction as a military commander when the Romans invaded the island in the 1st century B.C.E.

   Over the following centuries the island suffered repeated invasions by one world power after another until 1462, when it was taken by the Turks, who retained possession of it until 1912. German forces occupied the island between 1941 and 1944.

▲ **Fig. 30.** Sappho, the famed poet of Mitylene

Biblical Significance

Mitylene is mentioned only once in the New Testament (Acts 20:14–15): "When he [Paul] met us in Assos, we took him on board and went to Mitylene. We sailed from there, and on the following day we arrived opposite Chios." This incidence occurred on the **Apostle Paul's** third and last missionary journey as he was returning to Jerusalem from his final visit to Greece. Paul's companions had left Philippi before him and

▲ **Fig. 31.** The north harbor at Mitylene where Paul's ship landed

were waiting at Troas, where they stayed for seven days. Paul then went by land, for some reason, to Assos while his friends came by boat. Paul joined them on board and they sailed approximately 45 miles to Mitylene, where they docked at the present-day northern harbor, site of the ancient harbor, and not at the prominent southern harbor around which the modern city lies. (In ancient times a canal joined the two harbors.)

It is uncertain whether Paul actually set foot on the island. The text seems to imply that the ship stayed at Mitylene overnight, in which case it is probable that he did go ashore. As a tentmaker, Paul might have chosen to camp on shore in his own tent, as did most sailors, rather than sleep in the tight confines of the ship or in the notoriously disreputable, dirty, and frequently dangerous inns of the time. There are no other incidents in Mitylene regarding Paul and his companions mentioned in the text.

Site Visit

The only site on Mitylene pertaining to the Bible is the **northern harbor** (no longer in use), where Paul and his companions landed. The best view of the ancient port site is probably attained from the hill where the **castle** is located. Portions of the **ancient jetty** are still visible underwater. Only scattered fragments remain of other structures that once surrounded the port.

The castle is generally regarded as Venetian because it was first mentioned in a Venetian document of 1260, but some sections may date to the time of the emperor **Justinian**. Some remains of a **sanctuary of Demeter** have been found in the outer courtyard of the castle. The castle hill also provides an excellent view of nearby Turkey.

Slightly over a mile to the west of the castle, on the highest point in town, lie the ruins of the **ancient theater** (Hellenistic period; renovated during the Roman period), which may have seated as many as 15,000 spectators. The theater has undergone some restoration and has a spectacular view of the northern part of the island. (An automobile or taxi is necessary to reach the site.)

The remains of the **Menander House**, a mansion from the 4th century C.E., were discovered in a residential district below the theater (Zalagou Street). **Mosaics** from this house depicting scenes from the comedies of Menander are now in the Archaeological Museum of Mitylene.

Behind the cathedral (Ermou Street), ruins were discovered that have been identified as part of the remains of the ancient **agora**. Most notable among these remains is the foundation of an **ancient semicircular building**.

An especially fine collection of ancient objects can be found at the **Archaeological Museum of Mitylene**, which now occupies two separate buildings. The older building, close to the eastern end of the waterfront (southern harbor), is a classical mansion containing artifacts from the Early Bronze Age through the Hellenistic period. The newer building of the museum, a spectacular modern building just up the hill (also on Ogdois Noemvriou Street), houses an extensive collection of mosaics, as well as notable objects from the Archaic Greek period through the Roman period.

Approximately 4 miles outside Mitylene, near the village of Moria, stands an impressive section of the **Roman aqueduct** that brought water to Mitylene from the hills 15 miles away. (Take the main road north along the eastern coast toward Panagiouda and Thermiles.)

Neapolis

Neapolis, modern Kavala, still shows clearly why it was an obvious place for a port in ancient Greece. Nestled snugly about a half-moon bay, the city looks down upon a natural harbor that became the principal location in northern Macedonia for travel to and from Asia Minor.

Location and History

Kavala is the site of ancient Neapolis, the principal port of Philippi. Founded in the 7th century B.C.E. as a colony of Thasos, it was significant both for its port and for its commanding location along the coastal route from Thessalonica to Asia Minor. The fleet of **Brutus** was stationed at

▲ **Fig. 32.** The harbor at Neapolis

Neapolis at the time of the battle of Philippi. The **Apostle Paul** first set foot in Europe at Neapolis on his first missionary voyage. In later centuries the town was renamed Christoupolis, and it was burned by the Normans on their way to Constantinople in 1185. The city was under Ottoman rule until 1912, and on three separate occasions it has been under Bulgarian occupation, including more than two years during World War II.

Virtually nothing remains of the ancient city. The impressive **aqueduct** on the hills above the city dates from the 16th century, when it was built by **Sulëyman the Magnificent**. In 1769 **Mehmet Ali**, pasha of Egypt, was born in Kavala.

Biblical Significance

In Troas **Paul** had a vision in which he saw a man of Macedonia asking him to come to his country: "During the night Paul had a vision: there stood a man of Macedonia pleading with him and saying, 'Come over to Macedonia and help us.' When he had seen the vision, we immediately tried to cross over to Macedonia, being convinced that God had called us to proclaim the good news to them" (Acts 16:9–10). The rapid expansion of Christianity to the west largely was due to Paul's decision to follow the prompting of this vision. This biblical statement is significant also because it is the first use of the first-person plural, *we,* in the Acts narrative, possibly indicating that the writer of Acts, traditionally regarded as Luke, now accompanies Paul on this portion of his travels. (However, this also was a common device of ancient travelogues.)

Although sea travel was both quicker and easier than travel overland, the hazards of the sea prompted ancient travelers to make their journeys on the ocean short whenever possible. Neapolis therefore became the principal port through which Paul passed more than once on his various travels between Asia Minor and northern Macedonia. Neapolis is mentioned in Acts 16:11: "We set sail and took a straight course to Samothrace, the following day to Neapolis." From Neapolis Paul and his companions went straight to Philippi; there is no mention of missionary activity in Neapolis. Apparently the city served only as a port for their travels, though its proximity to Philippi makes it likely that work subsequently may have been done there also.

On his third missionary journey Paul sailed in the return direction, from Neapolis to Troas. The winds must have been less favorable for this trip; the return took five days instead of the two required on his first journey (Acts 20:6).

Site Visit

Since whatever may remain of ancient Neapolis, if anything, lies buried beneath modern Kavala, there is nothing left there to see from the 1st century except the **harbor** itself. Nevertheless, this harbor, with its busy docks and quaint seaside cafes, provides more than enough atmosphere to imagine the setting for Paul's historic first entry onto European soil.

From the sea, the hills that slope gently away from the shore appear as a natural amphitheater, and Paul and his companions must have greatly anticipated their landing at Neapolis and further journeys into Greece.

Kavala does have an **Archaeological Museum** at the western end of the harbor that contains numerous items of interest. The most ancient of these finds are from the Sanctuary of Athena (the patron goddess of Neapolis) at Kavala (6th–5th century B.C.E.), including **two columns** from the temple; Hellenistic and Roman sculpture; various amphorae and urns; and jewelry and ornaments.

▲ **Fig. 33.** Columns from the Temple of Athena at Neapolis (Kavala Museum)

Nicopolis

An ancient city whose name suggests the reason for its founding ("Victory City"), the site of Nicopolis today still gives indication of its power and size in the 1st century C.E. Caesar Augustus founded the city to celebrate his great victory at nearby Actium over the forces of Antony and Cleopatra. It has been called "the best site to appreciate the Roman conqueror's transforming hand on ancient Greece's landscape" (Christopher Mee and Antony Spawforth, *Greece: An Oxford Archaeological Guide* [Oxford: Oxford University Press, 2001], 389).

Location and History

Nicopolis lies on the northwestern shore of Greece in the province of Epirus. It can be reached on fine highways from Athens (approximately 5 hours), or by flights from Athens to Aktion (also known as Preveza airport), only 7 miles away, where an automobile ferry crosses every half hour to Preveza. (A tunnel has been recently completed that will make the future use of the ferry unnecessary.) Taxis are available for the short trip 5 miles west to Nicopolis. Taxis from the airport also can be reserved in advance; be sure to ask if the driver will wait for a visit to the site (approximately an hour), and always get the negotiated price in writing. The area is idyllic and beautiful, particularly the harbor and city of Preveza.

The first cities in the area were established by **Pyrrhus**, king of the region of Epirus (who lent his name to the term "Pyrrhic victory," referring to a costly battle, generally without real resolution). Nicopolis was founded by **Octavian**, later known as Caesar Augustus, to commemorate his epic victory over the combined fleets of **Antony** and **Cleopatra** at Actium (31 B.C.E.), one of the most important battles of antiquity. The crews of Antony's warships had been weakened by the malarial fever they contracted in the area, and due to their fatigue they were never able to execute the head-on ramming techniques for which his heavier ships were noted. Octavian's ships stayed well out of range until he perceived that the enemy was tiring, then they blocked the exit to the sea and destroyed much of Antony's fleet of five hundred ships. Antony was able to escape, as was Cleopatra, but only sixty ships managed to make it back to Egypt. Within a year both Antony and Cleopatra were dead, and one of the greatest eras in Roman history began.

Octavian had watched the battle from a hill overlooking the bay and subsequently erected Nicopolis on the adjacent plain. He also erected a battle monument on top of the hill, the remains of which may be visited today. Much of the initial construction of the city, including a city wall, was paid for by **Herod the Great**, a client of Augustus, to curry favor for his rule in Israel. Octavian populated the new colony and free city, typically, with legionnaires, freedmen, and the inhabitants of whole villages in the area he had ordered to relocate to his new city. An aqueduct, large portions of which still exist a few miles west of the site, conducted water from springs to the twin fountain houses at the entrance gate to the city. Octavian also transferred the Actian Games from Actium and increased their prominence until they rivaled the other great games at Olympus, Corinth, and Delphi. These festivities attracted great crowds until well into the 3rd century C.E.

Soon Nicopolis became the most important city in the region, a position it retained well into the Christian era (9th century C.E.). The famed philosopher **Epictetus** (60–140 C.E.), the greatest Stoic philosopher of the 2nd century, had a school there. Crippled in one leg and poor, he was a former slave who had settled in Nicopolis. Travelers from its port frequently visited Epictetus in order to be able to say they had heard his teaching. His impact also was lasting, as he was the greatest influence on Marcus Aurelius. In 67 C.E. Nicopolis became even better known when it was named the capital of the province of Epirus.

Evidence of its prominence in the Christian era still exists in the remains of five basilicas constructed within and around the city. **Hadrian** once visited Nicopolis (128 C.E.) and likely made donations for civic improvements. After suffering repeated raids by invaders over the centuries, Nicopolis declined during the Byzantine period and finally disappeared altogether sometime between the 9th and 10th centuries, when invaders from the area of Bulgaria overran the region.

Biblical Significance

Nicopolis is mentioned only once in the New Testament, in **Paul**'s Letter to Titus: "When I send Artemas to you, or Tychicus, do your best to come to me at Nicopolis, for I have decided to spend the winter there" (Titus 3:12).

In many ways, this is a curious text. Nowhere is any previous contact by Paul with Nicopolis mentioned in the New Testament, nor is there any reference to any church at Nicopolis or, indeed, anywhere west of the heavily populated eastern coastline of Greece. On the other hand, Paul's mission strategy seems to have been to plant churches in newer, vigorous, Romanized cities in strategic trade areas. (A more traditional, older Greek city such as Athens, for example, seems to have received less attention, and no church at Athens is ever mentioned in the New Testament.) Probably the greater openness and dynamism of such cities, coupled with the greater likelihood of a new movement spreading from these more cosmopolitan places, influenced his thinking.

As unlikely as it seems today to the visitor standing on the quiet and deserted site of ancient Nicopolis, in the 1st century C.E. the city was the most prominent trading center between Rome and Greece in the northern and western parts of Greece. Favored with two ideal harbors and an easily accessible route from Italy, Nicopolis would have fit the image of other cities in which Paul chose to focus his mission (Corinth, Thessalonica, Ephesus, etc.). Furthermore, the entire coast where Nicopolis is situated is noted for its relative warmth, which might have figured in a decision to spend the winter there. On the other hand, the area is also noted, even today, for its humidity and prevalence of mosquitoes. The malaria that infected the sailors of **Mark Antony** gives proof of that problem in antiquity. Some scholars believe that the illness Paul contracted in his travels to his home coasts around Tarsus on his first missionary journey was malaria, characterized by repeated, lifelong episodes of stabbing headaches, and that this was his famous "thorn in the flesh" (2 Cor 12:7). Of course, Paul would have had no inkling that humid coasts, mosquitoes, and malaria (or persistent, recurring pain; his "thorn," if it was malaria) had any connection.

Finally, there is no evidence that Paul actually spent the winter in Nicopolis, though he may well have done so. Furthermore, many scholars seriously doubt, for several reasons, that the Letter to Titus was authored by Paul in the first place, believing that it came from the hand of a later disciple of Paul, though the letter may contain portions of earlier Pauline material.

Site Visit

The site of Nicopolis consists of three principal areas: the museum area, the odeion area, and the monument hill. Perhaps the best place to begin a visit to Nicopolis is at the small **museum**, opened in 1972, on the southern end of the site. Several objects of interest are displayed in the two rooms of the museum: an **impressive sculpture of a lion** from the 3rd century B.C.E.; a **bust of Marcus Agrippa**, Octavian's general at Actium; and jewelry and various pieces of column capitals and bases.

The ruins of a basilica from the 6th century C.E., known as **Basilica A**, lie near the museum. Known also as the **Basilica of Doumetios**, the ruins of the church include an outstanding group of mosaic floors (usually covered for preservation). According to inscriptions found there, the three-aisled basilica was named for the bishop who was its founder. Some remains of a building called the **Bishop's Palace**, originally a Roman structure but possibly used as the bishop's residence, lie farther to the northwest.

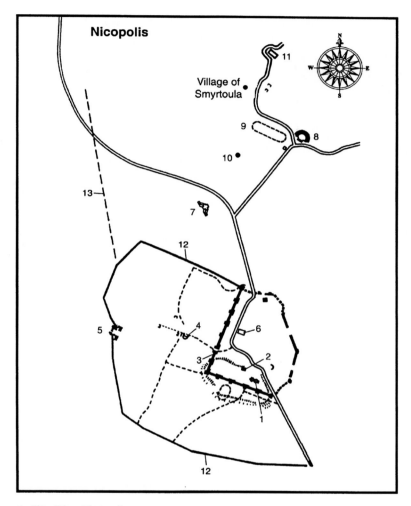

▲ Fig. 34. Nicopolis

1. Museum and Basilica A
2. Bishop's Palace
3. Byzantine City Wall
4. Odeion
5. Nymphaia
6. Basilica B
7. Baths

8. Theater
9. Stadium
10. Gymnasium
11. Camp Site Memorial
12. Ancient City Walls
13. Aqueduct

(Dotted Lines = Paths)

▲ **Fig. 35.** Byzantine walls at Nicopolis

To reach the **odeion**, walk north along the main road to the path leading left toward the **Byzantine** wall built by Justinian. Pass through the west gate, once flanked by two enormous towers that have been compared with those at Constantinople. Although this impressive wall once was more than a mile long (approximately a quarter of a mile of it remains today), it encompassed only a portion of the enormous area of the ancient city. The impressive odeion (1st century C.E.), once roofed, is on the left of the path. Recent restoration has enabled it to be used for an annual festival of ancient drama held each August.

Continue along the path to the left around the odeion. Turn right where the path divides to walk to the main ancient gate to the city, flanked by **twin fountain houses** (nymphaia). These fountains, still standing to a height of nearly 30 feet, were erected on either side of the principal west entrance to the city. Originally these impressive structures were covered with multicolored marble tile. They were supplied by an **aqueduct** (some portions still visible), likely built by **Hadrian**, bringing water from springs some 40 miles away.

To see the other places of interest around the site, take the main road toward Arta. On the right after leaving the museum area are the considerable ruins of the five-aisled **Basilica B** (450–516 C.E.), also known as the **Basilica of Alkison,** named for its first bishop. Some fragments of mosaics remain. Just past the fork to the left to Igoumenitsa, the unexcavated ruins of **public baths** (fenced) can be seen (probably 2nd century C.E.).

▲ **Fig. 36.** The odeion at Nicopolis

Continue on the Arta road to a sign for the **Monument of Augustus**; turn left on the road to the village of Smyrtoula. The road passes the outline of the ancient **stadium** on the left, where inscriptions to two athletes of Nicopolis were uncovered. On the right, portions of the auditorium and proscenium of the **theater** still stand. The slots along the top of the auditorium wall were for poles that held the awning that covered the seating. (The stones are in poor repair and climbing on the structure is forbidden.)

At the top of the hill where Octavian's command tent once stood are the remains of the **monument base**, or **podium**, renovated in 2000, which once held the bronze prow rams from more than thirty of the 350 ships captured by Octavian in the battle of Actium. Some of these enormous rams weighed nearly 4,000 pounds and were elaborately decorated. One of these prows, astoundingly, was found on the shores of Israel, where storms and tides had carried it. Ongoing underwater investigations in the Ambracian Gulf have located hundreds of small catapult stones such as would have been fired from the ancient warships. Attempts to locate prow rams and other artifacts continue in the area. According to the inscription on the face of the podium, the monument was dedicated, appropriately, to the gods Neptune and Mars. Portions of the inscription remain. Corinthian columns once stood on top of the podium, and a stoa there likely held more trophies of the victory.

Patmos

Famous for being the location for the writing of the book of Revelation (the Apocalypse), the island of Patmos is a jewel in the Aegean. This small island combines the charm and beauty of a typical Greek island with the tranquility and reverence of a sacred space. Visitors today might very well wish that they, like John, could be sentenced to exile on this island so rich with tradition, faith, and wonder.

Location and History

The northernmost island of the Dodecanese Islands (part of the Southern Sporades chain) in the Aegean Sea, Patmos, a part of the country of Greece, is 22 miles southwest of the island of Samos and about 38 miles from ancient Miletus on the mainland of Turkey. Patmos is a small, mountainous island, about 7 miles long and 3 miles wide, with a ragged coastline. The island has two narrow isthmuses that divide it into three parts. Primarily known for its association with the author of the New Testament book of Revelation, the island today displays the charm of a typical Greek island. The three main towns or villages on the island are Hora, Skala, and Kambos.

Patmos is mentioned only briefly by ancient writers (Thucydides, Strabo, Pliny the Elder, and Tacitus), and little is known of its ancient history. The island was settled by the Dorians and later by the Ionians. Ancient ruins on the island attest to the inhabitation of the island during the Hellenistic period, a time when Patmos, along with the islands of Lipsos and Leros, belonged to the territory controlled by Miletus. These islands served as "buffer" islands, guarding and protecting the city of Miletus. Inscriptions from the island provide evidence of a temple of Artemis and a gymnasium on the island.

Information about Patmos during the Roman period is scarce. Christian tradition, based on Revelation 1:9, claims Patmos as the site where **John** was exiled at the end of the 1st century C.E. by the Roman emperor **Domitian**. Whereas the Roman historian Tacitus does name three other islands in the Aegean (Donusa, Gyarus, and Amorgus) as islands where the Romans exiled or banished political prisoners, Patmos is never mentioned by ancient writers as a place of punishment. A 4th-century inscription mentions that the Temple of Artemis on the island was torn down and a Christian basilica was built over its ruins.

Between the 7th and 11th centuries, the island seems to have been basically deserted, like many other Aegean islands, due to heavy activity of pirates in the area. In 1088 **Christodoulos Latrenus**, a monk from

⚓ **Fig. 37.** View across the island of Patmos

Nicaea (modern Iznik, Turkey), received permission to establish a monastery on Patmos from **Emperor Alexios I Comnenos**, who granted him possession of the island. That same year **Christodoulos** (which means "servant of Christ") started construction of the monastery, known as the Monastery of St. John the Theologian, supposedly over the remains of the Christian basilica and the Temple of Artemis. He also built the Chapel of St. Anne near the Cave of the Apocalypse in honor of either (or both) the mother of the Virgin Mary or the mother of Alexios I Comnenos, both of whom were named Anne. Aside from John, the author of Revelation, the most important inhabitant of Patmos was Christodoulos, whose memory is honored twice a year, once on the anniversary of his death (March 16) and again on October 21, the anniversary of the day his remains were brought to Patmos from the island of Euboea, where he died.

In the subsequent centuries the island was raided by Arabs and Normans and came under the control of the Venetians (from 1204 to 1261) and the Turks (from 1456 to 1912). In 1821 the island gained its independence during the Greek War of Independence from the Turks, but this status was short-lived, as Patmos, along with the other Dodecanese Islands, came back under Turkish control in 1832. During the period of Turkish control, Patmos experienced periods of unprecedented prosperity, as well as times of destruction and poverty. During the 15th century, Patmos had a fleet of forty ships involved in commercial ventures throughout the Mediterranean. During the 16th century, the Patmian fleet was destroyed by the

Venetians, and much of the island was sacked by them. Patmos experienced a renaissance during the early 18th century when **Makarios Kalogeras** founded the Patmian School. The success and fame of the school helped fuel economic growth for the island. Control over the Dodecanese Islands changed again in 1912, when Italy gained possession of them. Briefly controlled by Nazi Germany (1943–1945), all the Dodecanese Islands were made a part of Greece by the Treaty of Paris in 1947.

Biblical Significance

The author of Revelation, the last book of the New Testament, describes himself with these words: "I, John, your brother who share with you in Jesus the persecution and the kingdom and the patient endurance, was on the island called Patmos because of the word of God and the testimony of Jesus" (1:9). The traditional view of authorship sees **John** as having been exiled or banished to Patmos by the Roman government on account of his Christian faith. The 4th-century church historian Eusebius reports that John wrote Revelation in 95 c.e., during the time when **Domitian** was the Roman emperor. According to Eusebius, John was released from the island after the death of Domitian and took up residence at Ephesus. Church tradition often identified John of Patmos with **John the disciple of Jesus**. Evidence from the book of Revelation renders such identification unlikely, however. (For example, in 21:14 the author referred to the twelve apostles, whose names were written on the foundations of the new Jerusalem. The writer was looking back on a venerated group of heroes of the faith. This description would have been an odd way for the disciple John, if he were the author, to refer to himself.) The author of Revelation is best understood as an otherwise unknown John living in Asia Minor in the closing years of the first century. He was obviously well known to the Christians in Asia Minor and was recognized as an authoritative leader in the churches. An outspoken figure, John apparently ran into trouble with the government authorities and as a result was sent to the island of Patmos, where he received a revelation from God.

A 5th-century apocryphal writing called the *Acts of John by Prochorus* contains legendary stories about the activities of John. According to this work, John was accompanied to Asia Minor by **Prochorus**, one of seven people chosen by the Jerusalem church to assist in the daily distribution of food (Acts 6:5). In addition to describing other events in the life and work of John, this work narrates John's exile to Patmos. Prochorus accompanied John there and served as his scribe, recording the visions dictated to him by John that became the book of Revelation. Although the story of Prochorus is likely nonhistorical, the traditions are strongly followed on the island of Patmos. The memory of Prochorus is celebrated on June 28 in Orthodox churches.

Site Visit

Visitors to Patmos arrive at the port of Skala. For those who make only a one-day visit to the island by cruise ship or by excursion from a neighboring island (such as Samos), the most important places to visit are the **Monastery of St. John the Theologian** and the **Cave of the Apocalypse**. The Monastery of St. John the Theologian, whose imposing structure looms over the island, is located in the town of Hora, approximately 1.5 miles from Skala. Grab a taxi for a quick ride (less than ten minutes) to the monastery. The driver will likely offer to return to pick you up at a set time. A better option is to walk back down to Skala, stopping on the way back at the Cave of the Apocalypse.

The Monastery of St. John is built on one of the high points of the island, giving it a commanding view over the island and its ports. The walls of the monastery resemble those of a medieval fortress. They were built this way to provide protection for the monastery from attacks by pirates and other intruders. The entrance to the monastery is by a cobblestone stairway at the north of the complex. Just prior to reaching the main entrance, notice on the right the **Chapel of the Holy Apostles**, built in 1603. Adjacent to it, on the west, is an open space (a bastion) from which there is a splendid view over the northern part of the island, including Skala. Across from the bastion is the entrance to the monastery, above which is a mosaic of St. John.

Beyond the tunnel-like entrance is the central cobblestone courtyard with its graceful arches, built during the 12th century. The large circular stone structure in the courtyard contains a huge **wine jar** that formerly was used for storage of wine but is now used for storage of holy water. Hanging from the columns in the courtyard is a long wooden beam called

⛰ **Fig. 38.** Monastery of St. John the Theologian on Patmos

a **simandron**. At certain times the monks strike the simandron (as well as a smaller iron simandron) rhythmically with special mallets to call the faithful to prayer. If you are fortunate enough to be in the monastery when the simandron is sounded, return to the courtyard to watch as well as listen to this memorable ritual.

On the east side of the courtyard is the **main church**, built in the 11th century by Christodoulos. Some of the building materials of the outer narthex of the church are said to be from the 4th-century Christian basilica that stood on this site, and some possibly even from the Temple of Artemis. Built in the 17th century, the outer narthex is decorated with frescoes. The frescoes on the lower part of the eastern wall are from the end of the 19th century. Many of the ones along the top are from the 17th century. They portray legendary scenes from the life of St. John, such as the resurrection of Domnus at Ephesus, the rescue by John of the young man who fell overboard on the journey to Patmos, and the drowning of the magician Kynops in the harbor of Skala. On the lower left (north) wall is a depiction of the story of the forty martyrs of Sebaste. Beyond the outer narthex is the inner narthex, built in the 12th century and containing frescoes from the 12th, 17th, and 19th centuries of New Testament scenes. The large icon of St. John holding the Fourth Gospel is originally from the 11th century, although much of what is seen today is not the original but the result of a repainting in the 19th century. The partially buried columns in the inner narthex are reused materials, possibly from the 4th-century basilica.

At the southern end (on the right) of the inner narthex is the **Chapel of the Blessed Christodoulos**. This 16th-century chapel contains the marble sarcophagus of Christodoulos and a wooden, silver-covered reliquary containing the relics (including the skull) of the founder of the monastery. The nave of the main church is dominated by the large, ornate wooden iconostasis, which was a gift in 1820 from **Bishop Nectarios**, a native of Patmos who was the metropolitan of Sardis. The large icon of the Apocalypse on the north wall, given to the monastery in 1625 by **Nicephoros**, the bishop of Laodicea, hides the entrance to the **Outer Treasury**. Off-limits to visitors, this room, built by the same Nicephoros for his library, is used today for storage of vestments and other items used in worship.

East of the main church, and also off-limits to visitors, is the **Ancient Treasury**, in which are stored the revered treasures and relics of the monastery, including supposed parts of the skulls of the Apostle Thomas and Antipas (the martyr of Pergamum), parts of Titus, Timothy, and Philip (the "deacon"), and a piece of the cross of Jesus. On the south side of the main church is the entrance to the **Chapel of the Virgin**. Built in the 12th century, the walls are painted with murals from the end of that century. These were painted over with other frescoes in the 18th century. In

▲ **Fig. 39.** Bell tower on the Monastery of St. John the Theologian on Patmos

1958, the older frescoes were discovered underneath and were subsequently uncovered. The paintings include one of the enthroned Virgin holding the Christ child on her knees, with the archangels Michael and Gabriel standing on either side; the Trinity, represented by the three angels receiving hospitality from Abraham; John Chrysostom; Jesus with the Samaritan woman at the well; the Virgin in the temple; the healing of the paralytic; and the healing of the crippled woman. The stone with ancient Greek inscriptions that is now a part of the threshold step of the iconostasis is possibly from the Temple of Artemis.

Return to the central courtyard and go to the left into the inner courtyard. East of the inner courtyard is the **refectory** (dining hall). Built in the 11th century, the room contains two long stone dining tables. The frescoes were begun in the 12th century and completed the following century. The refectory also contains ancient inscriptions collected from various places on the island. From the refectory, cross back through the inner courtyard. A short flight of stairs in the southwest corner (directly across from the small souvenir shop) leads to a second-floor walkway that goes to the bakery and the treasury museum. The **bakery**, a dim and almost empty room, contains a large 11th-century wooden kneading trough carved out of the trunk of a plane (sycamore) tree. At one end of the room are two large ovens that the monks used for baking the bread for the monastery.

The **treasury museum**, which has a small admission fee, displays some of the monastery's most important possessions. Among the many items on display is a portion of a **6th-century copy of the Gospel of Mark**. Written in silver letters on purple vellum, this document is the monastery's oldest manuscript. The monastery possesses thirty-three pages of this manuscript (known as the **Codex Purpureus Petropolitanus**). The rest of the manuscript is in various museums and libraries around the world, including the Leningrad Library, the Vatican Library, and the British Museum. The second oldest manuscript in the monastery museum is an **8th-century illuminated copy of the book of Job**. Of special interest also are two other items: the **12th-century chrysobull** (official Byzantine imperial document) from Emperor Alexios I Comnenos to Christodoulos granting control of Patmos in perpetuity to Christodoulos and the monastery; and a **4th-century-B.C.E. marble inscription** stating that Orestes (son of Agamemnon and Clytemnestra) visited Patmos and established a temple to Artemis on the island, supposedly in the same location as the Monastery of St. John. In addition to these items, the museum contains other important biblical manuscripts and an impressive collection of icons, jewelry, and vestments.

The monastery's **library**, not open to the public, contains one of the most important collections of ancient books in that area of the world, manuscripts, and other documents, dating back to the 6th century C.E. In previous centuries visitors to the library frequently "borrowed" valuable works and never returned them. Because of these losses, the library is now accessible only by special permission to scholars and others with valid reasons who need access to the library's materials.

After completing the visit to the monastery, walk downhill on the path to the **Cave of the Apocalypse**, the traditional site for the writing of the book of Revelation. The walk should take about ten to fifteen minutes. Located on the hill, halfway between the Monastery of St. John and the town of Skala, the Cave of the Apocalypse is located inside the Monastery of the Apocalypse. Before entering the monastery, notice the mosaic above the entryway that depicts John dictating the book of Revelation to his disciple Prochorus. The cave, located down a flight of stairs, is enclosed by the **Chapel of St. Anne**, built in 1090 by Christodoulos and then reconstructed in 1703. The narthex of the chapel leads into the nave (the main room) of the chapel and into the cave. The nave of the chapel is on the left, the cave on the right. At the rear of the nave is the chancel, separated from the nave by a carved and gilded wooden screen. The three large icons on the screen are (from left to right) of the Virgin Mary, Christ, and St. Anne (the mother of Mary). On the ceiling between the chapel and the cave is a **three-branched crack** in the rock. This split has traditionally been identified as a symbol of the Trinity, created when the voice of God spoke to John, commanding him to write the Apocalypse.

▲ **Fig. 40.** Interior of the Cave of the Apocalypse on Patmos

Hanging from the ceiling of the cave are **seven silver oil lamps**, representing the seven lamp stands that John saw in his vision. The engraved silver shrine in the casé between the chapel and the cave contains the skull relic of **Makarios Kalogeras**, the 18th-century founder of the Patmian School. (The ruins of the original school building are immediately behind the monastery. Its modern replacement is above it on the hillside.) To the right of this case, in the cave itself, is the 16th-century wooden iconostasis with **two icons** painted by Thomas Vathas of Crete. The large icon shows John receiving his revelation, with the Son of Man (Christ) figure above. To the right is another icon by Vathas with a depiction of Christodoulos (the large figure) and two smaller scenes of John's resurrection in Ephesus (top) and John dictating to Prochorus (bottom). On the rock wall to the right of the iconostasis near the floor is a **hole encircled by silver** (behind the decorative fence). Tradition claims that this is where John laid his head when he rested. Further to the right and a little higher is a **smaller niche encircled with silver** that is supposedly a handhold John used to help him get to his feet. The embroidered cloth covers a flat, sloping surface of the rock that is said to be the desk Prochorus used for writing down John's visions as John dictated them to him.

Try to allow plenty of time to appreciate the significance of this holy site. Fortunate is the visitor who is able to visit the cave when it is not crowded with other tourists. The wooden benches in the cave are a wonderful place to sit and experience the serenity and mystique of the Cave of the Apocalypse. Even if (as is likely) the cave has no actual historical significance, it serves as a powerful reminder of John's encounter with God.

When you have experienced sufficient revelation for the day, head back down the path to Skala. This walk is a delightful stroll that provides a beautiful view of the island and passes by some of the charming houses and chapels on the island. If time allows, visit the site of the ancient **acropolis** of Skala, located on Mt. Kastelli. The walk to Kastelli takes about twenty to thirty minutes from the center of Skala. The best way to find the site is to buy a city map of Skala, which has the place marked. On the summit are the remains of the **Hellenistic fortifications** (probably 3rd century B.C.E.), along with the modern chapel of St. Constantine. The view from the summit is one of the best on the island.

Once you are back down in Skala, you may want to stop by the place that is venerated as the **baptismal font** where St. John baptized the first Christian converts on the island. This site, a large rock surrounded by a wrought-iron fence, is located past the marina at the far end of Skala beach. A plaque (written in Greek) inside the fence identifies the site. The little chapel next to the site is dedicated to John. Note the mosaic on the front of the chapel that portrays the scene from the apocryphal *Acts of John by Prochorus* in which the wicked magician Kynops (in league with the devil) jumps into the sea, only to be turned into stone by John. According to local legend, the rock in the Skala harbor (about 75 yards from shore and 12 feet below the surface), marked today by a red buoy, is this very same petrified Kynops.

Philippi

An important city in the Roman and early Christian period, Philippi exists today only as an archaeological site. The impressive remains of this once flourishing city on the Via Egnatia, the important Roman highway in the area, are frequently visited by modern pilgrims retracing the steps of the Apostle Paul, who started a Christian church in the city.

Location and History

The ruins of ancient Philippi are easy to find. The archaeological site is located in the region of Macedonia, alongside highway 12 between Kavala and Drama, next to the village of Krenides. Settlement in the area occurred as early as the Middle Neolithic period (ca. 5000 B.C.E.). In 360 B.C.E., Greek colonists from the island of Thasos, led by the exiled Athenian politician **Kallistratos**, founded the colony of Krenides on the site of what later became Philippi. The colony at Krenides (which means "spring," because of the abundant streams in the area) provided the Thasians with access to the rich resources of the area, particularly its silver and gold mines. Threatened by the Thracian tribes in the area, the colonists at Krenides asked **Philip II** of Macedonia for military assistance in 356 B.C.E. Eager to gain control of the area, and particularly its rich resources, Philip conquered the city and renamed it Philippi in his honor. Philip fortified the city with new walls, increased the city's population with Macedonian mercenaries, and extracted large amounts of gold and silver from the mines in the area. Although little is known of the city during the Hellenistic period, this was apparently a prosperous time for Philippi. In the 2nd century B.C.E., the Romans occupied Macedonia and turned the area into a Roman province.

During the Roman period, the most important event associated with Philippi took place. In 42 B.C.E. the forces of **Octavian** (later known as Augustus) and **Mark Antony** defeated the armies of **Brutus** and **Cassius** (the murderers of Julius Caesar) on the plains just outside the west wall of Philippi. This battle brought to an end the Roman Republic. Following the battle, Roman veterans and other colonists were settled at Philippi and the city became the political center of a large Roman colony, eventually covering more than 700 square miles, including the seaport of Neapolis (modern Kavala) to the south. After Octavian defeated Antony at the battle of Actium in 31 B.C.E., he settled more veterans in the city and renamed the city Colonia Augusta Julia Philippensis in honor of his daughter. The Via Egnatia, the major Roman road that connected the Adriatic Sea with Byzantium, underwent major repairs during the time of Trajan (r. 97–117 C.E.). Along with this renovation, the city experienced a flourish of building activity in the 2nd century. Most of the ruins in the forum area date from the 2nd century.

Another famous event associated with Philippi occurred during the Roman period. Around 49–50 C.E., the Christian missionary **Paul** visited the city and there made the first Christian converts on European soil. Christianity took root in Philippi and prospered. One of the earliest known Christian church buildings in Greece, a church dedicated to St. Paul, was constructed at Philippi during the 4th century. During the 5th and 6th centuries at least four additional Christian basilicas were built in the city. Philippi suffered from several damaging earthquakes. Such damage, coupled with the incursion of Slavs into the area, likely led to the decline of the city, which was evident by the 7th century. In the 10th century, a Byzantine fortress was located at Philippi. By the 16th century only five or six houses were still occupied at the site.

Biblical Significance

According to the information given in Acts 16, the **Apostle Paul** visited Philippi in the company of **Silas** and **Timothy**. This visit, in response to a vision Paul had at Troas of a man from Macedonia saying, "Come over to Macedonia and help us," probably occurred around 49–50 C.E. The travelers sailed from Troas to the island of Samothrace (Samothraki) and from there to Neapolis, the port city for Philippi. On the sabbath, looking for "a place of prayer," they met a group of women outside the city gate by the river. Among these was **Lydia**, a Gentile from the city of Thyatira in Asia Minor who worshiped the God of the Jews. Support for the existence of a Jewish community in Philippi comes not only from this passage in Acts, but also from some grave inscriptions discovered in the city, although the latter are two or three centuries after the time of Paul. Among the most important of these inscriptions is a marble grave stele from the late 3rd or the 4th century C.E. that makes reference to a synagogue that was in the city. Also a tombstone from the same time period was found in Philippi bearing the name "Simon of Smyrna." Simon was a common Jewish name, and Smyrna was home to a large population of Jews.

After listening to the message of Paul, Lydia accepted the Christian faith and was baptized, whereupon she prevailed upon the visitors to stay at her house during their visit to the city. Paul and Silas ran into trouble in the city because of their healing of a slave girl who had the "spirit of divination" and were arrested, flogged, and imprisoned. (Paul apparently refers to this experience in 1 Thessalonians 2:2 when he writes that he had "suffered and been shamefully mistreated at Philippi.") Refusing to escape after an earthquake miraculously rattled the prison doors open and unfastened the prisoners' chains, Paul and Silas converted the jailer and his household to the Christian faith. The next morning the town magistrates freed Paul and Silas, who then departed the city and traveled to Thessalonica. Paul maintained contact, however, with the Christians in Philippi, both by letter and by sending messengers (Acts 19:22; Phil 2:22–23). On several occasions Paul visited the region of Macedonia, likely visiting the Christians at Philippi during some of these travels (2 Cor 2:13; 7:5; Acts 20:1–2). Later in his ministry, at the end of his third missionary journey, Paul apparently visited the city again. Acts 20:1–6 describes Paul as traveling through Macedonia, and verse 6 says, "We sailed from Philippi . . . and joined them in Troas." To sail "from Philippi" likely means that he departed from Neapolis.

Paul's initial work at Philippi bore fruit, as the church there increased in numbers and later supported Paul in his ministries elsewhere. The Letter to the Philippians in the New Testament bears witness to Paul's deep affection and appreciation for the congregation at Philippi. Writing the letter from prison (probably in Ephesus or Rome), Paul sent the letter

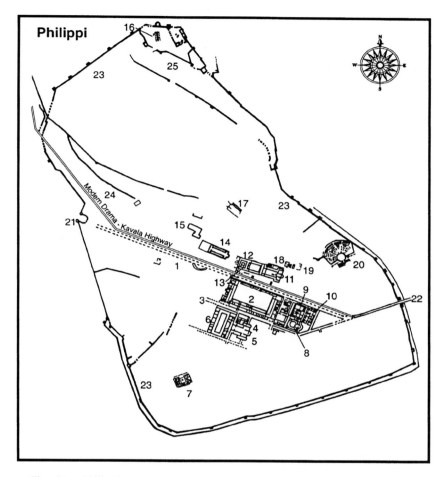

▲ **Fig. 41.** Philippi

1. Via Egnatia
2. Roman Forum
3. Commercial Road
4. Commercial Agora
5. Basilica B
6. Palaestra
7. Roman Bath
8. Octagon Church
9. Bath Complex
10. Episkopeion
11. Basilica A
12. Heroon
13. Cistern ("St. Paul's Prison")
14. Basilica C
15. Museum
16. Acropolis
17. Sanctuary of the Egyptian Gods
18. Sanctuary of Silvanus
19. Sanctuary of Artemis
20. Theater
21. Krenides Gate
22. Neapolis Gate
23. Hellenistic Walls
24. Roman Aqueduct
25. Byzantine Wall

to the church at Philippi not only to deal with some problems in the church there but also to express his gratitude and indebtedness to the Philippian congregation. Of all the Pauline writings in the New Testament, the Letter to the Philippians is the most affectionate. In the letter Paul thanked the Philippians, who had not only prayed for his release from prison but also sent one of their own members, **Epaphroditus**, to take gifts to Paul and to minister to his needs. With gratitude, Paul mentioned their earlier assistance to him: "You Philippians indeed know that in the early days of the gospel, when I left Macedonia, no church shared with me in the matter of giving and receiving, except you alone. For even when I was in Thessalonica, you sent me help for my needs more than once" (Phil 4:15–16).

Site Visit

The archaeological site lies on both sides of highway 12, approximately 9 miles northwest of Kavala. Excavations at the site, first conducted in 1917 by the French School of Archaeology at Athens, continue today by the Greek Archaeological Service, the Aristotelian University of Thessaloniki, and the French School of Archaeology at Athens. Begin the visit with the part of the site that lies on the south side of the highway (across the highway from the ticket booth).

Immediately beyond the entrance to the site is an exposed section of the **Via Egnatia** with its large marble paving stones. The Via Egnatia was the main east-west road through the city, passing through the city gates in the east and west walls of Philippi. This road, built by the Romans, was built on top of an earlier Hellenistic road. Adjacent to the road is the **Roman agora**, or **forum**, which served as the administrative center of Philippi. The ruins visible today are from the forum built during the reign of **Marcus Aurelius** (r. 161–187 C.E.), which was built over the location of an earlier forum. The forum consisted of a large central square, surrounded on the east, south, and west by stoas. The main entrances were on the north side, as were also two public fountains and a speaker's platform (a tribunal, or bema). On the west side were a **temple** (northwest corner), a **Roman basilica**, and other buildings. The temple was likely a part of the imperial cult, used to honor the emperor **Antoninus Pius**. On the east side were a **temple** (northeast corner; matching the temple on the northwest corner), a **library**, and other buildings. The temple in the northeast corner, which had two Corinthian columns, was also likely used for emperor worship. Attached to the south stoa were several small **shops**. In the southeast corner was another entrance to the agora.

South of the Roman agora, running parallel to the Via Egnatia, was another road, the so-called **Commercial Road**. South of the Commercial

◀ **Fig. 42.**
A portion of the
Via Egnatia at
Philippi

▲ **Fig. 43.** Shops along the Commercial Road south of the Roman agora
in Philippi

Road was a building complex from the Roman period known as the **Commercial Agora**. Parallel streets, perpendicular to the Commercial Road, ran along the east and west sides of the Commercial Agora. The Commercial Agora consisted of several shops surrounding a central colonnaded court. Entrance to the Commercial Agora was through a colonnaded stoa on the north side. Notice the games incised in the floor.

Around 550 C.E. a large Christian basilica was built that covered the southern half of the Commercial Agora and extended to the east. This basilica, referred to as **Basilica B** (or, in Turkish, Direkler Basilica, meaning "the pillars basilica"), contained three aisles and a square nave covered by a dome supported by four pillars. A large freestanding dome was supposed to cover the major portion of the church, but the dome collapsed prior to completion of the church. Later a smaller church was built using the narthex of the former structure.

To the west of the Commercial Agora are the ruins of a 2nd-century Roman **palaestra**. The central part of the palaestra was a colonnaded courtyard that was used as an exercise area. On the east side of the palaestra was a small **theater** with small rooms on each side. Several small rooms lined the west side of the palaestra. When Basilica B was built, it was constructed over the theater. Steps in the southeast corner lead down to a **latrine**. Originally the latrine contained forty-two seats in a continuous bench around the walls. Some of the seats are still intact. Underneath the seats a continuous flow of water carried away the wastes. Further south, between the palaestra and the city walls, are the remains of a 3rd-century **Roman bath**, which had mosaic floors, hot and cold rooms, and dressing rooms. The bath complex was built over an earlier temple for the worship of Liber Pater, Libera, and Hercules.

In the area between the Via Egnatia and the Commercial Road, east of the Roman agora, are the remains of the **Octagon**, Philippi's cathedral church built around 400 C.E. over the ruins of an earlier building that served as a chapel. This chapel, built in the middle of the 4th century, was dedicated to the **Apostle Paul**. A mosaic inscription found here reads: "Porphyrios, bishop, made the embroidery of the basilica of Paul in Christ." ("Embroidery" is a reference to the mosaic floor.) The Octagon, which survived until the beginning of the 7th century, had an entryway from the Via Egnatia. Entrance was through a three-aisled portico that led to the narthex of the church.

North of the Octagon were associated rooms and structures, including a fountain and a four-part **baptismal area** (containing a dressing room, a baptismal font, a room for catechetical instruction of those to be baptized, and a room for anointing the newly baptized with oil). The Octagon complex incorporated an earlier 2nd-century **Hellenistic funerary heroon** (a cult shrine for a hero). The remains of the heroon include the underground vaulted **tomb** and three steps of the platform on which

△ **Fig. 44.** Basilica B at Philippi

rested a temple-like structure. An inscription on the tomb gives the name of the person who was buried in the tomb: Euephenes, son of Exekestos. The name of this same person appears on a list of initiates into the cult of the "Great Gods" at Samothrace. Because the heroon was incorporated into the church, it has been suggested that it was reused as a Christian cult building of some sort.

Between the baptistery and the Via Egnatia are the remains of a **bath complex** dating from the time of Augustus and containing the usual rooms: hot room, warm room, cold room, changing room, and latrine. This bath supplied the hot water for the church's baptistery.

The large courtyard and rooms west of the three-aisled portico and narthex of the Octagon have been variously identified as storerooms, workrooms, and an atrium, or as a courtyard and guesthouses for Christian pilgrims to Philippi. To the northeast of the Octagon was a large rectangular building complex that has been identified as the **episcopeion**, or bishop's residence. Built on the site of an earlier Roman building, the episcopeion was elaborately decorated with mosaics and wall paintings. The episcopeion, part of which was two stories, contained not only the residence of the bishop but also apartments for personnel employed by the bishop, offices, storerooms, workshops, reception rooms, winepresses, and courtyards.

The remainder of the archaeological site is across the Drama-Kavala highway. The first major building on the north side of the highway is a large three-aisled basilica, called **Basilica A**. Built at the end of the 5th century C.E., the church had a peristyle courtyard at its west end, a four-sided atrium in the middle with steps leading to the narthex of the church. In the north end of the narthex were stairs leading to the second story of the church. The apse of the church was at the east end. The floor of the church was covered with marble paving, and the church was ornately furnished with elegant frescoes and sculptural decorations. In the center of the courtyard at the west end of the church complex are the remains of a two-roomed, temple-shaped building that has been identified as a Hellenistic **heroon**, possibly dedicated to **Philip II**. During the Roman period an impressive stairway was built, leading to the west entrance of the heroon. When Basilica A was built, the heroon was incorporated into its structure, with the main room of the heroon converted into a water cistern.

To the right (east) of the stairway is a structure that is popularly identified as **St. Paul's Prison** and is claimed to be the place where **Paul** and **Silas** were imprisoned, as described in Acts 16. Since Hellenistic times, however, this area had been the location of various religious buildings and shrines and thus would not have been a place where a prison would have been located. Instead of a prison, this structure was a Roman double **cistern** that was incorporated into Basilica A. After the destruction of Basilica A, the cistern was used for Christian worship and a cult center for the Apostle Paul. Inside the cistern are remains of Christian frescoes. Above the cistern a small chapel was built.

West of Basilica A is another large, early Christian church, **Basilica C**, dating from the 6th century. Discovered during work for the construction of the museum, the basilica had three aisles, chapels, auxiliary rooms, and a gallery that was accessed by means of a spiral staircase. Like Basilica A, this church also had elegant sculptural decorations and a marble-paved floor. A large amount of colored glass was found in the ruins, possibly coming from a stained-glass window. After the church was destroyed in the 7th century, part of it was used as a cemetery.

The **Philippi Archaeological Museum** is nearby. Built in 1961, the museum has been closed since 1997 for renovations. It mainly contains items from Philippi and the surrounding area, including some items from Megalo Lithari (Dikili Tash), a prehistoric settlement near Philippi. Among the numerous interesting exhibits are the upper part of a **statue of Nike** (2nd century C.E.); a Roman-period marble **portrait bust of Lucius Gaius Caesar**, the adopted son of Augustus; and a **fragmentary inscription** recounting that Philippi was settled because of a decree from **Alexander the Great** and stating his plans for the city and the use of the area's natural resources.

A path on the north side of the museum leads to the ancient **acropolis**. Visitors who have the time and are adventurous might want to make the climb. On the top of the acropolis, portions of the **ancient fortifica-**

tion wall are still intact. The earliest phase of the wall was built by Phillip II, with additions during the Byzantine period. The four-sided tower on the acropolis dates from the late Byzantine era. The best reason to climb to the acropolis is for the spectacular view over the ruins of Philippi and the surrounding landscape.

On the lower slope of the acropolis hill are several **sanctuaries** and **rock reliefs** that date from the 2nd century C.E. Among these are the **Sanctuary of the Egyptian Gods,** north of Basilica C, which consists of five small rooms along the north side of a large room and was dedicated to the worship of the Egyptian gods Isis, Serapis, Horus (Harpocrates), and probably Telesphorus. Further east is the **Shrine of Cybele,** which contains a relief of the goddess and a votive inscription. Nearby is the **Three Niches Sanctuary,** which consists of three rock-cut niches and a rock-cut bench. The niches likely originally held statues of deities. Approximately 100 feet to the east is the **Sanctuary of Silvanus.** Here are several votive inscriptions in Latin that record the names of worshipers of Silvanus, the Roman god of woods and forests. Nearby is the **Sanctuary of Artemis,** with reliefs of the goddess Artemis, the hunter.

The path that runs from the basilicas and below the sanctuaries and shrines eventually leads to the **theater.** Built by **Philip II** around the middle of the 4th century B.C.E., the temple was renovated and expanded in the 2nd and 3rd centuries C.E. During these renovations, the theater was

▲ **Fig. 45.** Theater at Philippi

modified for gladiatorial contests. The first three or four rows of seats were removed, protective walls were added to keep the animals from the audience, new rows of seats were added on the upper part of the theater, and, in the 3rd century, an underground tunnel was constructed underneath the orchestra for the purpose of bringing in the wild animals. Also, in the 2nd century, a new two-story *skene,* or stage building, was erected.

In the modern village of Krenides, outside the city walls of ancient Philippi to the east, are the remains of another Christian basilica, the so-called **Extramuros Basilica**, "the basilica outside the walls." Built in the latter half of the 4th or the 5th century, the church is located in a cemetery used during the late Roman and early Christian periods. The basilica was significantly modified during the 6th century, perhaps as a result of repairs due to earthquake damage. Near this basilica excavators have discovered another, even larger basilica, from the 4th century. Since the Acts account of Paul's visit to Philippi mentions that Paul found Lydia and others worshiping "outside the gate by the river" (16:13), some have conjectured that the baptism of Lydia occurred in a stream near the east (or Neapolis) gate. The presence of the churches here was perhaps an early attempt to memorialize the baptism of Lydia by Paul.

Other scholars have proposed the location for Lydia's baptism as the Krenides stream, which flows near the western (or Krenides) gate. This site, approximately one-half mile from the center of ancient Philippi, is located on the road toward Drama in the small village of Lydia (named after Paul's convert from Thyatira). Here has been built a modern **Baptistery of St. Lydia** (the octagonal building) to commemorate her baptism. A modern baptismal area with bench seats has also been constructed near the stream. This area was apparently an ancient cemetery (the so-called **West Cemetery**), since several sarcophagi and grave monuments have been discovered here, as well as a circular funerary **heroon** (in front of the Baptistery of St. Lydia). Excavations have also revealed **Roman paving** in the area, perhaps part of the Via Egnatia. (A third proposed site for the baptism of Lydia is the River Gangites, approximately 2 miles west of the center of ancient Philippi. The distance of this site from the center of the city, however, renders it unlikely to have been the place where the Jews would have gathered for worship.)

Rhodes

Nearly two million visitors a year come to the historic island of Rhodes to enjoy its sun, beaches, and famous medieval city. Rhodes is the largest island of the Dodecanese, or Twelve Islands, although there are actually two hundred small islands that compose the group. Historically it was the home of the world-renowned Colossus of Rhodes, one of the seven wonders of the ancient world. It is also mentioned in the Bible as one of the ports visited by the boat carrying the Apostle Paul to Jerusalem on his return from his third, and last, missionary journey.

Location and History

The island of Rhodes lies much closer to Turkey than to Greece, but it can be easily reached by frequent flights from Athens or by ferry from Piraeus (14 hours), the port of Athens; from Kusadasi through Samos (6 hours); or from Bodrum, Marmaris, or Fethiye (between 1½ and 2 hours). Flights are also available from Thessaloniki and Crete, and in summer from Santorini and Mykonos as well.

Because of its favorable location close to the shoreline of Asia Minor and between Greece and Israel, Rhodes was favored for development in antiquity. Both its eastern and western ports were frequented by traders and merchants, and numerous ancient writers mention it as a place of both economic and cultural achievement. In the 4th century B.C.E. Rhodes even surpassed Athens as a center for trade and commerce. The island also became renowned for its school of rhetoric, founded in 324 B.C.E., at which such distinguished Romans as **Cicero, Julius Caesar, Pompey,** and **Tiberius** studied. Famous citizens of Rhodes included the poet **Apollonios** and the sculptors **Pythocretes** (who created the famed Nike of Samothrace, which was dedicated by the citizens of Rhodes to commemorate their victory over Antiochus III in 190 B.C.E.) and **Chares of Lindos** (sculptor of the Colossus of Rhodes). The world-famous Laocoön, a sculpture that depicts the priest of Apollo and his children in the grip of two great snakes, was produced by three sculptors from Rhodes, **Agesander, Athinodoros,** and **Polydoros**. This work was taken to Rome in the 1st century C.E. and later discovered (1506) in the palace of Nero in Rome. Today it resides in the Vatican Museum.

The most familiar work associated with Rhodes, however, continues to be its legendary statue, the Colossus of Rhodes. This remarkable sculpture, nine stories (90 feet) high, stood on a 10-foot stone base and probably served as a lighthouse. Created to commemorate deliverance from a siege by **Demetrios** in 305 B.C.E., one of the successors to Alexander the

Great, the bronze statue of the god Helios stood for only 66 years before it was toppled in a great earthquake (226 B.C.E.). The pieces of the Colossus remained where it collapsed until 653 C.E., when Arab raiders carried them to the mainland of Asia Minor, where they were sold. (According to tradition, it took a thousand camels to carry the remains of the statue.) This work probably achieved its great renown in part because of the legend that it straddled the entrance to the harbor of the city of Rhodes. Even today, at Mandraki Harbor, twin columns surmounted by a stag and a hind (patron animals of the island) mark the supposed location of the Colossus. In fact, archaeologists believe that the great statue more likely stood in the courtyard of the Temple of Helios, now buried under the reconstructed Palace of the Grand Masters.

Rome assumed control of the island in 44 B.C.E. following the assassination of Julius Caesar, with whom Rhodes had allied itself, after a lengthy siege by **Cassius**. Subsequently, the island slowly began to decline. **Herod the Great** visited Rhodes in 30 B.C.E. after the battle of Actium in order to seek the favor of **Octavian**, who ratified Herod's appointment as king of Judea. Rhodes, like the rest of the Greek world, eventually fell prey to one nation after another, including the Byzantine Empire. When Constantinople fell to the Crusaders (1204), Rhodes was granted its independence. The **Knights of St. John** took control of the island in the 14th century and ruled it until they were defeated by the Ottoman Empire under **Sulëyman the Magnificent** (1522). In more recent history, Rhodes was occupied by the Italians from 1912 to 1947, when finally it was returned to Greece.

Biblical Significance

The island of Rhodes is mentioned once in the Old Testament (Ezek 27:15), once in the New Testament (Acts 21:1), and once in 1 Maccabees 15:23. In Ezekiel, Rhodes is listed as one of the nations that traded with Tyre. In Acts, the **Apostle Paul** is said to have stopped there in his journey to Jerusalem. According to local tradition, Paul's ship landed in a small harbor at Lindos, which is known today as St. Paul's Harbor. Another tradition suggests that Paul conducted missionary work on the island. The text of Acts, however, does not support either of these theories: "When we had departed from them and set sail, we came by a straight course to Kos, and the next day to Rhodes, and from there to Patara." (Some ancient authorities add "and Myra.") Notice that no point of landing is named, and the text seems to imply a departure from Rhodes without other incidents. Of course, it is entirely possible that the ship did dock at Lindos, and Paul may have spent a brief time on Rhodes, but there is no evidence of that.

Site Visit

The island of Rhodes offers much of interest, but little of it relates to the biblical narrative. Even the tiny harbor where Paul is said to have landed is a matter of speculation. Nevertheless, Rhodes was known to writers of both the Old and New Testaments, and every visitor to this picturesque island will want to include three places with relevance to the background of the Scriptures: the **acropolis of Lindos**, with its temples and spectacular view of **St. Paul's Harbor**; the **acropolis of Rhodes**, on Monte Smith Hill; and the **Archaeological Museum of Rhodes**, housed in the most important and best-preserved medieval building of the Knights of St. John, the **Hospital of the Knights**.

Acropolis of Lindos

To reach the **acropolis of Lindos** from Rhodes town (approximately 38 miles), take the road to Koskinu, Arkhangelos, and then Lindos. This magnificent acropolis contains structures from the 6th century B.C.E. to the 16th century C.E. These include temples, stoas, defensive fortifications, and an ancient theater. The area was excavated over a ten-year period (1902–1912) by the Danish Archaeological School. Today the climb to the top may be made by a broad stone stairway with numerous

▲ **Fig. 46.**   St. Paul's Harbor at Lindos, viewed from the acropolis of Lindos on Rhodes

spots for resting along the way. If the climb is regarded as too rigorous, however, donkeys are available for hire.

The various structures of the acropolis are located on four different levels on the ascent to the summit. At the first level are **wheat storage bins** and **underground water tanks** from the Byzantine period, surrounded by numerous **statue bases**. Most of the statues that once stood on the acropolis were sent to Rome in 42 B.C.E. by **Cassius**, who was angered at the support of the citizens of Rhodes for Julius Caesar in the struggle between the two for Roman supremacy. Also on this level is the famous **relief of a trireme** (ship) commemorating a naval victory in 180 B.C.E., as well as the **Exedra**, a stone bench that likely once was literally the seat of government. At the next level the stairway enters the **Castle of the Knights**, also once used by the Turks. To the left are the remains of a **temple**, believed to be Roman. The third level holds a dramatic **Hellenistic stoa** (approximately 200 B.C.E.), nearly 250 feet long. A monumental staircase leads up to the **Propylaea** and the restored **Temple of Lindian Athena** on the fourth and final level at the summit of the acropolis. The remains of this temple date from the 4th century B.C.E. It replaced an earlier temple built by the ruler **Cleoboulos** in the 6th century B.C.E., the period of greatest dominance by Lindos. A magnificent statue of Athena once stood in the temple, but it was carried to Constantinople by the emperor **Theodosius II** and destroyed. Ongoing restoration is taking place on both the third and fourth levels of the acropolis.

Be sure to cross to the far back corner of the summit of the acropolis to view the **ancient theater** below and to obtain a spectacular view of **St. Paul's Harbor** (Agios Pavlos). The harbor was once the location of the fleet of Lindos and the only natural harbor on the island of Rhodes.

Acropolis of Rhodes

The **acropolis of Rhodes** is located on a hill with the modern name Monte Smith, named for the British admiral who watched for **Napoleon**'s fleet from this location in 1802. (To reach the acropolis on Monte Smith Hill, take either a taxi or city bus no. 5; unenclosed site, no admission fee.) At the top of the hill are the ruins of the **Temple of Pythian Apollo**, marked by four standing columns that have been re-erected on the site. Below the hill on the south side is the reconstructed and impressive **stadium** (2nd century B.C.E.) where the athletes of Rhodes trained for the Olympic Games. Though much of it consists of modern refurbishing, it provides the visitor with one of the better opportunities in Greece for understanding an ancient stadium. Nearby is a small **theater**, also mostly of recent reconstruction, with a few ancient remains of the original. This may have been the location for the famous **school of rhetoric of Rhodes**, where numerous great Romans studied.

▲ **Fig. 47.** The stadium at the acropolis of Rhodes

Archaeological Museum of Rhodes

Every visitor to the island is intrigued by the fascinating **Old City** and its fortress and buildings erected by the Knights of St. John. Perhaps the finest of these structures is the **Hospital of the Knights**, which houses the **Archaeological Museum of Rhodes**. The building itself is well worth a visit, but the collection inside houses several antiquities of great significance. Among these should be noted **two statues of Aphrodite**, the finest and most famous of which is known as the **Aphrodite of Rhodes** (1st century B.C.E.); a marble **funerary stele** (5th century B.C.E.) of a mother, **Timarista**, saying farewell to her daughter, **Crito** (hair cropped in mourning over the death of her mother); and a **marble head of Helios**.

▲ **Fig. 48.** The Aphrodite of Rhodes in the Archaeological Museum of Rhodes

Samos

The island of Samos, one of the most pleasant of all the Greek islands, played an important role in both Greek and Roman history. The significance of Samos was due to its strategic location and its fame from three sources: the Great Temple to Hera, one of the most renowned in the ancient world; the Tunnel of Eupalinus, one of the great engineering feats of antiquity; and two of its most famous citizens, the moralist Aesop and the mathematician Pythagoras, of Pythagorean theorem fame.

History and Location

Samos is located only 1 mile from the shore of western Turkey. It received its name, according to Herodotus, because of its mountainous terrain. *Samos* means "high land" and seems to have been derived either from the Phoenician word *sama* or from the Ionian word *samo,* both of which have the same meaning. (Another island to the north has a similar name, Samothrace, which means the *samos* of nearby Thrace.) This relatively small island, 14 miles wide and 27 miles long, shows evidence of occupation at least as early as the 4th millennium B.C.E. Later, abundant evidence attests to further occupation in the Early Bronze Age by the Mycenaeans. Likewise, the Ionians established colonies on the island during the early Iron Age and it subsequently became a great naval power. Sometime during the 8th century B.C.E., Samos obtained land on the opposite coast of Asia Minor, which led to ongoing conflict with neighboring Priene.

The most famous, and infamous, ruler of Samos was **Polycrates**, the tyrant who ruled from approximately 550 B.C.E. until 522 B.C.E., when he was lured to Asia Minor and subsequently crucified by the Persians. During his reign, according to Strabo, the naval fleet of Samos became the first to rule the Aegean Sea since the days of the Minoan civilization. Polycrates established a cultured court, encouraged fine arts, and invited the famous hydraulics engineer **Eupalinus of Megara** to construct the great water tunnel that became known as the Tunnel of Eupalinus. Other public works projects included the construction of great walls around the city. (The city of ancient Samos was located at the site of present-day Pythagoria.) These walls were approximately 4 miles long, nearly 15 feet thick, and up to 15 feet tall, with fourteen entrance gates, and were protected by thirty-one round towers. The jetty on the south side of the port at Pythagoria, still in use after 2,600 years, was also built by Polycrates. Due to a series of military victories during this period, first against the Persian fleet, then on various islands and around the coast of

Asia Minor, Herodotus called Samos the most famous of all Greek and foreign city-states.

When the Ionian states rebelled against Persia in 499 B.C.E., Samos joined them in their struggle. The Persians were finally defeated after battles at Salamis and the destruction of their fleet in the narrow strait of Mycale, which separates Samos from Turkey (ancient Asia Minor). Typical of the Greeks and their city-states, however, Samos vacillated in its allegiances, sometimes aligning with the Athenians, as in the Peloponnesian wars, and sometimes fighting against them. For centuries the island passed from independence to occupation by various warring powers and back to independence again.

The philosopher **Epicurus** (341–270 B.C.E.) was born on Samos to Athenian parents and went to Athens at the age of eighteen to fulfill his military service. He later became famous as the founder of the Epicurean school of philosophy and founder of the Garden, a philosophical community and school in Athens.

During the years that followed the reign of Alexander the Great, Samos was caught in the center of the conflict between the rival successors to Alexander's kingdom. But when the Romans seized control of the Mediterranean world, Samos was attached to the administrative province of Asia (the western coast of present-day Turkey). Many notables were connected with Samos during the Roman age, including the famous Cicero brothers, for whom a monument was erected beside the Temple of Hera: **Quintus Cicero**, honored as a wise governor of the province of Asia during perilous times, and his more famous brother, **Marcus Cicero**, the orator, who tried the notorious Roman consul **Verres** after his looting of the Temple of Hera in 82 B.C.E.

In the years that followed, many other famous persons visited the island. In 39 B.C.E., according to Plutarch, **Antony** and **Cleopatra** brought their fleets to the island. **Augustus Caesar** spent two winters (20–19 B.C.E.) in Samos after his naval victory over Antony and Cleopatra at Actium, and subsequently granted autonomous status to the island. In 22 B.C.E. **King Herod of Judea**, also called Herod the Great, visited Samos. In 58 C.E. a ship carrying the **Apostle Paul** anchored at Samos during his last missionary journey.

In 267 C.E. the Herulians raided the island and destroyed the city of Samos and its magnificent Heraion. The further fate of Samos followed the unfortunate history of that part of the Mediterranean world, as subsequent invaders such as the Goths, the Huns, Turkish pirates, the Venetians, the Franks, and the Genoans pillaged and briefly ruled the island. Eventually both Greeks and Turks settled upon Samos, and even the Russians under Catherine the Great briefly held the island (1771–1774). But after years of struggle between Turkey and Greece for its possession, in 1913 Samos finally was officially adopted as a part of Greece, and so it has remained. During World War II, however, the island was heavily bombed and occupied by the Italians and then the Germans. The city now known as Samos (traditionally called Vathy by its inhabitants), as well as other parts of the island, suffered severe damage. A bloody period of resistance by the islanders and reprisals by the Nazis ensued, until the island finally was liberated on October 5, 1944.

Biblical Significance

The island of Samos has little connection with the biblical story. The only reference to Samos is in the book of Acts (20:15) regarding **Paul**'s third and last missionary journey. Paul had traveled north from Greece by land through Macedonia to Philippi, where he took a ship to Troas. For some reason he then decided to proceed by land to Assos. There he met up with his companions, who had made the journey by ship, and together they sailed south to Chios and Samos. The harbor at which Paul's ship docked was near Pythagoria, at ancient Samos, not at the modern city of Samos.

Some confusion has existed over whether Paul's ship actually docked at the harbor of Samos for an overnight stay or whether his ship simply passed near the island. The best textual evidence seems to indicate that his ship did land at Samos. It was customary for ships to pick a safe anchorage in the evening to wait for more favorable morning winds rather than risking a hazardous night crossing. Not surprisingly, there is a tradition on Samos that Paul not only visited the island but crossed it and made converts. However, neither biblical nor non-biblical sources give any evidence that Paul ever set foot on the island, though of course he may have done so. In any event, he was there only one day: "And sailing from there we came the following day opposite Chios; the next day we touched at Samos; and the day after that we came to Miletus" (Acts 20:15).

Site Visit

A few small sites of some interest, though mostly overgrown, lie along the road from Pythagoria to the Heraion, the principal archaeological site of interest. The site of the ancient **agora** is adjacent to the Olympic Airways office on Lykourgou Logotheti Street. Diagonally across from it can be seen the few remains of the **Temple of Aphrodite**. Farther along the road, on the left at the Pythagoria beach sign, is the location of an ancient **athletic area**; just beyond it are the ruins of a **Roman bath**. Behind the baths, the outline of an ancient **stadium** is visible, as well as the **Tria Dhontia** ("three teeth"), three buttresses from an early Christian

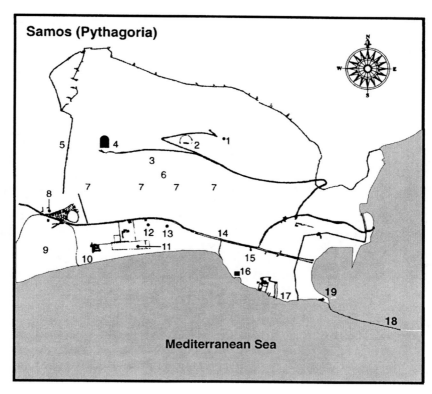

Samos (Pythagoria)

Mediterranean Sea

△ **Fig. 49.** Samos (Pythagoria)

1. Spiliani Monastery
2. Theater Site
3. Hellenistic Villa
4. Tunnel of Eupalinos
5. Ancient Walls
6. Roman Aqueduct
7. Ancient City
8. Artemision Site
9. Archaic Harbor
10. Early Christian Basilica
11. Stadium
12. Baths
13. Athletic Area
14. Ancient Agora
15. Temple of Aphrodite
16. Castle
17. Hellenistic Villa/Early Christian Basilica
18. Jetty of Polycrates
19. Greek/Roman/Modern Port

basilica. On the right, the ancient **fortification walls** of the city stretch impressively up the high hill to the right and down again. The **ancient city of Samos** was spread along the lower slopes of this hill. If traveling the area in a taxi, ask the driver to point out these areas of interest.

The principal site of interest on the island is the **Heraion**, which lies approximately 4 miles from Pythagoria. Without a rental automobile, it must be reached by taxi. (Some hardy visitors choose to ride bicycles or

▲ **Fig. 50.** The Heraion at Samos

walk, but the trip can be both hot and humid.) If a taxi is used, be sure to arrange return transportation. Taxis will wait (for a fee, usually reasonable), and some will return at a given time (although that may be more expensive than if they wait, due to the extra trip involved; ask before taking the cab). An hour should be ample time for a leisurely visit; those with less interest can walk across the site and return in even less time. Be aware that there are no telephones at or near the site; if for some reason you find yourself left with no vehicle for a return, walk the short distance out to the main road and hail one of the passing cabs. Failing all else, the village of Heraion is a fifteen-minute walk to the left at the main road. Taxis and telephones can be found there.

Within the site, which can be bewildering due to the large number of scattered monuments and ruins, four items should not be missed: the **Great Temple of Hera** itself, the platform of the **Cicero brothers monument**, the **Great Altar of Hera**, and the **Geneleos votive group**. Other remains of significance will be pointed out on the route to these principal attractions.

The site, and indeed the island, principally gained its fame from the **Great Temple of Hera**. Hera was the wife of Zeus, and legend has it that the goddess was born on Samos under a willow tree on the banks of the small river Imbrasos, which today flows near the Heraion. Herodotus wrote: "The Samians themselves think that the goddess was born on the island by the river Imbrasos and under the willow which even in my time

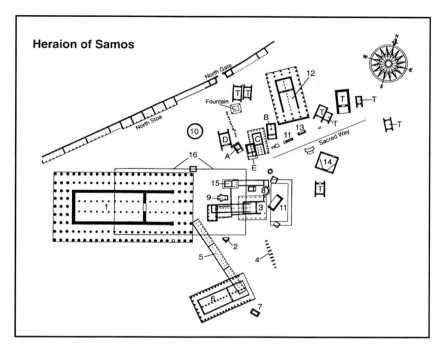

⚜ Fig. 51. Heraion of Samos

1. Great Hera Temple
2. Cicero Monument
3. Roman Temple to Hera
4. Ship Monument
5. South Stoa
6. South Building
7. Basin
8. Christian Basilica
9. Late Roman Baths
10. Rotunda
11. Geneleos Group
12. North Building
13. Monument to the Caesars
14. Hellenistic Building
15. Corinthian Temple
16. Temple of Rhoikos

T = Treasuries
A-E = Temples

still grew in the Heraion" (*Histories* 2.1.2). Several temples occupied this site over the centuries, beginning in the 8th century B.C.E. Because the temples from various centuries were sometimes built on top of each other, identification of each is difficult. Upon entering the site, however, the ruins of the Great Temple lie immediately on the left.

The first temple on the site was destroyed in 670 B.C.E. and replaced by a second one that was greatly enlarged over the years. These earliest temples were built of bricks rather than stone. But the first of the so-called Great Temples was built somewhere around 570 B.C.E. by the architect **Rhoikos of Samos**. Nearly 300 feet long and 150 feet wide, of the dipteron style, with 160 columns (8 by 20), it must have been an amazing structure. Herodotus called it the largest temple of its day, and other ancient writers called its forest of columns a "labyrinth." Unfortunately, this magnificent building enjoyed a short life of only thirty years due to its poor foundations and the instability of the moist soil upon which it was built. Around 530 B.C.E. the tyrant Polycrates commissioned the building of a replacement, but the work was often interrupted and it was never completed, though efforts continued until the 3rd century B.C.E. Today only a single column, itself incomplete, remains standing (the entire area derived its name, Kolona, from it). Nevertheless, the extensive foundations give an indication of the size and grandeur of this famous temple.

Proceed past the Great Temple; on the right stands the **semicircular base of the monument** erected to the **brothers Cicero**. Most likely their bronze statues stood in the central portion of the platform, Marcus on the right and Quintus on the left. To the right of Marcus stood the statues of his wife **Terentia** and his son **Marcus**; to the left of Quintus stood his wife **Pomponia** and his son **Quintus**. Another statue must have stood on the rectangular projection to the rear of the semicircle, likely that of a god. The monument probably was erected by the citizens of Samos following the term of Quintus as governor of Asia (58 B.C.E.) or perhaps following a visit to the island by Marcus (51 B.C.E.).

To the left of this platform are the remains of the small Roman-era **temple to Hera**, and on its left, the ruins of an **early Christian basilica** (5th century) that measured 90 feet long and 55 feet wide.

Behind the platform stands the **foundation** of an unusual votive offering to Hera, a **ship** approximately 80–90 feet long. Such offerings of ships, while not common, have been found in other locations in the Greco-Roman world (Samothrace, for one, and Delos, both islands). This monument seems to come from the late 7th century B.C.E. In the 6th century B.C.E. it was enclosed within a rectangular building.

Behind the early Christian basilica stand the remains of the **Great Altar of Hera**, in its day regarded as second in grandeur only to the Altar of Zeus in Pergamum. This altar was the central object of the cult of Hera, where burnt offerings and prayers were rendered to the goddess. At least seven earlier altars stood in the same location, the earliest dating to the Late Bronze Age. The latest altar was built around 560 B.C.E., together with the monumental Temple of Hera built by Rhoikos. The existing **foundations** suggest that the size of this altar was 110 feet by 50 feet. It was enclosed by a protective wall, likely three-sided, which was decorated with the familiar egg-and-dart pattern and the reliefs of sphinxes and fighting animals. The ends of the walls were finished with plaster columns.

Continuing along the same path, the **Geneleos votive group** stands on the left. The original monument consisted of six statues of a family group: three large figures standing; one smaller figure to their left; one figure, sitting, at the left end; and one figure, reclining, at the right end. Such monuments were erected by prominent individuals as gifts to the

▲ **Fig. 52.**   Geneleos group at the Heraion at Samos

god or goddess of the sacred precinct—and, no doubt, to immortalize themselves as well. The originals of three figures are today in the Samos Museum; one (of a female) is in the Staatliche Museum in Berlin. None of the heads of the figures has ever been found. This famous family group dates to the Archaic period, and **inscriptions** on it reveal the names of these persons and their sculptor, **Geneleos** ("Geneleos made us"). The reclining man holding either a drinking horn or a bird in his left hand is the father of the group. Only the last part of his name remains, "——arches." The sitting figure is his wife, **Phileia**; the four figures in between, their children. Only part of a foot remains of the smaller figure beside the mother. The female figure next to it was found in fragments, but the two other large figures (**Philippe** and **Orinthe**) were found virtually complete. The work dates to 560–550 B.C.E.

Farther along the path lie the remains of the **Sacred Road**, which was approximately 3 miles long and linked the site with ancient Samos. It was constructed in the 7th century B.C.E. and covered with marble slabs. The entire length of the road was surrounded by tombs, monuments, and statues. The most famous of these was the enormous **kouros** (figure of a young man), 15 feet tall, which was found in 1980 by German archaeologists and is now a featured attraction in the fine Samos Museum. A procession was held on the Sacred Road annually to celebrate the festival day known as Heraia, in honor of the wedding of Hera to Zeus.

Return to the east down the same path, past the Geneleos group. The remains of the **Temple of Aphrodite** lie on the right, and on the left are those of a **Roman peripteral temple**. Numerous other ruins dot the area, most of them well labeled.

After returning to Pythagoria, do not fail to observe the **ancient breakwater** of Polycrates on the south side of the **harbor**, still in use after 2,600 years. Also in Pythagoria there is a small **museum** that contains a very few items, but several of them are of interest: fine **busts of the emperor Claudius and of Caesar Augustus**; a larger-than-life-size **statue of the emperor Trajan** (2nd century C.E.); and, most unusual, an extremely rare scene on a **wall plaque depicting a slave**, prostrate, **being beaten with rods** by two men. Outside, there is a **bust of Pythagoras**, greatly beloved by the pigeons.

From Pythagoria, signs indicate the road that leads to the remarkable **Tunnel of Eupalinus**. On the way to the tunnel, three other sites can be observed. First, at the fork in the road that leads to the **monastery of the Spiliani**, on the right is the **ancient theater**; farther along the main road, on the left, are ruins of a **Hellenistic villa**; and below them, a portion of the **Roman aqueduct** is still visible. The road then leads farther to the **south entrance to the Tunnel of Eupalinus**. (Some work has been done to open the north entrance as well.)

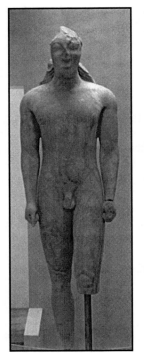

▲ **Fig. 53.** Colossal figure of a kouros from the Sacred Road at the Heraion of Samos

The tunnel was constructed to bring water from north of the acropolis to a point at the south, near the city. Eupalinus employed two teams of workers, working simultaneously from both north and south. Amazingly, the teams met with only a slight error. Herodotus described it as one of the great engineering feats of the ancient world. The tunnel is over 3,000 feet long and approximately 7 feet wide and 7 feet high. It can be entered for a short distance. Those who are in poor health should be cautious about going in to view the tunnel, since the footing can be slippery and considerable caution is required of all visitors.

The **Samos Archaeological Museum** (located next to the town hall in Samos Town) is outstanding and should be included on any tour of the island. This collection is remarkably extensive and well presented. The museum consists of two buildings, an older museum to the left of the main steps and a new museum to the right. Begin with the **old museum**, which houses a fine collection of small votive objects from many surrounding countries and a large assortment of pottery and amphorae. Continuing in the **new building**, one finds the most striking and important object in the museum: the **colossal figure of a kouros**, 15 feet tall, found at the Sacred Road, the largest such statue in Greece (except for the Apollo of Naxos, which never left its quarry); a large collection of wooden objects (7th–5th centuries B.C.E.), including an unusual **cabinet door** with nine wooden hinges; a collection of ivory figurines (8th–6th centuries B.C.E.) from Greece, Egypt, and Syria; perhaps the largest collection of **bronze griffins** in existence, both hammered and cast, which were attached to cauldrons and tripods, popular votive offerings at the Temple of Hera (Homer mentions such items as generous gifts and prizes in athletic contests); unusual figures of **worshipers with dogs**, from Babylonia (8th–7th centuries B.C.E.); and a hammered **bronze figure of a Syrian man with a flower** (8th century B.C.E.).

Samothrace

Unfortunately, fascinating Samothrace does not receive the attention from foreign visitors it deserves. Except for the peak of the summer period, when many Greeks and a few others make mostly day trips to the island, Samothrace is largely ignored as a tourist destination. Weather in the winter can be harsh and windy, but otherwise the climate is inviting. Only a very few small hotels exist on the island (though there are many guest rooms available in private homes), and places to dine are limited, shopping even more so. But for an overnight visit, or perhaps a weekend, Samothrace is hard to beat for a sense of a Greek world that once was. The wild beauty that surrounds the once glorious buildings of the Sanctuary of the Great Gods, where the immortal Nike of Samothrace, now in the Louvre, once stood, is largely unmatched for a striking impression of Greek sanctuaries before they were surrounded by pavement and urban buildings. Do not miss this unique island if it is in reach of your journeys to Greece.

Location and History

The island of Samothrace (or Samothraki) can be reached easily by car ferry or hovercraft from Alexandroupolis, approximately 20 miles away. Although there is only one road that circles the island, an automobile or taxi is necessary to reach the site of the Great Sanctuary of the Gods, which lies 4 miles from the harbor at Kamariotissa. (Bus service is possible but infrequent.) If a taxi is used, be sure that a return is arranged; get a card from the driver with a phone number, and be aware that taxi service is not available on Sunday afternoon. The only telephone available is at the adjacent museum, and when it closes, if you are without transportation, be prepared to hike or use hitchhiking skills on the rare passing automobiles.

Samothrace was known historically as the most remote of the Greek islands, which certainly is not true in modern times, when the nearby Thracian shore is a part of Greece. Likewise, the island is virtually equidistant from the Gallipoli peninsula of Turkey as well. These proximities made Samothrace a natural stopping place for vessels plying the waters between both coasts.

The island was inhabited as early as Neolithic times, apparently by peoples from the region of Thrace. (Its name means "Thracian high place.") Greek colonists arrived around 700 B.C.E., and a century later the island achieved its zenith when its naval power enabled it to establish fortified trading colonies on the mainland. Within a hundred years that power had diminished, but the increasing fame of its **Sanctuary of the Great Gods** caused Samothrace to be known as the center of religious life in the northern Aegean. **Herodotus** and **King Lysander** of Sparta were initiated into its mysteries, which are mentioned by both Plato and Aristophanes.

Who were the Great Gods? Originally, twin gods known as the Cabeiri, or Kabeiroi—mysterious, fierce, and much-feared volcanic gods of the underworld—were the center of the cult. But by the 4th century B.C.E. they were identified with four gods, identified as Hermes, Hades, Demeter, and Persephone. In later times the central figure of the cult seemed to be related to the Anatolian Great Mother goddess, who came to be called Cybele. Initiation into the mysteries was open to all and consisted of two degrees, or stages, the *myesis* and the *epopteia*. The first of these was the basic initiation into the cult; the second, which could be taken without interval after the first, required a certain moral standard and the confession of sins. Like other mystery religions, this cult promised its initiates well-being and a blessed afterlife. The mysteries seemed to have been celebrated in an annual festival in midsummer, perhaps July, when pilgrims came from great distances for the nocturnal initiations. Details of the ceremonies are unknown—initiates were pledged to secrecy under penalty of death—but may have included ritual purifications, the carrying of lamps, and the wearing of an iron ring (perhaps related to the Cabeiri, who were portrayed as smiths) and special garments. Celebrations were also held in the various dining rooms, also by torchlight, where drinking wine to intoxication was part of the rites.

In 340 B.C.E. the island became part of the Macedonian kingdom, and a series of buildings were constructed at the Sanctuary of the Great Gods by **Philip II** and his successors. It was at Samothrace that Philip met his wife, **Olympias** (the future mother of Alexander the Great), who was also attending the mysteries. Likewise, **Queen Arsinoe II** of the Ptolemies was a benefactor of the sanctuary. The island subsequently became a Roman possession, and various notables of the Roman Empire, including **Varro, Hadrian,** and the father-in-law of Julius Caesar, **Piso,** attended its mysteries. Over the centuries Samothrace was largely independent, due to its sacred sanctuary, but at various times it served as a naval base for the Athenians, the Thracians, the Ptolemies, the Seleucids, and the Macedonians.

After an earthquake in 200 C.E. the island gradually went into decline, and with the rising dominance of Christianity, its cult finally ceased altogether after the 4th century. By the 7th century Samothrace was a poor and scarcely populated island, its only function a place of exile for the Byzantine Empire. In 1459 Samothrace came under Turkish control, and in 1912 it rejoined the mainland as part of Greece. Today Samothrace has approximately 3,000 inhabitants and only two towns, the tiny port town of Kamarioftissa, and Khora, or Samothraki.

Biblical Significance

The only biblical reference to Samothrace occurs in Acts 16:11: "We set sail from Troas and took a straight course to Samothrace, the following day to Neapolis, and from there to Philippi, which is a leading city of the district of Macedonia and a Roman colony." This was the beginning of Paul's first missionary journey. Paul chose to cross over into Macedonia because of a vision in which he saw a Macedonian man saying, "Come over to Macedonia and help us" (Acts 16:9). Therefore, he and his companions chose to terminate their plans to continue their missionary work down the western coast of Asia Minor (Turkey), a province then known as Asia, believing that they had been "forbidden by the Holy Spirit" (Acts 16:6) from entering Asia.

At this point the narrative of the Book of Acts shifts to the first-person plural, perhaps indicating that the writer now accompanies Paul in this phase of his work. (Some scholars believe that this style is a literary device typical of travel narratives.) This writer remains unidentified, but traditionally he has been identified as Luke, "the beloved physician" (Col 4:14). In any case, the writer describes the direct journey to Samothrace, apparently made in one day, where it was customary for ships to anchor for the night rather than risk a tricky and dangerous night voyage to the opposite coast. The winds must have been favorable for this trip, since the same return journey from Philippi to Troas on Paul's third missionary journey took five days instead of two (Acts 20:6).

There is no indication that Paul set foot on shore at Samothrace, where he would have been virtually at the foot of the Sanctuary of the Great Gods above the harbor. But if he did, likely he would have taken advantage of viewing this world-famous center of Greek worship. Conditions on board the commercial ships of the day had no facilities for sleeping other than on the decks or in the hold upon the cargo, so sailors and travelers generally went ashore to sleep. The inns of the Roman period were notoriously dirty and frequently dangerous, so many of the sailors owned small tents that they utilized for sleeping onshore. As a tentmaker, Paul may have carried a tent for such purposes during his travels, but if so, it is never mentioned. In any event, the next day their ship set sail, and they proceeded on to Neapolis.

Site Visit

The site of the **Sanctuary of the Great Gods** is relatively large, but good paths make it easy to visit. If time or interest is limited, a visit to the central buildings takes little time. Other ruins both east and west of these primary structures, however, are well worth seeing.

The main path begins at the parking lot beside the small museum and runs directly south. The ruins of the first building on the right are known as the **Milesian Dedication** (3rd century B.C.E.), so named because it was a gift of a woman from Miletus. This rectangular Ionic building seems to have been a place for ceremonial banquets.

For a continuous circuit through the sanctuary area, visitors may continue up the path past the **principal cult structures** above and on the left until they reach the site of the ancient **theater** (2nd century B.C.E.), opposite the last of the central buildings. Only two seats of the theater remain.

Proceed to the right up the western hill to the site of the **stoa** (3rd century B.C.E.), once the largest building at the sanctuary. This structure seems to have been built to accommodate the many visitors to the site. A colonnade of thirty-five Doric columns, surmounted by a terra-cotta tiled roof, provided entrance to the building, which was constructed of three walls and sixteen Ionic columns that supported the main roof. On the eastern edge of the stoa the foundations of a number of monuments remain.

The building whose foundations lie immediately north of the stoa is known as the **Neorion** (3rd century B.C.E.), a building that housed a ship that was an offering to the gods (a similar ship offering was made at the Heraion at Samos, the foundation of which may still be seen). Farther beyond the northern end of the stoa, the outlines of several **Hellenistic buildings** can be observed. The purpose of most of these buildings is not yet known, though they may have been **ceremonial dining rooms**.

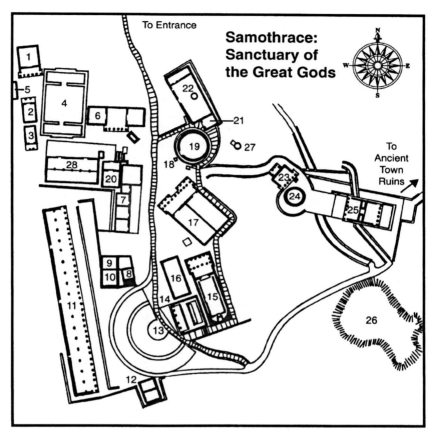

▲ **Fig. 54.** Samothrace: Sanctuary of the Great Gods

1.–4. Late Hellenistic Buildings
5. Medieval Fort Ruins
6. Milesian Dedication
7. Ritual Dining Rooms
8. Unidentified Room
9. Niche
10. Unidentified Room
11. Stoa
12. Nike Monument
13. Theater Site
14. Altar Court
15. Sanctuary (Hieron)
16. Hall of Votive Gifts
17. Hall of Choral Dancers (Temenos)

18. Sacred Rock
19. Rotunda of Arsinoe
20. Orthostat Foundations
    (within Rotunda)
21. Sacristy
22. Anaktoron
23. Dedication of Philip and
    Alexander
24. Circular Area
25. Propylon of Ptolemy II
26. Southern Necropolis
27. Doric Rotunda
28. Neorion

To the southeast of the stoa, portions of the foundation of the **Nike monument** remain. The most famous find from Samothrace was located here. The statue known as "**Winged Victory**," or the **Nike of Samothrace**, now in the Louvre, is one of the world's great art treasures. Terrace walls from the early imperial period surrounded the monument on three sides. Its base was a marble ship's prow upon which the statue stood. Beneath the fountain was a reflecting pool, so that from below, the figure of the goddess Nike appeared to be standing on the prow of a ship gliding over the sea. Other fountain statues attempted the same effect, but this one was regarded as the ultimate example of such art. A replica of this figure stands in the museum at the entrance to the site.

Continue along the upper path some distance to the east to the **Propylon of Ptolemy II**, or return down the hill to the central buildings if a longer walk is prohibited by time. The **road** from the ancient city to the sanctuary terminated at this monumental gatehouse dedicated to the Great Gods by **Ptolemy II Philadelphus** (285–281 B.C.E.). Originally the small stream from the mountains above was channeled through the vaulted tunnel in the lower portion of the structure; its upper portion contained porticoes on both east and west sides, separated by a double wall. The **inscription** above the six columns on both sides of this temple-style building reads, "King Ptolemy, son of Ptolemy and Bernice, the saviors, to the Great Gods."

From this point continue in the same direction as the ancient visitors to the sanctuary and proceed to the **circular paved area** (5th century

▲ **Fig. 55.** The circular paved area at the Sanctuary of the Great Gods on Samothrace

B.C.E.) with its five rows of steps and central altar. Candidates stood on these steps and perhaps learned the requirements for initiation or participated in other portions of the ceremony, including sacrifice. A rectangular building was added on the northwest (323 B.C.E.) and then replaced (317 B.C.E.) by a more elaborate marble building, a gift of two of the successors of Alexander the Great, **Philip III** and **Alexander III**.

Below these remains, toward the central buildings of the sanctuary, are the foundations of a tiny **Doric Rotunda** (4th century B.C.E.). Continue down the hill as the path leads to the **temenos**, or **Hall of the Choral Dancers**, and the **Rotunda of Arsinoe II**.

The temenos came to be known as the Hall of the Choral Dancers because of the frieze, depicting a chorus of dancers, discovered there. The processional of the initiates terminated at this building (340 B.C.E.), which consisted of an open court flanked by an Ionic propylon. Likely, within stood a famous statue of Aphrodite by Skopas. The structure contained a sacred hearth for burnt sacrifices and a pit for libations. This was the earliest sacrificial area in the sanctuary (7th century B.C.E.). The building may have been a gift of **Philip II**.

The **Rotunda of Arsinoe II** to the north (erected sometime between 289 and 281 B.C.E.), the largest known circular building in Greek architecture (more than 60 feet across), was used for sacrifices and official gatherings during the ceremonies. The **walls** visible in the center of the floor of the rotunda are the remains of a building that was an early predecessor (4th century) of the **Anaktaron** (550 B.C.E.), the hall of initiation to the north of the rotunda. It was used for the first stage of initiation, the *myesis*.

The inside of the Anaktaron, similar to the temple in Jerusalem, had a Holy of Holies at its far end with a higher floor, which constituted an inner sanctuary. Entrance within this building was permitted only after initiation. The walls of the main hall were coated with white plaster. A wooden platform stood in the center, and wooden grandstands stood along two walls. The initiates must have sat or stood there while cult officers gave instructions from the platform in the center. In the southeast corner of the building, a stone structure surrounded a pit into which libations were poured. Two bronze statues of the Cabeiri, with raised hands, stood on either side of two doors in the western wall. The initiates entered through the sacristy, where they may have been given symbols of the cult and to which they returned for certificates of initiation.

Return through the Hall of the Choral Dancers. To the south are the foundations of two structures, a large building (the **Hieron**) and a small building (the **Hall of Votive Gifts**). The Hall of Votive Gifts (5th century B.C.E.) displayed the many gifts dedicated to the sanctuary. The Hieron ("sanctuary") was used for the initiation into the higher degree of the mysteries. It was constructed between 325 and 150 B.C.E. A sacred hearth was within, and a hole in a marble block was used for pouring libations.

⬕ **Fig. 56.** The Hieron at the Sanctuary of the Great Gods on Samothrace

This Doric building had a colonnaded façade, a double porch of fourteen columns, and a sculptured pediment. The floor was originally of marble. **Spectator benches** still remain on either wall. Outside, the master of the initiation heard the confession of the initiates. The **Altar Court** lies to the west of the Hieron.

The **museum** at the site contains a small but interesting collection: vases and seals from various areas, architectural remains from the sanctuary, a **marble stele** in both Greek and Latin prohibiting the uninitiated from entering the inner sanctum of the Anaktaron, **oil lamps** used during the mysteries, a terra-cotta **statue of Eros**, and a **copy of the Nike of Samothrace**.

Thessalonica

In 315 B.C.E. Cassander, king of Macedonia, once a general in the army of Alexander the Great, founded a new city in his kingdom. He named it for his wife, Thessalonike, daughter of Philip II of Macedon and the half sister of Alexander. In the centuries that followed, Thessalonica became the premier city of northern Greece, enduring and flourishing under Hellenistic, Roman, and Greek control. Many famous figures in world history played important roles throughout its lengthy and colorful existence, including Alexander the Great, Cleopatra, Cicero, Pompey, and Suleyman I the Magnificent, among others. But no resident or visitor to Thessalonica had a greater influence on the city than an obscure Christian missionary who visited there in the first century, Paul of Tarsus. The first New Testament writing is believed to be Paul's First Letter to the Thessalonians.

History and Location

Modern Thessaloniki (biblical Thessalonica), second only to Athens among the cities of Greece, is easily reached by automobile or by frequent flights from Athens. Although its ancient ruins and monuments are overshadowed by those of Athens, this city is well worth visiting for its fine archaeological museum and as a point of departure for the spectacular Royal Tombs at Vergina, home to the amazing riches of the family of Alexander the Great. Increasingly, more of ancient Thessalonica is being unearthed by archaeologists and made available to public view.

According to Strabo, Thessalonica was established at the site of ancient Therme and formed from the incorporation of twenty-five smaller villages. The ancient city was laid out according to the Hippodamian plan, that is, in rectangular blocks. Its development was encouraged by its fine port and, during the Roman period, by being made the capital of Macedonia. When the Romans connected the Via Egnatia, the historic road linking east and west, to Thessalonica, the city prospered even more. The Roman orator **Cicero** was exiled in Thessalonica (58–57 B.C.E.) and wrote to his friend Atticus on July 21, 57 B.C.E., that he had delayed leaving the city "owing to the constant traffic along the road" (the Via Egnatia; M. Tullius Cicero, *Letters* 69). Under Caesar Augustus, Thessalonica became the most important military center in Macedonia. Later it served as the headquarters of **Pompey** and his armies in 49 B.C.E. when he sought refuge from Julius Caesar. The city further prospered under the emperors Hadrian, Trajan, and Diocletian, and boasted splendid temples and monuments.

In the 3rd century C.E. (254 C.E.), Thessalonica was successful in defending itself against the Goths. The emperor **Galerius** lived in the city when he became ruler of the eastern half of the Roman Empire upon the retirement of Diocletian. Galerius, however, instituted persecutions against the strong Christian community in Thessalonica. One of the martyrs of that time was named **Demetrius**, later St. Demetrius, who became patron saint of the city. Under Constantine the Great, a new artificial harbor and other improvements further advanced Thessalonica as the preeminent city in northern Greece. **Theodosius the Great** (r. 379–395 C.E.) was converted to Christianity in the city during a critical illness. Later he issued the Edict of Thessalonica (380) that eliminated the toleration of pagan gods, worship of which formerly was allowed under the emperor Julian. In 904 C.E., Thessalonica was besieged and captured by the Saracens, who sold 22,000 of its citizens into slavery.

The city fell to the Ottoman Turks in 1387, and centuries of Turkish control followed. In 1492, some 20,000 Jews who had been banished from Spain were relocated in the city. By the 16th century, Jews were said to constitute the majority of the city. **Suleyman I the Magnificent** (r. 1520–1566) made extensive repairs and additions to the famous White Tower (1430), which was first a part of the coastal defenses and later a jail. During the First Balkan War, Thessalonica was liberated from Turkish rule (1912) and the city was ceded to Greece. In 1917 a devastating fire swept through much of the city, and extensive areas had to be rebuilt. During the German occupation in World War II, some 60,000 Jews were deported to Poland, and the Jewish population never recovered. Earthquakes in 1978 caused extensive damage to the city. The city was also the birthplace of Mustafa Kemal, later known as Atatürk, the father of modern Turkey. Thessalonica is now home to the largest university in Greece, with more than 60,000 students.

Biblical Significance

The **Apostle Paul** and his companions traveled to Thessalonica on his second missionary journey (49–50 C.E.). They arrived there after having been beaten and imprisoned in Philippi on the charge of disturbing the peace. Their route took them through Amphipolis and Apollonia; whether they pursued their mission in those cities is unclear. Perhaps, as in Philippi, there was no synagogue in Thessalonica, as Acts 17:1 may imply, but Luke's narrative is condensed in these travel excerpts. In any case, the journey of more than 95 miles would have taken several days. The events at Thessalonica that followed are told in Acts 17:1–15:

> After Paul and Silas had passed through Amphipolis and Apollonia, they came to Thessalonica, where there was a synagogue of the Jews. And Paul went in, as was his custom, and on three Sabbath days argued with them from the scriptures, explaining and proving that it was necessary for the Messiah to suffer and rise from the dead, and saying, "This is the Messiah, Jesus whom I am proclaiming to you." Some of them were persuaded and joined Paul and Silas, as did a great many of the devout Greeks and not a few of the leading women. But the Jews became jealous, and with the help of some ruffians in the marketplace they formed a mob and set the city in an uproar. While they were searching for Paul and Silas to

bring them out to the assembly, they attacked Jason's house. When they could not find them, they dragged Jason and some believers before the city authorities, shouting, "These people who have been turning the world upside down have come here also, and Jason has entertained them as guests. They are all acting contrary to the decrees of the emperor, saying that there is another king named Jesus." The people and the city officials were disturbed when they heard this, and after they had taken bail from Jason and the others, they let them go.

That very night the believers sent Paul and Silas off to Beroea; and when they arrived, they went to the Jewish synagogue. These Jews were more receptive than those in Thessalonica, for they welcomed the message very eagerly and examined the scriptures every day to see whether these things were so. Many of them therefore believed, including not a few Greek women and men of high standing. But when the Jews of Thessalonica learned that the word of God had been proclaimed by Paul in Beroea as well, they came there too, to stir up and incite the crowds. Then the believers immediately sent Paul away to the coast, but Silas and Timothy remained behind. Those who conducted Paul brought him as far as Athens; and after receiving instructions to have Silas and Timothy join him as soon as possible, they left him.

It is impossible to determine how long Paul and his companions remained in Thessalonica. Acts says that he spoke on three Sabbaths in the synagogue there, but that should not be taken to mean that three weeks was the extent of his stay. From his later writings we learn that he worked "night and day" in Thessalonica to support himself and his companions (1 Thess 2:9). Acts also says that he required supplementary income for his subsistence, which was provided more than once by the church at Philippi (Phil 4:16). Together, these scriptures lead to the conclusion that Paul must have remained at Thessalonica for several weeks, if not months.

The Jewish community became upset in this situation, not only because of the proselytizing of their numbers by the Christian missionaries, but also because they feared the wrath of the secular authorities concerning the preaching of loyalty to another "king." (This same fear was expressed in Jerusalem by the religious authorities prior to the arrest of Jesus.) At this time Thessalonica enjoyed the status of a free city, which meant that Romans did not occupy the local offices and government although a Roman procurator was headquartered in the city. Instead, local rulers were known as politarchs, a name peculiar to Macedonia and found by archaeologists on the **Vartar Gate** in Thessalonica. Exactly the same word for officials, *politarchs,* is used in this account, Acts 17:8. The populace was understandably agitated at any suggestion that their favored status might be in jeopardy.

As at Philippi, Paul's friends quickly ("that very night") escorted him out of the city, they supposed, to a safer, out-of-the-way city, Beroea. But after some time (again, indeterminable from the text), those who had opposed the Christian mission in Thessalonica came to Beroea and stirred up the populace there also. Subsequently, Paul left Thessalonica and Macedonia for Athens, presumably by sea. **Silas** and **Timothy** (previously not mentioned in these accounts) were instructed to join him as soon as possible.

Site Visit

Fortunately for visitors to Thessalonica, virtually all the significant ancient sites are located near the center of the city and can be visited on foot. Any hotel near the center of the city, or the university area, is in easy walking distance of the antiquities. Even the **White Tower** (now a Byzantine museum) on the attractive waterfront area can be reached on foot. Two days is ample time to visit the sites and the outstanding **Archaeological Museum**. Definitely consider a day trip to the Royal Tombs at Vergina, one of the top attractions in all of Greece (see "Other Sites of Interest," below).

Perhaps the most visible ancient monument in Thessalonica is the **Arch of Galerius**, a triumphal arch beside the **Via Egnatia** (Egnatia Odhos), erected in 304 C.E. to commemorate the emperor's victories over the Persians (297 C.E.). Originally two additional spans extended across what is today the street of Egnatia. Reliefs on the piers of the better-preserved arch depict (top to bottom, east side): a sacrificial scene depicting **Diocletian** and **Galerius** (to his right) and **Caesar**, in military garb, celebrating the victories of Caesar; Galerius addressing his troops; prisoners begging for mercy; and beneath the central arch, Galerius riding in his chariot; Galerius fighting on horseback; and various battle scenes.

Next, up Apostolou Pavlou Street, stands a massive brick building, the **Rotunda**, which has served as a church (5th century), a cathedral (15th century), and a mosque (16th century). Originally erected to serve as a **mausoleum for Galerius** (probably in his lifetime), today this building is known as **Agios Georgios** (St. George), the name it took from the small church adjacent to it. It is used now for cultural events.

In the opposite direction from the Arch of Galerius, follow Germanou to Odhos Gounari, which leads to Navarinou Square (Plateia Navarinou), to reach the **Palace of Galerius**, the most important part of this entire complex erected by the emperor. The principal entrance to the palace was on the seaward side of the building. The impressive octagonal-shaped ruins probably served originally as a **throne room**. Images of the gods and a bust of Galerius on an architectural medallion were found in this area. Although the site is closed to visitors while restoration is being done, it is possible to walk completely around the outside of the site and

see most of the ruins. (To visit the White Tower and the waterfront, proceed south and follow Pavlou Mela, which leads directly to the tower,
approximately eight blocks.)

To visit the Roman Forum and Agios Dhimitrios: from the White
Tower, it would be best to take a taxi to Agios Dhimitrios, then walk one
block south to the Roman Forum in Dhikastirion Square (Plateia
Dhikastirion). From the Arch of Galerius, walk north on Leonida
Iassonidhou to Agiou Dhimitriou; turn left to the church (a total distance
of 10–12 blocks).

When ground was broken (1963) for new law courts in this extensive
square, left bare following the great fire of 1917, the remains of the **Roman Forum** from the 2nd and 3rd centuries C.E. were discovered. Extensive, ongoing excavations are being conducted in this area. Likely the
same site was the location for the **Hellenistic agora** as well. The forum
originally covered two extensive terraces. The one to the north contained
a large courtyard surrounded on four sides by two-story **stoas**; to the
rear of the stoa on the east side stood the **odeion**, originally a theater for
music and performances, later converted into an arena for gladiatorial
contests. The upper level of the stoa on the south side was supported by
columns decorated with large figures of gods and goddesses (now in the
Louvre in Paris).

▲ **Fig. 57.** The Roman Forum at Thessalonica

Agios Dhimitrios, the shrine to Demetrius, the patron saint of Thessalonica martyred by Galerius, is a basilica erected in the 5th century but gutted by fire in 1917. It was reconstructed from the original materials, so far as possible, between 1926 and 1948. The cavernous **basement and crypt area** of the church, likely the location of part of the **Roman baths** in which Demetrius traditionally was said to be imprisoned, contains a niche that is said to be the area where Demetrius was kept prisoner. There is also a small section of an ancient **Roman street**, evidence that this room originally was at ground level.

The **Archaeological Museum** is located a few blocks northeast of the White Tower at the intersection of Tsimiski and Angelaki Streets. Although the treasures of Philip II and Alexander the Great are no longer here following the opening of the modern museum within the Royal Tombs of Vergina, this outstanding museum still contains notable treasures: spectacular **floor mosaics** from a villa in Thessalonica; an outstanding **statue of Augustus**; a famous **bronze krater** (urn) from Derveni (320–300 B.C.E.), finest of its kind in the world; a **bust of Alexander the Great**; and many notable examples of pottery, jewelry, and gold and silver burial objects from Sedes.

▲ **Fig. 58.** Alexander the Great, Thessalonica Museum

Near the Archaeological Museum is the fine **Museum of Byzantine Culture**. Note especially the **oriclinium**, a reconstructed entrance room to a 5th-century home featuring elaborate wall and floor mosaics and a display of domestic life; also, a **wall painting of Susanna and the Elders** (5th century) from Thessalonica's **east cemetery**, as well as many interesting grave stelae from the 3rd and 4th centuries.

Extensive remains of the **ancient walls** of Thessalonica are still standing. The walls visible today are basically Byzantine with later Ottoman additions, although in some places traces of earlier Hellenistic construction is evident. Originally these walls ran for nearly 5 miles and surrounded the entire city, but during the 19th century and afterward the sections along the seafront, as well as other portions, were torn down. Major sections of the wall, including some impressive towers, are still intact, particularly on the northeastern side of the city. One of the best places to view the wall is on the city's acropolis, whose wall is almost totally intact. The southern section of the acropolis wall is especially well preserved.

Other Sites of Interest

The **Royal Tombs of Macedonia** are located at Vergina, a short distance from Thessalonica. As one of the finest specialty museums in the world, this site should not be missed. It is a true world-class attraction, rivaling even the treasures of King Tut in the Cairo museum. Frequent local buses from the west bus station (do not confuse it with other bus stations; they do not have connections to Vergina) provide transportation from Thessalonica to Vergina (approximately one hour). Vergina features two sites of interest, the Royal Tombs and the site of the palace, although the first holds much greater attraction for most visitors.

From ground level, the visitor enters the **Royal Tombs** via a sloping passageway that leads to the first underground level, which has been transformed into an impressive, ultramodern museum. The spectacular treasures of the Macedonian royal family are displayed about the circular room. Preeminent among these are the **golden casket** that contained the cremated bones of **Philip II**, a unique **gold and ivory shield** from the tomb of Philip II, a large **silver amphora** and an ornate **bronze lantern**, an intricately wrought **gold wreath** and **diadems** that were perfectly preserved in their marble and stone underground tombs, and **ivory figures** that once adorned the funerary couches.

On this level also is located the first of three Macedonian tombs, the so-called **Tomb of Persephone**, which depicts the abduction of Persephone by Pluto. Much of the color of the frieze still remains. This tomb is believed to be the burial place of **Amyntas III** (d. 369 B.C.E.), as well as that of an adult female and a newborn baby, which suggests that the woman may have died in childbirth.

Two other tombs, however, are the featured attraction of the museum. Both of these tombs lie at a second underground level, and their **monumental façades** may be viewed, though the tombs themselves may not be entered. Archaeologists long suspected that the tombs discovered at Vergina (1997–1998) might have belonged to the royal family of Macedonia. Examination of a skull with a damaged eye socket and a pair of **ceremonial greaves** (ornate shin guards), one shorter than the other— Philip II had suffered such an eye wound from an arrow eighteen years earlier, and one of his legs was shorter than the other—confirmed one of these tombs as belonging to none other than the powerful king and father of **Alexander the Great**, Philip II of Macedon. A second tomb is believed to belong to the boy king **Alexander IV**—the grandson of Philip II, the son of Alexander the Great by his Iranian wife, the famed beauty **Roxane** (the child was born after the death of Alexander). He was murdered along with his mother in 310 B.C.E. by **King Cassander**.

The burial place of Alexander himself has never been discovered, although it is believed that he may have been buried in Alexandria, Egypt, the most famous of his many namesake cities. (Alexander died in Babylon at the end of his famous eight-year campaign against the Persians.)

On the hill above Vergina (approximately a twenty-minute walk) lie the extensive ruins of the **Royal Palace of the Macedonians** at **Aigai**, the name of the ancient village once at this location. The palace area is impressive for its vast size, and because it is the only ancient Greek palace still in existence. This enormous complex (350 feet by 290 feet) was one of the largest buildings of ancient times. Likely it was built by Cassander around 300 B.C.E. A series of **dining rooms** encircled the colonnaded courtyard in the center on all four sides (off-center doors indicate a room for serving). It has been estimated that nearly three hundred guests could be seated in these rooms. The circular room on the east side of the building may be the **throne room**. A few mosaics remain among the ruins (some covered with gravel for preservation).

Just below the palace can be seen the partially excavated remains of the **theater** (4th century B.C.E.) where Philip II was murdered by one of his bodyguards, **Pausanias** (an offended lover), at the wedding of his daughter. Both Alexander, who became king, and his mother, who wished to rule (but was made governor of the province of Asia on the western shore of Asia Minor, modern Turkey), have been suspected as accomplices in the plot. Some of the seating in the small theater is visible.

Either on the way to the palace or returning, take a moment to look at the so-called **Macedonian Tombs** beside the road. The tomb on the east (closed) dates to around 340 B.C.E. It may have been occupied by the mother of Philip II, **Eurydike**. A highly decorated throne was discovered inside. The **adjacent tomb** is accessed by a ramp that descends to a vaulted interior containing a **marble throne**. Its date and occupant are uncertain.

Part II

Sites in Turkey

Turkey was the arena for much of the biblical story. Haran, the city to which Abraham and Sarah moved after having left Ur, is near the Euphrates River in modern Turkey. The ancient Hittites, ancestors of those mentioned in the Hebrew Bible, controlled a powerful kingdom in ancient Turkey. In the New Testament, Antioch, then a part of Syria but now in Turkey, was the place where the name "Christians" was first used in reference to the followers of Jesus. Paul, the leading missionary of the Christian faith, was a native of the city of Tarsus (in Turkey) and traveled extensively through Asia Minor (ancient Turkey) spreading the message of Christianity. All seven of the churches mentioned in the book of Revelation were located in the area of modern Turkey. Even beyond the biblical period, Turkey was crucial for the development of Christianity. Constantinople became the center of the church in the east, and several important early church councils, at which major issues of church doctrine were debated, were held in Turkey (the Councils of Nicaea, Chalcedon, Ephesus, and Constantinople). Still today, the patriarch of Constantinople has the primacy of honor, the "first among equals," over all the Eastern Orthodox patriarchs.

Antioch on the Orontes

At one time Antioch on the Orontes was one of the three largest and most important cities of the Greco-Roman world, along with Rome and Alexandria (Egypt). Although Antioch faded from prominence centuries ago, the present city, with its population of approximately 150,000, is still a rewarding place to visit. The museum of the city, the Hatay Archaeological Museum, contains one of the best collections of ancient mosaics of any museum in the world.

Location and History

In ancient times Antioch on the Orontes was a part of Syria and thus is sometimes referred to, especially in biblical studies, as Antioch of Syria. (Fifteen other cities in the ancient world were named Antioch as well.) Today the city, now known as Antakya, is just north of the Syrian border, in the Hatay province of southern Turkey. The Orontes River (today called the Asi) connected the city to the Mediterranean Sea. **Seleucus I Nicator**, one of the generals of Alexander the Great, founded the city. At first **Antigonus**, another general, controlled Syria, but he was defeated in 301 by Seleucus and other leaders. Seleucus then gained control of Syria and established his own cities, including Antioch and its port city of Seleucia Pieria. Seleucus named the city, which soon became the capital of the Seleucid kingdom, after his father, Antiochus. Subsequent Seleucid rulers, including **Antiochus I Soter** (r. 281–261 B.C.E.), **Seleucus II Callinicus** (r. 246–225 B.C.E.), and **Antiochus IV Epiphanes** (r. 175–164 B.C.E.), enlarged and enhanced the city. **Tigranes** of Armenia captured the city in 83 B.C.E., but in 66 B.C.E. he was defeated by the Roman general **Pompey**, who made Antioch the capital of the Roman province of Syria. Both **Julius Caesar** and **Augustus** visited the city, and both erected various buildings there. (The wedding of **Mark Antony** to **Cleopatra** likely took place in Antioch. Ancient sources indicate it occurred in Syria but do not specify the city. As the capital, Antioch was the likely location.)

During the Roman period, Antioch was a large, cosmopolitan city, the third largest city in the Roman world after Rome and Alexandria. (Some scholars claim that Ephesus may have had a slightly greater population than Antioch.) Not only was the city important militarily as a staging ground for Roman activities in the east, but Antioch was also a major commercial and cultural center. Antioch was truly a city where East met West. The emperor **Claudius** began the Olympic Games of Antioch. Held every five years, these athletic events became one of the most celebrated festivals of the Roman world. **Septimius Severus** (r. 193–211 C.E.) bestowed the coveted title of Roman colony on the city.

Antioch continued to enjoy prestige and prosperity during the Byzantine period, when it was famous as a center of learning and culture. The city also saw its share of disasters, from both natural and military causes. The area was prone to earthquakes, several of which did extensive damage to the city at various times. A severe earthquake struck the city in 37 C.E. To help the city recover from the extensive damage, the emperor **Caligula** provided large sums of money. During a visit to the city by **Trajan** in 115, the city suffered one of its most destructive earthquakes. Trajan himself barely escaped harm. (**Hadrian**, who would succeed Trajan as emperor, was also in the city at the time.) In 458 C.E. another major earthquake struck Antioch, doing extensive damage to certain sections of the city. The most disastrous quake, however, occurred the following century. A quake shook the city in 526, reportedly killing 250,000 people, with aftershocks continuing for a year and a half. These aftershocks culminated with a second major earthquake in 528, which leveled most of the remaining buildings and walls of the city.

As if the earthquakes were not problem enough, Antioch also had to deal with military attacks. On three different occasions during this period (253 C.E., 260 C.E., and 540 C.E.) the Persians captured the city and/or burned it. Rebuilt on a smaller scale by the emperor **Justinian**, Antioch never regained its former importance. In the 7th century Syria (including Antioch) was overrun by the Persians and a large number of people carried away as captives. Later that same century, when the Muslim Arabs conquered the entire region, Antioch came under Arab control and remained in Arab hands for the next three hundred years. In the following centuries Seljuk Turks, Crusaders, Egyptian Mamluks, and Ottoman Turks ruled over the city. At the end of World War I Antioch was transferred to Syria, which was then a protectorate of France. In 1937–38, for a brief period, the autonomous Republic of Hatay came into existence, which included Antioch. In 1939 this area was joined to Turkey and became the Turkish province of Hatay.

Jews comprised part of the population of Antioch since the founding of the city. According to the 1st-century-C.E. Jewish historian Josephus, Jews were among the mercenaries who served in the army of Seleucus I Nicator, the founder of the city, and were granted citizenship rights in the cities he founded. The accuracy of the claims of Josephus that the Jews were given citizenship and special privileges by Seleucus has been questioned. However, his claim that Jews served in the army of Seleucus and settled at Antioch is plausible, since throughout much of the Hellenistic and Roman periods a strong Jewish community existed at Antioch. The Jews seem to have been well integrated into the social and economic life of Antioch in a variety of professions at every economic level. Their religious beliefs and practices were not only tolerated but apparently also accepted by many, for Josephus reports that the Jews in Antioch made converts of many non-Jews (*Jewish War* 7.45).

In 167 B.C.E. **Antiochus IV Epiphanes** attempted to bring all of Palestine under the worship of Zeus and to turn the temple in Jerusalem into a temple to Zeus, an action that ultimately led to the Maccabean Revolt in 166 B.C.E. Although the plight of the Jews in Antioch at that time is not reported, undoubtedly their situation must have been rather difficult. A few years later, under the reign of **Demetrius II** (r. 145–139 B.C.E.), a revolt against Demetrius occurred in Antioch. The Jewish ruler **Jonathan**, who had earlier allied himself with Demetrius, sent three thousand Jewish soldiers from Judea to help put down the revolt. Although ancient sources do not describe any retaliation by the residents of Antioch against their Jewish neighbors, this use of Jews from Judea likely worsened the relations between the Jews and Gentiles in Antioch.

After the Jewish revolt against the Romans led to the fall of Jerusalem in 70 C.E., a group of Antiochene citizens asked the Roman general (and future emperor) **Titus** to banish the Jews from Antioch. When he refused to do so, they asked him to rescind certain privileges enjoyed by the Jews. This he also refused to do. Josephus cites this action as examples of the fair-mindedness of Titus in his dealings with the Jews, even after the Jewish revolt in Judea (*Jewish War* 7.96–111; *Jewish Antiquities* 12.121–124). All of Titus's actions toward the Jews of Antioch were not benevolent, however. While in Antioch, Titus presented to the city several items to serve as memorials to the defeat and humiliation of the Jews in Judea. Near one of the gates of Antioch, in the Jewish quarter of the city, he set up bronze figures that were supposed to represent the cherubim that had been taken from the temple. On the gate itself he placed a figure of the moon to serve as a reminder that Jerusalem fell during the night. Furthermore, he built a theater in Daphne, a suburb of Antioch, reportedly destroying a synagogue in order to build the theater on the same site.

During the Byzantine period, Judaism continued in Antioch. Although the increasing influence of Christianity in politics and other areas of society at times made life difficult for the Jews, Judaism continued to be a vibrant religion in the area, as evidenced by the warnings from the 4th-century Christian leader **John Chrysostom** to his congregation not to participate in Jewish worship or other activities.

Antioch became one of the leading centers of Christianity in the early centuries. As noted below, the city played a large role in the opening chapters of the Christian movement, being visited by both **Peter** and **Paul** as well as serving as the home base for Paul's missionary activities. Antioch has also been the most widely supported scholarly conjecture for the location of the writing of the Gospel of Matthew. The Gospel nowhere identifies the place where the work was written, but the city of Antioch does fit the characteristics that many scholars see reflected in the Gospel—it was a cosmopolitan city, it had a large population of Jews as well as a strong Christian community, and it had a Greek-speaking population. Furthermore, the earliest evidence for the use of the Gospel of Matthew is in quotations of the work by a church leader from Antioch, **Ignatius**.

Ignatius (ca. 35–ca. 107 C.E.) is remembered as the third bishop (some traditions say the second) of the city of Antioch. During the reign of **Trajan**, Ignatius was arrested and sent to Rome for execution under a guard of ten soldiers. Along the way he wrote letters of encouragement and instruction to six churches and to Polycarp, bishop of Smyrna. In his letters, particularly the letter to the Roman church, Ignatius made it clear that he did not wish to avoid his impending death. He welcomed martyrdom as his means of having a closer and enduring relationship with God. Ignatius's acceptance of and even yearning for martyrdom became a model and an inspiration for many Christian martyrs who followed in his path. With the death of Ignatius, the church of Antioch had not made its final contribution to the roll of martyrs, however, for Antiochene Christians were victims of major persecutions against the church during the 3rd and early 4th centuries.

Antioch was also important for its contributions to biblical scholarship in the early years. The approach to interpretation known as the "Antioch school" stressed a more literal and straightforward approach to the scriptures, emphasizing historical and grammatical studies. This approach was in contrast to that advocated at Alexandria by such figures as Origen, who applied an allegorical interpretation to the texts. One of the leading proponents of the "Antioch school" was John Chrysostom (John the Golden Mouth), famous for his powerful and effective preaching and interpretations. He later became bishop of Constantinople.

A rather bizarre act of Christian piety and devotion was associated with Antioch during the early centuries. In the 5th century a monk named Simeon moved to a hillside southeast of Antioch where he climbed atop a pillar upon which he stayed for forty-two years, dying in his seventies. The pillar was initially low but was gradually increased in height to approximately 60 feet. (He is known as **Simeon Stylites the Elder**. "Stylites" comes from a Greek word meaning "pillar.") Simeon lived on a platform on the pillar with no shelter, spending his time in prayer and contemplation. Once a week he ate; the remainder of the time he fasted. Simeon attracted many visitors who came seeking miracles and spiritual guidance. From his pillar he preached, exhorted, reconciled enemies, healed, and worked on behalf of the poor. So great was his influence that even the emperor at times followed his advice. Simeon had several imitators, among them **Simeon Stylites the Younger**, who set up his pillar on a mountain west of Antioch during the 6th century. Like his namesake, this pillar saint also preached, healed, performed miracles, and exerted tremendous influence over the people.

At the Council of Nicaea in 325, Antioch was officially recognized, after Rome and Alexandria, as an episcopal see of special authority. Later councils added Constantinople to the list (after Rome) and Jerusalem (after Antioch). The bishop in each of these cities was designated a patriarch. Thus the tradition developed of five patriarchates, with one of those being the partriarchate of Antioch. Today the bishop of Antioch does not reside in the city but instead lives in Damascus, the capital of Syria, from where he performs his duties as the patriarch of Antioch.

Biblical Significance

Ancient Antioch played a major role in the story of early Christianity. One of the seven men in the Jerusalem church who were chosen "to wait on tables" (that is, to handle the practical matters of the church) when a dispute arose among different groups in the church ("Hellenists" and "Hebrews") was from Antioch, a man named **Nicolaus** (Acts 6:5). Acts 11:19 states that Antioch was also one of the places to which many Christians fled after persecution arose in Jerusalem following the stoning of Stephen. The Christian faith prospered so well in Antioch that the Jerusalem church sent **Barnabas** to investigate the situation there. Seeing the success of the Christian work in the city, Barnabas went to Tarsus and brought back **Paul** to help him instruct and strengthen the new converts. According to Acts, the followers of Jesus were first called "Christians" in Antioch (11:26). Soon after, the church at Antioch demonstrated its compassion and its indebtedness to the Jerusalem church by sending a relief offering to the Jerusalem Christians during a time of famine (11:27–30).

The church at Antioch was instrumental in the missionary endeavors of the early church, for it was the Antioch church that first sent Paul and Barnabas on their so-called first missionary journey. At the end of this missionary journey they returned to Antioch. When a conference was needed in Jerusalem to deal with the issue of Gentiles becoming Christians, Paul and Barnabas went from Antioch to Jerusalem to attend the meeting. At the conclusion of the meeting Paul and Barnabas returned to Antioch, where "they taught and proclaimed the word of the Lord" (Acts 15:35). Shortly thereafter Paul and Barnabas decided to embark on another mission trip, but, as a result of a disagreement, they separated, with each going on a separate missionary journey. Paul, along with **Silas**, traveled through Asia Minor and Greece and eventually returned to Antioch (Acts 18:22). After remaining in the city for some time, Paul departed from Antioch to begin his third and final missionary journey.

Paul himself, in writing to the Galatian Christians, mentioned his stay in the city of Antioch. Paul was in Antioch when a dispute arose over the issue of inclusion of Gentiles in the Christian movement. Some people in the early church believed that Gentiles had to submit to certain practices and requirements within Judaism (particularly circumcision) before they could become Christians. Paul strongly opposed such requirements, arguing that in Christ "there is no longer Jew or Greek" (Gal 3:28). In Galatians 2 Paul described an incident in which he confronted **Cephas (Peter)** about his hypocritical actions related to this issue. Peter, who was also in Antioch at the time, had previously been willing to associate with and accept Gentiles as equals in Christ. Yet when a group of Jewish Christians who were opposed to the full acceptance of Gentiles arrived from Jerusalem, Peter "drew back and kept himself separate for fear of the circumcision faction" (2:12). Antioch does not appear again in the New Testament, but the work of Paul and Barnabas and other early Christian leaders in the city was apparently successful, for Antioch became a major center for Christianity in the following centuries.

Site Visit

On the basis of literary evidence and archaeological findings, archaeologists have a good idea of many of the buildings and streets that existed in ancient Antioch. Unfortunately, not much remains from antiquity for the modern visitor to see. The city was situated between Mt. Silpius on the east and the Orontes River on the west. The streets of the city were laid out on a Hippodamian grid plan (i.e., with streets intersecting at regular right angles). During Roman times a great colonnaded street, which served as the main street of the city, ran through the city for almost 2 miles. The street had triumphal arches at each end and a large forum, with a nymphaeum, in the center. **King Herod** of Judea supplied the paving stones for the street, whereas **Emperor Tiberius** (or Herod—ancient sources differ) erected the colonnades along both sides of the street. (Today the main route through the city, the Kurtuluş Caddesi, basically follows the path of the Roman street.) Among the buildings of the city were a hippodrome (or circus) and a palace (both on the island in the Orontes), two theaters, an amphitheater (for gladiatorial contests and other events), the Pantheion, the Kaisareion (a basilica built by **Julius Caesar** for the promotion of the cult of Rome), public baths, aqueducts, and several temples (including ones to Jupiter Capitolinus, Dionysus, Pan, Artemis, Ares, and Hercules).

A portion of the **Roman aqueduct** can be seen in the eastern part of the city, near the city hospital. This part of the aqueduct, built during the

▲ **Fig. 59.** The Church of St. Peter at Antioch (Antakya)

time of Trajan (r. 98–117), is today used as a bridge, called the **Memikli Bridge** by the locals. The **Church of St. Peter** (Senpiyer Kilisesi) is located on the northeast edge of Antioch, about 2 miles from the center of the city. Follow Kurtuluş Caddesi northeast and look for a sign on the right pointing the way to St. Peter's. The older part of the church is a natural cave on Mt. Staurin, which is an extension of Mt. Silpius. Local tradition claims that this cave was the meeting place for the early Christians of Antioch, including **Peter**, who supposedly preached and taught in this church. Another tradition claims that the property originally belonged to **Luke the Evangelist**, who supposedly was from Antioch and who donated the property for use by the Christians as a worship site. A narrow tunnel on the left side of the apse (now blocked) is claimed to have been an escape route used by the Christians during times of danger.

The actual early history of the cave is difficult to determine. At least as early as the 4th or 5th century the cave was used as a Christian church, because the mosaic floors in the cave apparently date to that period. To the right of the modern altar are traces of frescoes on the wall, also from the early period. The façade at the front of the cave was added during the 12th or 13th century, when the Crusaders were in control of the city. The present façade is a restoration dating to the middle of the 19th century.

On the slope of Mt. Staurin, about 220 yards northwest of the Church of St. Peter, is a carved relief known as **Charonion**. The relief is the head and shoulders of a figure wearing a veil, with a smaller figure standing on the right shoulder of the bust. The smaller figure, which is shrouded, is very badly eroded. The carving was never completed. Although the source and identity of the relief are not certain, the 6th-century-C.E. monk and local chronicler John Malalas reported that it was carved during the time of Antiochus IV Epiphanes (r. 175–164 B.C.E.) in order to bring to an end a plague that was wreaking havoc in the city. It has been suggested that it was called the Charonion (after Charon, the ferryman of Greek mythology, who carried the souls of the dead across the River Styx to the underworld) because it was a bust of some god or goddess of the underworld who, having been appeased, brought the plague to an end and thus stopped sending people to death and the underworld.

Like most ancient cities, Antioch was surrounded by defensive walls. Today little remains to be seen of the city walls of Antioch, which reportedly were approximately 8 miles in length. About all that is left of the **walls**, as well as the **citadel** of the ancient city, is on Mt. Silpius. To visit the ruins, go east on highway 420 for approximately 3 miles, turning right onto the road to Altinözü. After traveling approximately 15 miles, turn right onto another road that leads to a small parking area. The remains of the citadel are mainly from the time of Nicephorus II Phocas (r. 963–969).

The most impressive place to visit in Antakya is the **Hatay Archaeological Museum**, located on Gündüz Caddesi, on the west bank of the Asi River. The museum is famous for its spectacular collection of mosaics discovered in the excavations of Antioch, Daphne, Seleucia Pieria, and other nearby locations. The mosaics, which are from the 2nd to the 6th centuries C.E., are primarily floor mosaics from private homes, although some are from public buildings such as baths. With their rich colors and detailed scenes, the mosaics bear testimony to the great skill of the artists who produced them. Bordered by intricate geometric designs, the panels of the mosaics depict mythological scenes, animal and plant life, and scenes from the everyday lives of the ancient people.

Rooms 1–4 and the hallway at the end of room 4 display the museum's collection of mosaics. Among the mosaics not to be missed are the following: **the four seasons** (room 1), **the personification of Soteria** (room 1), **the buffet mosaic** (room 2), **the happy hunchback** (room 3), **the Negro fisherman** (room 3), **the evil eye** (room 3), **the infant Hercules strangling serpents** (room 3), **Oceanus and Thetis** (room 3), **the drunken Dionysus** (room 4), **the jugglers** (room 4), **the Megalopyschia hunt** (room 4), **the Bacchic dancers** (room 4), and **the boat of the Psyches** (room 4). In these rooms are displayed various statues and statuettes also, including representations of **Hygieia, Fortuna, Artemis, Faunus,** and **Hades**. In the hall behind room 4 are several additional mosaics, including one of **Dionysus** and one of **ducks and fish** amid water lilies. Room 5 contains various Mitanni, Assyrian,

▲ **Fig. 60.** Mosaic of the drunken Dionysus in the Hatay Museum, Antakya

Hittite, and post-Hittite items (idols, altars, an Assyrian inscription, a relief of Assyrian soldiers, column bases, and figures of lions), mostly made of basalt. Room 6 consists of a collection of small items found in Antioch, in the nearby tells (mounds), and in the surrounding area. In addition to some statues, the room also contains a collection of coins dating from the 5th century B.C.E. to the Ottoman period. In the garden and on the porch are several other items, including additional mosaics, statues, and some sarcophagi.

Other Sites of Interest

Although the site has no biblical significance, visitors interested in early church history might enjoy a brief visit to ruins of the **monastery of St. Simeon Stylites the Younger**. As noted above, Simeon Stylites the Younger, like Simeon Stylites the Elder, whom he imitated, spent his life perched upon a column (from the age of seven on) as an act of piety and devotion. To reach the monastery, take the road from Antioch toward Samandağ. Just past Karaçay, turn left. The road leads uphill for approximately 2.5 miles before there is a fork to the right that leads to the ruins.

Antioch of Pisidia

Although overshadowed in the New Testament by a different Antioch (Antioch on the Orontes), Antioch of Pisidia was an important city during Hellenistic and Roman times. Archaeological excavations have uncovered the remains of a thriving city, complete with theater, baths, temples, stadium, nymphaeum, paved streets, and aqueduct. Augustus had a copy of his famous Res Gestae, the list of his accomplishments, inscribed on his sanctuary in the city.

Location and History

Several cities in the ancient world were called Antioch, named for various members of the Seleucid dynasty who bore the name of Antiochus. Antioch of Pisidia was located approximately 0.5 mile northeast of the modern town of Yalvaç and 22 miles southwest of Akşehir. (Pisidia was a mountainous region in the south-central section of Asia Minor.) Antioch was actually not a part of the Pisidian region but lay just north of Pisidia in the region of Phrygia. The city was sometimes called Pisidian Antioch (see Acts 13:14), meaning "Antioch near Pisidia," as a way of distinguishing it from other cities named Antioch. When the Romans established the province of Galatia in 25 B.C.E., Antioch became a part of Galatia. In 295 C.E. the Romans redivided the area, creating the province of Pisidia, with Antioch as its capital.

Antioch is situated on the southern foothills of the Sultan Mountains, on the northwest side of the Yalvaç River (ancient Anthius River). The city was spread over seven small hills, reminiscent of the seven hills of Rome, a similarity that was not lost on the Romans, who divided the city into seven districts, one on each of the seven hills. Backed up to the Sultan Mountains, Antioch enjoyed good natural defenses. Strategically located, the city was important both militarily and commercially. The land around Antioch was fertile, producing a variety of fruit and grains.

Although a precise date cannot be determined, the city of Antioch was founded in the first half of the 3rd century B.C.E. by the one of the

Seleucid rulers, either **Seleucus I**, **Antiochus I**, or **Antiochus II**. The Seleucids established several cities in the region, including Apollonia, Seleucia (Seleucia Sidera), and Laodicea Catacecaumene. These cities apparently served to protect the major road that ran from the Aegean Sea through the northern part of the Pisidian region of Asia Minor to Syria. The original settlers of Antioch, at the invitation of the Seleucid ruler, were from Magnesia on the Meander, a town near the Aegean coast. Few archaeological remains from the Hellenistic period have been uncovered at the site. One significant exception is the nearby Temple of Men Askaenos, the Anatolian moon god, built during the 2nd century B.C.E. The theater in the city also may come from the Hellenistic period but was later enlarged, possibly as late as the 3rd and 4th centuries. In 188 B.C.E., after the Romans had defeated Antiochus III, Antioch was declared a free city. Sometime around 39–36 B.C.E. the Romans put the city under the control of **Amyntas**, the client king of Galatia. At the death of Amyntas in 25 B.C.E., Augustus placed the area under direct Roman control, creating the province of Galatia, which encompassed a large portion of central Asia Minor, including the city of Antioch.

In order to gain better control over this part of Asia Minor, Augustus established several colonies of military veterans in the region. Antioch was the first such Roman colony in the area. Settled by veterans from the Roman legions V and VII, the city was called Colonia Caesarea Antiochia. This refounding of the city as a Roman colony inaugurated the most illustrious period of Antioch's history. The next one hundred years witnessed a flurry of building activity in the city. A large temple and sanctuary for the promotion of the imperial cult was built, as was a grandiose triple-arched gateway and stairs leading to the sanctuary, a colonnaded street, an aqueduct, and a nymphaeum. One of the factors contributing to the growth of the city was the network of new roads built by the Romans. One of the most important of these highways, the Via Sebaste (Sebastian Way), was built by Augustus in 6 B.C.E. The juncture of the two portions of the road was in Antioch. The road ran west and then south from Antioch to Perga near the Mediterranean coast. The other section of the road ran eastward from Antioch to Iconium and Lystra, thus connecting the interior of Asia Minor with the coast. The inhabitants of Antioch were a mixture of Roman military veterans and their families, descendants of the Hellenistic settlers, and people of Phrygian and Pisidian background. Several of the Roman colonists eventually achieved notable success in the Roman military and administrative arenas, some even becoming members of the Roman senate.

During the 2nd and 3rd centuries Antioch continued to prosper. When **Emperor Diocletian** created the new province of Pisidia in 295 C.E., Antioch was established as the capital of the province. The theater was enlarged and a new agora and porticoes were built. No evidence survives of any Christian presence in Antioch before the 4th century. **Valerius Diogenes**, governor of Pisidia early in the 4th century, actively persecuted Christians. By the end of the 4th century, however, when persecution of Christians had ceased, Antioch had at least one if not three church buildings. The city was also the seat of the metropolitan bishop for Pisidia, including **Bishop Optimus**, who was present at the Council of Constantinople in 381. Early in the 8th century Arabs invaded and destroyed the city. Never fully recovering, the city did continue, however, as the seat of the metropolitan bishop into the 12th century.

Biblical Significance

According to the itinerary in Acts 13, **Paul** and **Barnabas** visited Pisidian Antioch on their first journey to Asia Minor, having first arrived in Perga on their journey from Cyprus. From Perga they would have followed the Via Sebaste to Antioch. The book of Acts states that on the sabbath Paul and Barnabas went to the synagogue in Antioch and were invited to speak to the people there. Their message was so well received that on the following sabbath "almost the whole city gathered" to hear them (13:44). While they were able to make some converts to Christianity, their popularity created jealousy on the part of some of the Jews, who "incited the devout women of high standing and the leading men of the city, and stirred up persecution against Paul and Barnabas, and drove them out of their region" (13:49). Paul and Barnabas then traveled to Iconium, Lystra, and Derbe. Acts says that while they were in Lystra, some Jews came from Iconium and Antioch and turned the people against them, forcing them to leave that city and go to Derbe (14:19). Passing through Antioch on their return to Perga, they encouraged the new believers.

In describing Paul's second journey, Acts reports that Paul revisited several churches in southern Asia Minor that he had established on his first journey. Although Antioch is not mentioned, Acts does say that after visiting Derbe and Lystra, Paul "went through the region of Phrygia and Galatia" (16:6), perhaps implying a return visit to Antioch. Similarly, Acts 18:23 mentions Paul visiting Christians in Galatia and Phrygia on his third journey. The only other biblical reference to Pisidian Antioch is in 2 Timothy 3:11, in which the pseudonymous writer mentions the unpleasant experience in Antioch.

Even though Acts mentions a synagogue in Antioch, no remains of one have been found (see the discussion below on the Byzantine church in the center of the city). Josephus, the 1st-century-C.E. Jewish historian, mentions that the Seleucid ruler **Antiochus III** ordered that two thousand Jewish families in Babylonia be transported to trouble spots in Lydia and Phrygia because he was convinced that they would be loyal guardians and supporters of the Seleucids (*Jewish Antiquities* 12.146–153). If accurate, then Josephus's statement could explain the origin of the Jews around Antioch.

An inscription discovered at Antioch has sometimes been linked to an episode in Acts. According to Acts, Paul and Barnabas visited Cyprus prior to going to Antioch. In the city of Paphos they met the proconsul **Sergius Paulus,** who was converted to Christianity (Acts 13:4–12). An inscription discovered near Antioch in 1912 mentions the name "L. Sergius Paullus the younger, son of L." On the basis of this inscription it has been claimed that the proconsul whom Paul converted was a member of the same family as this "L. Sergius Paullus" and that Antioch was the hometown of the proconsul of Cyprus. Furthermore, it is sometimes argued, the reason that Paul made the trip inland to Pisidian Antioch was that Sergius Paulus convinced Paul to visit his hometown. As intriguing as this suggestion may be, the identification of the proconsul with the family at Antioch is not convincing, since it is a conjecture based on slim evidence. The name Sergius Paulus was too common in the Roman world for the proposed identification to be accepted.

Antioch also appears in an early apocryphal tradition about Paul. The *Acts of Paul*, a popular work containing legendary material about Paul and written during the 2nd century, describes Paul's conversion of **Thecla,** a native of the city of Iconium. She and Paul traveled to Antioch (likely Pisidian Antioch rather than Syrian Antioch, although the text is not clear), where Thecla ran into trouble. After rebuffing the amorous advances of Alexander, one of Antioch's leading citizens, she was accused of sacrilege (perhaps for dishonoring the imperial symbols that Alexander wore). Thecla was arrested and condemned to death by wild beasts. Although various wild animals were released against Thecla, she was miraculously preserved from harm and eventually set free.

Site Visit

Although several European travelers visited the site of ancient Antioch and published accounts of their explorations in the 1800s, the earliest archaeological work at Antioch occurred in 1912, when W. M. Ramsay and others excavated the nearby sanctuary of Men Askaenos. In 1913 and again in 1914 Ramsay partially excavated the site of the city itself. From 1924 to 1927 the site was the focus of excavation and study by a team of archaeologists led by D. M. Robinson of Johns Hopkins University under the sponsorship of the University of Michigan, along with Ramsay. Excavation of the site continues today by Mehmet Taşlialan, director of the Yalvaç Museum.

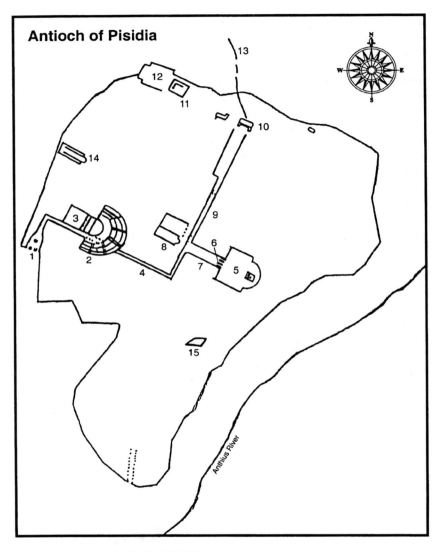

A Fig. 61. Antioch of Pisidia

1. Triple-Arched West Gate
2. Theater
3. Agora
4. Decumanus Maximus
5. Temple of Augustus
6. Propylon
7. Tiberia Plateia
8. Byzantine Church

9. Cardo Maximus
10. Nymphaeum
11. Palaestra
12. Roman Bath
13. Aqueduct
14. Church of St. Paul
15. Byzantine Structure

Approaching the site from Yalvaç, the visitor first encounters the **triple-arched gateway** on the western side of the city. Although in ruins, the gate is being reconstructed with the original stones. This monumental gate was approximately 26 feet wide and was decorated with reliefs of kneeling captive soldiers, floral motifs, weapons, and winged figures (Nikes?) on pedestals holding garlands. Near the top on the front and back of the gate were inscriptions in bronze letters, one a dedicatory inscription to **Emperor Hadrian**, the other an identification of the person who paid to have the gate built. Previously thought to have been built in 212 C.E., the gate is now dated to around 129 C.E., during the reign of Hadrian. During that year Hadrian and his wife visited the interior of Asia Minor, possibly including Antioch.

The street from the city gate ran north until it intersected the main east-west street (the **decumanus maximus**) of the city. In the middle of this short (ca. 100 feet long), wide street leading from the gate was a series of stepped stone basins with running water that created a decorative waterfall. The *decumanus maximus* ran eastward for approximately 350 feet until it ended at the main north-south street (the **cardo maximus**). Ruts worn in the paving stones of the street by chariots can be seen today. Approximately at the midpoint of the *decumanus maximus* on its northern side was situated the **theater** in Antioch. The date of the theater is uncertain, built perhaps as early as the Hellenistic period. During the late 3rd or early 4th century C.E. the theater was enlarged, increasing the seating capacity and the stage area. The most remarkable aspect of the renovated theater was a tunnel (approximately 61 feet long) on its southern side through which the *decumanus maximus* passed. By means of this vaulted tunnel, part of the seating of the theater was built over the street. The estimated capacity of the theater was approximately 15,000 people, with twenty-six rows of seats. When the theater was enlarged, a large square surrounded by porticoes was built adjacent to the theater on its western side. This square likely functioned as an **agora** or **forum** for the city.

The *cardo maximus* traversed the city north to south, with a gate in the city wall at each end. These gates were neither large nor elaborate. Little remains of them today. On the eastern side of the *cardo maximus,* about 80 feet north of its intersection with the *decumanus maximus,* was the most important structure in the city. Here was the **imperial sanctuary** with its **temple to Augustus**, built on the highest point of the city. The front of the temple contained a stairway of twelve steps leading up to the porch, which had four columns along the front with Corinthian-style capitals. Portions of some of the columns can be seen at the site. As is evident, the foundation of the temple was mostly carved out of the rock that composed the hill on which the temple was built. The temple covered an area approximately 15.5 feet wide by 30 feet long. Surrounding the temple on the rear and most of two sides was a semicircular two-story portico, largely

▲ **Fig. 62.** Temple of Augustus at Antioch of Pisidia

carved out from the rock of the hillside. Along the rock face can still be seen the holes cut into the rock to support the wooden beams of the second-story floor of the portico.

In front of the temple was a large square, surrounded by a single-story portico. On the western side of the square was a **three-arched propylon**, which was the entrance to the imperial sanctuary. Built at the beginning of the 1st century C.E., this gate contained an inscription in bronze letters dedicating it to Augustus and was richly decorated with sculptures and reliefs celebrating his victories. Attached to the propylon was a Latin copy of the Res Gestae Divi Augusti, fragments of which were discovered at the site. (The Antiochene copy of the Res Gestae is known as the Monumentum Antiochenum.) This document, written by Augustus shortly before his death, is a compendium of his achievements during his lifetime. He ordered copies of it to be inscribed on his sanctuaries throughout the empire. Twelve steps led down from the propylon to the **Tiberia Plateia** (Tiberias Square), a broad colonnaded street leading down to the *cardo maximus*. Behind the colonnades along the street were small shops, possibly bars and restaurants. In this area several game boards (with circles and rectangles) can be seen where they were etched into the paving stones for playing various games of dice.

Opposite the Tiberia Plateia on the west side of the *cardo maximus* are the remains of a **Byzantine church**, possibly from the 4th or 5th century B.C.E. In describing excavations at this site in the 1920s, W. M. Ramsay claims to have found evidence of a synagogue beneath this church. This was evidence, he claimed, that this church in the center of the city had been built over the site of the synagogue in which Paul had preached as recorded in Acts 13. These claims are unsubstantiated, however. Between the church and the Tiberia Plateia evidence of several small **shops** or **workshops** were found. The northern end of the *cardo maximus* opened into an elongated square, at the northern end of which was a large **nymphaeum**, or monumental fountain. Some of the foundations of the nymphaeum can still be seen. To the northwest of the nymphaeum is the **palaestra** (exercise area) and adjoining **Roman bath**, which together constituted the gymnasium complex for the city. The palaestra, situated in front of the bath (between the bath and the nymphaeum), was a rectangular courtyard surrounded by colonnaded porticoes. Including the porticoes, the palaestra measured about 40 feet by 32 feet. Only the paving stones of the floor have survived from the palaestra. The bath, a typical building in a Roman city, included a frigidarium (cold room), a tepidarium (warm room), a caldarium (hot room), and an apodyterium (changing room). Several smaller rooms also were a part of the bath. A large part of the bathhouse has survived and is still being excavated. The date of construction of the bathhouse complex, while uncertain, probably was during the latter half of the 1st century or early 2nd century.

Along the western wall of the city, approximately halfway between the bathhouse and the triple-arched western gate, are the remains of a **large church** built in the basilica style. The church consisted of an apse, a nave, two narrower side aisles (separated from the nave by a row of thirteen columns on each side), an outer narthex, and an inner narthex. The church

⊿ **Fig. 63** The "Church of St. Paul" at Antioch of Pisidia

contained a mosaic floor, portions of which are still in place. One of the inscriptions in the mosaic refers to **Optimus**, the bishop of the city between 375 and 381 C.E. This inscription allows the church to be dated to around the end of the 4th century. The church was later renovated and expanded, perhaps during the 5th or 6th century. The remains of the church walls come from this later period. The church has sometimes been labeled the **"Church of St. Paul"** due to a large font (dated to after the 6th century C.E.) found in the nearby town of Yalvaç. Reportedly the font originally came from the site of the basilica. On one side of the font is an inscription that reads "Saint Paul." This church is one of the largest ever discovered in early Christian Asia Minor. It served as the seat of the metropolitan bishop at Antioch.

Two structures or complexes outside the city wall are also of interest. Just north of the city are the remains of the **aqueduct** that brought water to the city from springs approximately 6 miles away in the hills northeast of Antioch. Part of the aqueduct ran through tunnels, while other sections were carried over bridges or arched supports. Three impressive sections of the arches of the aqueduct can still be seen today. The aqueduct likely was constructed during the early 1st century C.E.

West of the city are the partially excavated remains of a **stadium**, possibly built during the Hellenistic period and renovated during the 2nd century C.E. Built in a horseshoe shape, the stadium was approximately 208 feet long and 33 feet wide. The stadium would have served the city as a place for various sporting events and games.

Other Sites of Interest

Approximately 3 miles southeast of Yalvaç, near the village of Gemen (Özgüney), is a hill known locally as Karakuyu. On the top of this hill is the **sanctuary of Men Askaenos**, the principal god of ancient Antioch. This sanctuary, dated to the 2nd century B.C.E., was in use until the 3rd or 4th century C.E., when, according to conjecture, it was destroyed by Christians in Antioch. The main structure of the sanctuary was a **temple to Men**, the Anatolian moon god, with its colonnaded enclosure. The remains of the wall and part of the paving of this enclosure, or temenos, are visible today. The ruins belonging to the foundations of the temple itself are also visible. Numerous votive inscriptions can be seen on the southwest wall of the temenos. In addition to this temple, ruins of several other buildings are present on the site, including another, **smaller temple**, a **stadium**, and several **small buildings**. The stadium would have held games in honor of Men, while some of the small buildings were likely used for meals, banquets, and meetings associated with the worship of Men. The sanctuary site also contains the unexcavated ruins of a 4th- or

5th-century church. Much of the material used in the construction of the church was reused from other buildings at the sanctuary, including the Temple of Men.

Many of the artifacts found at Antioch are in the **museum** in the nearby town of Yalvaç. Inside the museum are numerous statues, busts, figurines, coins, votive inscriptions, and other items from Antioch and the surrounding area. Fragments of the **Monumentum Antiochenum** (Antioch's copy of the Res Gestae) are also on display here, as is the **font** with the inscription for St. Paul. Outside in the garden and under the covered walkways are milestones, votive altars, sarcophagi, grave stelae, inscriptions, and architectural fragments from the site, including columns and friezes.

Assos

With its acropolis perched on a steep hill overlooking the Aegean Sea, the city of Assos provides a spectacular view for the visitor. From the acropolis one can look down on the ruins of the ancient buildings on the slope and also see the remains of the city's harbor in the Aegean. On a clear day the island of Lesbos is visible approximately 7 miles south across the Bay of Edremit. From this island came the first settlers of ancient Assos.

Location and History

The site of ancient Assos is located in the southern part of the Troad area of Turkey, on the modern highway that runs along the Aegean coast and connects the towns of Geyikli and Ayvacïk. Assos was in the ancient region of Mysia. Today the village of Behramkale occupies the site of ancient Assos. During the 7th century B.C.E. Aeolian Greeks from the town of Methymna (modern Molivos) on the island of Lesbos crossed the Edremit Bay and founded the city of Assos. During the first half of the 6th century, **King Croesus** of Lydia (whose capital was at Sardis) captured and controlled Assos. Lydian domination ended in 546 B.C.E., when **Cyrus** of Persia defeated Croesus and brought this area of Asia Minor under Persian control. During the following century Assos gained its freedom when a coalition of Greek city-states defeated the Persians. Assos then became a part of the Delian League under the leadership of Athens. One of the rulers of Assos in the 4th century was **Hermias**, who had been a student, along with **Aristotle**, of the philosopher Plato. At the invitation of Hermias, Aristotle went to Assos and lived there from 348 to 345 B.C.E., marrying Hermias' niece. The Persians recaptured the city and killed Hermias, but their control ended with the conquests of **Alexander the Great**. After Alexander's untimely death the Seleucids ruled Assos.

In 241 B.C.E. the city became a part of the Pergamene kingdom and remained under the control of the kings of Pergamum until the death of **Attalus III** in 133 B.C.E., at which time the city passed into Roman hands. One of the most famous natives of Assos was the philosopher **Cleanthes** (331–232 B.C.E.). Born in Assos, Cleanthes went to Athens, where he studied with Zeno, the founder of the philosophical system known as Stoicism. After the death of Zeno in 246 B.C.E., Cleanthes succeeded him as the head of the Stoic school. Although Cleanthes was the author of nearly fifty works, only fragments of his writings have survived, of which the most famous is his "Hymn to Zeus."

During the Roman period, the **Apostle Paul** visited the city, leaving from its harbor to travel by ship to Caesarea in Palestine. The Byzantine period saw the decline of Assos to a small village. Reused building materials from a 6th-century church were incorporated into a mosque constructed in the 14th century, when Assos was under Ottoman rule.

Biblical Significance

At the end of **Paul**'s third missionary journey as he was returning to Palestine, he traveled overland from Troas to Assos, a distance of approximately 20 miles. At Assos, his traveling companions, who had come by ship from Troas, met Paul and took him aboard with them. From there they sailed to Mitylene on the island of Lesbos, to Samos, and then to Miletus. Leaving Miletus, they eventually returned to Caesarea and then went down to Jerusalem. The account of this visit to Assos, found in Acts 20:13–14, does not mention whether Paul spent any time in Assos or whether he preached or made any converts in the city. Assos is not mentioned again in the Bible.

Site Visit

The **acropolis** of Assos sits above the modern village of Behramkale and is reached by walking along the steep, narrow main street of the village up to the ruins. The **fortification walls** that are encountered first on the acropolis are from the Byzantine period (6th century). To the northeast of these walls is a 14th-century **mosque** partially built with materi-

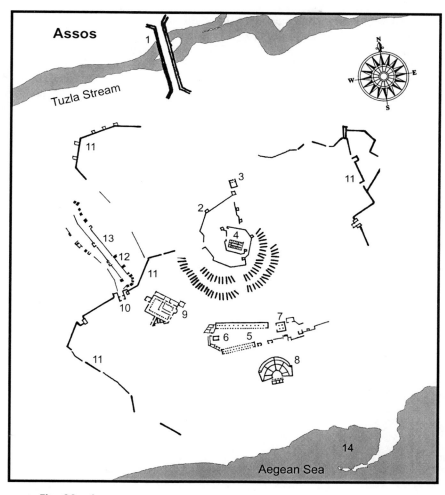

▲ **Fig. 64.** Assos

1. Ottoman Bridge	6. Agora Temple	11. Hellenistic Walls
2. Byzantine Walls	7. Bouleuterion	12. Necropolis
3. Mosque	8. Theater	13. Ancient Main Road
4. Temple of Athena	9. Gymnasium	14. Harbor
5. Agora	10. West Gate	

als from a 6th-century church (note the cross and the chi-rho symbol over the door of the mosque). This area provides a great view to the north, encompassing the village of Behramkale, the landscape, and the 14th-century **Ottoman bridge** over the Tuzla Çay. The main structure on the acropolis is the **Temple of Athena**. Built around 530 B.C.E., the temple was constructed in the Doric style (with some Ionic elements) and was made of andesite stone. The temple originally had thirteen columns on each of the two longer sides and six columns on the two ends, with two additional columns in the front porch area. Some of the columns have been restored and placed on the temple platform, which measures approximately 46 feet by 100 feet. Reliefs from the temple are in the Archaeological Museum in Istanbul, the Louvre in Paris, and the Museum of Fine Arts in Boston.

A small path leads down the south slope of the acropolis toward the harbor, where the remains of several buildings are located on terraces cut from the hill. Unfortunately, not much can be seen of the buildings; in some cases only the foundations survive. The major building complexes, all of which are from the Hellenistic or Roman periods, are the agora, the theater, and the gymnasium. The north side of the **agora** had a two-story Doric stoa approximately 380 feet long, while the south stoa of the agora was three stories. The top floor of the south stoa was open to both the

▲ **Fig. 65.** Temple of Athena at Assos

agora to the north and the sea to the south, providing a pleasant area in which the ancient citizens of Assos could stroll, converse, and socialize while enjoying the cooling breeze from the sea and the spectacular view across the bay. The middle floor contained shops, while the bottom floor contained two cisterns and rooms for bathing. At the west end of the agora was a 2nd-century-B.C.E. **temple**, later converted into a church. Northwest and southwest of the temple were located several additional shops. At the east end of the agora was a Hellenistic **bouleuterion** (council chamber), in front of which was a **bema**, the platform used for public pronouncements and speeches. Several other buildings were also located in this area.

South of the agora, on a lower terrace, was the **theater**. Built in the 3rd century B.C.E., the theater was later altered by the Romans. Recent excavations have restored much of the seating (the cavea) and the orchestra areas of the theater. The low wall separating the seating from the orchestra, part of which has been restored, is from the Roman alteration of the theater. Oriented toward the bay, the theater provides a spectacular view. To the west of the agora was a **gymnasium**, built during the Hellenistic period. The gymnasium contained a paved courtyard measuring 105 feet by 131 feet that was surrounded by colonnades on all four sides. During the Byzantine period a **church** was built in the northeast part of

▲ **Fig. 66.** Harbor at Assos

the courtyard. A cistern is in the southwest corner of the courtyard. West of the gymnasium was the main gateway of the city, the **west gate**. Flanked by two **towers**, the gate is a part of the city's defensive **wall**. The wall, which is one of the best-preserved Hellenistic walls in all of Turkey, dates from the 4th century B.C.E. Part of the wall is still intact to a height of 45 feet. The city's **necropolis** was located outside the west gate. Several large Hellenistic and Roman sarcophagi and grave monuments are still present. Several sections of the **paved roads** of ancient Assos have been uncovered. A portion of the main road into the city through the west gate is visible, as is part of the road along the western part of the city that leads down to the harbor.

At the base of the hill on which the acropolis stands is the city's **harbor**. The ancient harbor where Paul would have joined his companions aboard ship after he had traveled to Assos from Troas (Acts 20:14) no longer exists, but it was in the same general area. In fact, ancient Assos apparently had two harbors. As in antiquity, a **mole** has been constructed out into the bay in order to create a safe harbor for ships. The present mole is a restored one from the 19th century. Some of the stones from the ancient mole can still be seen.

Attalia

Antalya, the modern name for ancient Attalia, is a delightful city perched on the Mediterranean coast of southern Turkey. The eleventh largest city in modern Turkey, Antalya is a thriving tourist center. Although many visitors to the city use it as a base for visiting beaches along Turkey's Mediterranean coast or archaeological sites in nearby locations, Antalya has plenty of charm and interest of its own.

Location and History

Attalia was a city in the region known as Pamphylia, an area bounded by the Taurus Mountains on the north and the Mediterranean Sea on the south. Situated on what is now called the Gulf of Antalya, the city served as the major port in Pamphylia during Hellenistic, Roman, and Byzantine times. **Attalus II**, who was king of Pergamum from 159 to 138 B.C.E., founded the city and named it after himself. When **Attalus III** (r. 138–133 B.C.E.) bequeathed the Pergamum kingdom to Rome in his will, Attalia was one of the areas excluded and thus became a free city for a while. In

77 B.C.E. Attalia was annexed by the Romans. During the 2nd century C.E. **Emperor Hadrian** conferred the status of colony on the city and visited Attalia in 130 C.E. The Hadrian Gate was built to commemorate this visit. Dedicated to the emperor, the triple-arched gate was made of marble and contained a dedicatory inscription in bronze letters.

During the Byzantine era the city was known as Adalia and continued to serve as an important port city. Used by the Crusaders as a harbor on their way to the Holy Land, the city was conquered by the Seljuk Turks in 1207. The Seljuks left their mark upon the city by means of several buildings, some of which still decorate the city's landscape. Around the end of the 14th century, the Ottomans gained control of the city. During this period Antalya continued to flourish and serve as an important harbor on the Mediterranean. When the Allies dismantled the Ottoman Empire at the end of World War I, Antalya was given to Italy, only to be retaken by the Turkish army in 1921.

Biblical Significance

When **Paul** and **Barnabas** were at the end of their first missionary journey, which took them through several cities in southern Asia Minor, they left Perga and went to Attalia. From Attalia they left by ship and returned

▲ **Fig. 67.** Harbor of Antalya (ancient Attalia). In the background are portions of the ancient wall at the harbor.

to Antioch (Acts 14:25–26). The Acts account does not give any indication that Paul and Barnabas spent any time in Attalia. Although Attalia is not mentioned elsewhere in the Bible, Paul and Barnabas possibly also passed through Attalia earlier on their first journey, when Acts says they sailed from the city of Paphos on Cyprus and traveled to Perga (Acts 13:13). Perga was located approximately 7 miles inland but apparently had access to the Mediterranean by means of a port on the nearby Cestrus River, which emptied into the Mediterranean. Thus Paul and Barnabas possibly could have sailed directly to Perga from Paphos up the Cestrus River, or alternatively they could have landed at Attalia and gone overland to Perga.

Site Visit

The symbol of Antalya is the **Yivli Minare**, or Fluted Minaret. Located along Cumhuriyet Caddesi, this 125-foot-tall minaret is the oldest Seljuk monument in Antalya. Constructed of bricks, the minaret was built in 1230. The most impressive reminder of Attalia's ancient history is **Hadrian's Gate**, located on Atatürk Caddesi. Built to commemorate **Hadrian's** visit to the city in 130 C.E., this richly decorated marble structure originally had two stories. The gate provided entrance to the city through three arched entryways. The gate has eight unfluted granite columns on pedestals, one column on both sides of the four piers that support the three arches of the gate. The tower to the left of the gate dates to Roman times, whereas the tower on the right was partially restored during the late Byzantine period. The gate is a part of the **ancient wall** surrounding the old city. The two streets, Cumhuriyet Caddesi and Atatürk Caddesi, basically follow the path of the old city walls. The area framed by these streets, which surrounds the harbor, is the historic area of the city known as Kaleiçi. In the Kaleiçi district are several old Turkish houses as well as some monuments from Hellenistic, Roman, Byzantine, Seljuk, and Ottoman times. This area is now a designated historic area and protected from destruction and modern development. Wandering among the small, winding streets of this section of the city with its restaurants, bars, and small shops intermingled with old houses is an enjoyable way to spend a few hours.

About 350 yards southwest of Hadrian's Gate on Hesapçi Sokak in the historic area is **Kesik Minare Camii**, which means "mosque with the truncated minaret." (A fire damaged the mosque and burned the wooden top of the minaret.) Although the mosque is closed, one can walk around the outside of it. This building has a long history. Originally a Roman temple from the 2nd century C.E. stood here. In the 6th century a church dedicated to the Virgin Mary was built on the foundations of the old Roman temple. In the 13th century the building was converted to a mosque, only to be turned back into a church the following century. Late in the 15th century it became a mosque once more and continued to function as a mosque for the neighborhood until the disastrous fire in the 19th century forced its closure. Continue southwest on Hesapçi Sokak to its intersection with Hïdïrlïk Sokak. Nearby is the **Hïdïrlïk Kulesi**, a 44-foot-tall stone structure composed of a square base with a round tower surmounted by a wall on top. The main part of the structure was likely built in the 2nd century C.E., while the wall, or parapet, on top was added during the Byzantine era. The purpose of the structure is still uncertain. Although some have suggested that it was a fort, a lighthouse, or a watchtower, its similarity to Roman mausoleums has led others to conclude that it was likely the burial place for a local Roman dignitary.

▲ **Fig. 68.**   Hadrian's Gate in Attalia (Antalya)

Near the Hïdïrlïk Kulesi is the modern Yacht Harbor (Yat Limani), which is the site of the **ancient harbor** of Attalia. Restored in the 1980s, the harbor area is filled with nice restaurants, cafes, and shops. The beautiful waters of the Mediterranean form a pleasant backdrop for a stroll, a meal, or ice cream from one of the sidewalk vendors. This ancient harbor, built during the 2nd century, would have been the place from which **Paul** and **Barnabas** sailed when they left Asia Minor to return to Antioch (Acts 14:25–26). Around the harbor are portions of the **ancient city walls and towers**. Built on Hellenistic foundations, the walls were rebuilt and enlarged by the Romans, the Byzantines, and the Seljuks.

Antalya boasts one of the best museums in Turkey. Located on the western edge of the city on Konyalti Bulvari, the **Antalya Museum** won the European Museum of the Year Award in 1988. The exhibits in the museum are attractively displayed and are labeled in English as well as Turkish. The majority of the museum is devoted to archaeological finds, although it also contains some excellent ethnographical exhibits. Room 1 in the museum is a children's room, with archaeological and ethnographical displays of particular interest to children. Room 2 is devoted to the natural history and prehistory of the area, containing displays from as early as the Paleolithic era. The reconstructed **pithos-jar burial** from the 3rd millennium B.C.E. is especially interesting.

Room 3 contains some examples of red-figured pottery from the classical period (5th–4th centuries B.C.E.) and numerous Phrygian artifacts. The **silver statuette of a priestess** and the **ivory statuette of a female figure** (both from the late 8th or early 7th centuries) are small but striking. Room 4 is the "Gallery of the Gods," exhibiting a variety of statues of ancient gods and goddesses. Among the deities and their offspring represented are **Zeus, Artemis, Hygieia, Apollo, Asclepius, Athena, Hermes, Aphrodite, Dionysus, Nemesis**, the **Dioscuri (Castor and Pollux), Tyche, Serapis, Isis**, and **Harpocrates**. Most of the statues date to the 2nd century C.E. and came from Perga.

Room 5 displays a variety of small objects discovered in the region, including items recovered from the Mediterranean Sea. Of particular note are the marble statuette of **Priapus**, the bronze head of **Attis**, the bronze statuette of **Apollo**, the bronze statuette of **Hercules**, the marble statuette of **Tyche**, the two marble statuettes of **Aphrodite**, the marble heads of **Zeus, Serapis**, and **Athena**, and the statue of **Marsyas**. Room 6, known as the Gallery of the Emperors, contains some excellent statues of the emperors **Trajan, Hadrian**, and **Septimius Severus** (2nd and 3rd centuries C.E.), some of their family members, a **priest of Apollo**, an **imperial priest**, and a **priestess of Artemis**. One of the most interesting statues in the room is that of a **dancer**. The sculptor has captured the swift motion of the dancer and has used both white and black marble in the statue. Also included in the collection is a group statue of the **Three Graces**. All of these sculptures were discovered at Perga.

Several impressive sarcophagi with elaborate frieze decorations are displayed in room 7. Found at Perga, these marble sarcophagi are excellent examples of the skill of the sculptors at Perga. Grave stelae and other items from the burial grounds of Perga and nearby locations are also displayed, including a **Lycian votive stele** with a relief depicting the twelve gods of Lycia.

The Gallery of the Icons is the name given to room 8, which contains 19th- and early-20th-century icons depicting scenes from the life of Christ, the Evangelists, John the Baptist, the Virgin and Child, and St. Nicholas of Myra. A small reliquary purportedly contains some of the **bones of St. Nicholas**, bishop of Myra and the person behind the legend of Santa Claus. Also on display is a portion of the 6th-century-C.E. collection of silver objects from Corydalla (modern Kumluca). Room 9 is devoted to mosaics from Seleucia and Xanthos. It also contains some sculptures and other artifacts. In room 10 are several display cases with ancient coins and jewelry, and rooms 11, 12, and 13 contain ethnographic exhibits of items representative of Anatolian life in the past.

Other Sites of Interest

Antalya is a great location for several day trips to nearby archaeological sites. Even though these sites are not mentioned in the Hebrew Bible or the New Testament, they do provide valuable insights into the Hellenistic and Roman worlds out of which the Bible developed. Turkey is so rich in such sites that mention of all them is beyond the scope or purpose of this book. A few of them, however, deserve to be mentioned. Southwest of Antalya on highway 400 is the site of ancient **Phaselis**. Founded around the beginning of the 7th century B.C.E. by Greek colonists from Rhodes, the city possesses some of the only good harbors on this part of the Mediterranean coast. In fact, Phaselis had **three harbors**, all of which can still be seen. The best-preserved is the southern harbor, which served as the military harbor and the harbor for larger ships. Most of the ruins at Phaselis date from the Roman period, although some are from Hellenistic and Byzantine times. Among the remains at the site, in addition to the harbors, are a **theater**, the **main street**, **two baths**, **three agoras** (one from the time of **Domitian**, one from the time of **Hadrian**, and the third from late Roman or Byzantine times), an **aqueduct**, a **necropolis**, and a **monumental gate** dedicated to Hadrian.

Approximately 20 miles northwest of Antalya on highway E87/350 lie the ruins of ancient **Termessos**, which today is part of a national park, the Güllük Daği Milli Parkï. Due to its rugged location in the mountains, Termessos has the distinction of being one of the few cities that **Alexander the Great** was not able to conquer, although he did put the city under siege. The site is a little difficult to visit because the ruins are spread out and somewhat overgrown, and the terrain is sometimes steep and rocky. Among the remains here are an **agora**, the **Stoa of Attalus II**, the **Temple of Zeus**, the **Temple of Artemis**, the **bouleuterion** (or an odeion), the **Stoa of Osbaras**, a **colonnaded street**, a **gymnasium**, a **necropolis**, and a **theater**. The view from the theater is spectacular; a trip to Termessos is worthwhile for this alone, if for no other reason. Built in the Hellenistic period, then renovated during the Roman era, the theater provides a breathtaking view across the Pamphylian plain to the twin peaks of Mt. Solymus.

Travelers to this area of Turkey should certainly visit **Side**, a resort city known more in modern times for its splendid beaches than for its antiquities. However, a number of outstanding ancient remains also make it well worth a visit. There is no evidence that Paul or any of the early Christian missionaries visited Side, but their route along the coast of the Mediterranean in Asia Minor would most naturally have passed through the city. Apparently Side could have used a bit of missionizing. The city did not enjoy a good reputation in ancient times, as it was principally known as a center of the slave trade along this coast. One Roman critic,

Stratonicus, is reputed to have referred to the men of Side as the most "rascally" in the whole world.

On the western outskirts of the city, portions of a **Roman aqueduct** are visible that brought water to the city from a source 25 miles away. Some of the **Hellenistic walls** (2nd century B.C.E.) that circled the city remain, although those on its seaward side have disappeared. Near the entrance to the city from the west (highway 400), two large **defensive towers** stand on either side of the **main gateway** of antiquity, and a fine **nymphaeum** also remains nearby. The most outstanding structure remaining from ancient Side is the impressive **Roman theater**, still standing to a height of more than 40 feet. The elaborate stage building of the theater originally stood more than 60 feet high. Other notable structures in the precinct of the old city include a **monumental archway** that once spanned the entrance to the inner city of Side, portions of a 5th-century **Byzantine basilica**, and **columns of the Temple of Apollo** looking out over the Mediterranean. Additionally, many lesser structures and monuments are to be found among the extensive ruins. A **museum** contains numerous objects of interest from the site.

Colossae

At one time a thriving city in the fertile valley of the Lycus River, the city of Colossae is almost forgotten today. If not for its significance to the Bible, the site of ancient Colossae, now only an unexcavated mound, would be visited very seldom.

Location and History

Colossae was situated near the Lycus River (today the Aksu Çay), the chief tributary of the Meander River. Located in the Phrygian region of Asia Minor, the city was approximately 120 miles east of Ephesus. During the 5th and 4th centuries B.C.E. Colossae was a large and prosperous city. At that time the leading city of the Lycus Valley, Colossae was eventually eclipsed in importance during the Hellenistic and Roman periods by the neighboring cities of Laodicea and Hierapolis. The textile industry flourished in the Lycus Valley, particularly because of goods made from the exceptionally fine wool produced in the area. Colossae was well known for its purple-colored wool. The economic prosperity of the city was also due to its being located on the main trade route from the

Aegean coast to the Euphrates. Like Laodicea and Hierapolis, Colossae likely was damaged by the severe earthquake that struck the Lycus Valley in 60 C.E. By the 9th century the site was abandoned, its remaining inhabitants having moved to the nearby town of Chonae (modern Honaz).

To reach the ruins of ancient Colossae, take highway 320 east from Denizli toward Dinar. Approximately 12 miles from Denizli, turn right onto the road for Honaz. After traveling approximately 4 miles, turn left. The site of ancient Colossae, a low hill in a field, is about 6 miles on the right.

Biblical Significance

The ancient city of Colossae is remembered today primarily because one of the letters in the New Testament is addressed to "the saints and faithful brothers and sisters in Christ in Colossae" (Col 1:2). Aside from this one reference, the city of Colossae does not appear in the New Testament. The Letter to the Colossians claims to be a letter from the **Apostle Paul**, although its authorship is sometimes attributed to an anonymous disciple of Paul's who wrote in the name of Paul. If the letter was actually by Paul, he apparently had not visited the Christians in Laodicea prior to writing the letter. (Colossians 2:1 refers to the Christians at Laodicea as among those who had never seen Paul.) The founder of the church at Colossae was likely **Epaphras** (Col 1:7; 4:12), who had ministered not only at Colossae but at Laodicea and Hierapolis as well (Col 4:13). According to Colossians 4:9, the slave **Onesimus** was also from Colossae. On behalf of this runaway slave, Paul wrote to **Philemon**, the slave's master, who would have lived in Colossae, informing him of Onesimus' return and urging Philemon to treat Onesimus as a Christian brother. The Letter to Philemon is addressed not just to Philemon but also to the entire church that met in his house in Colossae.

Site Visit

Discovered in 1835 by W. J. Hamilton, the site of Colossae still awaits archaeological excavation. The visitor to the site will likely be disappointed, for not much can be seen of this once important city in the Lycus River valley. The paved road to the site passes over the Lycus River. On the south side of the river is a low mound, the site of the acropolis of ancient Colossae. The mound and its surroundings are now part of a wheat field. On the sides and the top of the site, which is quickly climbed, a few scattered remains of **building fragments** and the remains of a **defense wall** can be seen. The top provides an excellent view across the

▲ **Fig. 69.** Unexcavated mound of ancient Colossae

Lycus Valley. On the eastern side of the mound the concave outline of the **theater** at Colossae is still discernible. To the north of the Lycus River was located the **necropolis** of the city, where several tombs with flat slabs have been discovered.

Derbe

One of the cities visited by the Apostle Paul during his travels, Derbe has almost vanished today. A few inscriptions, coins, and literary references and an unexcavated mound bear scant testimony to a city that was one of the early recipients of the preaching of Paul and Barnabas.

Location and History

The ancient city of Derbe was located southeast of Iconium (modern Konya) in the ancient region of south-central Asia Minor known as Lycaonia. Several sites have been proposed for the precise location of

Derbe, most of them located near the modern town of Karaman. The location that has the strongest claim to being the authentic site of Derbe is the tumulus (mound) Kerti Höyük, which is situated approximately 15 miles northeast of Karaman (ancient Laranda) and near the village of Aşïran (Ekinözü). On the side of this mound in 1956, Michael Ballance discovered a white limestone block approximately 41 inches high, 27 inches wide, and 27 inches thick. The stone block is inscribed with a dedication by the council and the people of Derbe honoring **Emperor Antoninus Pius**. In the inscription, which has been dated to 157 B.C.E., the city was likely referred to as Claudioderbe, a special title given to the city during the time of **Emperor Claudius**. (Part of the face of the stone immediately preceding the word *Derbe* is broken off. The name *Claudioderbe* appears on 2nd-century-C.E. coins from Derbe.)

Another inscription mentioning Derbe, this one from a tombstone from the 4th–5th century C.E., was discovered in the nearby village of Suduraği. This inscription, surrounded by five engraved concentric circles, mentions "the most God-loving Michael, bishop of Derbe." Michael Ballance says he was shown this inscribed marble slab in 1958 and was told by the villagers of Suduraği that the inscription was found nearby at Devri Şehri, about 2.5 miles southeast of Kerti Höyük. Bastiaan van Elderen reported seeing the slab in 1962 and said that the people of Suduraği were adamant that the inscription came from Kerti Höyük. Because the first inscription mentioned above, discovered in 1956, and likely this second inscription as well, came from Kerti Höyük, that mound is probably the location for the ancient city of Derbe.

Not much is known about the history of Derbe, owing to the scarcity of ancient literary references to the city and the absence of any archaeological excavations at the site. Scattered fragments on the surface of Kerti Höyük indicate that the site was occupied at least as early as the Hellenistic and the Roman periods. The Greek geographer Strabo (1st century B.C.E.–1st century C.E.) mentions Derbe as the headquarters during the 1st century B.C.E. of a local chieftain named **Antipater Derbetes**, who also controlled the nearby city of Laranda (*Geography* 12.6.3). After the defeat of Antipater by **King Amyntas** of Galatia, Derbe came under the control of Amyntas, who ruled as a client king of the Romans. When Amyntas died in 25 B.C.E., Derbe may have become a part of the newly created Roman province of Galatia. Exactly where the eastern border of the Galatian province was located cannot be determined with certainty. Derbe may have been a part of Galatia, or it may have belonged to the Cilician kingdom of **Antiochus IV of Commagene**. (Or, if the boundaries shifted, it may have belonged to each of the areas at different times.)

Little more is known about Derbe. Second-century coins from the city indicate that it had been given the honorific title Claudioderbe (or Claudiaderbe) in honor of Emperor Claudius. In 381 C.E. **Bishop Daphnus** of Derbe was present at the Council of Constantinople. The "Michael" inscription described above bears witness to the presence of another bishop in Derbe, this time during the 4th or 5th century.

Biblical Significance

Derbe was one of the cities visited by **Paul** and **Barnabas** during their first missionary journey. Acts 14:20–21 briefly describes their visit to the city after they had preached in Pisidian Antioch, Iconium, and Lystra (see also Acts 14:6): "After they had proclaimed the good news to that city [Derbe] and had made many disciples, they returned to Lystra, then on to Iconium and Antioch." Derbe was also on Paul's itinerary during his second preaching campaign, this one taking him back through the cities in southern Asia Minor that he had visited on his first trip. Acts 16:1 simply mentions that Paul visited the city, without giving any details of what took place during the second visit. At the beginning of his third missionary journey, Paul "went from place to place through the region of Galatia and Phrygia, strengthening all the disciples" (Acts 18:23). If Derbe was a part of the Galatian region at that time, Paul may have visited the city for a third time. During this third journey one of Paul's traveling companions was a native of Derbe, a man named **Gaius** (Acts 19:29; 20:4).

▲ **Fig. 70.** Inscription mentioning Bishop Michael of Derbe in the Karaman Museum

Site Visit

Aside from providing a view of the general area in which Derbe was located, a visit to Kerti Höyük is not very informative for the modern visitor. The site is unexcavated and offers little evidence of the ruins of the ancient city that likely lie buried in the mound. The Derbe inscription discovered by Michael Balance in 1956 can be seen in the Konya Archaeological Museum. The inscription that mentions Bishop Michael is in the Karaman Museum. Both museums also contain various coins, pottery, and other artifacts found in the area.

Ephesus

Often crowded with tourists, Ephesus is a must-see stop on any itinerary through western Turkey. Few archaeological sites in Turkey are as impressive as Ephesus. The excavated and reconstructed buildings bear eloquent testimony to this important and grand city of ancient Asia Minor. Strolling the streets of Ephesus, past fountains, statues, monuments, temples, a great library, residences, the agora, and the theater, the modern visitor can easily imagine the ancient city thronged with crowds engaged in the various activities of their society.

Location and History

Ephesus is situated near the Aegean coast, east and slightly north of the island of Samos and approximately 40 miles south of Izmir. The modern city of Selçuk is located in the general area of ancient Ephesus. In antiquity Ephesus was a major port city situated on the Aegean coast. Over the years alluvial deposits from the Cayster River, which ran near the city, filled in the harbor, and as a result, the site of the city today lies approximately 5 miles inland from the coast. In addition, Ephesus was the beginning point for the main highway that ran from the Aegean coast to the eastern part of Anatolia, which along with its harbor allowed the city to flourish as a commercial and transportation center.

According to the geographer Strabo, the earliest inhabitants of Ephesus were a group of peoples called Leleges and Carians. Sometime around 1100–1000 B.C.E., a group of Ionian Greek colonists, supposedly led by the legendary Athenian prince **Androclus**, established a Greek settlement at the base of the northern slope of Panayïr Daği (Mt. Pion), one of three hills in the vicinity of ancient Ephesus. An ancient legend claims that Androclus chose this site on the basis of an oracle that said the city should be established at the site indicated by a fish and a wild boar. When Androclus and his companions landed on the coast of Asia Minor, Androclus joined some locals who were grilling fish. One of the fish, along with a hot coal, flipped off the grill. The burning coal ignited the grass, and the ensuing fire caused a wild boar to bolt from the burning grass, whereupon the boar was killed. Taking this as a fulfillment of the oracle's sign, Androclus built his city on that location. The locals worshiped the mother goddess Cybele. The Greek colonists assimilated this native religion, identifying Cybele with the Greek goddess Artemis, the virgin hunter. (Later the Romans identified Artemis with their goddess Diana.)

Around 560 B.C.E. **Croesus** of Lydia conquered Ephesus and most of western Asia Minor. Under Croesus' rule, the city was moved farther south to an area southwest of the hill Ayasoluk. A magnificent temple, the Artemision, was constructed for the worship of Artemis. In 547 B.C.E., following the defeat of Croesus by **Cyrus** of Persia, Ephesus came under Persian control. One of the city's most famous citizens, the philosopher **Heraclitus**, lived during the latter part of the 6th and the early part of the 5th centuries B.C.E. Disaster struck the city in 356 B.C.E., when fire destroyed the Artemision. **Alexander the Great**, who was reportedly born on the same day as the Artemision fire, took over the area in 334 B.C.E. His offer to finance the ongoing reconstruction of the temple was diplomatically declined by the Ephesians, who said that it was not fitting for one god to make a dedication for another god. The rebuilt temple became known as one of the seven wonders of the ancient world. (The other six were the Great Pyramid [of Khufu, or Cheops] of Egypt, the lighthouse at Alexandria, the statue of Zeus at Olympia, the Colossus of Rhodes, the Mausoleum at Halicarnassus, and the Hanging Gardens of Babylon.)

Lysimachus, one of Alexander's generals, ruled over Ephesus from approximately 301 to 281 B.C.E., when he was killed by **Seleucus I**. Under Lysimachus the city was moved again, this time to higher ground to escape the danger of flooding, to the area between Panayïr Daği and Bülbül Daği (Mt. Coressus). Lysimachus built city walls, part of which are still visible on the slope of Bülbül Daği, constructed a new harbor, and laid out new city streets. After the death of Lysimachus, Ephesus came under the control of the Seleucids, then the Ptolemies, and then back to the Seleucid rulers. After the Romans defeated the Seleucid king **Antiochus III** in 189 B.C.E., Rome rewarded **Eumenes II** of Pergamum for his military assistance by giving him large areas of western Asia Minor, including Ephesus. In 133 B.C.E., at the death of the last Pergamene ruler (**Attalus III**), the city came under direct Roman control.

Ephesus thrived under the Romans, reaching the pinnacle of its greatness during the 1st and 2nd centuries of the Christian era, and served as the capital of the Roman province of Asia. During this time Ephesus was probably the third or fourth largest city in the Roman Empire, with a population estimated at 225,000–250,000. (It ranked behind Rome, Alexandria, and maybe Antioch.) Most of the remains of the city visible today date from this period. The city proudly boasted that it was the first and greatest metropolis of Asia and was honored on at least four occasions with the title of *neokoros,* or temple warden, for temples for the imperial cult.

Two of the reasons for the city's economic success through the centuries were the Temple of Artemis and the commercial harbor at Ephesus. Eventually the city lost both of these assets. The Temple of Artemis was important economically because it drew visitors from all over the ancient world, served as a bank, and employed many people. In 262 C.E. Goths attacked the western part of Asia Minor, including Ephesus. They plundered the Artemision and set it on fire. Even though the temple underwent repairs, it never regained its former glory. When Christianity became the official religion of the empire in the following century, the Temple of Artemis was abandoned and eventually used as a stone quarry. The depositing of silt from the Cayster River in the city harbor was a problem throughout the city's history, with several efforts made to dredge the harbor and deepen its entrance. In fact, it is believed that the city's harbor was located at three different sites throughout history, as silting forced the moving of the harbor and also the city. **Hadrian** even shifted the course of the river to try to alleviate the problem. Sometime during the late Byzantine period, however, the battle against the silting was lost and Ephesus was no longer a harbor city.

During the Byzantine period, much of the city shifted from the harbor area to Ayasoluk Hill. On top of the hill in the 6th century C.E. the emperor **Justinian** constructed a large basilica, the Basilica of St. John, which replaced an earlier church built over the supposed grave of St. John. In order to protect the city from Arab raids in the 7th and 8th centuries, walls and a fortress were constructed on the hill. Much of the harbor area seems to have been abandoned around this time, and the city was primarily located on Ayasoluk Hill. Around 1300 C.E. Ephesus came under the control of the Seljuk Turks and experienced a new period of growth and prosperity. At the beginning of the 15th century the Ottoman Turks seized power. They had little interest in Ephesus, and the city went into a steep decline, never to recover. Much of the older city was in ruins by this time anyway, the victim over the years of earthquakes, Arab attacks, and the silting of the harbor.

No remains of a synagogue or Jewish artifacts have been found in ancient Ephesus. Likewise, few Jewish inscriptions have been found. Several literary works, however, attest to the presence of Jews in the city. The 1st-century Jewish historian Josephus on several occasions mentions Jews in Ephesus, pointing out certain privileges they enjoyed (such as exemption from Roman military service and the freedom to practice their religion). The book of Acts (see below) also describes a Jewish community in Ephesus, including a Jewish synagogue there.

Christianity arrived early in Ephesus, apparently introduced by **Paul**, **Priscilla**, and **Aquila** (Acts 18:18–19). The book of Revelation gives evidence of Christians in the city at the end of the 1st century C.E. (2:1–7). When **Ignatius**, the bishop of Antioch, was being escorted as a prisoner to Rome, where he would die as a martyr around 107 C.E., he wrote letters along the way to several churches, including the church at Ephesus. In 431 C.E. the city was the location for the Third Ecumenical Council, an important gathering of church officials at which **Nestorius**, the patriarch of Constantinople, was condemned and deposed. Nestorius and his followers argued that the divine and the human natures of Christ were separate and that **Mary** was mother of only the human nature of Jesus. The council confirmed the doctrine that the two natures of Christ were indivisible, and thus the designation of Mary as "Mother of God" (*theotokos*, "bearer of God") was officially accepted. A second church council was held in Ephesus in 449, called by **Emperor Theodosius II** to deal with the disputed condemnation of **Eutyches** by **Flavian**, the patriarch of Constantinople, a condemnation supported by **Pope Leo I**. When the council reversed the condemnation of Eutyches and instead condemned Flavian, Leo denounced the council, calling it a "synod of robbers." Accordingly, the council has subsequently been known as the "robber council of Ephesus."

Biblical Significance

Of all the cities mentioned in the New Testament that were visited by **Paul**, Ephesus is the only one that was also addressed in the book of Revelation. According to Acts, Paul visited the city of Ephesus on both his second and third missionary journeys. On his second journey his visit was brief. **Priscilla** and **Aquila** (wife and husband) accompanied Paul to Ephesus. After engaging in a discussion in the synagogue, Paul left Ephesus, leaving Priscilla and Aquila in the city, and promised to return (Acts 18:18–20). Sometime after Paul left Ephesus, another Christian, **Apollos** of Alexandria, came to Ephesus. Discovering that his understanding of the Christian faith was deficient in some areas, Priscilla and Aquila instructed him more fully (Acts 18:24–28). After Apollos left to go to Greece, Paul returned to Ephesus during his third journey. This time he spent a considerable length of time in Ephesus. (Acts 19:8–10 says Paul spent two years teaching and preaching in the hall of Tyrannus in Ephesus, after having spent three months teaching in the synagogue there. Acts 20:31 says he spent three years in Ephesus.)

During this stay in Ephesus Paul aroused the anger of the city's guild of silversmiths, who had a prosperous business selling silver shrines of Artemis, the goddess whose impressive temple was located in Ephesus. Paul's preaching was harming their business and challenging the worship of Artemis. The silversmiths began to chant, "Great is Artemis of the Ephesians!" A near riot ensued, in which the people of the city gathered in the theater, dragging two of Paul's traveling companions, **Gaius** and **Aristarchus**, with them. Paul wanted to go into the theater, presumably to rescue his companions or to help quell the disturbance, but his friends and even some of the city officials persuaded him not to go. After the disturbance had lasted for two hours, the town clerk was able to bring order to the crowd and end the outbreak. Shortly after this event Paul left Ephesus and traveled to Macedonia (Acts 19:1–20:1). At the end of this third journey Paul bypassed Ephesus on his eventual return to Jerusalem. Acts 20:16 states that Paul bypassed the city because of his eagerness to return to Jerusalem. Perhaps the disturbance during his previous visit contributed to that decision as well. Rather than stopping at Ephesus to visit the Christians, Paul sent a message to them from Miletus and asked the elders of the church at Ephesus to come meet him there (Acts 20:17).

When Paul wrote the letter of 1 Corinthians he was in Ephesus, likely during the lengthy stay mentioned in Acts 19 (see 1 Cor 16:8). He perhaps also wrote portions of 2 Corinthians from Ephesus. Some scholars suggest that Paul may have been imprisoned at Ephesus for part of this period and that during this imprisonment he wrote the letters of Philippians and Philemon, as well as Colossians (if actually by Paul). Whereas there is no evidence that Paul was indeed a prisoner in Ephesus, he does state that he had been imprisoned on numerous occasions, one of which may have been in Ephesus (2 Cor 11:23). In 1 Corinthians 15:32 Paul says that he "fought with wild animals at Ephesus." This, however, is probably only a figure of speech for the difficulties he encountered from opponents in the city.

The New Testament contains a letter supposedly from Paul that is traditionally called the Letter to the Ephesians. Since there are no personal references in the letter and the earliest Greek manuscripts of the letter do not include a reference to Ephesus in the greeting, many scholars consider this a circular letter that was intended to be read to several churches and not addressed just to the church at Ephesus. The First Letter to Timothy claims to be written by Paul to **Timothy**, his younger coworker. (The majority of New Testament scholars would say that all three of the Pastoral Letters—1 and 2 Timothy and Titus—are not actually by Paul but were written by an unknown writer who wrote in Paul's name to give his writing more authority.) Paul urges Timothy to remain in Ephesus to help the Christians there, particularly to help them deal with false teachings that had arisen (1 Tim 1:3). Ephesus is mentioned twice in 2 Timothy. In 1:16–18 Paul praises **Onesiphorus**, who had rendered special service to him, both in Rome and in Ephesus. In 4:12 he informs Timothy that he has sent **Tychicus**, one of his traveling companions, to Ephesus.

The other appearances of Ephesus in the Bible occur in Revelation, written by **John** of Patmos. The church at Ephesus is the first of the churches addressed in the book. As the most important city of Asia Minor, Ephesus was a fitting recipient of the first message. In the message, found in Revelation 2:1–7, Christ praised the Ephesian Christians for their works, their labor, and their endurance. The church's faithfulness was particularly evident in its resistance to false teachers, or false apostles. Although John gives no details about the false apostles at Ephesus, they were possibly connected with the people labeled "Nicolaitans" (2:6, 2:15). In addition to problems from false leaders within the church, the Christians at Ephesus were also suffering from unnamed external threats. Christ praises them for their patient suffering and endurance. Praise quickly turns to criticism, however, as Christ rebukes the Ephesians for their loss of love in dealing with others. Christ commands the Ephesian church to repent, to return to the love and compassion that formerly characterized their lives.

Early Christian tradition identified Ephesus with the disciple John. The tradition, found in various forms in different early writers, basically claimed that John moved to Ephesus after he left Jerusalem. There he taught and preached until he ran into trouble with the local authorities and was sent into exile to the island of Patmos. Later, allowed to return from exile, he lived out the rest of his life in Ephesus, from which he wrote the Gospel of John and the three Letters of John. While on Patmos (or after returning to Ephesus) he also wrote the book of Revelation. According to this tradition, John died in Ephesus and was buried there, his grave being eventually housed in the Church of St. John the Theologian. When he moved to Ephesus, John supposedly took along with him Mary, the mother of Jesus. This latter tradition is based on the scene in the Gospel of John in which Jesus, looking down from the cross and seeing his mother and "the disciple whom he loved" (or the Beloved Disciple), said, "Woman, here is your son," and to the disciple, "Here is your mother." The Gospel of John adds, "And from that hour the disciple took her into his own home" (John 19:26–27).

Several problems exist with this tradition, however. New Testament scholarship generally disputes the claim that all five works (the Gospel of John, the Letters, and Revelation) were written by the same person. Furthermore, whether the disciple John wrote any of them is highly doubtful. The identification of the disciple John with John of Patmos is almost certainly erroneous, based on clues from the book of Revelation itself (see the article on Patmos). The early church apparently confused John of Patmos with John the disciple. Furthermore, the Gospel of John never identifies the Beloved Disciple, who supposedly took Mary under his care. In the opinion of many scholars, the Beloved Disciple was an otherwise unknown disciple. With all the doubts about the association of John the disciple with Ephesus, the modern visitor should view the traditions with suspicion. Even if the identifications (of John with the Beloved Disciple; of John as the writer of the Fourth Gospel; of John the disciple as the author of Revelation; of John living, dying, and being buried in Ephesus; and of Mary with Ephesus) are incorrect, however, the visitor to this city associated with John and Mary can still appreciate the intention of these traditions—to pay homage and offer gratitude to these two important figures of early Christianity.

Site Visit

A visit to ancient Ephesus should include time to visit several associated sites, such as the museum, the House of Mary, the Church of St. John the Theologian, and the Cave of the Seven Sleepers.

Main Site

The main site has two entrances, one at the north end of the site (the lower entrance) and the other at the southeast edge of the site (the upper entrance). Ticket booths and parking areas are located at each entrance. The following itinerary begins at the upper entrance and ends at the lower entrance, which has more gift shops and food and drink vendors, the latter likely much appreciated after the walk through the site. The other advantage in beginning at the upper entrance, which is located on the road between Selçuk and the House of Mary, is that the walk through the city then follows a more downhill route.

Approximately 500 yards to the right (east) of the upper entrance is the **Magnesian Gate**, which led to Magnesia on the Meander. An earlier gate was possibly built here by **Lysimachus** as a part of the city walls he erected, although the date is uncertain. Originally the gate consisted of a single entryway and a paved courtyard. The present remains date mostly from the 1st century B.C.E., when the gate was expanded by the addition of two additional entrances and flanking towers. Around the 3rd century C.E. the gate underwent restoration and repairs. North of the Magnesian Gate is the **East Bath-Gymnasium** complex, dating from the 2nd century C.E. The south end of the complex fronted the street leading from the Magnesian Gate. This side of the complex consisted of a colonnaded stoa with shops. Behind the stoa was the palaestra, with a lecture hall adjoining it on the east and another hall on the west. Behind the palaestra was the bath complex. During the 4th or 5th century a church was built

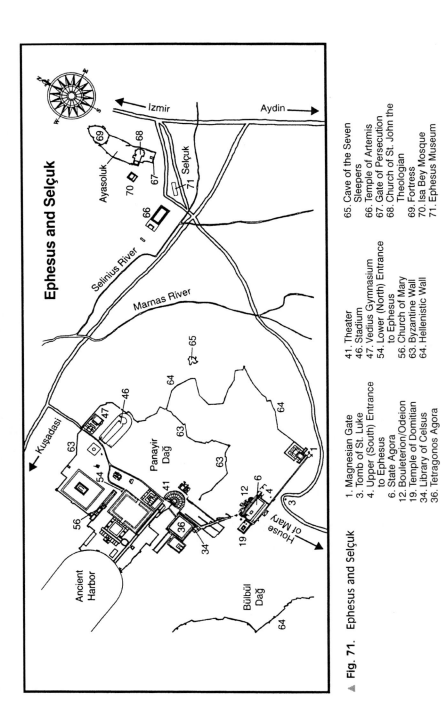

Ephesus and Selçuk

Izmir ← → Aydin

Selinius River

Marnas River

Ayasoluk

Selçuk

Kuşadası

Ancient Harbor

Panayir Dağ

House of Mary

Bülbül Dağ

◢ **Fig. 71.** Ephesus and Selçuk

1. Magnesian Gate
3. Tomb of St. Luke
4. Upper (South) Entrance to Ephesus
6. State Agora
12. Bouleterion/Odeion
19. Temple of Domitian
34. Library of Celsus
36. Tetragonos Agora

41. Theater
46. Stadium
47. Vedius Gymnasium
54. Lower (North) Entrance to Ephesus
56. Church of Mary
63. Byzantine Wall
64. Hellenistic Wall

65. Cave of the Seven Sleepers
66. Temple of Artemis
67. Gate of Persecution
68. Church of St. John the Theologian
69. Fortress
70. Isa Bey Mosque
71. Ephesus Museum

east of the lecture hall (over the Hellenistic wall). This was soon converted into a three-aisled basilica church.

West of the Magnesian Gate and the bath complex, near the upper entrance, is the **State Agora**. First built in the late Hellenistic period and later modified by the Romans, the State Agora and its surrounding buildings served as the administrative and civic center for Ephesus. The eastern end of the agora was built over an archaic necropolis. The agora was approximately 525 feet long and 190 feet wide, with a two-aisled colonnade on its south side. At the east end of the colonnade was a gatehouse. South of the colonnade of the agora was a colonnaded road, the **South Road**, which ran parallel to the south colonnade of the State Agora and led from the Bülbül Daǧï area in the west and through the Magnesian Gate to the east. To the south of the South Road was a **nymphaeum**, built in the 1st century C.E. and enlarged in the following century. The nymphaeum was an important part of the city's water distribution system. A colonnade similar to the south colonnade likely existed on the east side of the State Agora.

Running the length of the north side of the agora was originally a one-aisled stoa. This was replaced in the first decade of the 1st century C.E. with the three-aisled **Basilica Stoa**, dedicated in 11 C.E. to Artemis, **Augustus, Tiberius**, and the city of Ephesus. The original columns that divided the stoa into its three aisles were Ionic. Additional columns, Corinthian in style, were added later to provide additional support for the structure. The Basilica Stoa was likely used for judicial and administrative functions. At the western end of the open square of the State Agora was a **small temple** built during the third quarter of the 1st century B.C.E. The identity of this temple is disputed. It has been variously interpreted as a temple of Isis, a temple of Dionysus, a temple to Augustus, and most recently a temple dedicated to the divine Julius Caesar and to Dea Roma. In the southwest corner of the State Agora the governor **Caius Laecanius Bassus** erected a **nymphaeum** (or fountain) around 80 C.E. This structure, a two-story façade elaborately decorated with statues of goddesses, sea creatures, and river gods, contained a large water basin and fountains. It provided water for several of the buildings in the area.

Adjoining the northeastern end of the State Agora is the **Upper Bath-Gymnasium**, only partially excavated (until recently often incorrectly identified as the Baths of Varius or the Baths of Scholasticia). This complex followed the typical pattern of Roman baths of including a caldarium, a tepidarium, and a frigidarium, along with other rooms (including a latrine in the west end of the complex). A palaestra, though not yet excavated, is presumed to have been in the south of the complex.

West of the Upper Bath-Gymnasium, across from the Basilica Stoa, is a small, restored theaterlike structure built into the south slope of Panayïr

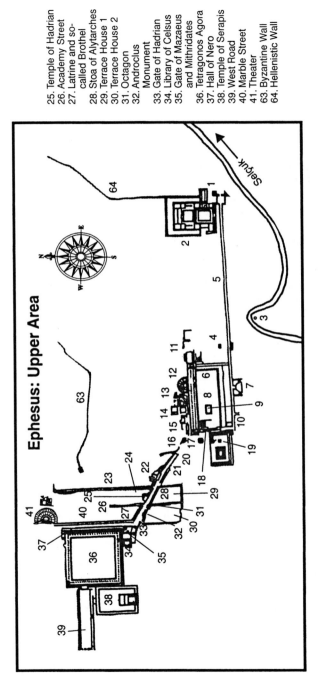

Fig. 72. Ephesus: Upper Area

Ephesus: Upper Area

1. Magnesian Gate
2. East Bath-Gymnasium
3. Tomb of St. Luke
4. Upper (South) Entrance to Ephesus
5. South Road
6. State Agora
7. Nymphaeum
8. Basilica Stoa
9. Temple (to Divine Julius Caesar and Dea Roma?)
10. Nymphaeum of C. Laecanius Bassus
11. Upper Bath-Gymnasium
12. Bouleuterion/Odeion
13. Temenos
14. Prytaneion
15. Banqueting House/Residence
16. Memmius Monument
17. Chalcidicum
18. Pollio Fountain
19. Temple of Domitian
20. Hercules Gate
21. Curetes Street
22. Fountain of Trajan
23. Bath Street
24. Baths of Varius/Scholasticia Baths
25. Temple of Hadrian
26. Academy Street
27. Latrine and so-called Brothel
28. Stoa of Alytarches
29. Terrace House 1
30. Terrace House 2
31. Octagon
32. Androclus Monument
33. Gate of Hadrian
34. Library of Celsus
35. Gate of Mazaeus and Mithridates
36. Tetragonos Agora
37. Hall of Nero
38. Temple of Serapis
39. West Road
40. Marble Street
41. Theater
63. Byzantine Wall
64. Hellenistic Wall

Daği that has been variously identified as a **bouleuterion** (city council chamber) or an **odeion** (a concert hall). The building probably served both functions. Built in the mid-2nd century, the odeion would seat approximately 1,500 people. Like most such buildings, the odeion likely had a permanent roof (perhaps of wooden beams and clay tiles) to provide protection from the sun and rain. Entrance to the odeion was through arched doorways on both sides near the stage area, as well as through doorways that connected the odeion with the Basilica Stoa. Adjacent to the odeion on the left is an open courtyard that was surrounded on three sides by colonnades, which likely was the **temenos** (sacred precinct) of a temple. On the west side is a podium, on which was built an altar or a small double temple. Scholars disagree over the identification of this site. Some experts consider that it was likely a double temple of Divus Julius and Dea Roma. Others believe that it was an altar dedicated to the worship of Artemis and Augustus. Since later buildings were erected over this area, it is difficult today to make out the outlines of the earlier structures.

The **Prytaneion**, located to the west of the courtyard, was one of the most important buildings in ancient Ephesus. Here the sacred fire of Hestia Boulaia, goddess of the hearth, was kept burning continuously. This building, which functioned like the city hall of Ephesus, served several purposes, including as a place for conducting political business, entertaining official guests, and hosting banquets and receptions. The remains that can be seen today date from the Prytaneion built in the 1st century C.E., which underwent alterations in the 3rd century. Scholars assume that an earlier Prytaneion from the time of Lysimachus likely was located in the same area. The structure consisted of a large courtyard with Doric columns, on some of which were inscribed long lists of names of the *curetes,* cult personnel in the Prytaneion. (The *curetes* were originally a class of priests who served in the Temple of Artemis in Ephesus. During the time of Augustus they were transferred to the Prytaneion.) Some of these columns, which had been reused in the 4th century C.E., have been reconstructed today. Behind the broad north colonnade of the courtyard was the major building of the Prytaneion. The main room, in the east part of this building, was possibly used for religious banquets or public feasts honoring important individuals. Heart-shaped columns stood in each of the four corners of the building. The purpose of the rectangular stone foundation in the center of the room is uncertain. It was perhaps the location of the sacred hearth of Hestia. The two famous statues of Artemis Ephesia, now on display in the Ephesus Museum, were discovered in the Prytaneion, where they had been ritually buried, likely after the disastrous earthquake of the 4th century. (They also might have been buried to keep them from being destroyed by zealous Christians after Christianity became the official religion of the empire in the 4th century.) Smaller rooms of unknown purpose were located to the north and west of the main room. To the west of the Prytaneion excavators uncovered the ruins of a **banqueting house** or **residence**.

The colonnaded street that runs west from the Prytaneion was known as **Kathodos** (which simply means "the way down"). Where this street ends at **Domitian Square** there are **stone bases**, one on each side, perhaps on which statues originally stood. On both of these bases is a similar pair of reliefs. The reliefs that face the Kathodos portray the tripod of Apollo. The other reliefs depict a nude Hermes with a ram (or goat). Domitian Square is the name given to the area at the juncture of Kathodos and Curetes Street. The monumental structure on the north side of Domitian Square is the **Memmius Monument**, a monument built in the last half of the 1st century B.C.E. to honor **Caius Memmius**, a grandson of the Roman dictator Sulla. The figures on the side of the monument may represent members of his family. Within a few decades after the construction of the monument, a fountain with four columns, referred to as the **Hydreion**, was built on the west side of the monument. Around 300 C.E., statues of the emperors Diocletian, Maximian, Constantius Chlorus, and Galerian were added in front of the fountain.

On the east side of Domitian Square, just south of Kathodos, is a structure that connects to the west end of the State Agora. This structure, called the **Chalcidicum**, was an extension of the Basilica Stoa. The lower part of the building, visible today, consisted of three rooms accessible from Domitian Square, while the upper part opened onto the center aisle of the Basilica Stoa. West of the Chalcidicum is a **round structure** with garlands and bulls' heads. This was moved here from another part of the city in the 4th century C.E. Adjacent to this structure is a relief of a flying **Nike** figure holding a wreath. This architectural fragment was a part of the Hercules (Heracles) Gate, located at the eastern end of Curetes Street.

South of the Chalcidicum, next to the western edge of the State Agora, is the location of the **tomb monument for C. Sextilius Pollio**, a leading citizen and benefactor of Ephesus. Pollio donated the funds for building both the Basilica Stoa and an aqueduct for the city. Built at the beginning of the 1st century C.E., this tomb monument was renovated or rebuilt into a fountain (the **Pollio Fountain**) in 93 C.E. The arch in front of the apsidal room has been reconstructed. The pool for the fountain was located within this apsidal room, with water flowing into the fountain through the apsidal wall. South of the Pollio Monument/Fountain are the remains of several shops. The street that these shops, as well as the Pollio Monument/Fountain, faced has been called **Domitian Street**.

The major structure in Domitian Square was the large temple called the **Temple of the Flavian Sebastoi**, or the **Temple of Domitian**. The temple, built during the reign of Domitian (81–96 C.E.), stood on a terrace on the south side of Domitian Square and was originally dedicated to Domitian and his predecessors, Titus (his brother) and Vespasian (his father). These three emperors were known as the Flavian Sebastoi, since *Flavius* was the "family name" for these emperors. (*Sebastoi* is the Greek word for "augustus," a title given to the emperors.) After the assassination of Domitian, instigated in part by his wife, he suffered the official condemnation of his memory (*damnatio memoriae*), which led to the obliteration of his name and image. Consequently the temple was transferred to his father, Vespasian. As a result of the building of this temple, Ephesus acquired the title of *neokoros,* meaning it possessed a provincial temple of the emperors.

About all that remains of the temple is the terrace on which it stood. The terrace, measuring 164 feet by 328 feet, was built over a vaulted substructure. Portions of a colossal statue of an emperor were found in the substructure. This statue, which possibly stood nearly 25 feet tall, was for a long time identified as a statue of Domitian. Recently many scholars have argued that it represents his brother Titus instead. The head and forearm of this statue are in the Ephesus Museum. The substructure, still mostly preserved, served as storerooms. The long eastern hall of the substructure is used today as the **Inscription Museum**, which contains a collection of various inscriptions from the 7th century B.C.E. until Byzantine times uncovered at Ephesus. Unfortunately, the museum is rarely open. A two-story (or perhaps multistory) terrace façade stood in front of the substructure to partially conceal it. A portion of this columned façade has been reconstructed and stands today. The temple itself was reached by means of a double stairway that led to the top of the terrace, where a row of columns surrounded the temple, with eight columns in the front and in the back and thirteen columns on each of the two sides. Four columns lined the front porch (the pronaos). Archaeologists uncovered an altar, elaborately decorated with reliefs, that is now on display in the Ephesus Museum. Northwest of the temple terrace, adjoining the terrace façade, was an east-west hall with columns in the center.

As noted above, **Curetes Street** (known in ancient times as Embolos or Plateia) is the street leading northwest from the north area of Domitian Square. It is called Curetes Street today because some of the columns lining the upper part of the street are reused columns from the Prytaneion that were inscribed with lists of the names of *curetes*. This street is one of the oldest in Ephesus. Whereas the other streets of the city are basically laid out according to the Hippodamian grid plan and thus intersect at right angles, Curetes Street cuts diagonally through the city. It is a part of the older Processional Way that led to the Artemision. The view looking down Curetes Street to the Library of Celsus is one of the most impressive views in the entire city. The street, paved with marble blocks and with a sewer running underneath, was lined with columns and statues on statue bases at its upper end. The lower end had shops, houses, and public buildings on each side. At the eastern end of Curetes Street is the

▲ **Fig. 73.** Curetes Street in Ephesus

Hercules Gate, probably built during the 5th century C.E., although some of its elements are reused pieces from earlier periods. Its name is derived from the reliefs of Hercules on pillars of the gate. The architectural fragment with a relief of a flying Nike, now in Domitian Square, was part of an arch that spanned the gateway.

Farther down the street is the **Fountain of Trajan,** built to honor the emperor after his visit to Ephesus between 102 and 104 C.E. The monumental fountain was a two-story structure containing numerous columns with Corinthian capitals. In the center of the fountain was a long rectangular pool into which the water flowed. The pool was surrounded on three sides by the two-story façade. In the center of the rear wall was a large statue of Trajan, twice life size. One of the feet of this statue has survived and has been placed in its original position. Various other statues also decorated the fountain.

Beyond the Fountain of Trajan are the **Baths of Varius**, or the **Scholasticia Baths**, a public bath originally built in the late 1st century or early 2nd century by **P. Quintilius Varius Valens** and his family. The bath had two entrances, one from Curetes Street and the other from the street running east of the bath, referred to today as **Bath Street**. Bath Street runs uphill to the theater and beyond. The street itself has been excavated but not the sides of the street, which were probably lined with residential buildings. The entrance from Bath Street led into the apodyterium (changing room), and from there one entered the various other rooms of the bath complex—the frigidarium, the tepidarium, the caldarium, and the sudatorium. During the 4th century a wealthy Christian woman of Ephesus named Scholasticia sponsored a renovation of the bath complex, reusing some materials from the Prytaneion. The seated statue of Scholasticia was placed in a niche at the entrance from Bath Street. A street, called **Academy Street** by the archaeologists, is on the west side of the baths.

One of the most popular sites in Ephesus to modern visitors (and likely to ancient residents as well) is the **latrine**, located in the area on the west side of Academy Street. Built at the same time as the bath complex, these public toilets consist of bench seating (with appropriately cut holes) around three sides of an open courtyard. (The area over the seats was roofed.) Fresh water flowed in a channel in front of the seats, while running water underneath the seats carried the wastes away. Sponges attached to sticks were used for wiping and then rinsed in the channel in front of the seats. Going to the toilet was not a private affair but a chance to socialize with one's neighbor, as evidenced by the close seating arrangements. The adjacent building with several rooms is frequently described, by tour guides and publications alike, as a **brothel**. This identification is primarily based on two factors: the discovery in a well in the building of a well-endowed (and probably much envied) phallic statue of the Egyptian god Bes (sometimes identified as Priapus, god of fertility and virility), the god of childbirth, dance, and pleasure (now in the Ephesus Museum), and an inscription on a reused architrave mentioning the presence of a *paidiskeion*, a word that could mean either "brothel" or "public latrine." The view held by many recent scholars is that the building was probably a **residential building**, not a brothel. The architrave with the word *paidiskeion* was likely brought from the latrine and reused here.

The ornate building facing Curetes Street that was incorporated into the Baths of Varius is the **Temple of Hadrian**. Built during the 2nd century C.E. and renovated in the 4th century, the temple consists of a pronaos (front porch) with a small cella (the room behind the pronaos). The pronaos originally had a pediment (a triangular structure) supported by two columns and two pillars, all with Corinthian capitals. The corners of the pediment and its arched architrave have been restored. The relief in the middle of the arch is of Tyche, goddess of fortune. The four statue bases in front of the temple held bronze statues of the emperors Galerius, Maximian, Diocletian, and Constantius Chlorus.

On the south side of Curetes Street was a colonnaded stoa, the **Stoa of Alytarches**, named after the person who sponsored its construction. The stoa contains a beautiful multicolored mosaic composed of geometric patterns, birds, flowers, and plants. The stoa was built in the 1st century C.E., whereas the mosaic was added in the 5th century. Behind the stoa are several **shops** that opened onto the stoa. These shops had two stories, with the top floor likely used as living quarters by the owners. One of the shops seems to have been a restaurant.

On the terrace behind the shops was a wealthy residential area. Two of the **terrace houses** located here have been excavated. Terrace House 2 has been completely placed under a protective roof and is open to the public. The houses contain several residential units, similar to modern condominiums. The residential units contained several rooms and usually consisted of two or more floors, following the contours of the terrace. The homes were elaborately decorated with beautiful mosaics, frescoed walls, ornate columns, and marble constructions. The earliest houses here date back to the 1st century B.C.E. Some of the units continued to be used for residences as late as the 7th century C.E. During that time period, many renovations and reconfigurations of the residential units occurred. The elaborate decorations of the houses rival the famous finds at Pompeii and Herculaneum. The visit to the terrace houses is well worth the additional admission fee that is charged.

On Curetes Street in front of Terrace House 2, the westernmost of the two terrace houses, are two honorific monuments, the **Octagon** and the **Androclus Monument**. The Octagon, built between 50 and 20 B.C.E., was a monumental grave with Corinthian columns and a stepped pyramid roof. In a sarcophagus in the monument archaeologists discovered the skeleton of a young female, fifteen or sixteen years old, that is now thought to be the remains of **Arsinoe IV**, the youngest sister of **Cleopatra**, who had been killed in Ephesus in 41 B.C.E. by **Mark Antony** at the request of Cleopatra. To the west of the Octagon are the remains of a heroon (an honorific monument for a hero) for **Androclus**, the mythical founder of Ephesus. The building was a two-story structure with Doric columns and a fountain in the recessed middle section. The panels in front of the structure (decorated with crosses) were added in Byzantine times to convert the water basin in front of the fountain into a reservoir. (For this reason this structure is sometimes called the Byzantine Fountain.)

A three-story monumental gate, the **Gate of Hadrian**, stood at the lower end of Curetes Street on its southern side. The gate, today partially reconstructed, was situated across the southern end of Marble Street. From this gate another road led west to Ortygia, the location the Ephesians claimed as the birthplace of Artemis and where they celebrated her birth annually. (Outside Ephesus, the most widely held view was that the birthplace of Artemis was the island of Delos.) Built in the 2nd century C.E., the gate was heavily damaged by an earthquake in the 3rd or 4th century and subsequently rebuilt. West of the Gate of Hadrian are the foundations and the stairway of an **altar**, possibly an altar to Artemis, from early Roman times. West of the altar was a **peristyle house** from Hellenistic or early Roman times. During the 4th century a **hall** was built over the location of the altar and the house.

Probably the most recognized building in Ephesus, the **Library of Celsus** was built in the first quarter of the 2nd century C.E. as a grave monument for **Tiberius Julius Celsus Polemaeanus**, the proconsul of the Roman province of Asia from 105–107 C.E., by his son. The sarcophagus of Celsus is in a burial chamber underneath the apse in the

▲ **Fig. 74.** Library of Celsus in Ephesus

interior of the library. The reerected two-story façade of the building, with its Corinthian columns, is reached by a flight of nine steps. Decorating the lower story of the façade are statues of four women personifying the virtues of *sophia* (wisdom), *arete* (moral excellence), *ennoia* (thought), and *episteme* (knowledge). (The statues are copies. The originals are in the Ephesus Museum in Vienna.) The interior of the building consisted of three stories. On the top two stories were cupboardlike niches containing the scrolls and balconies that provided access to the niches. One of the largest libraries in the ancient world, the Library of Celsus contained approximately 12,000 scrolls. An earthquake in 262 c.e. destroyed the interior of the library. The façade was destroyed in the 10th century, likely by an earthquake as well.

The restored monumental gate located east of the library is the **South Gate**, or the **Gate of Mazaeus and Mithridates**. According to an inscription on the gate, written in Latin and Greek, the gate was erected by **Mazaeus** and **Mithridates**, two wealthy freedmen, in honor of **Emperor Augustus**, his wife **Livia**, his daughter **Julia**, and his son-in-law **Agrippa**. The two men, former slaves of the imperial family, erected the gate in 4 or 3 b.c.e. (A bit of graffito scrawled on the gate warns that "whoever shall relieve himself here shall suffer the wrath of Hecate," the goddess of crossroads.) East of the South Gate was discovered a burial chamber, formerly vaulted, that contained the 2nd-century-c.e. **sarcophagus of Tiberius Claudius Flavianus**, a sophist of Ephesus. During Roman times a staircase led above the burial chamber to the Hall of Nero. The purpose of the nearby **brick barrel vault**, built in the 2nd century c.e., is unknown. Near the street are the remains of a **circular Hellenistic building** with a conical roof. This was perhaps a decorative fountain.

The South Gate, with its three arched entranceways, served as the south entrance to the **Tetragonos Agora** (or **Square Agora**), the major commercial agora of Ephesus. The agora was first built here in Hellenistic times, then later rebuilt and renovated several times by the Romans. The agora, forming a square approximately 370 feet long on each side, was surrounded on all four sides by double-colonnaded stoas that apparently had two stories. Nearly one hundred rooms, which served primarily as shops and other commercial facilities, were located behind the colonnades. On the east side of the agora, running behind the east colonnade and facing Marble Street, was a two-aisled basilica called the **Hall of Nero**. An inscription indicates that the hall was dedicated to Artemis Ephesia, **Nero**, his mother **Agrippina**, and the citizens of Ephesus. The agora had three entrances: the South Gate, the **North Gate**, and the **West Gate**. The West Gate opened onto the so-called **West Road**, which led to the harbor.

Adjoining the southwest side of the agora, with an entrance from the West Road, is a **temple complex**, often called the **Temple of Serapis**, or the **Serapeion**. The identification of the deity to whom the temple was dedicated is uncertain. (Other proposals argue that it was an imperial temple or perhaps a nymphaeum.) One of the major arguments for assigning the temple to Serapis is the complex water system that was a part of the building. Water rituals were an important part of the Serapis cult. Built in either the 2nd century C.E. or the beginning of the 3rd century C.E., the temple was heavily damaged by an earthquake and fires, likely during the 3rd century. During the 4th century the temple was converted into a Christian church.

The street that runs north from the Gate of Hadrian is **Marble Street**. The marble paving, from which the street derives its name, was added in the 5th century C.E. A part of the Processional Way that led to the Artemision, the street was lined on its east side by a colonnade, behind which were shops and residential buildings. The west side was flanked by the Hall of Nero, whose floor level is approximately 5.5 feet above the street and thus inaccessible from Marble Street except by means of an entrance at the north end. This entrance platform provides a good location from which to view the agora and Marble Street. Note the ruts worn in the pavement from wheeled traffic (chariots, carts, and wagons). Near the middle of the street, on the west side, is a marble block in the street with drawings on it. The drawings represent a woman's face, a foot, and a heart-shaped object. These drawings are popularly interpreted as an advertisement for the supposed brothel at the southern end of Marble Street (see discussion above about the brothel), with the symbols supposedly being a representation of a prostitute, a heart (or a woman's pudenda), and a woman's foot pointing the way to the brothel. This interpretation is highly speculative and even unlikely, since, among other reasons, the building at the end of Marble Street was likely not a brothel. (Other problems with identifying the drawings as a brothel advertisement include the claims that the woman represented is not a prostitute but the goddess Tyche; that the foot is that of a man, not a woman; that the marble block is too far away from the supposed brothel to be a clear advertisement for it; and that the block possibly dates from the 5th century C.E.)

At the north end of the street is one of the most magnificent structures in Ephesus—the **theater**. Beginning as a smaller structure possibly as early as the 2nd century B.C.E., the theater was enlarged and renovated during the 1st to 3rd centuries C.E. As a result of these renovations, the second and third tiers of seats were added to the theater, bringing its total seating capacity to nearly 25,000 spectators. The stage building was also enlarged, resulting in a three-story, richly decorated façade. The cavea (the seating area), which was divided vertically by three diazomata (walkways), was partially covered by an awning. When the preaching and actions of **Paul** the apostle in Ephesus led to a near riot, it was into this theater that his companions **Gaius** and **Aristarchus** were dragged by the crowd. (See "Biblical Significance," above.)

▲ **Fig. 75.** Theater in Ephesus

A paved, colonnaded street running north from the theater, the so-called **Theater Street**, passes along the east side of the remains of the **Theater Gymnasium**. This bath-gymnasium complex, built in the 2nd century C.E., consisted of a palaestra and the various rooms typical of a Roman bath. The large palaestra, with colonnades on three sides, is located on the south side of the complex. The north side of the palaestra has four rows of seats, where observers could watch the activities in the palaestra courtyard. These seats served also as steps leading to the bath portion of the building. Theater Street continues north, going past an **apsidal building** (possibly a church but more likely a secular building) and a **Byzantine palace**. The palace, earlier identified as a bath, was possibly the residence of the governor of the area. (The building may have been a bath during the 1st century and later converted into a palace complex.)

The **stadium** and the **Vedius Gymnasium** are at the northern edge of the city and can be reached from Theater Street. The stadium, although only partially excavated, is still recognizable from the horseshoe-shaped depression in the landscape. Originally built during the Hellenistic period, the stadium was greatly expanded during the time of Nero. The seats in the south side of the stadium were built into the southern slope of the hill, while on the north a vaulted substructure was constructed to support the seating. (During the 5th century a **church** was built in the west end of the tunnel under the north seats.) The main entrance to the stadium was through a monumental gateway on the west. At the east end of the stadium is an elliptical area that was likely separated from the interior of the stadium. This area was probably used for gladiatorial contests. Much of the building stones of the stadium were removed during the Byzantine period to be reused for buildings on Ayasoluk Hill.

North of the stadium is the Vedius Gymnasium. Built in the middle of the 2nd century c.e. by **M. Claudius P. Vedius Antoninus Phaedrus**

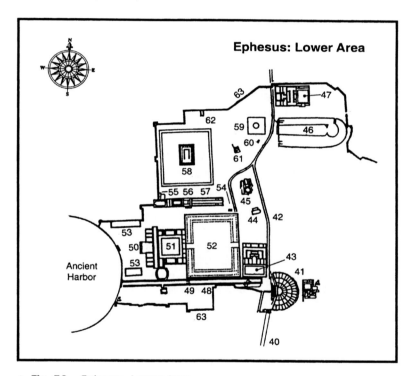

▲ **Fig. 76.** Ephesus: Lower Area

40. Marble Street
41. Theater
42. Theater Street
43. Theater Gymnasium
44. Apsidal Building
45. Byzantine Palace
46. Stadium
47. Vedius Gymnasium
48. Arcadian Way/Harbor Street
49. Monument of the Four Evangelists
50. Harbor Baths
51. Harbor Gymnasium
52. Halls of Verulanus
53. Market Buildings
54. Lower (North) Entrance to Ephesus
55. Baptistery
56. Church of Mary
57. Episcopeion
58. Olympieion
59. Macellum
60. Byzantine Well House
61. 3rd Century c.e. House
62. Crevice Temple
63. Byzantine Wall

Sabinianus, a generous benefactor of the city who was given the honorary title of *ktistes*, or founder of the city, because of his generosity in constructing public buildings, the Vedius Gymnasium was a bath-gymnasium complex consisting of a palaestra and a bathing area. The entrance to the palaestra, located on the east side of the complex, was through a monumental, three-aisled propylon. To the left of the propylon was a latrine. The courtyard of the palaestra, 130 feet by 64 feet, was surrounded by a colonnade. The west side of the palaestra led into a small, elaborately decorated room that was likely an imperial hall dedicated to the cult of the emperor **Antoninus Pius,** to whom the complex was dedicated. West of the imperial hall were the various rooms of the bath. (To continue the visit at the site, return to the theater area.)

The broad street leading from the theater to the harbor is known as the **Arcadian Way,** or **Harbor Street.** (Presently visitors to the site cannot travel the entire length of the Arcadian Way to visit the structures named below. To visit them, follow the dirt path beside the restrooms at the north entrance. The path will eventually fork. Follow the left fork to find the harbor ruins. The right fork leads to the Church of Mary. The area around the harbor is heavily overgrown and somewhat difficult to visit.) Initially constructed during Hellenistic or early Roman times, the street was remodeled during the reign of **Emperor Arcadius** (395–408 c.e.). Approximately 36 feet wide and 1,750 feet long, the street had mosaic-paved colonnades on both sides, with shops located behind them. During the 5th century lamps were added along the street so that the street could be lit at night. Whether arriving by day or night, a visitor passing from the harbor up the marble-paved, colonnaded Arcadian Way could not help but be impressed by the magnificence of the city. Approximately in the middle of the Arcadian Way was a four-column monument, often known as the **Monument of the Four Evangelists.** Erected in the 6th century, this monument is thought to have contained statues of each of the writers of the four New Testament gospels, one statue on each of the four columns.

On the north side of the Arcadian Way, west of the Theater Gymnasium, was the largest bath-gymnasium complex in the city. This complex stretches all the way from the west side of the Theater Gymnasium to the harbor. This area, consisting of the **Harbor Baths,** the **Harbor Gymnasium,** and the **Halls of Verulanus,** has been only partially excavated and is difficult to visit (as well as to excavate) because of the heavy vegetation and marshy terrain. The Halls of Verulanus were located next to the Theater Gymnasium. (Today the path to the north entrance passes through this area.) This large athletic field, which measured 650 feet by 790 feet, was surrounded by a three-aisled colonnade paved with marble. The athletic field is known as the Halls of Verulanus because the imperial priest **Claudius Verulanus** paid for the marble paneling of the colonnaded walls during the time of Hadrian (117–138 c.e.).

West of the Halls of Verulanus was a smaller exercise area, the Harbor Gymnasium. Consisting of a square peristyle courtyard (a palaestra) surrounded on three sides by rooms for various purposes, this structure had elaborate architectural features and lavish furnishings. It contained a marble hall in honor of the emperor **Domitian**. The west side of the Harbor Gymnasium was connected to the various rooms that constituted the Harbor Baths. All of the structures that make up the large bath-gymnasium complex were built either at the end of the 1st century or the early years of the 2nd century C.E. West of the Harbor Baths, at the edge of the ancient harbor, are the ruins of two similar structures that have frequently been identified as **harbor warehouses**. Recent studies, however, have concluded that they were probably open **porticoes** used for business and trade.

The path to the modern north entrance to the site of Ephesus leads along the eastern edge of the Halls of Verulanus. Prior to the exit from the site, a path beside the restrooms leads to the **Church of Mary**, also known as the **Council Church**. Recent research has indicated that the church complex was constructed by modifying the 860-foot-long south stoa of the **Olympieion**, a large temple complex built after 130 C.E. (Earlier proposals had incorrectly identified the temple stoa as a commercial building associated with the harbor or as a *museion*, a school of arts and learning dedicated to the Muses.) This temple, which served as the imperial temple to **Emperor Hadrian** as Zeus Olympios, was approximately 80 feet tall, built in the Corinthian style, and surrounded by stoas. The building was destroyed around 400 C.E., presumably by Christians who despised the imperial cult. The south stoa of this complex, divided into three aisles by two rows of columns, was reconstructed into a church and an **episcopeion**, or bishop's palace. In the initial phase of the building, perhaps as early as the late 5th century, the church consisted of a peristyle atrium at the west end and a three-aisled church hall, with a narthex in between. The east end of the church hall had a large apse, beyond which was built the bishop's palace. North of the atrium a **baptistery** was constructed. The baptismal basin, with steps leading down into it, can be seen in the center of the room. This basin would have been used for adult baptisms.

In the 6th century the church underwent extensive alterations, perhaps necessitated by earthquake damage, with the western part of the church hall being turned into a separate church with its own apse of brick construction. The large marble basin in front of this apse is suspected of being a reused item from one of the baths in the city. It perhaps served in the church as a font. Due to the Arab raids of the 7th century and the shifting of the population from the harbor area to Ayasoluk Hill, the Church of Mary dwindled in importance. From the 7th to at least the 11th century, the church functioned as a cemetery church, with burials in and around the building.

This church is sometimes called the **Council Church** because it has been thought that this was the meeting place for the important Third Ecumenical Council in 431. The latest archaeological studies indicate that the church had not yet been built at that time. Perhaps the council met in the stoa prior to its reconfiguration as a church building. Archaeological finds do support the possibility that some reconstruction of the stoa had begun prior to 431, but the building now referred to as the Church of Mary had not yet been completed.

Beyond the north entrance of the site are numerous gift shops and kiosks. North of the parking lot and west of the stadium is a small hill thought to be the **acropolis** where the Ionians, supposedly led by **Androclus**, settled in the 10th century B.C.E. During the 6th century B.C.E. the Lydians, led by **King Croesus**, destroyed the buildings on the acropolis and forced the people to resettle near the area where the Temple of Artemis was built. Remains of a building that had a columned courtyard from approximately the 2nd century C.E. lie on the plateau of the hill. Often called the **Macellum** (meat market), the actual purpose of this building is unknown. Inscriptions locate the meat market not here but in the agora. This building may have been an imperial cult site. South of this building, near Theater Street, are the remains of an **early Byzantine well house**. On the southwest edge of the hill are the remains of a **3rd-century-C.E. house** that incorporated the **walls of a Hellenistic fortification**, likely erected as a defense against the Romans in 191 B.C.E. Near the northwest edge of the hill are the remains of a small temple from around 400 B.C.E., called the **Crevice Temple** because the temple was built over a natural crevice in the rock.

Cave of the Seven Sleepers

On the east side of Panayïr Daǧï is a cave area first used as a cemetery around the end of the 4th century C.E. Soon after that time a church was built over the site. Eventually several hundred burials took place in the area. Popular tradition claims that this is the place where seven young men from Ephesus took refuge in a cave during the persecution of Christians by **Emperor Decius** (249–251). Here they fell asleep and did not awaken for nearly two hundred years. When they went into town and found that the persecution had ended, they became heroes to the people. When the men died, years later, they were buried in the cave, which became a popular shrine and place of pilgrimage. Several variations of the legend of the Seven Sleepers circulated in antiquity, with many locations claiming to be the site of this miraculous event.

Tomb of St. Luke

Near the south entrance to the Ephesus site, on the opposite side of the modern road, are the remains of a 2nd-century circular building. The function of this building, erected over an earlier structure, is unknown.

Around the 5th or 6th century the building was renovated into a Christian church. When the explorer J. T. Wood first excavated the site in the 19th century, he found a pillar with a relief of a bull and a cross. He interpreted the bull as a symbol of **Luke the Evangelist** and thus called the building the tomb of St. Luke. The building, which had been richly decorated with wall paintings, apparently has no connection with St. Luke.

The House of Mary

In the 19th century a German nun, Catherine Emmerich, claimed that the location of the house of **Mary**, the mother of Jesus, was revealed to her in a dream at a location near Ephesus. Based on the details described by the nun, Lazarist fathers from Izmir explored the area and found the house she described several miles south of Selçuk at Panaya Kapulu. The existing house is clearly not the home of Mary, since according to archaeological examination the house dates from Byzantine times, perhaps as late as the 13th century. The house is built on the remains of a much earlier structure, however, perhaps dating to the 1st century c.e. A place of pilgrimage for Catholic and Orthodox Christians, as well as Muslim visitors, the place attracts many visitors who come to pay homage to the Blessed Virgin. The site, approximately 5.5 miles from Selçuk, is reached via the road from Selçuk that passes by the Magnesian Gate and then continues up the slope of Bülbül Daği. The trip to the site provides a great view of the ruins of Ephesus and the **Hellenistic city walls** on the hillside.

Roman Aqueduct

Approximately 3 miles from Selçuk on the road toward Aydïn is a portion of an aqueduct from the time of Augustus. Spanning the valley of

▲ **Fig. 77.** Pollio Aqueduct near Selçuk

the Dervenddere River (the ancient Marnas River), this two-story section of the aqueduct has three large arches in the lower section and six smaller arches on the top. Because an inscription on both sides of the aqueduct names **C. Sextilius Pollio**, his wife, and his stepson as the ones who provided the funds for building the aqueduct, it is sometimes known as the **Pollio Aqueduct**.

St. Paul's Prison

One of the watchtowers that are part of the Hellenistic city walls built by Lysimachus on the slopes of Bülbül Dağï is popularly known as **St. Paul's Prison**. There is no valid basis for associating this structure with Paul. The tower, on the southwest slope of the hill, can be seen easily from the highway that runs from Selçuk to Kuşadasi.

Temple of Artemis

Known as one of the seven wonders of the ancient world, the **Temple of Artemis** (or the **Artemision**) drew visitors from throughout the Mediterranean world who came to offer sacrifices and gifts and seek the favor of Artemis. The initial excavation of the Artemision was by J. T. Wood, who discovered the long-lost site in 1869 after a seven-year search. Wood located the temple site by following the route of the Processional Way, which led from Ephesus to the Artemision. Excavations were continued by D. G. Hogarth in 1904–1905 under the auspices of the British Museum (for whom Wood also worked). From 1965 to the present, the Austrian Archaeological Institute has been excavating the site. The results of these excavations have revealed that in the 8th century B.C.E. a small temple (measuring 44 feet by 21 feet) stood on the site. The temple had four columns along its front and back and eight columns on the two sides. Inside the open cella of the temple, a rectangular structure supported on six columns housed the temple's cult figure, a wooden representation of the goddess. In a later renovation a tiled roof was placed over the cella. In the late 7th or early 6th century B.C.E. another temple (called Temple C) was built over the site of the 8th-century-B.C.E. temple. Also in the late 7th century B.C.E. a small temple, sometimes called the *hecatompedos* (hundred-footer) because its length of 113 feet is approximately 100 Ionic feet, was constructed west of Temple C. This temple, like Temple C, was apparently never finished. South of the southwest corner of the *hecatompedos* temple is a base for a structure that apparently served a cultic purpose, as evidenced by the animal bones and votive gifts discovered nearby.

In the 6th century three small structures were built west of the *hecatompedos*. Two of these have **square bases** measuring approximately 11.5 feet. North of these two square bases was a **ramp** or **stairway-ramp**. These three structures were probably used for sacrificial purposes. Around

560 B.C.E. the Ephesians, with donations from **King Croesus** of Lydia, began construction on a **monumental marble temple** approximately 185 feet wide. Its length is unknown, although it has been estimated at approximately 378 feet. The temple was designed by three architects— **Chersiphron** and his son **Metagenes** from Knossos, Crete, and **Theodoros** from Samos. The temple, the largest structure at the time to be built solely of marble, had double rows of columns, eight rows on the front and back and approximately twenty on the sides. Many of the columns contained reliefs depicting people and animals on their way to sacrifice. The columns, which supported covered porticoes, surrounded the walls of the cella of the temple, which was unroofed. Inside the cella was a small building that contained the cult statue. During the 5th century an **altar** with a large courtyard surrounding it was constructed west of the temple. The altar courtyard incorporated the three bases from the 6th century mentioned above.

The Croesus temple suffered a disastrous fire in 356 B.C.E., set by a man named **Herostratus** who allegedly wanted to make himself famous. A few decades later, the temple was rebuilt. Alexander the Great, who reportedly was born on the same night of the fire, offered to pay for the reconstruction of the temple, but his offer was diplomatically declined. The new temple, built on the foundations of the Croesus temple, had

▲ **Fig. 78.** Remains of the Temple of Artemis Ephesia at Ephesus

basically the same dimensions as the earlier temple, although its plan was slightly altered. Built on a thirteen-step platform to avoid flooding, the temple had three rows of eight columns in the front and three rows of nine columns in the rear. The two sides likely had two rows of twenty-one columns each, approximately 59 feet tall. As in the Croesus temple, the Hellenistic temple contained a cult statue of Artemis in the cella of the temple. The U-shaped altar to the west of the temple apparently was rebuilt on the same foundations as the earlier altar.

During Roman times the temple suffered at the hands of people who robbed it of some of its treasures, although **Emperor Titus** provided major repairs to the temple. In 263 C.E. the temple was plundered by the Goths, and during Byzantine times it was abandoned with the rise of Christianity. During the 5th century a church was built in the Artemision. Eventually this once magnificent structure succumbed to neglect and pilferage, as some of its materials were reused in other structures.

A visit to the site today is rather disappointing. Not much remains to be seen. A lone **column**, erected from various column pieces, stands on the site, which is often partially or even completely covered with water. (The reerected column is approximately 13 feet shorter than the original columns.) Much of the earlier excavated areas have been reburied. What can be seen varies at different times of the year, according to the water level at the site. In addition to pieces of different columns and architectural fragments, the **foundations of the Croesus temple**, the **foundations of the hecatompedos**, and the **foundations of the altar, ramp, and associated bases** can sometimes be seen.

Ephesus Museum

Located in Selçuk, the Ephesus Museum exhibits many spectacular finds from the excavations at Ephesus and the surrounding area. A visit to Ephesus would not be complete without a tour of the museum.

Begin the tour with the room to the left of the entrance, the Room of the Terrace Houses. This room exhibits items discovered in the excavations of Terrace Houses 1 and 2 on Curetes Street. Among the many items of note displayed here are medical and cosmetic items and jewelry; **busts of Socrates, Marcus Aurelius, Menander, Tiberius,** and **Livia**; a **portrait head of Eros**; a **bronze statuette of Eros riding a dolphin**; the small terra-cotta **statue of the god Bes** found in the so-called brothel; a marble **statue of the god Priapus**; and the **statue of an Egyptian priest**. Especially noteworthy is the reproduction of a portion of the **"Socrates" room** from Terrace House 2. This display contains a **statue of Artemis the hunter** and a **wall painting of Socrates**.

Room 2, the Room of the Fountains, contains statues that were in three of the fountains of the ancient city—the fountains of Pollio, Trajan, and Laecanius Bassus. The **Odysseus and Polyphemus statue group**, a **statue of the river god Marnas**, and **statues of Dionysus and Aphrodite** are among the various pieces displayed in this room.

In room 3, called the Room of the New Finds and Small Finds, the museum exhibits some of the finds from recent excavations. Included here are an **ivory frieze** that was part of a lintel decoration from Terrace House 2, parts of an **ivory frieze from a casket**, a collection of lamps, and a case displaying coins and gold objects from graves.

Room 4 is an outdoor garden courtyard that displays grave stelae, sarcophagi, an **inscription of customs regulations from the time of Nero** (later reused as part of the pulpit for the Church of St. John the Theologian), a 3rd-century-c.e. **sundial**, and various architectural pieces.

The Room of the Grave Finds, room 5, primarily contains items found in graves in and near Ephesus. Some of these items date back to Mycenaean times. The room also contains some informative plaques, one telling the legend of the Cave of the Seven Sleepers and another one describing the evolution of the worship of the Great Mother in Anatolia, from Cybele to Artemis.

In room 6, the Room of Artemis Ephesia, are arguably the most famous objects in the museum. The room contains statues, architectural pieces, and various artifacts from the Artemision, as well as other objects related to Artemis. Note particularly the **small gold statuette of Artemis** from the 7th century B.C.E. The most spectacular displays are two large statues of Artemis Ephesia, both of which were uncovered from excavations of the Prytaneion in Ephesus. The one on the left, known as the **Great Artemis**, is from the 1st century c.e. The goddess wears a three-tiered headdress, the top tier of which is a representation of the Temple of Artemis. This statue is missing its arms below the elbows. The goddess is decorated with various animal figures, prominent among them bees, which were the symbol of Ephesus. Especially conspicuous are the many oval protuberances from her chest. These objects have been given a variety of interpretations, most frequently eggs, breasts, or bull testicles (bulls were often sacrificed to Artemis), any of which would have served

▲ **Fig. 79.** Statue of Artemis Ephesia (the "Beautiful Artemis") in the Ephesus Museum

as symbols of fertility. On the opposite side of the room is the so-called **Beautiful Artemis**, a shorter statue from the 2nd century C.E. made of fine-grained white marble. Like the Great Artemis, this statue is thought to be a Roman copy of the statue of the goddess that was in the Artemision. Her headdress, or polos, is missing. On either side of her are statues of a deer, sacred animal to Artemis, along with beehives.

The last room, room 7, is known as the Imperial Cult Room. In addition to the **altar from the Temple of Domitian**, the room contains **busts or portrait heads of Augustus, Trajan**, and **Commodus**; a **statue of the consul Stephanos**; and the **frieze from the Temple of Hadrian**. On the right wall are the head and left forearm of a **colossal statue** of one of the emperors. Usually considered to be a statue of **Domitian** from the end of the 1st century C.E., several scholars recently have argued that the statue is instead a representation of **Titus**, the brother of Domitian. In addition to the head and arm, smaller fragments of the arms and legs were also discovered, although these are not on display. Found in the area of the Temple of Domitian, the statue would have stood nearly 25 feet tall.

The Church of St. John the Theologian

Early tradition associated John, the disciple of Jesus, with the city of Ephesus. Early traditions also identified this John as the author of the Gospel of John and the book of Revelation. As the discussion above indicates (see "Biblical Significance"), these traditions are suspect. Regardless, however, of the veracity of the traditions, as early as the 4th or 5th century a Christian church was built over a simple grave, supposedly the grave of John the disciple. In the 6th century **Emperor Justinian** had an impressive domed basilica built to replace the earlier church. The church, known as the **Church of St. John the Theologian**, is located on Ayasoluk Hill, which can be reached by a street leading up from the center of Selçuk. The hill, including the church, is surrounded by defense walls erected in the 8th and 9th centuries C.E. as protection against the Arab raids. The major entrance to the hill is through the gate on the south side, the so-called **Gate of Persecution**. The arched gateway is flanked on each side by a square guard tower. Originally a reused frieze depicting the discovery of Achilles by Odysseus was above the arch. Misunderstood as a scene of persecution of Christians, the gate was named the Gate of Persecution.

The Church of St. John, now being partially restored, was built on an east-west axis with a cross-shaped ground plan. At the west end is an atrium that was surrounded on three sides by double-colonnaded halls. The atrium led into the exonarthex, the narthex, and then the nave of the multidomed basilica. At the junction of the north-south and east-west parts of the basilica is the alleged grave of St. John, marked today by a marble slab and four columns. The nave originally was roofed with six large domes, the largest of which was over the grave. The domes were supported by marble and brick pillars, between which were blue-veined marble columns that separated the central nave from the side aisles and supported the upper story. The supposed grave of John is underneath the mosaic and marble floor of the bema (altar) of the church, which is raised two steps above the floor of the church. A raised path leads from the bema to the ambo (pulpit) of the church. At the rear of the bema is the synthronos, the seating area for the clergy.

The octagonal **baptistery** is located on the north side of the nave. Three steps on each side lead down into the baptismal font. Small rooms on the east and west sides of the baptistery were probably used for preparation and prayers before baptism. East of the baptistery, at the end of the northern arm of the basilica, was a **treasure house** used to store the valuable possessions of the church and the items used for church services. During the 10th or 11th century the treasure house was converted into a chapel. Outside the church on the north side is an excellent scale model of the church.

Above the Church of St. John is the **fortress,** built during Byzantine times and later modified by the Seljuk and Ottoman Turks. On the southwest slope of the hill, outside the defense walls, is the **Isa Bey Mosque.** Built in 1375, it is an excellent example of Seljuk architectural style, especially the beautifully detailed ornamentation in the interior of the mosque.

Hierapolis

Hierapolis is a popular tourist site, featured frequently on travel posters and tourist advertisements because of the adjacent spectacular calcified cliffs. Equally as impressive as the white cliffs, however, are the remains of the ancient city and the excellent museum at the site.

Location and History

Along with Colossae and Laodicea, Hierapolis was one of the major cities of the Lycus River valley. While Colossae and Laodicea are on the southern side of the Lycus River, Hierapolis (today known as Pamukkale) is north (or northeast) of the river. The site of the ancient city is approximately 12 miles north of the modern city of Denizli. The most striking aspect of the city, in ancient as well as modern times, is the sight of the calcified white cliffs, formed by mineral deposits from the water flowing over the cliffs. From these white cliffs, which can be seen from the ruins of Laodicea, approximately 6 miles away, Hierapolis derived its modern name of Pamukkale (meaning "cotton castle").

The date of the founding of the city of Hierapolis is uncertain. Because the earliest inscription found at Hierapolis dates from the reign of **Eumenes II** of Pergamum (r. 197–159 B.C.E.), the founding of the city has usually been dated to the time of the Pergamene kingdom. But because of an inscription in the theater that lists various tribal names, some of which are derived from the names of members of the Seleucid family who ruled parts of Asia Minor during the 4th and 3rd centuries B.C.E. (such as Seleucidos and Antiochidos), the founding of the city should likely be moved back to the time of the Seleucid kings. Even the origin of the name of the city is uncertain. One tradition is that the Pergamene rulers named the city after **Hiera**, the wife of **Telephus** (son of Hercules and grandson of Zeus), the mythical founder of Pergamum. Another explanation is that the name means "holy city" (*hieros* in Greek means "holy") and that the city was so named because of the temples located there. The latter explanation may have arisen after the mythological connection was forgotten.

When the Pergamene king **Attalus III** bequeathed his kingdom to the Romans in 133 B.C.E., Hierapolis came under Roman control. In 129 B.C.E. it was included as a part of the Roman province of Asia. During the reign of Tiberius in 17 C.E., Hierapolis suffered from a major earthquake that struck the region. The city was rebuilt, only to be devastated by an even more severe earthquake in 60 C.E., when Nero was emperor. Rebuilt once more, the city continued to prosper. It reached its peak during the 2nd and 3rd centuries. One of the city's claims to fame was that it was the birthplace of the Stoic philosopher **Epictetus** (ca. 55–ca. 135 C.E.), who later moved to Rome to teach and, after being banished by Domitian, settled in Nicopolis in Greece. Hierapolis was also the home of the philosopher and rhetorician **Antipater**, whom Emperor Septimius chose as the tutor for his sons Caracalla and Geta, both of whom later became emperors.

As was the case with other cities in the Lycus valley, Hierapolis was famous for its textile industry, including wool workers, carpet weavers, and dyers. The city was particularly famous for its rich purple dye, made from the juice of the madder root. Strabo attributed the richness of the color to the mineral content of the water at Hierapolis, claiming that the purple dye made at Hierapolis rivaled the purple dye that was made from shellfish (*Geography* 13.4.14). In addition to the textile industry, the city was famous for its hot springs, which were thought to possess healing properties. People visited the city to bathe in the mineral-laden waters to seek cures for various ailments.

The chief god of Hierapolis was Apollo, who was honored as the city's divine founder. The Temple of Apollo presently visible at the site is of

Roman construction, dating from the 3rd century C.E. or later. Its foundations, however, may be from an earlier, Hellenistic temple. Among the many other gods and goddesses worshiped at Hierapolis was Pluto, the Roman god of the underworld. Adjacent to the Temple of Apollo was the Plutonium, a cave sanctuary dedicated to Pluto and believed to be the entrance to the underworld.

Hierapolis had a sizeable Jewish population in antiquity, as evidenced by various inscriptions, including some of the tomb inscriptions. Some of the Jews are named as members of the various craft guilds of the city. The Jewish presence in the city likely paved the way for the acceptance of Christianity among some of the residents of Hierapolis, a development that occurred during the 1st century (see Col 4:13), probably led by Paul and his associates. Traditions as early as the 2nd century associate Philip with Hierapolis, although which Philip is not certain. The early traditions confuse **Philip the Evangelist** with **Philip the Apostle**, one of the twelve disciples of Jesus, and even conflate the two. Philip the Evangelist, who was one of the seven men chosen by the Jerusalem church to handle certain administrative and service needs of the church (Acts 6:1–7), is remembered in Acts as having four virgin daughters who were prophets (21:8–9). Other traditions refer to the Philip who lived at Hierapolis and was buried in Hierapolis along with his virgin daughters as Philip the Apostle. Later church tradition (*Acts of Philip*) claimed that Philip the Apostle was martyred (by being crucified upside down). Since the Philip who lived at Hierapolis is remembered as the one having virgin daughters who were prophets, Philip the Evangelist seems to be the one intended; on the other hand, since Philip the Apostle is the one who was martyred, and a martyrion to Philip was erected in Hierapolis, then Philip the Apostle seems to be the one associated with the city.

Another early Christian figure associated with Hierapolis was **Papias** (ca. 60–130), a bishop of the city who was said to be a disciple of John and a companion of Polycarp. He was the author of a work called *Expositions of the Sayings of the Lord,* apparently a collection of oral and written traditions and legends about Jesus. The work survives today only in quotations in Irenaeus and Eusebius.

Biblical Significance

Hierapolis is mentioned only once in the Bible. In Colossians 4:12–13, **Epaphras**, a Christian from Colossae, is praised for his faithfulness and hard work. The Colossians are told, "He has worked hard for you and for those in Laodicea and in Hierapolis." Epaphras was likely the primary person responsible for spreading the Christian faith in the Lycus River valley and starting churches there, including in Hierapolis.

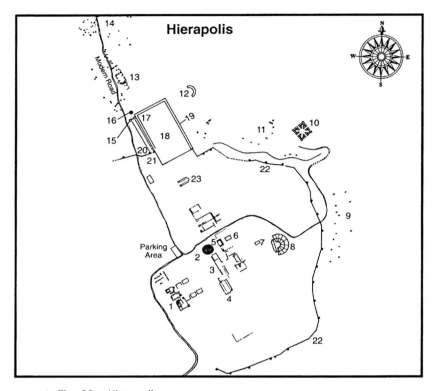

▲ **Fig. 80.** Hierapolis

1. South Baths/Museum	9. East Necropolis	17. Latrine
2. Sacred Pool	10. Martyrion of St. Phillip	18. Agora
3. Colonnaded Street	11. West Necropolis	19. Stoa Basilica
4. Basilica Church	12. Hellenistic Theater	20. Colonnaded Street
5. Nymphaeum	13. North Baths	21. Byzantine Gate
6. Temple of Apollo	14. North Necropolis	22. Byzantine Walls
7. Peristyle House	15. Gate of Domitian	23. Basilica Church
8. Roman Theater	16. Tomb of Flavius Zeuxis	

Site Visit

Hierapolis is a great place to visit, both for its archaeological finds and for its natural wonders. For both of these assets, Hierapolis/Pamukkale has been designated one of UNESCO's World Heritage Sites. Long before the visitor arrives at Pamukkale, the gleaming white calcified cliffs attract attention. Looking like snow on a mountainside, these limestone formations are the result of calcium deposits from the mineral-rich water that still flows over the cliffs. Stalagmites, stalactites, and limestone-covered pools of water add to the spectacular beauty of ancient Hierapolis. This natural treasure of Turkey features prominently in travel brochures and on travel posters. Until recently, visitors to the site were allowed to walk on the formations and to bathe in the various pools. Additionally, several hotels had been erected around the edge of the formations, diverting much of the water that flowed over the cliffs for their own pools. As a result, the terraces were being damaged by visitors and were losing their brilliance because the diminished water flow was not depositing sufficient new layers of calcium. In order to preserve the site, the Turkish government ordered the removal of the hotels from the summit and prohibited walking on most of the terraces. Current visitors to the site can enjoy the beauty of the limestone formations, some of which look like frozen waterfalls cascading down the cliffs, as well as swim in the designated public pool, the ancient Sacred Pool.

The ruins of Hierapolis, which lie above the modern town of Pamukkale, are spread over a large area. Perhaps the best way to visit the site is to begin at the **Pamukkale Museum,** now housed in part of the **south Roman baths,** which were built in the early 2nd century C.E. The museum is small but excellent. The displays are attractively presented and have good descriptive signs in Turkish and English. In addition to statues and reliefs, the museum contains coins, jewelry, medical objects, sarcophagi, and architectural fragments. Most of the objects are from

▲ **Fig. 81.** Relief of Dionysus and Pan in the Pamukkale Museum (from Laodicea)

Hierapolis, especially from the theater and the northern necropolis. Among the noteworthy objects are **statues of the god Hades**, a **relief of the marriage of Zeus and Leto**, a **relief of the birth of Apollo**, a **relief of King Eumenes of Pergamum**, and **reliefs of gladiators fighting**. The exhibit also contains some objects found at Laodicea, including a **statue of a priestess of Isis** and a **relief of Dionysus and Pan**. On display also is an excellent **color map** showing how ancient Hierapolis would have looked. A close examination of this map will help the visitor understand the remains of the city.

Northeast of the museum is the **Sacred Pool**, until recently a part of the Turizm Hotel and now a public swimming area. This pool has attracted visitors throughout its history. During the Roman period, columned porticoes surrounded the pool. As a result of earthquake damage, several of the columns and other architectural pieces tumbled into the pool, where they can still be seen today. A portion of the **colonnaded street** can be seen to the east of the Sacred Pool. This street, which was the major street of the city, ran approximately north to south. South of the Sacred Pool are the remains of a 6th-century **basilica-style church**, constructed of a central nave, two side aisles, and a semicircular apse.

Behind the Sacred Pool is the **nymphaeum**, a monumental 4th-century-C.E. fountain that has been partially restored. Three walls of the fountain partially surrounded a large basin of water. The entrance to the nymphaeum was on the open side, by means of a flight of steps. The niches in the walls originally contained statues, while columns and marble slabs contributed to the extensive ornamentation of the structure. Water flowed into the basin in the nymphaeum through a pipe in the center of the back wall. From the basin, the water was distributed throughout the city.

The nymphaeum is located in front of the **Temple of Apollo**. About all that remains of this structure are the foundations, platform, and entry steps. The foundations are thought to be from the Hellenistic period, when an earlier temple to Apollo had been constructed, although the latest temple was built during the 3rd century C.E. On the south side of the temple is an arched opening that leads to the **Plutonium**, the sacred cave believed to be the entrance to the underworld, the domain of the god Pluto. Today, as in antiquity, the cave emits poisonous vapors. For this reason, officials have closed the entrance. According to Strabo, the priests of Cybele were able to enter the chamber, while animals that entered or were brought into the cave died (*Geography* 13.4.14).

East of the temple (between the theater and the Temple of Apollo) are the ruins of a **peristyle house** with Ionic columns. Built in the 6th century C.E., the house contains a courtyard with a floor made using the opus sectile technique (pieces of highly polished colored stone or glass specially cut to form geometric patterns or images).

⚱ **Fig. 82.** Theater at Hierapolis

One of the most impressive structures at Hierapolis is the **Roman theater**. Built in the 2nd century C.E., the theater was renovated during the early part of the 3rd century and then again in the 4th century. During the 4th-century renovations, the orchestra area of the theater was altered to allow it to be filled with water for staging mock naval battles and other water presentations. Many of the elaborate, decorative friezes on the stage building are still in place, most showing scenes from the life of various gods and goddesses. The theater, restored by Italian archaeologists, had a seating capacity of 12,000 to 15,000. Note the special seating in the center of the first row for important dignitaries. East of the theater, beyond the Byzantine walls, is the **east necropolis** of the city.

Follow the dirt path north that goes beside the theater to reach the **Martyrion of St. Philip the Apostle**, located north of the ancient city walls. As mentioned above, the traditions concerning which of the two Philips (the Apostle or the Evangelist) lived at Hierapolis are confusing. Non-canonical writings from the early church describe the death of Philip at Hierapolis by being hung upside down by his ankles from a tree. The martyrion, built to commemorate and revere the life and death of Philip, was constructed during the early 5th century, supposedly on the site where he was martyred. The martyrion was apparently used neither as a church (no altar has been found) nor as a burial site (no tomb has been found), but rather served as a place for processions and special services in honor

▲ **Fig. 83.** Stage area of the theater at Hierapolis

of the saint. The outside of the building is in the shape of a square. On the outside of each of the four walls were small rooms, possibly used by pilgrims who came to honor St. Philip. The inner, domed structure was octagonal in shape. Of particular interest are the crosses and other Christian symbols carved over the entranceways of the arches. Between the inner octagonal room and the outer walls were eight rooms that possibly served as chapels.

From the martyrion visitors can either retrace their steps and return to the parking area and from there visit the northern portion of the ruins or go west over the hills from the martyrion. To the west is a **necropolis** and a little farther northwest are the ruins of the ancient **Hellenistic theater**. Not much remains of this early theater. Northwest of the theater are the **north Roman baths**. Built in the late 2nd or early 3rd century C.E., the baths were later completely altered and converted into a basilica-style church, likely during the 5th century. North of the bath/basilica is the major necropolis of the city, often called the **north necropolis**. For over a mile along both sides of the highway entering Hierapolis are numerous tombs representing a variety of styles, including sarcophagi, house and temple tombs, and tumulus tombs. This necropolis is one of the largest in Turkey, containing over a thousand tombs from the Hellenistic period to the early Christian period. Many of the tombs are quite large and elaborately decorated, and some were originally surrounded by gardens.

South of the necropolis, past the north baths, is the monumental entryway to the city, known as the **Gate of Domitian** (or **Arch of Domitian**, or sometimes the **Gate of Frontinus**). Built by **Julius Frontinus**, proconsul of Asia, and dedicated to **Domitian** around 83 C.E., the gate is a triple-arched construction with twin towers. Originally the gate had two stories, but the top story has disappeared. This gate served as the northern entrance to the city. To the right of the gate is the **tomb of Flavius Zeuxis**, a merchant of Hierapolis who claimed to have traveled from Asia Minor to Italy seventy-two times by sea. Just past the Gate of Domitian on the left is a large **latrine**. A groove along the walls indicates the location of the stone slabs that served as the seats.

The street that ran through the Domitian Gate was colonnaded and was the main north-south street through the city. This **colonnaded street**, known as **Frontinus Street**, was the heart of the commercial area of the city during Roman times. Covered walkways, 20 feet wide, lined both sides of the streets. Behind these were shops and public buildings. Immediately east of the street was the **agora**. Constructed during the 2nd century C.E., it is the largest uncovered agora ever discovered in the ancient world. Approximately 580 feet wide and 920 feet long, the agora was surrounded on three sides by marble porticoes with Ionic columns. On its east side was a large **stoa-basilica**, approximately 66 feet wide and 920 feet long, which was one floor above the level of the square.

▲ **Fig. 84.** Gate of Domitian at Hierapolis

▲ **Fig. 85.** Frontinus Street in Hierapolis

Entered from the agora by a flight of marble steps, the stoa-basilica was richly decorated with figures of sphinxes, lions attacking bulls, garlands, Eros figures, and Gorgon masks.

Near the southwestern corner of the agora, the **Byzantine Gate** sits astride the colonnaded street, where it guarded the entrance to the city in Byzantine times. This gate was erected at the end of the 4th or the beginning of the 5th century, when the **city walls** were built to protect the city from invasions. The city area was reduced, resulting in the agora and other portions of the city north of the Byzantine gate being excluded. Between the Byzantine Gate and the parking lot next to the museum are the remains of a **5th–6th century Christian basilica.**

Other Sites of Interest

For the person interested in archaeology or ancient history, a visit to the site of ancient **Aphrodisias** should not be missed. Aphrodisias is located west of Denizli, near the modern village of Geyre. From Denizli take highway E87 toward Nazilli, which is northwest of Denizli. Approximately 15 miles before arriving at Nazilli, turn left on the road to Karacasu and Geyre. Aphrodisias is approximately 1 mile past the village of Geyre. Named after the goddess Aphrodite, the city was an excellent example of a Roman-Hellenistic city. The ruins of the city are still spectacular. A modern visitor does not need much imagination to envision the splendor of ancient Aphrodisias. Especially noteworthy are the remains of the **Temple of Aphrodite**, the **agora**, the **theater**, the **colonnaded street**, the **odeion**, the **baths**, and the **stadium**. The stadium, with a capacity of approximately 30,000 spectators, is one of the largest and best-preserved stadiums from the ancient world. The **Aphrodisias Museum** is also well worth a visit. Its primary collection is of sculptures, most of which were produced in workshops in the ancient city. Aphrodisias was one of the primary centers for sculpture in Asia Minor and possibly throughout the Mediterranean area. An examination of the sculptures in the museum gives ample evidence of why the city was famous for its art.

The Hittites: Hattusa and Yazïlïkaya

In many ways the ancient Hittite sites of Hattusa and Yazïlïkaya are among the most distinctive sites related to the Bible in the entire Mediterranean region. Unlike the majority of ancient cities of the Bible in both Turkey and Greece, these sites are not related to the Apostle Paul and the New Testament. In fact, they are only marginally related to the Old Testament. Nevertheless, the identification of this city in 1906 by the German archaeologist Hugo Winckler created a sensation in archaeological and biblical studies. Since 1986 the site of Hattusa has been included on the World Heritage List of UNESCO (the United Nations Educational, Scientific, and Cultural Organization).

Location and History

Prior to the 19th century, the Hittites were entirely unknown to the world except for their mention in the Bible. The biblical references to such a powerful kingdom, for which no other evidence existed, were met by skepticism and even outright disbelief. Scholars did not believe that so dominant an empire could disappear without a trace. Following the discovery in 1799 of the Rosetta Stone in Egypt by Napoleon's soldiers, however, which unlocked the key to reading hieroglyphics, reference to the Hittites was also discovered in Egyptian sources. Most notable among these citations are references to a great battle between the Egyptians, led by **Ramses II** (likely the pharaoh of the Exodus tradition), and the Hittites at Kadesh (Syria). Also mentioned was a subsequent treaty, a nonaggression pact, wherein both nations pledged mutual support and agreed to establish Syria as the southern boundary of the Hittites' power and the northern boundary of the Egyptians' power.

Modern discovery of the Hittites began in 1834, when Charles Texier located the ruins of the capital city of the Hittites, Hattusa, which he believed to be a city of the Medes. Correct identification of the city was not made until 1906, when the discovery of 2,500 fragments of cuneiform tablets allowed Hugo Winckler to recognize that the extensive ruins were in fact the Hittite capital city. Since that time excavations by the German Archaeological Institute and others have continued. Today most of the Lower City, the temple precinct in the Upper City, the Great Temple, and virtually all of the Hittite Royal Citadel have been excavated. Nevertheless, extensive areas still remain untouched, and work is continuing.

To reach the site, from Ankara take highway E88/200 east for approximately 68 miles. Turn left (northeast) onto highway 190. After approximately 34 miles, turn right and follow the road to Boğazkale (approximately 14 miles). A second major site of the Hittites at Yazïlïkaya ("rock with writing"), a spectacular rock sanctuary of the Hittite gods, was also discovered by Texier. This site is approximately a mile northeast of Boğazkale.

The continuous occupation of the Boğazkale area began toward the close of the Early Bronze Age (ca. 2200 B.C.E.) when the Hatti, predecessors of the Hittites and native to northern and central Anatolia, founded a settlement there. Subsequently this settlement became an important trading post for Assyrian merchants who plied their trade to and from Mesopotamia. During this Hattian period the city was known as Hattus. Around 1700 B.C.E. the settlement was burned to the ground; subsequently the area was inhabited by Hittite kings who renamed it Hattusa.

The first of the great kings was **Hattusili I**, who built a powerful military empire that extended into northern Syria. Under his successor, **Mursili**, Aleppo was captured, and even mighty Babylon, more than 700 miles from Hattusa, fell to the Hittites. In the following years the fortunes of the Hittites fell on hard times, and in 1400 B.C.E. the city was burned by invading tribes from the north. Finally, under the great king **Suppiluliuma I**, the Hittites were able to defeat the kingdom of Mitanni and regain northern Syria and the Mesopotamian valley. (An interesting side note of history: The young **widow of King Tutankhamen** sent a letter to Suppiluliuma begging him to send one of his "many sons" to marry her, because she said she would never marry "a servant." The king was at first skeptical, but then sent one of his sons with a detail of soldiers to Egypt. However, the party was intercepted just outside the Egyptian border and the prince murdered. Subsequently, the queen had to marry one of her ambitious—and likely culpable—Egyptian court advisers.)

Since Mitanni was an ally of the Egyptians, the Egyptians were infuriated by the southern encroachments of the Hittites. In one of the most famous battles of ancient history, the armies of Ramses II met the armies of **King Muwatalli** (r. 1308–1285 B.C.E.) at Kadesh on the Orontes (Syria). The Hittites cleverly allowed two spies to be captured by the Egyptians in order to plant false information. In the resulting battle the Egyptians were nearly wiped out, but then were rescued at the last moment by a late-arriving division that Ramses had deliberately ordered to trail the main body of his army. Both sides subsequently claimed victory. In fact, the battle was a standoff, with the Egyptians agreeing to remain south of Syria and the Hittites agreeing to establish Syria as the southern extent of their boundaries. The nonaggression pact that they signed, three copies of which still exist, was the first of its kind in history.

Not long after the reign of Muwatalli, under **Hattusili III**, most of the buildings that are visible today at Hattusa were built or rebuilt. His grandson, **Suppiluliuma II**, was responsible for bringing the rock sanctuary at Yazılıkaya to its final form. By the end of the 13th century B.C.E., however, the glory of Hattusa had faded, and the end of the great city was not long in coming. By 1180 B.C.E. the city lay in ruins, destroyed in a fiery conflagration. Who brought about its final collapse? Scholars still debate that question. Some attribute the conquest of Hattusa to the Sea Peoples, Aegean invaders; others to the Kashkans or another of their Anatolian neighbors. In any event, this site subsequently was occupied by primitive squatters who lacked even the simple technology of the pottery wheel. A long period of "dark ages" fell over central Anatolia for over three hundred years. The great Hittite Empire had ended.

Biblical Significance

The word *Hittite* or *Hittites* occurs more than fifty times in the Old Testament. Yet none of these citations refers to the Bronze Age/Hattusa period of Hittite history; the name continued to be used for centuries in the Near East after the Hittite Empire had been destroyed. As in some Egyptian and late Assyrian sources, *Hittite* in the Bible refers to occupants of northern Syria and parts of Lebanon, people who perhaps traced their ancestry to the period of Hittite dominance of that region.

In both 2 Kings and 2 Chronicles the Bible refers to Syria as "the land of the Hittites" (2 Kgs 7:6; 2 Chr 1:17). Other passages refer to the kings of the Hittites (2 Kgs 7:6); **Solomon** was said to have exported chariots "to all the kings of the Hittites" (small city-states in northern Syria; 1 Kgs 10:29). Numerous individuals in the Bible are also called Hittites: Ephron, Judith, Zohar, Beeri, Ahimelech, Uriah, etc. Yet these names are Semitic, not Hittite. If these people in fact were descended from Hittite or Neo-Hittite ancestry, they already had been assimilated into the larger Semitic culture of the region. Some have suggested that the Hittite suzerainty treaties (treaties between a greater power and a lesser one) show significant similarities with the Sinai covenant between Yahweh and Israel. Characteristic elements of these Hittites treaties made with lesser kings included the name of the greater king making the treaty; a listing of prior beneficial acts by the great king for the lesser power; the requirements of the treaty, principally obedience and loyalty; an obligation to remember and recite the treaty; a list of divine witnesses; and future blessings or curses to those obligated by the treaty. Each of these elements is included in the account of the Sinai covenant (Exod 19–24), including the Hittites' traditional ceremonial meal and the depositing of the treaty in a sacred place (the Ark of the Covenant; Exod 25:16).

Site Visit

In order to fully appreciate the capital city of the Hittites, visitors should see both Hattusa and Yazïlïkaya, the rock sanctuary of the Hittite gods. The ruins of Hattusa are spread across a vast area (over 400 acres); a half day should be allowed for the average visit, although more time could easily be spent roaming the area. Yazïlïkaya, on the other hand, requires no more than an hour's visit. With an early start, both Hittite sites can be seen in a day trip from Ankara.

Hattusa

The visit to **Hattusa** begins at the parking lot. The path leads first past the remains of the so-called **Lion Basin** (on the left), which once had four lions at each of its rectangular corners and served either as a basin or as the base of a monument. Next is the gateway to **Temple 1**, the largest temple complex at the site and the principal temple of the Hittites. The temple proper measures some 200 feet by 130 feet, but with its surrounding storerooms it covers more than 40,000 square feet. In typical fashion, on either side of the threshold are rooms for temple guards.

Continue along the paved street of the temple. On the left there is a peculiar **green stone**, a block of nephrite, common in the area. The stone may have had some cultic purpose, but its use is unknown. A **water basin**, likely used in temple rituals, stands in the center of the **paved road**. The paved road passes on either side of the temple and is surrounded by long, rectangular **storage rooms** that were used for materials vital to the temple and its service. No walls remain. Originally they were of timber-frame construction, filled with mud brick/adobe, and covered with plaster. The ceiling also was made of wood, with mud used as

▲ **Fig. 86.**   Overview of the Temple District and dwellings at Hattusa

pitch. The many holes in the surface of the **foundation blocks** were drilled there for dowels of wood and bronze to connect them to the timber-frame construction above.

The entrance to the temple proper (right) crosses a **threshold** with evidence of the large wooden doors that pivoted at the corners on socket stones (and obviously dragged somewhat, from the scrapings on the threshold stones). Beyond the threshold is the spacious **Temple Court**, open to the sky, in which the great festivals of the Hittite religion took place. At the far end of the courtyard a stone stands on the right, which may have been an **altar**, and across the back of the courtyard, a series of stones served as **column bases** for a **stoa** (covered porch). Only the Hittite king and queen, who also served as the high priests of the land, and priests of the temple might pass this point into the twin **cult chambers** beyond (on the left). These small rooms likely served as sanctuaries for the chief gods of the Hittites, the weather god of the Hatti and the sun goddess of the city of Arinna.

Notice the low **windowsills** on either side of the **base for the cult statue**. Windows in such a sacred place are quite unusual. The various Holy of Holies in other principal temples (Jerusalem, Karnak) were shrouded in windowless darkness. These windows may have been regularly shuttered, but their function otherwise is a matter of speculation.

Perhaps sunlight was admitted in keeping with the nature functions of the gods, as at the outdoor sanctuary of the gods at Yazïlïkaya. Some of the other rooms in this temple served as the apartments of the gods, since it was also the year-round home to the two gods who were worshiped there.

At the west side of the temple (to the left, facing the doorway) are **large storage jars** in the storeroom area, with a capacity of up to 500 gallons. These once held grain, oil, wine, or other materials needed for the support of the temple. In the storage areas on the east side of the temple were found thousands of clay tablets written in cuneiform. Typically these would have been stored on wooden shelves in a library arrangement. Fortunately, when such structures were destroyed by fire, as was the case in Hattusa, clay tablets were only fired harder and thus were preserved.

Return along the paved **Temple Street** to the original entrance to the temple complex, then turn right. Another street borders the storerooms on the south. The **complex of rooms** on the right likely served as a work area for various artisans connected with the temple. Just past this complex there is an underground **springhouse** that served some cultic function, according to a stele now in the Museum for Anatolian Civilizations in Ankara. From here proceed up the hill toward the **upper city**. (Most visitors may prefer to drive, making stops at the notable sites.)

The first site of interest is the **House on the Slope**, a two-story building of impressive size. A large number of clay tablets were found here, indicating that this is not a house at all but a government building of some sort.

Continuing along the street, pass through a line of **fortifications** leading up to the **Royal Citadel**. Eight tunnels passed underneath the wall. The entrances to these tunnels are still visible, but their interiors are blocked with debris.

The road soon forks; take the right turn. This road leads to the **Lion Gate**, one of the monumental entrances in the southern wall of Hattusa. Two **towers** once stood on either side of the **great lions**, the remains of which still stand left and right of the entrance. The carving on the side of the lion to the right (facing the gate) gives some indication of the skill of the workmen in this 13th-century-B.C.E. city. Originally this gate was protected by a massive wooden door secured by wooden bolts. From outside the wall, the gate was reached by a **ramp** from the valley below.

Continue along the road to the highest point of the city, the **Sphinx Gate**. (The southern defense wall of Hattusa had three gates: the Lion Gate to the west, the Sphinx Gate in the center, and the King's Gate to the east.) Originally two sphinxes flanked this gate, but they were removed for safekeeping because of their poor condition following the conflagration that destroyed the city. One sphinx is in the Museum of Ancient Civilizations in Istanbul, the other in the Near Eastern Museum

▲ **Fig. 87.** Lion Gate at Hattusa

in Berlin. These sphinxes, unlike their Egyptian prototypes, seem to have female faces rather than male, and the style of the hair suggests the Egyptian goddess Hathor.

Beneath this gate is the only **tunnel** through which you can walk today. It is a spectacular example of the engineering ability of the ancient Hittites. This tunnel had to be constructed first, and then the great **earthen rampart** laid over it. The massive limestone blocks from which it is constructed are slightly offset to the inside and retained at the top with wedge-shaped keystones. The tunnel is over 200 feet long and is one of the greatest remaining structures of such antiquity (13th century B.C.E.). Originally its floor was covered with a white plaster, which would have aided the dim lighting inside. Both ends of the tunnel were secured with wooden doors. At the exterior of the rampart wall, two **stairways** on the east and west lead up again to the top of the rampart. Since this arrangement appears not to have aided defense, perhaps it was intended for special religious or civic events. In any case, the southern wall would have presented an impressive face to any travelers or foes who approached it.

Hittite texts refer to Hattusa as "the city of a thousand gods." From the vantage point of the Sphinx Gate, the foundations of many of the temples of the **Temple District** are visible. The Hittites prided themselves on including in their worship all of the gods with which they were familiar, and this in turn led to a proliferation of temples. Generally these temples followed the plan of the Great Temple in the Lower City. No statues or objects remain from these buildings, so it is impossible today to say which deities were worshiped there. Some of the smaller structures scattered about the Temple District were **dwellings** that grew up in the area, perhaps for the protection of the southern wall, toward the end of the glory days of Hattusa.

The **King's Gate** stands at the east end of the south-facing rampart. Like the lion gate, it also had twin towers on either side of its double gates. This gate was named for the **warriorlike sculpture** that decorated one side of its entrance. The original excavators assumed the figure was a king, but the horns on the helmet indicate that the figure was that of a god. Its identity remains uncertain.

Leaving the King's Gate and continuing along the road toward the north, on the right are the outlines of two ponds, or artificial lakes, which served as **water reservoirs** for the city. These reservoirs first were supplied by springs within the city walls, but an increasing need for water led the city to install a pipeline of clay pipes under the city walls to bring water from springs outside.

At the north end of **Pond 1** (actually the second pond on the descent from the rampart), two **domed chambers** stand at either end of the dam. The first chamber, nearest to the road, could be only partially restored. The second chamber, however, known as the **Hieroglyph Chamber**, has been completely restored and contains dramatic reliefs within. It is so called because of the **inscription** on one wall of six lines of Luvian hieroglyphics, a picture language of the region. Its text states that the great king **Suppiluliuma** won victories and made many sacrifices to the gods. The final line makes reference to "a divine earth-road," which may refer to the structure and its lake as an entrance into the underworld. On the back wall of the chamber is a **relief of the sun god**; to the left is the **figure of Suppiluliuma II**, last of the great kings of Hattusa, and builder of the chamber. His pointed hat with its horns, characteristic of gods, likely indicates that the king was regarded as a divinity in his lifetime.

Beyond the ponds on the right is the **Southern Citadel**, probably developed in the late Iron Age (ca. 700 B.C.E.), long after the Hittite period in Hattusa. Elements of the culture found in the citadel are Phrygian, including evidence of the worship of the goddess Cybele. Nevertheless, the identity of these inhabitants remains in question. On the opposite side of the road are the remains of **Temple 31**, which may have been connected with cult ceremonies of the chambers.

The road leads next to the **Royal Citadel**, the residence of the great kings. This large complex of buildings stands on a flat plateau surrounded by steep slopes, ideal for protection for its residents. Steps lead to its surface, but originally an elevated roadway led up to the **main gate** of the citadel. Only the right hand side of this gate remains today. Go through the gate and enter a **series of courtyards**, which were once flanked by long stoas. The structures on the left probably served as **residences** and **administrative buildings** for court officials. The pathway next passes through a second gate; on its left are smaller buildings that perhaps served as **palace shrines**. One of these structures, known as **Building C**, contained a **ritual pool** in which were found numerous offering vessels. Beyond these buildings lies the largest structure of the Royal Citadel, known as **Building D**. Originally a two-story building, the upper story is believed to have been the king's reception hall. The two buildings at the far end of the citadel are thought to have been the **king's private dwellings**. In this secluded area, protected by the various structures of the citadel on one side and the gorge on the other, the great kings would have found both privacy and safety—at least in theory.

When the palace was burned at the end of the 13th century B.C.E., some of its most important contents survived. Hundreds of clay tablets with invaluable records of the history, religion, business dealings, and oracles of its prophets were preserved. These tablets have provided an unusually detailed insight into the life of a once obscure people, the Hittites.

From the palace, the road leads past the Great Temple again to the exit. This completes the circuit visit of Hattusa.

Yazïlïkaya

Yazïlïkaya presents visitors with one of the truly unique archaeological sites in the world. In the middle of the 13th century B.C.E., Hittite sculptors carved a procession of the pantheon of Hittite gods on the walls of an already existing sacred rock chamber approximately a mile northeast of Hattusa.

Actually, there are two rock chambers at Yazïlïkaya, **Chamber A** and **Chamber B**. Of the two, the smaller Chamber B is the better preserved because it remained unexcavated until the 19th century. (Of course, the figures continue to undergo erosion since the chambers are open to the sky. It is to be hoped that some protection may be given them in the future.) These chambers were originally entered through a series of structures at the front of the rock cleft that no longer exist. The **foundation** of these buildings is still visible. Beyond the original entrance gate (at the northern end of the structures) was an open court that contained an altar for preliminary rites before entering the chambers themselves.

The larger chamber on the left, **Chamber A**, is a lengthy opening in the rock walls some 90 feet long and 30 feet wide at the entrance, tapering to less than 15 feet at its narrowest point. On the left side of the walls are portrayed **male gods**, on the right **female gods**. All of them appear to be moving toward the end of the chamber, where principal deities of the Hittites, the weather god **Teshub** and the sun goddess **Hebat**, greet

▲ **Fig. 88.** Twelve gods of the underworld at Yazïlïkaya

one another. Many of these figures have been identified by the **Luvian hieroglyphics** beside them, but some of the inscriptions have not yet been deciphered and others are the subjects of dispute. Beneath the figures was carved a **small ledge** in the rock, perhaps for votive offerings. From the gods arrayed on the walls, it is likely that some type of cultic ceremony pertaining to the seasons was held in the chamber, perhaps at the beginning of the Hittite new year to celebrate the coming of spring.

Beginning on the left side, the procession of **male gods** of the Hittites begins with twelve figures carrying curved swords. These are the **gods of the underworld**. (The same twelve figures are repeated in Chamber B.) The bearded gods ahead of them are **mountain gods**; their long skirts symbolize the mountains. Some of the next gods have not yet been identified, but the bull-like figures following them represent the **Bulls of the Heavens**, Hurri and Sheri. They stand on a symbol for the earth and hold over their heads a crescent moon, symbol of the heavens. Also on the left, the **sun god** and **moon god** can be identified: the sun god holds a long, curving staff, and a pair of wings with a sun disk in the center rests upon his head; the moon god wears a crescent moon on his hat.

On the end wall, the procession of figures reaches its climax. The figure standing upon two mountain gods is the **chief god Teshub**, the weather god, holding a mace in his right hand; he greets a female figure standing on a lion, the sun goddess **Hebat**. Following her is their son,

Sharruma (notice the smaller size of the figure, denoting a child). He holds a battle axe in his left hand; with his right, he holds a leash attached to a lion standing on two mountains. Sharruma is followed by his sister, **Alanzu**, and another female figure whose identity is uncertain. They stand above a double-headed eagle.

The wall on the right side of Chamber A portrays the **goddesses of the Hittites**. With some exceptions, they are not as individually distinctive as the male gods. The second goddess in the procession is the **goddess Hutellura**. Other goddesses whose hieroglyphic symbols are present include **Shalush**; **Tapkina**, wife of the water god, Ea; and **Nikkal**, wife of the moon god. The goddess Ishtar is also portrayed on a block now in the Boğazkale Museum.

The entrance to **Chamber B** is guarded by **two winged demons** with the heads of lions, their arms raised menacingly. Immediately to the right of the entrance, the **twelve gods of the underworld**, identical to those in Chamber A, again are shown hastening toward some task.

On the opposite wall are carved three spectacular reliefs. The first of these depicts **the god Sharruma**, the patron god of **King Tudhaliya IV**, shown with his arm about the shoulders of the king. The **cartouche of the king** appears behind the hat of the god. The **niches** in the rock beside this relief were used for either offerings or cultic objects. The second relief depicts the sword god, **Nergal of the Underworld**. This strange figure is portrayed with a human head as the grip of the sword; in place of arms, two lion heads protrude from his shoulders. Two other lions perhaps represent the legs of the figure. The remainder of the sword below appears driven in the rock. The last relief is the **cartouche of Tudhaliya IV**. In ancient times, it has been surmised, this cartouche identified a large statue of the king that stood at the north end of the chamber. Only the limestone block by the entrance, which may have been the **base of the statue**, and a matching **basalt slab with larger-than-life-size feet upon it**, found in a neighboring village, remain to suggest the existence of such an image.

▲ **Fig. 89.** Sharruma, patron god of King Tudhaliya IV, with his arm about the king (at Yazılıkaya)

It has been suggested that the purpose of this chamber is quite different from that of Chamber A. Much about the chamber suggests it functioned as a **memorial chapel** connected with death and the afterlife. For example, the god Nergal of the Underworld is depicted, in addition to the procession of the underworld gods common also to Chamber A. Likewise, the **cartouche** beside the relief of Tudhaliya IV has added the hieroglyphic for "hero" to the usual symbols for the king's name, further suggesting a memorial theme. Burials also were found in the surrounding rocks, including the burial of birds, traditionally known as offerings to the gods of the underworld. The overall impression is that of a special chamber memorializing **Tudhaliya IV** while at the same time honoring the gods of the afterlife. Likely this chamber was completed by **Suppiluliuma II**, son of King Tudhaliya IV, and dedicated to his father after his death.

To make it inaccessible from the rear, the back of the chamber had been sealed off in earlier times, even before the Hittites, with the **stone blocks** that are there today. At the left-hand end of the chamber, a **narrow staircase** provided an entry for cult officials.

Iconium

Although mentioned in the New Testament as one of the cities visited by the Apostle Paul, the ancient city of Iconium is more famous today because of its Muslim mosques, its theological schools, and its connection with the great Sufi mystic known as Mevlana. Considered by many to be Turkey's most religious city, modern Konya (ancient Iconium) is an intriguing place to visit because of its rich religious and architectural history.

Location and History

Known today as Konya, Iconium is located in south-central Turkey, approximately 170 miles south of Ankara. Situated in the Anatolian steppe, Iconium is one of the oldest cities in Turkey. Archaeological evidence indicates that the site of Iconium was occupied at least as early as the 3rd millennium b.c.e. During the 2nd millennium, the Hittites controlled the area. After the Hittite empire was destroyed, eventually the Phrygians gained control of the region and established a town at the site of Iconium. The Lydians took control of Iconium at the beginning of the 7th century, and then the following century the Persians ruled the area. When **Alex-**

ander the Great defeated the Persians in the 4th century, Iconium became a part of Alexander's empire. After Alexander's death, Iconium was controlled by the Seleucids and then by the Pergamene rulers. In 129 B.C.E., four years after the Pergamene kingdom was bequeathed to Rome, Iconium was made a part of the Roman province of Asia.

During the Roman period, Iconium was the seat of an archbishop and the location of an early church council (in 235). The city prospered under the Romans and also during the Byzantine time. From the 7th to the 9th centuries Iconium, like most of the towns and cities in the region, suffered from Arab raids. The Seljuk Turks unsuccessfully attacked the city in 1069, but by the next century they had taken control of the city, which they called Konya. As the capital of the Seljuk sultanate of Rum, Konya enjoyed a period of economic and cultural prosperity. Several of the mosques, mausoleums, and theological schools that can be seen in Konya today date from this period. When the Mongols defeated the Seljuks in 1242, Konya came under their control for a brief period until the Mongols were defeated approximately thirty years later by the Mamluks. In the 15th century, Konya and the surrounding area became a part of the Ottoman Empire.

Although for Christian visitors Iconium is best known as a place visited by the **Apostle Paul**, Konya is most important religiously as the city of **Celaleddin Rumi**, better known as **Mevlana**, the 13th-century Sufi mystic, poet, philosopher, and founder of the Mevlevi order of whirling dervishes. Born in Balkh in present-day Afghanistan, Mevlana moved to Konya in 1228 C.E. with his father, a renowned teacher. Mevlana followed in his father's footsteps, becoming a revered teacher and religious leader. A dervish Sufi (the Sufis are a type of Muslim mystic) named Tabrizi became a close friend of Mevlana's and exerted tremendous influence on him. To this friend, Mevlana dedicated his most important work, the *Mesnevi,* a six-volume work of religious and philosophical poetry. Mevlana died in 1273, but his mystical teachings continued to be studied and revered throughout the Islamic world. Mevlana's followers established Mevlevi dervish monasteries throughout Turkey. The Mevlevi order ended in 1925, when the Turkish government banned all dervish orders in Turkey because Atatürk saw them as an obstacle to the modernization of Turkey. Today, performances of the dervish ceremony, the *sema,* are presented annually in Konya in December on the anniversary of Mevlana's death. The dance of the dervishes is seen as a means of reaching mystical union with God.

Biblical Significance

During his first missionary journey described in the book of Acts, the **Apostle Paul** traveled through the southern region of Asia Minor, spreading the Christian faith in several cities, including Iconium (Acts 13:51–14:7). After preaching in Antioch of Pisidia, Paul and **Barnabas** went to

Iconium, where they preached in the synagogue. Initially successful in making converts to Christianity, they soon ran into opposition. Later, after learning of an attempt to stone them, Paul and Barnabas left and went to Lystra and Derbe. At Lystra, some of Paul's opponents came from Iconium and Antioch and turned the people of Lystra against him. After being stoned and left for dead, Paul left Lystra and traveled to Derbe (Acts 14:19–20). Finishing his itinerary in Derbe, he retraced his steps through Lystra, Iconium, and Antioch on his way back to Antioch of Syria. When Paul returned to Lystra on his second missionary journey, **Timothy**, a resident of Lystra who "was well spoken of by the believers in Lystra and Iconium" (Acts 16:2), joined Paul as he continued on his travels. The difficulties that Paul experienced during his visits to Iconium and the surrounding region are mentioned also in 2 Timothy 3:11, the only other mention of Iconium in the Bible.

Iconium was the setting for several episodes in the *Acts of Paul,* a work from the latter half of the 2nd century that contains legendary stories about the missionary activities of Paul. The episodes in Iconium involved **Thecla**, a young woman from the city who was so impressed by Paul's preaching that she left her fiancé and followed Paul on some of his travels.

Site Visit

The visitor to Konya today will find no trace of the ancient city of Iconium of Paul's day, except with some of the artifacts in the **Konya Archaeological Museum**. The museum, located on Sahip Ata Caddesi, is small but definitely worth a visit. In the courtyard are an assortment of sculptures, sarcophagi, column heads, and inscriptions. Of particular note for visitors interested in **Paul** are **two inscribed stone monuments**. One is a limestone block with the name of the city of Derbe; the other is an altar stone from the city of Lystra that mentions the city. (See the Derbe and Lystra entries for further descriptions of these inscriptions.) The interior of the museum exhibits works belonging to the Neolithic, Bronze, Iron, Classical, Hellenistic, Roman, and Byzantine periods. The exhibits include pottery, stone and bronze sculptures, sarcophagi, jewelry, and inscriptions. Particularly noteworthy are the **3rd-century-c.e. marble sarcophagus** with beautifully carved scenes from the life of Hercules, a **Roman-period clay sarcophagus**, a **marble sarcophagus with carved garlands**, a 2nd-century **statue of Poseidon**, and a **votive stele dedicated to the goddess Cybele** (the Anatolian mother goddess.)

The most popular site in Konya is the **Mevlana Museum**, or Mevlana Tekkesi, the former monastery of the whirling dervishes, recognizable by its attractive fluted dome of turquoise tiles. Visited not only by tour-

▲ **Fig. 90.** Third-century-c.e. sarcophagus with scenes of Hercules in the Konya Archaeological Museum

ists but also by faithful Muslims who come to pray and pay homage to Mevlana, the building served for several centuries as a center for religion, art, literature, and music. Today it is a museum and mausoleum containing the tombs of Mevlana, his father, his wife and children, and several important religious and civic figures. The museum contains personal items belonging to Mevlana as well as various illuminated manuscripts, musical instruments, furniture, carpets, and other artifacts.

Even though they have no connection to the Bible or the biblical world, the many Seljuk, Karamanid, and Ottoman mosques (*cami* in Turkish), theological schools (*medrese* in Turkish), and tombs in the city are well worth a visit. Among these would be the **Ince Minare Medresesi** ("the medrese with the slender minaret"), which has a fluted minaret decorated with red and blue glazed tiles and is now a museum of Seljuk wood and stone carvings; the **Sïrçalï Medrese** ("glazed medrese"), built in 1242, which now houses a museum of Seljuk, Karamanid, and Ottoman tombstones; the **Büyük Karatay Medresesi**, founded in 1251, which presently contains a large collection of beautiful Turkish ceramics and tiles from the 13th to the 18th centuries; the **Alaettin Camii**, the largest Seljuk mosque in Konya, whose construction began in 1155; and the **Sahip Ata Külliyesi**, a 13th-century complex consisting of a mosque, a mausoleum, a monastery, and baths.

Laodicea

Ancient Laodicea, once a thriving city, now lies in ruins, awaiting a more thorough excavation than it has so far received. Overshadowed by the more spectacular nearby site of Hierapolis (Pamukkale), Laodicea receives the occasional busload of tourists who stop to view the remains of this city that the book of Revelation imagined as having boasted, "I am rich, I have prospered, and I need nothing" (3:17).

Location and History

Laodicea is south of the modern village of Goncalï and north of the village of Eskihisar. The site is located on a plateau between two small rivers that are tributaries of the Lycus River. The Asopus River runs along the western part of the ancient city, while the Caprus River runs along the east. To visit the site, take the road from Denizli that leads to Pamukkale. Two different roads from the Denizli-Pamukkale highway lead to Laodicea, both of which are on the left and marked with a sign indicating the way to Laodicea.

Laodicea is situated 10 miles from Colossae and 6 miles from Hierapolis. This area was a part of the region of Phrygia, although it was sometimes considered a part of Lydia or Caria. Pliny the Elder claims that Laodicea was built on the site of an earlier settlement known as Diospolis and later as Rhoas (*Natural History* 5.105). Because of its location near the Lycus River, the city was known as Laodicea ad Lycum in order to differentiate it from several other cities named Laodicea. Of particular importance to the commercial success of the city was its position at the junction of two roads—one that ran from the Aegean coast near Ephesus through the Meander River valley and on to the Euphrates, and another that ran from Pergamum to Sardis and then to Perga and Attalia (modern Antalya).

Antiochus II, the Seleucid king (r. 261–246 B.C.E.), founded the city during the middle of the 3rd century B.C.E. He named the city in honor of his wife **Laodice**, whom he later divorced. After the Romans, with the aid of the Pergamene kingdom, defeated **Antiochus III** at Magnesia in 189 B.C.E., Laodicea came under the control of Pergamum. When **Attalus III**, the last king of Pergamum, bequeathed his kingdom to Rome in 133 B.C.E., Laodicea came under Roman control. In 129 B.C.E. Rome created the province of Asia out of a portion of the former kingdom of Pergamum, including Laodicea. When **Mithradates VI**, king of Pontus, waged war against Rome in 88–85 B.C.E. and unsuccessfully sought to free Asia Minor from Roman control, Laodicea was one of the few cities that refused to support Mithradates. Later the city was a judicial and administrative center, and because of that status **Cicero**, governor of Cilicia, spent several weeks there in 50 B.C.E. administering justice.

In 26 B.C.E., Laodicea competed against ten other cities in Asia Minor for the honor of building a temple for the worship of the emperor **Tiberius**. Smyrna was awarded the privilege, while Laodicea was rejected because of insufficient resources. The economic situation of the city seems to have improved by the middle of the century, however. When an earthquake in 60 C.E. devastated the region, including Laodicea, the city refused offers of assistance from Rome. Rather, the people of Laodicea rebuilt the city from their own resources. In 129 C.E. the emperor Tiberius visited Laodicea during one of his travels through Asia Minor. Toward the end of the 2nd century, the city was honored by being named *neokoros,* or temple warden, giving it the right to erect a temple for the worship of the emperor **Commodus**. The city lost the title of *neokoros* a few years later, when, after the death of Commodus, the Roman Senate condemned the memory of the emperor and ordered his name removed from public inscriptions. During the reign of **Caracalla**, however, Laodicea regained the honor when it was declared *neokoros* for both Commodus and Caracalla. A severe earthquake in 494 damaged the city so severely that it never fully recovered. It continued to exist on a smaller scale under the Byzantine, Seljuk, and Turkish rulers until it was abandoned sometime around the 13th to the 15th centuries.

Laodicea was famous in the ancient world for its raven-black wool, which was especially soft, and for its textile industry. According to Strabo (*Geography* 12.8.20), a great medical school was located in (or near) Laodicea, a claim that is supported by coins from Laodicea that bear the names of leading physicians of the school. The city was apparently also a banking center, as Cicero mentions that when he arrived in Laodicea he cashed his letters of credit in the city (*Epistulae ad familiares* 3.5.4).

The major god worshiped at Laodicea was Zeus. Thirteen miles from the city was a temple to the Anatolian god Men Karou (which may have been associated with the Laodicean medical school). Laodicea also apparently had a sizeable Jewish population. Cicero mentions that in 62 B.C.E. the collection of the Jewish temple tax (a half shekel per Jewish male annually) for the temple in Jerusalem was confiscated by **Flaccus**, governor of Asia, because no gold was supposed to be sent out of Asia Minor. The amount of the tax collected in the region of Laodicea equaled twenty pounds of gold (*Pro Flacco* 68). This amount of gold has been estimated to equal around 7,500 to 9,000 half shekels, indicating that at least that many Jewish males lived in or around Laodicea, in addition to the women and children. Further confirmation of a Jewish presence in Laodicea comes from the Jewish historian Josephus, who records a letter from the officials of Laodicea in 45 B.C.E. confirming that they would

abide by the requirement to allow Jewish residents to practice their religion without interference (*Jewish Antiquities* 14.241–243).
   The earliest reference to a Christian presence in Laodicea comes from the book of Colossians in the New Testament. The people in the church at Colossae are told to read "the letter from Laodicea," and the Colossian letter is to be read "in the church of the Laodiceans" (4:16). During the latter part of the 2nd century, one of the Laodicean Christians, a man named **Sagaris**, who was a bishop of the church at Laodicea, was killed as a Christian martyr (Eusebius, *Ecclesiastical History* 4.26.3; 5.24.5). In the 4th century an important church council met at Laodicea.

Biblical Significance

Laodicea is mentioned in two New Testament writings, Colossians and Revelation. **Paul** apparently had not visited either Colossians or Laodicea, since Colossians 2:1 states, "For I want you to know how much I am struggling for you, and for those in Laodicea, and for all who have not seen me face-to-face." Rather than Paul, a man named **Epaphras** was the leader and likely founder of the Colossian church (1:7), as well as one who had "worked hard for you and for those in Laodicea and in Hierapolis" (4:13). Epaphras probably spread the Christian message throughout the cities of the Lycus valley, including Laodicea. (Even if, as many scholars argue, Paul did not actually write Colossians, but one of his followers wrote it at a later date, the letter still represents a strong tradition concerning the origin of the Laodicean church.) According to Colossians 4:15, the church at Laodicea met in the home of **Nympha**, an otherwise unknown woman who was apparently a leader in the Laodicean church. The author of Colossians instructs the Colossian church and the Laodicean church to exchange the letters that had been sent to each of them (4:16). The "letter from Laodicea" that is mentioned in Colossians no longer exists, although some have made the unlikely suggestion that the New Testament letter to the Ephesians is actually the Laodicean letter.
   The church in Laodicea is one of the seven churches of the book of Revelation (1:11; 3:14–22). The church is condemned for being lukewarm, complacent, self-satisfied, and spiritually bankrupt. John writes, "You say, 'I am rich, I have prospered, and I need nothing.' You do not realize that you are wretched, pitiable, poor, blind, and naked" (3:17). Of the seven churches, the one at Laodicea is the only one that receives only condemnation and no praise. Several statements in the message to Laodicea appear to reflect specific knowledge of the history or situation of Laodicea. The criticism of the Laodicean church that they are "lukewarm, and neither cold nor hot" (3:16) perhaps alludes to the water situation in and near Laodicea. The city of Hierapolis, only 7 miles away,

was famous for its hot springs. Colossae, 11 miles away, had a good supply of cold water. The water at Laodicea, however, was of poor quality and possibly lukewarm. The lime-encrusted water pipes that brought water to the city (and which can still be seen near Laodicea) are a testimony to the hardness of the Laodicean water supply.

The Laodiceans' proud claim—"I am rich, I have prospered, and I need nothing" (3:17)—is reminiscent of the city's refusal to accept **Emperor Nero**'s offer of financial assistance to rebuild the city after the earthquake of 60 C.E. The Son of Man (Christ) tells the Laodicean church, "You do not realize that you are wretched, pitiable, poor, blind, and naked. Therefore I counsel you to buy from me gold refined by fire so that you may be rich; and white robes to clothe you and to keep the shame of your nakedness from being seen; and salve to anoint your eyes so that you may see" (3:17–18). This passage may have had special significance for the Laodicean readers. As a banking center, Laodicea dealt with much gold and money, thus the appropriateness of the reference to gold and commercial transactions. The white robes likely allude to the textile industry of the area, and the eye salve is perhaps an allusion to the medical school at Laodicea.

Site Visit

The site of ancient Laodicea was partially excavated by Canadian archaeologists from 1961 to 1963. A visit to the ruins today requires much imagination and diligence, since the site has only a few signs to help the visitor. Since 1993 archaeologists from the University of Venice (Università Ca' Foscari di Venezia) have been engaged in new topographical and archaeological surveys of the site. These new studies have already led to some changes in earlier locations and identifications of structures at the site. (For example, most previous site maps, based on a drawing of the site made by Gerhard Weber at the end of the 19th century, indicate the location of an Ionic temple at Laodicea. Unfortunately, no remains of this temple are evident today.) The site description given below, as well as the accompanying site map, is based on these initial new studies. The visitor needs to be aware that, whereas some of the structures on the map and described below have substantial remains (the nymphaeum, the stadium, the baths, the theaters), all that is visible of many of the structures are a few building blocks or architectural fragments. A new excavation of the site, started in 2002 by a joint team of archaeologists from the University of Venice, Pamukkale University, and Denizli University, is beginning to uncover additional streets and buildings from the ancient city.

At the southern end of the site are the remains of the **aqueduct** and **stone water pipes** that brought water from a spring near Denizli into

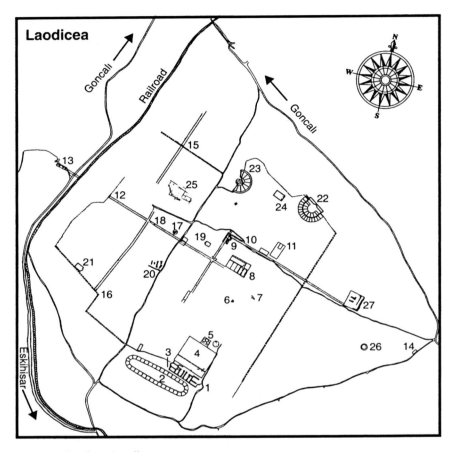

▲ **Fig. 91.** Laodicea

1. Water Tower
2. Stadium
3. Gymnasium-Bath Complex
4. Civic Agora
5. Bouleuterion/ Odeion
6. Small Structure (Baptistery ?)
7. Reservoir
8. Bath Complex
9. Nymphaeum
10. Colonnaded Street
11. Temple (?)
12. Ephesus Gate
13. Roman Bridge
14. Blocks from the Syrian Gate
15. Hierapolis Gate
16. Aphrodisias Gate
17. Circular Building
18. West Agora
19. Basilica-Style Building
20. Unidentified Structure
21. Basilica South
22. Larger Theater
23. Smaller Theater
24. Basilica North
25. Byzantine Church
26. Octagonal Structure
27. Unidentified Building

the southwest part of the city. Note the heavy lime deposits in the pipes. The aqueduct led to a **water tower** (the conical structure), part of which is still standing. Several terra-cotta water pipes, running vertically up the tower, can be seen. The tower was perhaps part of a monumental fountain or water distribution building for the city. The aqueduct continued north from the fountain and terminated at a **reservoir**.

Adjacent to the fountain are the remains of a large building that was a **gymnasium-bath complex**. Built in the first half of the 2nd century C.E., the complex consisted of a series of rooms on the south side and a long rectangular area (perhaps a palaestra, or exercise area). According to an inscription found on the building, it was dedicated to Hadrian and his wife Sabina. To the west of the gymnasium-bath are the ruins of a **stadium**, one of the most impressive remains at the site. Built in 79 C.E. and dedicated to the emperor Titus and to the people of Laodicea, the stadium was approximately 306 yards long (ca. 275 yards long inside the stadium) and 77 yards wide and was enclosed with curved ends. According to Cicero, the stadium was used for both athletic contests and gladiatorial shows.

Approximately 100 yards north of the stadium and the gymnasium are the unimpressive ruins of a **bouleuterion** (a council meeting house) or an **odeion** (frequently the same structure served both purposes). Some scattered stone fragments and the remains of a few rows of seats are all that are visible. The area between the bouleuterion and the bath-gymnasium is the location of the city's **civic agora**. The ruins of a **small structure** lie approximately 200 yards north of the bouleuterion. The few remains seem to indicate a building that had a vestibule on the west connected to a circular structure with three internal apses. A portion of a marble capital decorated with a cross was found nearby. The structure is thought to have served some religious purpose, perhaps as a baptistery or a small church. Further north are the substantial remains of a large **bath complex**, apparently from the Roman period. This structure, which covers an area of approximately 180 feet by 280 feet, contained four, or possibly five, rooms along its southern side; along the north was a long hall. Sometime, perhaps as early as the 4th century, the building was apparently converted into a church.

Northwest of the bath is the **nymphaeum**, a monumental fountain that was elaborately decorated with various statues, including a life-size statue of Isis (or a priestess of Isis). Built in the early 3rd century C.E., the nymphaeum was renovated four times prior to the 5th century. Originally the nymphaeum contained a large square water basin in the northwest corner of the structure, with a colonnade on its east and south. During one of the alterations, this basin was converted into a walled room with a raised floor, which was apparently used as a meeting room by the Christians. Because of all the alterations of the nymphaeum, few distinctive features of the structure can be distinguished.

▲ **Fig. 92.** Colonnaded street in front of the nymphaeum in Laodicea

A **colonnaded street** ran along the north side of the nymphaeum. Portions of the paved street, as well as some of the column fragments, are visible. This street was the main east-west route through the city. Facing the street on the north side are the remains of a **large complex** with a courtyard that likely had porticoes on its east, south, and west sides. A large building was at the north end of the complex. (A short section of the west wall of the building is visible.) This complex, likely built after the middle of the 2nd century C.E., was possibly a **temple** dedicated to the imperial cult. As noted above (see "Location and History"), Laodicea was honored with the title *neokoros* for both Emperor Commodus and Emperor Caracalla.

At the west edge of the city are the remains of the **Ephesus Gate**, a triple-arched entryway so named because the road led from there to Ephesus. The upper part of the three arches of the gate is relatively intact (although the entablature, or stonework that ran across the top of the arches, is missing); the lower portion is now below ground level. West of the Ephesus Gate, the road crossed the Asopus River by means of a **Roman bridge**, the remains of which are still present. The **Syrian Gate** was located at the east side of the city. Some building blocks from this gate are situated at the far eastern edge of the site, where apparently they were relocated. (The gate was probably located in the eastern wall at the colonnaded street.) An inscription on an architrave from the gate indicates that the gate was dedicated to Zeus and to the emperor Domitian and was built by Tiberius Claudius Tryphon, a freedman of the emperor Claudius. The gate was likely erected around 84–85 C.E. Little remains of a third gate, the

Hierapolis Gate, located at the northwest edge of the city, or a fourth gate, the **Aphrodisias Gate,** on the southwest side of the city.

Between the Ephesian Gate and the nymphaeum is an area with scattered architectural remains, including some blocks from a **circular building.** This area has been identified as the **west agora,** the commercial agora of the city. The plan of the circular building is similar to that of butcher shops found in other ancient cities. Between the west agora and the nymphaeum are the remains of a **basilica-style building** of unknown purpose. In the southwest area of the city, south of the west agora, are the substantial remains of another **unidentified structure.** Several arches, as well as parts of the walls of this building, are still standing. Suggested identifications of this edifice have included a cathedral and a basilica-style bath. Near the southwest corner of the city by the city wall is the so-called **Basilica South.** This structure, which was a Byzantine-era church, contained an apse on its southeast side, portions of which remain.

North of the nymphaeum, on the edge of the plateau, are **two theaters** carved out of the side of the hill. Neither is well preserved, nor have they been reconstructed. In the larger theater, which faces northeast, several rows of seats (in poor condition) and a small portion of the stage are visible. This theater was likely built in the Hellenistic era and then modified in Roman times, perhaps in the 2nd century C.E. To the left of the larger theater is a smaller one. Built possibly in the middle of the

▲ **Fig. 93.** The smaller theater in Laodicea

2nd century C.E., the smaller theater, which faces west, contains several rows of seats along the top that are relatively intact. Unfortunately, not much else remains of this theater. It has been suggested that the smaller theater may have functioned as an odeion.

Between the two theaters are the remains of a basilica-style building, referred to as **Basilica North**. This structure, perhaps a Byzantine-era church, apparently consisted of a central nave with two side aisles. Both of the side aisles and the nave had an apse at their east end. (The large Corinthian capital standing near the area of the apses is from an earlier structure, possibly 2nd century C.E., and was either moved to this area or perhaps reused in construction here.) A group of ruins in the northwest section of the city, located on a small hill near the Ephesian Gate, has been identified as a **Byzantine church** and some additional buildings and fortifications. The church was a basilica with three apses at its eastern end.

The remains of two buildings lie east of the city wall. One of these buildings, in the southeast area of the site, seems to have consisted of a central **octagonal structure**, surrounded by a circular wall. (Only a few foundation blocks of the building are visible.) The similarity of the ground plan of this structure to the martyrion of Philip at Hierapolis has led to the suggestion that perhaps this building was also a martyrion (a building dedicated to the veneration of a martyr). North of this structure is another **building**, located where the colonnaded street originally ended. The purpose of this building, which apparently had a monumental set of steps on the east, is unknown.

Lystra

Few visitors seek out the ancient site of Lystra. Neither its unexciting location in the Anatolian plain nor its unexcavated mound offer much enticement except to the hard-core adventurer seeking to trace the route of the Apostle Paul.

Location and History

The ancient city of Lystra was located near the modern village of Hatunsaray, approximately 24 miles southwest of Konya in south-central Turkey. In 1885, about a mile north of Hatunsaray, on a mound called Zoldera (or, variously, Zordula), J. R. Sitlington Sterrett discovered a stone block approximately 3.5 feet tall and 1 foot thick. On the stone was the Latin inscription "DIVVM AVG COL IVL FELIX GEMINA LVSTRA CONSECRAVIT D D," which uses the Latinized version "Lustra" for the name of the city. The discovery of this monument, erected to honor Caesar Augustus, who founded the Roman colony of Lystra, made identification of the site of ancient Lystra possible. Lystra was a part of the Lycaonian region of Asia Minor, an area bordering Phrygia on the west, Cappadocia on the east, and the ethnic Galatian region on the north. To the south were the Taurus Mountains. Earlier made a part of the province of Cilicia, Lycaonia was put under the control of **Amyntas**, an ally and client king of the Romans, in 36 B.C.E. When Amyntas died in 25 B.C.E., Lycaonia became a part of the Roman province of Galatia.

Because the site of Lystra has yet to be excavated, little can be said with certainty about the earliest settlements on the site. The evidence of Hellenistic-style pottery and Greek inscriptions from the Roman period would suggest that at least a small village existed here during the Hellenistic period. Of the coins that have been found that originated from Lystra, none predates the time of the Roman colony, perhaps indicating that any pre-Roman settlement was not significant enough to issue coins. **Emperor Augustus** established Lystra as a Roman colony, likely in 25 B.C.E. at the same time that several other Roman colonies, including Pisidian Antioch, were founded. While all the colonies were established to help secure Roman control over Asia Minor, Lystra was likely founded specifically to suppress the Homanadenses and other mountain tribes in south-central Asia Minor who were hindering Roman control of the area. Augustus settled Lystra with Roman military veterans and named the colony Julia Felix Gemina Lustra. A branch of the Via Sebaste (the important road built by Augustus that connected the Mediterranean coast in Pamphylia to Pisidian Antioch and then Antioch to Iconium) split off and ran to Lystra, thus connecting the colony with the other Roman colonies in that part of Asia Minor.

▲ **Fig. 94.** Stone monument with Lystra inscription in the Konya Archaeological Museum

In contrast to Pisidian Antioch, which consciously modeled itself after Rome, Lystra appears not to have been thoroughly Romanized. Rather than the language and customs of the Roman settlers transforming the Lycaonian and Hellenistic cultures of the area, the settlers and their descendants seem to have eventually adapted to the native cultures. Whether the incident is authentic or not, the statement in Acts 14:11 that the people in Lystra shouted out to **Paul** and **Barnabas** in the Lycaonian language reflects the belief that the native culture of Lycaonia was still strong in Lystra. One modern scholar has described Lystra during this period as "an active and prosperous community, not one to care much for its status as a Roman colony, a thriving, rather rustic market town" (Barbara Levick, *Roman Colonies in Southern Asia Minor* [Oxford: Oxford University Press, 1967], 154).

The ultimate fate of Lystra is unknown. Evidence from coins, inscriptions, and ancient records show that Lystra continued to exist at least until the 13th century. Specific bishops from Lystra are listed as being present at the councils of Nicaea (325 C.E.), Constantinople (381 C.E.), Chalcedon (451 C.E.), and Constantinople (879 C.E.). During Byzantine times, Lystra was overshadowed in ecclesiastical importance by Iconium, which served as the metropolis of Lycaonia.

Biblical Significance

The city of Lystra first appears in the Bible when **Paul** and **Barnabas** visited the city on their first missionary journey, which took them to Cyprus and the southern area of Asia Minor. After visiting Pisidian Antioch and Iconium and encountering resistance, Paul and Barnabas traveled to Lystra (Acts 14:5–20), where they healed a crippled man. Impressed, the inhabitants of Lystra mistakenly believed that Barnabas and Paul were Zeus and Hermes in human form. This misidentification of Barnabas and Paul recalls a legend popular in the nearby region of Phrygia that told how Jupiter and Mercury (equated by the Romans with Zeus and Hermes) appeared in human form to various villagers (see Ovid, *Metamorphoses* 8.611–724). Led by the local priest of Zeus, the people attempted to offer sacrifices of oxen to Barnabas and Paul, who were barely able to dissuade the people from carrying out their intentions. Afterward, some Jews from Antioch and Iconium arrived and turned the people against Paul and Barnabas. After stoning Paul, the people dragged him outside the city and left him for dead. The following day Paul and Barnabas traveled to Derbe, then passed through Lystra, Iconium, and Antioch again as they reversed their travels to head back to Antioch of Syria (Acts 14:21).

During what the book of Acts presents as Paul's second missionary journey, the apostle revisited the cities in southern Asia Minor, including Lystra (16:1–3). When he left Lystra, he took with him **Timothy**, son of a Jewish mother and a Greek father. This native of Lystra became one of

Paul's most faithful and untiring co-workers. When Acts 18:23 describes the beginning of Paul's third journey, it states that Paul "went from place to place through the region of Galatia and Phrygia, strengthening all the disciples." Since the area in which Lystra was located was a part of the Roman province of Galatia, the text may intend to imply that Paul once more visited the believers in the southern area of central Asia Minor, including the city of Lystra. Paul's experiences in Lystra are mentioned in 2 Timothy 3:11 also.

Site Visit

Ancient Lystra was likely located on and around Zoldera Höyük, the mound (or tell) about a mile north of Hatunsaray. Unfortunately, because the tell has not been excavated, there is little for the visitor to see of ancient Lystra. Scattered on the tell are some broken pieces of pottery and some stone fragments of building materials. Acts 14:13 states that a temple to Zeus was located just outside the city, but no evidence of it is presently visible. In nearby Hatunsaray a few marble pillars, gravestones, and monuments found in the vicinity are displayed in a small fenced-off area in the center of the town. The stone monument discovered in 1885 by Sterrett with an inscription that mentions Lystra is on display in the Konya Archaeological Museum.

Miletus

Originally famed for its philosophers of nature, Miletus became one of the great cities of commerce of the ancient world. Its four harbors and strategic location on the west coast of Asia Minor gave the city unique advantages as a vital port in both peace and war. Yet these factors also were the cause of repeated periods of invasion and destruction. Eventually Miletus ceased to be a major player in world affairs, not because of the fortunes of war, but because of the slower but deadlier effects of the gentle Meander River, which silted its harbors and created malaria-ridden marshes.

History and Location

Miletus is easily reached from Izmir by taking E87 south to Selçuk, then proceeding on highway 525 through Söke to Akköy, then north through

Balat to the site of Miletus. Today it is difficult to imagine that Miletus once was situated on a narrow peninsula and boasted of four harbors, three on the west and one on the east. Due to the continual silting effects of the Meander River, the ruins of Miletus now are situated in a broad plain some 5 miles from the sea. The island of Lade, where the Persian armada burned and destroyed the Ionian fleet in 494 B.C.E., was once to the west of the coast of Miletus. Now it is merely a hill 4 miles west of Miletus.

A Mycenaean colony that had cultural contacts with Crete and Greece existed in this location from 1400 B.C.E. Greeks settled in the area by at least the 10th century B.C.E. The city prospered and grew wealthy from its colonies on the Mediterranean, the Black Sea, and even in Egypt. It was one of the first cities in the ancient world to mint coins. Soon Miletus became the most important of the twelve cities of the region of Ionia. The city came under Persian control in 546 B.C.E. and later opposed them in the Battle of Lade, but the result was the loss of their fleet and the complete destruction of their city in 494 B.C.E. Herodotus, in fact, said that Miletus was reduced to slavery. Subsequently, Ephesus surpassed Miletus as the first city of the region.

Nevertheless, during the classical period that followed, Miletus achieved fame in its rebuilt state (479 B.C.E.). The city was unique for the orderly fashion in which its streets were laid out, known as "the Hippodamian grid." Named for one of its citizens, **Hippodamus**, the design was subsequently adopted by countless cities in the centuries that followed. Other famous citizens of Miletus included **Thales, Anaximander,** and **Anaximenes,** all noted for their theories of the nature of the essential matter of the universe; the historian and geographer **Hekataios,** who is credited with first using the word *history* in its modern sense; and later **Isidorus,** one of the designers of St. Sophia in Istanbul.

Over the next century Miletus passed in and out of Persian hands until **Alexander the Great,** in a battle that took place on both land and sea, seized the city and launched it upon a new era of trade and prosperity (ca. 334 B.C.E.). After the death of Alexander, the city came under the control of **Lysimachus,** one of his generals, and his donations to the city caused it to flourish.

The Romans annexed the area in 133 B.C.E., but their excessive taxes led to a revolt and the slaughter of tens of thousands of Roman citizens in one day (ca. 129 B.C.E.). Shortly thereafter the Romans reasserted control of Miletus, and for most of the remainder of the Roman period relations with Rome were satisfactory. Monumental structures, the remains of which may be seen today, were constructed throughout Miletus by Roman authorities. During the reign of Trajan (2nd century C.E.) the **Sacred Way** was constructed, a monumental road paved with limestone slabs that connected the **Sanctuary of Apollo** in Miletus with the Sanctuary of Apollo in Didyma (see other sites of interest, below).

Following the 3rd century C.E., Miletus went into a slow decline, and the marshes created by the silting of the Meander River led to malaria and the reduction of the city to an inferior village by the Ottoman period. The site was completely abandoned in the 17th century.

Biblical Significance

By the time the **Apostle Paul** visited Miletus at the conclusion of his third and final missionary journey, the city boasted numerous temples, including the Temple of Athena and the Sanctuary of Apollo adjacent to the harbor of the Bay of Lions, as well as an impressive harbor gate with sixteen columns that recently had been erected. Miletus also had three large market places, including its South Market, the largest market known to have existed in the ancient Greek world. The bouleuterion between the South and North Markets was there at the time, as was the theater, a gymnasium, and a stadium. The spectacular Market Gate now in Berlin was not built until the 2nd century C.E.

When Paul came to Miletus, he was hurrying to arrive in Jerusalem in time for Pentecost (Acts 20:16). So he had bypassed Ephesus, where his past connections would have obligated him to spend considerable time, and traveled directly from Troas to Miletus. There he summoned the elders from the church at Ephesus to meet with him and delivered a lengthy and poignant farewell speech to them (Acts 20:17–35). At the conclusion of this address he quoted an otherwise unknown saying of Jesus that has become famous, "It is more blessed to give than to receive" (Acts 20:35).

Another visit to the city, not identified in Acts or elsewhere, is suggested by 2 Timothy 4:20, where Paul is described as leaving **Trophimus**, who was from Ephesus, in Miletus due to illness.

Site Visit

The **theater** is a good place to begin a visit to Miletus since it is directly across from the **ticket office** and **entrance**, and also because the upper levels of the theater provide an excellent view across the site. This well-preserved structure is one of the most impressive theaters of the ancient world. Begun at the end of the 4th century B.C.E., enlarged in Hellenistic times, and finally completed by the Romans, its seating capacity grew from 5,300 in the Hellenistic period to 15,000 in the late Roman period (2nd century C.E.; some authorities say 25,000). Today the theater stands over 90 feet high, but in the Roman period additional upper galleries, now missing, added another 30 feet to its height. The front of the theater,

Miletus

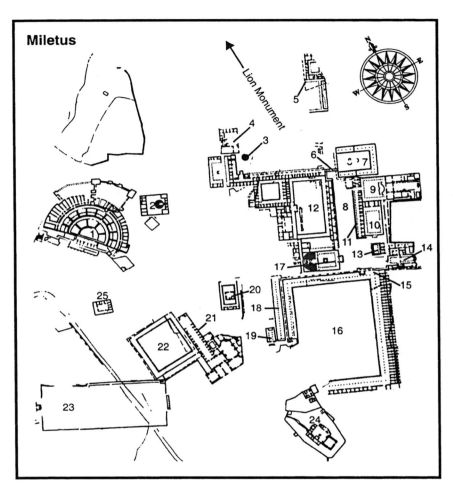

▲ **Fig. 95.** Miletus

1. Theater
2. Hellenistic Heroon
3. Large Harbor Monument
4. Synagogue
5. Roman Baths
6. Harbor Gateway
7. Delphinion
8. Sacred Way
9. Capito Baths
10. Gymnasium/Palaestra
11. Ionic Stoa
12. North Agora
13. Nymphaeum
14. Byzantine Church
15. North Gate
16. South Agora
17. Bouleuterion
18. Storehouse
19. Temple of Serapis
20. Roman Heroon
21. Baths of Faustina
22. Gymnasium
23. Stadium
24. Ilyas Bey Mosque
25. Caravansary

▲ **Fig. 96.** The theater at Miletus

which originally faced the harbor, is nearly 450 feet wide. In the Roman period a third floor was added to the stage building, which was decorated with columns and hunting scenes of Eros. In the center of the first rows, four columns, two of which remain, designated a special **box for the emperors**.

An interesting feature of the theater is the presence of an **inscription** in Greek on one of the rows that seems to designate an area for the seating of Jews. (This was not segregation; it was customary for various interest groups or guilds to sit together.) If so, such an inscription would indicate both a sizeable Jewish community and its participation in the theater, unthinkable among more conservative Palestinian Jews.

The wording of the rough inscription lends itself to two interpretations, however. It could be translated "Place of the Jews and the God-fearers" (Gentiles who followed certain Jewish beliefs but were not full converts). This is the usual interpretation, although the order of the Greek words is not entirely correct for such a reading. Others insist the inscription should be translated as "Place of the Jews [called] God-fearers." In this case, it would refer to the God-fearers (non-Jews), whom the inhabitants of Miletus regarded as part of the Jewish community and who had continued to attend the theater. But since Jews in Asia Minor in general were more liberal in their practices than those in Israel, it is not impossible that the inscription might include fully practicing Jews as well as the Gentile God-fearers.

▲ **Fig. 97.** The inscription, "Place of the Jews and the God-fearers," in the theater at Miletus

From the theater, visitors with little time may choose only to look across at the **Ionic Stoa** reflected in the standing water before it and then visit the **Faustina Baths**, the only other structure of any size still standing on the site. The route described below, however, will take the visitor past the most significant ruins of the ancient city.

Go first between the entrance to the theater on the left and the Baths of Faustina off to the right. Turn left down the hill past the **Hellenistic heroon** and the ruins of a **Byzantine church** on the left to reach the **Harbor Monument**. The **heroon** was a monumental tomb, built in the Hellenistic period in honor of a distinguished but as yet unidentified person who was subsequently deified. On the west side of the vaulted tomb chamber are five small niches to hold the remains of family members. In the center of the floor of the tomb chamber lies a rectangular hole for sacrifices. The large **Harbor Monument** stood 25 feet high, on top of which stood a tripod with a cauldron above it. The structure was decorated with reliefs of dolphins and tritons (lesser sea gods, half man, half fish). Apparently it was built in 63 B.C.E. and originally dedicated to **Pompey** for his victory over pirates in the area, though it was subsequently rededicated to **Emperor Augustus** for his victory in the Battle of Actium (31 B.C.E.). Originally this monument stood beside a marble-paved quay that stretched around three sides of the harbor. On its south side a Doric-style stoa built in Hellenistic times, known as the **North Agora**, was 500 feet long with sixty-four columns and contained thirty shops.

Just beyond the northwest corner of the Harbor Monument lie the poorly preserved remains of a **synagogue** from the Roman period. The New Testament does not mention any contact by **Paul** with a synagogue in Miletus, though, according to his pattern elsewhere, he likely did so.

On the plain stretching out below the monument, a long finger of the bay entered from the north in the direction of the Harbor Monument. Two **lion statues** stood on either side of the bay, toward its mouth. This port was called the **Lions' Harbor**, the oldest, largest, and most secure of four harbors at Miletus. One of the lions still stands in place; the other has disappeared. (If the plain is not wet and marshy, it is possible to walk across it in five minutes and view the remaining lion.)

Above this harbor, on its northeast side, stand the **Roman baths** built toward the end of the 1st century C.E. The caldarium and the apodyterium (changing room) are still standing.

Return in the direction of the Faustina baths. On the right is the **Harbor Gateway** that stood between the harbor and the city. Double rows of columns, 12 feet apart and covered with a flat roof, provided a dramatic entrance to Miletus. This gate led into the **Sacred Way** and stood beside the **Delphinion**, the principal worship place of Miletus, an open-air court surrounded by stoas. Here Apollo Delphinios (Apollo of the Dolphins), protector of ships and harbors, was worshiped at least as early as Greek and Hellenistic times. Altars dating from the Archaic period, 6th century B.C.E., also were found there. One of the round, portable **altars** that still stand there was dedicated to the goddess Hecate. A **temple structure** was added and later modified during the Hellenistic and Roman periods. The Delphinion was also used in the Roman period as the state archives.

Adjacent to this area on the south is a building that contained Roman baths known as the **Capito Baths**. These elaborate baths were built by **Vergilius Capito**, procurator of Asia Minor (according to the inscription found there, "Governor of Asia and Egypt"), during the reign of the emperor Claudius (r. 41–54 C.E.). In the front of the building is the tepidarium, partitioned into three sections. The rooms on the right and left are the apodyterium (changing rooms); in the center is the caldarium with two areas, one behind the other. The hypocaust (furnace room) for the baths was located in the southeast corner of the building. The **gymnasium** and **palaestra** (exercise court) of the baths, an area 120 feet square to the rear of the building, was surrounded by a two-story stoa. Originally a semicircular swimming pool stood in front of the stoa.

The monumental street called the **Sacred Way** began at the Harbor Gate and extended southward for 300 feet to the **square** in front of the **bouleuterion**. The street was 90 feet wide, with sidewalks 18 feet wide on either side. It led southward to link the city with Didyma (see "Other Sites of Interest," below). On its east side stood the spectacular **Ionic Stoa**, and on the west it fronted the **North Agora**. First built in the 5th century B.C.E., the North Agora was surrounded by stoas and shops in the Roman period.

▲ **Fig. 98.** Ionic Stoa and Capito Baths at Miletus

Perhaps the most dramatic remnant of ancient Miletus besides the theater is the **Ionic Stoa**, usually reflected in a large pool of standing water. Built in 58 C.E. by **Tiberius Claudius Sophanes**, this dramatic structure had thirty-five Ionic columns in front of nineteen shops. Behind the shops stood the Hellenistic gymnasium, with five rooms for study, and the palaestra of the Capito Baths.

Just beyond the Ionic Stoa are the remains of a monumental three-story fountain, or **nymphaeum**, which once was 55 feet high and 65 feet wide. Statues of gods and goddesses stood in the roofed niches on all three levels. The statues on the first level poured water from the amphorae they held and the fish beside them spouted water from their mouths, which cascaded down the steps before them into a large pool. Some statues and architectural pieces from this fountain are in the Berlin Museum and the Archaeological Museum in Istanbul. Originally a marble Temple of Asclepius stood beside the nymphaeum on the south; the ruins there today are the remains of a **Byzantine church** built in the 5th century C.E., though its façade dates to a Roman complex of the 3rd century C.E.

The **bouleuterion**, where the council of the city cast (Greek, *boule*) their votes, stands directly across the Sacred Way from the nymphaeum and the Byzantine church. The bouleuterion was built between the years 175 and 164 B.C.E. by two brothers from Miletus, **Timarchus** and **Heracleides**, and was dedicated to Antiochus IV (the same Antiochus

who incensed the Jews by desecrating the temple in Jerusalem). The structure had a colonnaded courtyard and an auditorium that could seat 1,500
persons. Its west wall contained windows.

The monumental entrance to the **South Agora**, or marketplace, was
constructed in the last half of the 2nd century C.E. (ca. 165 C.E.). The
agora itself, however, was established in Hellenistic times as a colonnaded courtyard of approximately 500 by 600 feet. Multiple shops surrounded the courtyard within the stoas on all sides. This was the largest
agora of antiquity. The colossal gate that opened onto the Sacred Way,
the **North Gate**, or **Market Gate**, is one of the great artifacts of ancient
times. It was removed from the site and completely reconstructed in the
Berlin Museum, where it now resides.

Built in the Hellenistic period (2nd century B.C.E.), the enormous **storehouse** (500 feet long by 40 feet wide) was used as a granary. In the Roman
period, a **latrine** was built between the storehouse and the South Agora.

Only fragments of the foundation and portions of columns remain of
the **Temple of Serapis**. The temple was dedicated to the Egyptian god
Helios Serapis, portrayed with a crown of sunrays, and was built during
the reign of Emperor Aurelius (270–275 C.E.). At the north end of the building there was a special partition where the cult statue stood. Between the
Temple of Serapis and the **Baths of Faustina** are the ruins of a 3rd-
century-C.E. **Roman heroon**, dedicated to an unidentified individual.

The tour of Miletus concludes at these spectacular baths, erected by
Faustina II, wife of the emperor Marcus Aurelius (r. 161–180 C.E.). From
the Temple of Serapis, a series of **furnace rooms** lies to the right (west)
of the path. The entrance to the building on the south leads to the two
rooms of the **caldarium** (hot room). The vaulted, central caldarium is
the largest hall in the building, measuring 90 feet by 45 feet and reaching
a height of approximately 75 feet. This room was heated by furnaces that
circulated hot air through clay pipes in the walls and a space beneath the
floors.

Beyond the caldarium on the west is the **tepidarium** (lukewarm room);
beyond that, the three rooms of the **frigidarium** (cold room). The central room of the frigidarium contains a large **pool** and two original **statues**, both of which were fountains, one of a **lion** and one of a **river god**
(likely Meander).

Beside the tepidarium extends the lengthy **apodyterium** (changing
room), 245 feet long, with small rooms for changing on both sides.
Benches for resting still exist in some of the rooms. **Niches** in the walls
of the room to the north of the apodyterium, called the **Hall of the Muses**,
originally held statues of Apollo, Asclepius, Telesphorus, the nine Muses,
and a head of Aphrodite. Parallel to the apodyterium on the west lies the
palaestra, or exercise area, for the baths.

▲ **Fig. 99.** Pool in the Baths of Faustina at Miletus, with two fountains, one of a lion and one of a river god, likely Meander

Just south of the South Agora and outside the central archaeological area is a famed mosque dating to the early 15th century (1404), well worth a visit. Noted for its beauty and antiquity, the **Mosque of Ilyas Bey** displays outstanding architecture and colorful marble surfaces.

Parallel to the bouleuterion, and at right angles to the North and South Agoras, is an unusual **stadium**, only partially excavated. The structure, 700 feet long and 250 feet wide, was built in the 2nd century B.C.E. and enlarged during the Roman period to a capacity of approximately 15,000 persons. Its track was 600 feet long, with three water clocks at each end. Unlike the typical Roman stadium, in which each end was enclosed in a horseshoe shape, this stadium terminated in **monumental entrance gates**. Its **west gate** is typically Hellenistic; the **east gate**, however, is Roman, though the well-fitted stones in the **east wall** date to the earlier Hellenistic period. Beyond the stadium on the west was the newest of the market areas of Miletus, the **West Agora**, likely dating to late Hellenistic times.

The Sacred Way, which linked Miletus to Didyma (see "Other Sites of Interest," below), passed through the town walls on the southwest at a **Roman gate**, restored by **Trajan** (100 C.E., according to an inscription found at the site) from earlier Hellenistic and Greek gates. Considerable remains of all these gates have been discovered. The massive **Hellenistic walls**, in places more than 30 feet thick, were stormed by **Alexander the Great** in his conquest of the city in 334 B.C.E.

Other Sites of Interest

Two other must-see sites are within easy reach of Miletus, one to the north, **Priene**, and one to the south, **Didyma**. Neither of these famous cities is mentioned in the Bible, but it is likely that contact with them was established by the early Christians in Miletus.

Priene is distinctive among the ancient cities of this region. Unlike its other well-known neighbors, the population of Priene was limited, never exceeding 5,000 persons. No doubt this was partly due to its cliffside location. The layout of the city, after it was rebuilt around 350 B.C.E. following frequent attacks by the Persians, was arranged in completely regular grids according to the Hippodamian approach to city planning, unlike the sprawling, accidental arrangement of most ancient cities (and modern ones as well). Priene was originally a port city, but the continuous silting caused by the Meander River eventually blocked the city's access to the sea and led to its gradual decline. Famous residents of Priene include **Bias**, one of the Seven Sages of Greece, and **Alexander the Great**, who briefly resided there during the lengthy siege of Miletus.

The climb to reach the city is well worth the effort. The ruins today are peaceful in their sheltered location, and the many side streets and remaining structures are fascinating in their uniqueness. Above the city, lengthy stretches of the **Hellenistic walls** have remained intact, in some places 6 feet wide and 18 feet tall. Several columns still are standing from the extensive **Temple of Athena** (4th century B.C.E.), and the **terrace walls** of the temple are particularly fine. Numerous other **temples** dot the area.

The seating of the **bouleuterion** (council chamber) remains, as does its **altar**, built in the 2nd century B.C.E. The **theater** of Priene is also well preserved. Five **armchair seats**, some with lion's-paw armrests, are intact. Portions of the **stadium**, the **Upper** and **Lower Gymnasium**, and numerous **houses**, one identified as the **Alexander House**, also may be seen.

To the south of Miletus, **Didyma** ("twin"), so named because of its famous shrine to Apollo, the twin of the goddess Artemis, is one of the most spectacular and popular tourist destinations in Turkey. Had the enormous structure been completed, modern authorities believe this magnificent temple would have been one of the seven wonders of the ancient world.

The two cities of Miletus and Didyma were connected by the **Sacred Road**, portions of which have been excavated. Impressive statues and monumental tombs of notable personages lined the way, which was approximately 10 miles long and 15 to 20 feet wide. In the spring of each year many pilgrims traveled from Miletus to the **Didymaion** (Temple of Apollo) to celebrate the annual festivities. This shrine was a notable rival of the famous Temple of Apollo at Delphi, where the oracle of Delphi was famed for her pronouncements. The same type of oracular prophecies brought thousands of pilgrims to Didyma to find answers to their future and also brought fame and enormous wealth to the Temple of Apollo.

The temple that is seen today was constructed over a lengthy period of time during the 3rd and 2nd centuries B.C.E., although portions of it were still under construction in the Roman period. This **Hellenistic temple** was begun in 313 B.C.E. over the site of the Archaic temple, which was built in the 6th century B.C.E. and destroyed in 494 B.C.E. by the Persians during the battle of Lade. Famous personages known to have visited the temple include **Lysimachus**, **Seleucus I**, and the emperors **Augustus** and **Trajan**. In the 5th century C.E. the emperor **Theodosius** had a **basilica** built in the adyton (sacred precinct).

Most arresting among the many fascinating elements of this splendid temple are the **enormous columns** and column bases atop the impressive **platform**, with its fourteen steps, upon which the temple rested. Once a forest of 122 columns surrounded the temple; today only three remain standing (2nd century B.C.E.). These columns stand 60 feet tall, the height of a six-story building, and they are 6 feet in diameter at the base. From ground level, the complete temple structure stood a total of 90 feet high.

Perhaps equally impressive is the **adyton**, to which only the priests and oracles had access. Narrow, vaulted corridors, some with the Meander motif on the ceiling, gave access to this area. Overall, the temple shows the influence of the Artemision at Ephesus and the Heraion at Samos, as it was designed by **Paionius of Ephesus** and **Daphnis of Miletus**, renowned architects who had also worked on the previous temples.

Myra

At one time one of the most important cities in Lycia, Myra almost has passed into obscurity. In addition to some interesting tombs and a theater, the most enduring legacy of ancient Myra is the tradition that developed around its most famous resident and bishop, St. Nicholas, who was the historical person behind the legend of Santa Claus. Popular etymology explained the name of the city as being derived from the Greek word for myrrh, an aromatic spice, but this is unlikely.

Location and History

Myra was a city in the Lycian region of Anatolia, along the Mediterranean coast approximately 85 miles southeast of modern Antalya. The ruins of ancient Myra lie about a mile north of Demre (or Kale), a small town along highway 400, the coastal road. Signs in the town point the way to Myra. The ancient city was considered a port city, even though it was about 3.5 miles from the coast. Its port was actually Andriace, but the name Myra often included the city proper and its port at Andriace. Thus, for example, when Acts 27:5 states that the ship carrying Paul landed at Myra, the actual port would likely have been Andriace. Whether Paul and the others with him went to Myra after disembarking from the ship is not known. The Myrus, or Andracus, River (Demre Çayï) flowed past the city on its way to the Mediterranean.

Settled probably as early as the 5th century B.C.E., Myra became one of the leading cities of the Lycian League by the 2nd century B.C.E. Myra was one of the six most important members of the league, which consisted of twenty-three cities. As such, it was entitled to three votes in the league (the maximum allowed). In spite of its importance, the city does not seem to have played a major role in ancient history. During Roman times the city apparently enjoyed good relations with Rome. **Augustus** (and after him, **Tiberius** as well) was honored by the people of Myra by their bestowing on him the title of "imperator of land and sea, benefactor and savior of the whole universe." **Germanicus**, the adopted son of Tiberius, and his wife **Agrippina** visited in 18 C.E. In their honor, statues of each were erected, and Germanicus was proclaimed savior and benefactor. In the 5th century C.E., Myra was named the capital of the province of Lycia. Beginning in the 7th century, the city suffered from various Arab raids. Eventually, the inhabitants of the city deserted it.

How or when Christianity first came to Myra is unknown. The apocryphal *Acts of Paul* tells of **Paul** preaching at Myra, performing miracles, and being joined there by **Thecla**, but this story has no historical basis. Whatever the origins of the Christian faith in the city, by the 4th century Christianity was firmly rooted there, for it is during the 4th century that its most famous bishop, St. Nicholas, served in the city. Born to wealthy parents around 300 C.E. in nearby Patara, Nicholas eventually became the bishop of Myra. According to some accounts, he was imprisoned during the persecution by **Diocletian** and later attended the Council of Nicaea in 325, where supposedly he slapped the face of Arius (who was declared a heretic) so hard that he made Arius' bones rattle.

These traditions are probably more legendary than historical, but they bear witness to the esteem in which St. Nicholas was held. Other, more incredible legends developed about St. Nicholas. In one story, a father of three young girls was so poor that he could not afford the dowries for his daughters to marry. As a result, the girls were destined to become prostitutes. St. Nicholas rescued them from this fate, however, by secretly tossing three bags of gold into their house. This story is apparently the basis for the tradition of giving gifts on the occasion of St. Nicholas' feast day, December 6. (The custom has been transferred to December 25 in some cultures.) In another tale, during a time of famine three young boys came to a butcher's house. While they were sleeping, the butcher killed them, cut them up, packed them in salt, and planned to sell them. Informed by an angel of the horrendous deed, Nicholas went to the butcher's house and restored the boys to life. Highly revered in Greece and Russia, St. Nicholas is known as the patron saint of children, sailors, merchants, and scholars. From his life of piety, kindness, and generosity arose the legendary figure celebrated today as St. Nicholas, Father Christmas, or Santa Claus.

Biblical Significance

Myra receives only brief mention in the Bible. It was one of the cities at which the ship transporting **Paul** from Caesarea to Rome landed around 59 C.E. According to the narrative in Acts, Paul was being sent as a prisoner to Rome under the guard of "a centurion of the Augustan Cohort, named Julius" (Acts 27:1). One of Paul's partners in his missionary work, **Aristarchus** from Thessalonica, accompanied him on the trip. When they landed at Myra, they changed ships because the ship they were on previously was not headed toward Rome but was sailing along the ports of Asia. The new ship was a grain ship from Alexandria, Egypt, that was bound for Italy. (Myra was a usual stopping place for Egyptian grain ships headed to Italy.)

Some ancient Greek manuscripts of Acts include Myra as one of the stops on Paul's third missionary journey as he was returning to Caesarea. According to those texts, Acts 21:1 includes "and Myra" after "Patara." Most textual critics, however, doubt the authenticity of that reading.

Site Visit

The **theater** and the **rock tombs** nearby are the most frequently visited parts of ancient Myra. An earthquake destroyed the original theater in 141 C.E., but thanks to the generosity of **Opramoas**, a citizen of Rhodiapolis and benefactor of many cities in Lycia who gave ten thousand denarii to Myra, the theater was rebuilt. The theater is still well preserved and contains thirty-five rows of seats, twenty-nine of them below the diazoma (the passageway separating the tiers of seats) and six above it. In the center of the wall above the diazoma is a representation of Tyche (the goddess of fortune) with an inscription that reads, "Fortune of the city, be ever victorious, with good luck." Steps on either side of the Tyche figure lead up to the upper tier of seats. Along the wall of the diazoma are painted several names, possibly as a way of reserving seats in the theater. The theater, which probably had a capacity of 10,000 spec-

▲ **Fig. 100.** Lycian house-type rock tombs at Myra

tators, has fourteen aisles, or stairways. A sizeable portion of the stage
building and part of the stage are intact.

On the side of the cliff to the west (left) of the theater is the **Sea
Necropolis**, which contains some of the rock tombs of ancient Myra.
Many of these are quite spectacular. Most are of the Lycian house-tomb
type, in which the cliff face that surrounds the entrance to the tomb is
carved to resemble the façade of a house (including carvings to resemble
wooden beams). Some are of the temple type. Adjacent to many of the
tomb façades are relief carvings of various scenes, frequently farewell
scenes involving the deceased and family members, servants, and friends.
One of the reliefs depicts two warriors with shields in combat. Originally many of the reliefs were painted, but little of the paint remains
today. These tombs date from the 4th century B.C.E.

Another necropolis, the **River Necropolis**, is a little farther away to
the east of the theater. This area contains even more tombs than does the
Sea Necropolis. One of the most impressive of the tombs in this area is
the so-called **Painted Tomb**. Originally the relief carved by the tomb
was painted in red, blue, yellow, and purple. Unfortunately, the colors
have disappeared. The scene in relief contains eleven life-size figures,
including a bearded man reclining on a couch and other figures likely
representative of his family engaged in various activities. North of these

tombs in the River Necropolis is an open channel cut into the rock about 10 feet above the ground. This channel served as an **aqueduct** to bring water to the city.

The **acropolis** of ancient Myra is reached by an ancient stepped path that leads to the top of the cliff northeast of the theater. Parts of the **Byzantine outer wall** and the **Lycian inner wall** from the 5th century B.C.E. still remain. At the southeastern end of the acropolis are the remains of a few buildings, one of which seems to be the foundation of a **Roman temple**.

Adjacent to the highway that leads from Myra to Demre are the ruins of a **brick building** from the Roman era, perhaps a basilica or a bath complex.

Other Sites of Interest

In Demre is located the **Church of St. Nicholas**. The precise history of the church, which has undergone extensive renovation and repair throughout the centuries, is not clear. St. Nicholas died in the 4th century, and it is possible that a church or chapel was built shortly afterward over his grave or to contain his tomb. There is no evidence to support this tradition, however. Literary evidence supports the existence of the Church of St. Nicholas as early as the 6th century. The present building was extensively restored in the 11th century and in the 19th century; various renovations were undertaken at other times as well. In 1087 a group of merchants from Bari, Italy, conspired to steal the remains of St. Nicholas. According to tradition, they found the bones in a tomb underground in the church. They transported the saint's bones back to Bari, where the supposed remains of St. Nicholas now rest in the church of San Nicolò. The sarcophagus in the church in Demre said to be that of St. Nicholas is located in the south aisle of the church behind a broken marble screen. The sarcophagus, made of plain marble, has an ornately carved lid with the figures of a man and woman. Even if the sarcophagus is authentic (which is doubtful), the lid certainly did not originally belong to that sarcophagus.

West of Demre, at a place called Karabucak, there is a junction of the small road with the main highway. At the junction stands a large **Roman monument tomb**, around 42 feet tall. The smaller road leads to **Andriace**, the ancient port for Myra. As noted above, it is likely that Paul stopped here and changed ships while being transported to Rome. Although somewhat overgrown and sometimes marshy, the site is worth a visit. The remains of several buildings from the Roman period still survive. The most impressive of these remains is the **granary** built by **Hadrian**. Constructed with eight rooms, the granary has two busts over the main door— the emperor Hadrian and a female figure who is variously identified as his wife **Sabina** or **Faustina**, the wife of Antoninus Pius. North of the granary are the remains of **houses** and **streets**. Beyond them is the **harbor**, which is now silted up. The ruins of a **watchtower** are to the west. Across the river are the **necropolis** and the ruins of a building that was likely either a **nymphaeum** or a **bath complex**.

Patara

In ancient times Patara possessed one of the best harbors on the Lycian coast. Modern visitors will be forced to use their imaginations to visualize the port of Patara, since the harbor eventually fell victim to the effects of silting from the Xanthos River. Today a beach and sand dunes cover the mouth of the ancient harbor, while the inner part of the harbor is now a marsh. Patara served as the port city for Xanthos, the leading city of the region of Lycia, which was located about 6 miles up the Xanthos River.

Location and History

Patara is located on the southwestern shore of Turkey, due east from the island of Rhodes. It is situated about halfway between Fethiye and Kale, near the present-day village of Gelemiş, about 3.5 miles south of the modern road (highway 400) that runs along Turkey's Mediterranean shore. Patara is approximately 6 miles east of the mouth of the Xanthos River. A stream from the Xanthos flowed into the sea at Patara and deposited the river's silt there. Important in the past because of its harbor, the area around Patara is known today for its 11 miles of excellent, sandy beaches.

Supposedly named after Patarus, a son of Apollo, the city was famous in antiquity for its Temple of Apollo (no archaeological evidence of the temple has yet been found) and the oracle of Apollo. According to ancient tradition, Apollo liked to spend the winter at Patara and thus the oracle of Apollo was operative only during the winter months. Pottery finds at Patara provide evidence for a settlement here as early as the 6th century B.C.E. In 334–333 B.C.E. Patara, along with several other Lycian cities, surrendered to **Alexander the Great**. During the subsequent Hellenistic period, the city came first under the control of the Ptolemies and then the Seleucids. **Ptolemy II Philadelphus** (r. 282–246 B.C.E.) expanded the city and renamed it Arsinoe in honor of his wife, but the new name never took hold. In 196 B.C.E., the Seleucid ruler **Antiochus III** of Syria captured several Lycian cities, including Patara. After Rome defeated the Syrians in 189 B.C.E., Patara was given to Rhodes, which had been an ally of the Romans in the war. After a brief period under Rhodian rule, Patara was given its independence by the Romans in 167 B.C.E.

Patara became an important city in the region because of its excellent and strategic harbor, one of the few good harbors on that part of the Lycian coast. The Roman period saw the creation of the Lycian League, a confederation consisting of twenty-three cities and towns. One of the six largest cities in the league, Patara was allowed three votes in the league's assembly, the maximum number of votes allowed to any city. The archives for the league were stored in Patara. When **Mithradates VI Eupator**, the king of Pontus in northern Asia Minor, waged war against the Romans in Asia Minor, he laid siege to Patara in 88 B.C.E. The city regained its independence two years later when the Romans were able to drive Mithradates from the region.

Aside from a brief period in 42 B.C.E. when the Roman general **Brutus** forced the city to surrender, Patara enjoyed relative freedom throughout most of the 1st century B.C.E. and the first half of the 1st century C.E. When the Romans combined Lycia and Pamphylia into one Roman province in 43 C.E., Patara became the residence and judicial seat for the Roman governor. In 129 C.E. the Roman emperor **Hadrian** and his wife **Sabina** visited Patara and endowed the construction of a large granary in the city, the ruins of which are still visible at the site.

Christianity apparently came early to Patara and prospered in the area, as evidenced by the remains of four different churches at Patara. Early in the 4th century, Patara was the seat of a bishopric, whose bishop, **Eudemus,** was present at the Council of Nicaea in 325 C.E. The city was reportedly the birthplace of **St. Nicholas**, the 4th-century bishop of Myra, about whom the legend of Santa Claus arose. As late as the 12th century, Patara's harbor was still being used by Christian pilgrims on their way to the Holy Land. After the silting from the Xanthos River clogged the harbor, however, Patara declined and eventually was abandoned, being buried beneath the sands and marsh.

Biblical Significance

Patara is mentioned only once in the Bible. According to Acts 21:1 the **Apostle Paul** stopped at Patara and changed ships on his way back to Jerusalem at the end of his third missionary journey. Paul and his companions sailed from Miletus and "came by a straight course to Cos, and the next day to Rhodes, and from there to Patara." Finding a ship bound for Phoenicia, they "went on board and set sail" (21:2); some ancient manuscripts of Acts add "and Myra" to the first sentence, reading "and from there to Patara and Myra." According to this reading, which is not considered by most scholars to be the original wording, Paul sailed on to Myra before changing ships.

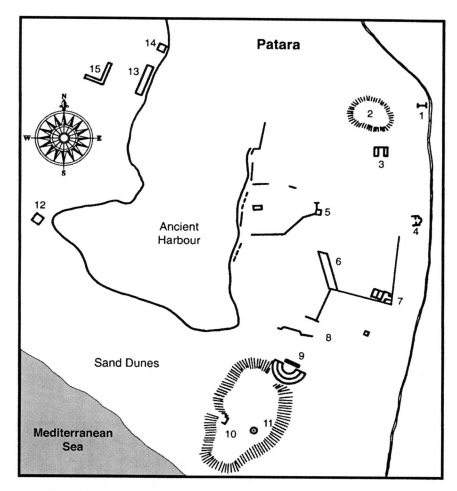

⚜ Fig. 101. Patara

1. Gate of Mettius Modestus
2. Mound (Possible site of Temple of Apollo)
3. Roman Baths
4. Byzantine Basilica
5. Corinthian Temple
6. Main Avenue
7. The Baths of Vespasian
8. Administration Building
9. Theater
10. Tomb or Temple
11. Cistern
12. Tomb
13. Granary of Hadrian
14. Pseudoperipteral Temple-Tomb
15. Agora

Site Visit

Although some archaeological work has been undertaken at Patara and an entrance fee is charged at the entry gate, the site offers few aids for the visitor. Apart from the sign containing a map of the site located adjacent to the entry gate, no signs are posted identifying the various ruins; paths (if existent) are barely discernible; and marsh and dense undergrowth make some of the ruins difficult to reach and at times virtually inaccessible. The paved road entering the site, on the eastern side of the ancient harbor, leads past the **triple-arched gateway of Mettius Modestus**. This gateway, which served as the entrance to the city, was erected around 100 C.E., when Modestus was governor of the province of Lycia-Pamphylia. The consoles (projecting brackets) on both sides of the gateway originally held busts of Modestus and his family. Several **sarcophagi** from the Roman period can be seen near the gateway. Along the roadside leading to the gateway can be seen several **Roman and Lycian tombs**. To the southwest of the gateway is a small **mound** where a large bust of Apollo was discovered, leading some people to speculate that this was the site of the ancient Temple of Apollo. Excavation of the mound sufficient enough to determine its purpose has not been undertaken, and the location of Apollo's temple remains unknown.

South of the mound lies one of the **bath complexes** found at Patara. Built during the Roman period, these baths continued to be used during the Byzantine era as well. Farther south are the **Vespasian Baths**. An inscription on one of the walls indicates that the Roman emperor **Vespasian** provided the funds for the building of this bath complex. These

⚊ **Fig. 102.** Gateway of Mettius Modestus at Patara

baths, measuring approximately 345 feet by 160 feet, contained five inter-connecting chambers. Near the baths are remnants of a **defense wall** constructed around part of the city. Between these two bath complexes, along the side of the paved road, are the ruins of a **Christian basilica** from the Byzantine period. Southwest of the Vespasian Baths lies Patara's most impressive ruin, the ancient **theater**. Much of the theater still lies under the sand that has accumulated over the centuries. The theater is possibly originally Hellenistic. An inscription on one of its walls records that the theater was repaired when **Tiberius** was emperor (14–37 C.E.). Another inscription mentions reconstruction of and renovations to the theater in 147 C.E. following a devastating earthquake that struck the area.

Behind the theater (to the south) rises a hill on whose summit is located a circular pit approximately 30 feet in diameter and 30 feet deep, with a square pillar in its center. Some investigators have claimed this is the base of the **lighthouse** for the harbor of Patara. The prevailing view now is that the structure was a **cistern** to supply water for the city prior to the construction of aqueducts for this purpose. West of the circular pit are remains that some scholars have identified as the stylobate (the top step, which served as the platform for the columns) of a **temple** (some have suggested the Temple of Athena). Other scholars identify the structure as a **tomb**.

Perhaps the most important reason to make the relatively easy climb to the top of this hill is not for the architectural remains but for the spectacular view that the summit provides. From the top of the hill one can look south and see the Mediterranean Sea and miles of beautiful beaches. The view to the north provides an excellent overview of the ancient city

▲ **Fig. 103.** Area of the ancient harbor at Patara

of Patara. From this vantage point, the general area of the ancient harbor and many of the buildings on both sides of the harbor are clearly discernible. The view from the summit alone is worth the trip to Patara.

North of the theater is a large structure that has been identified as an **administration building**. North of this building and west of the Vespasian Baths is the **main avenue** of Patara, paved with marble slabs. Along this street, which is often covered with water, lie broken columns that originally lined the street. Further north, west of the basilica, is a small, 2nd-century-C.E. **Corinthian-style temple**. This building, which sits at the base of the low **acropolis** of the city, is one of the best-preserved buildings at Patara. Its architectural style is that of a *templum in antis,* that is, a temple with no rows of columns surrounding it. Most of the other buildings in the area of the acropolis have not been identified. A **defense wall** from the Hellenistic and Byzantine periods surrounds the acropolis.

To the west of the acropolis, across the marsh (which in ancient times was the city's harbor), is located a huge **granary** built with funds given by Emperor Hadrian. (The western side of the ancient harbor can be reached by walking west along the beach and sand dunes.) This structure is basically intact except for the roof. Although the façade of the building is two-story, the granary bins appear to have been only one-story. The granary had eight large storage rooms for grain; each storage bin had its own entrance door. North of the granary are the ruins of a building that was likely a **temple-tomb**. This tomb was originally a rather striking structure, being built in the Corinthian pseudoperipteral style (i.e., the columns around the building were partially made into the wall of the temple, rather than being freestanding). Other tombs in the vicinity suggest that this area was likely a necropolis for the city. To the west of the granary is an area that may have been the **agora** of Patara. Approximately 400 yards southwest of the granary, at the edge of the sand dunes, are the remains of a **round building** on a rectangular foundation. This structure is located at the western edge of the entrance to the ancient harbor. Earlier tentatively identified as the base of a lighthouse, the structure is now thought to be an ancient **tomb**.

Perga

Certainly a striking city in its day, Perga (also spelled *Perge*) today still is an impressive place to visit. Its theater, stadium, agora, towers, baths, and colonnaded streets give the visitor a good sense of what an ancient city was like.

Location and History

Perga is located in the ancient region of Pamphylia, approximately 9 miles east of Antalya. To visit the site, take highway 400 east from Antalya to the town of Aksu, in which there is a yellow sign on the left that points to Perga, which is a little more than a mile north of Aksu. The Aksu Çayï (the ancient Cestrus River) comes within 3 miles of the site on its way to the Mediterranean, approximately 7 miles away. In ancient times Perga apparently had a port on the river, which was navigable, thus allowing the city to benefit commercially from the river.

Ancient tradition claims that Perga was founded after the Trojan War by Greek settlers under the leadership of **Calchas** (a seer whose prophecies helped the Greeks in the war) and **Mopsus** (another ancient seer). The acropolis at Perga, however, was inhabited much earlier than this, even during the Bronze Age. When **Alexander the Great** came through the area in 333 B.C.E., the city of Perga offered no resistance to him. Some of the people from Perga even served as guides to lead a part of Alexander's army from Phaselis into Pamphylia. After Alexander's death, the city was controlled by the Ptolemies and then by the Seleucid rulers. One of the most famous natives of Perga during the Hellenistic period was **Apollonius**, a 3rd-century-B.C.E. mathematician who wrote a nine-volume work on conics. His works were important contributions to astronomy and geometry. He studied in Alexandria and later lived in Pergamum. After the defeat of the Seleucids by the Romans in 189 B.C.E. at the battle of Magnesia, Perga became a part of the Pergamene kingdom. Bequeathed to Rome in 133 B.C.E. by the last Pergamene king, **Attalus III**, the city came under Roman control four years later, as a part of the Roman province of Asia Minor.

The 2nd and 3rd centuries C.E. were prosperous times for Perga, as evidenced by the large amount of building activity that occurred during this time period. The city's theater, stadium, baths, and agora were built during this period of prosperity and growth. One of the leading citizens and benefactors of the city was **Plancia Magna**, a woman who served as a priestess of Artemis Pergaea and also held the office of *demiourgos* (magistrate), the highest civic office. She came from a wealthy and distinguished family. Her father, **M. Plancius Varus**, was a Roman senator and at one time the proconsul of Bithynia, and her brother **C. Plancius Varus** was a Roman consul. Statues of her were found in the city, as well as several inscriptions mentioning her. The Temple of Artemis Pergaea, well known in antiquity, has never been found.

During the 3rd century C.E. the city acquired the title of metropolis (leading city of the province), a title it apparently shared with the city of Side. Perga seems to have been an important city for Christianity during the early Byzantine period, as evidenced by the presence of representatives from Perga at the Council of Nicaea in 325 and at the Council of Ephesus in 431, as well as by the remains of two basilica churches in the city, one from the 5th century and the other from the 6th century. Arab attacks beginning in the 7th century weakened the city, causing many of the inhabitants to move away. Seljuk Turks captured the region in the 11th century, and the Ottoman Turks gained control at the end of the 14th century, by which time (if not before) the city seems to have been mostly deserted.

Biblical Significance

Perga is mentioned twice in the New Testament, both times in connection with Paul's first missionary journey. When **Paul** and **Barnabas**, accompanied by **John Mark** (described in Col 4:10 as the cousin of Barnabas), left on their journey, their first stop, according to the book of Acts, was the island of Cyprus. When they left Cyprus, sailing from the city of Paphos, they went to Perga, the first city mentioned on their journey through the southern region of Asia Minor. At Perga, for some unexplained reason, John Mark left Paul and Barnabas and returned to Jerusalem (Acts 13:13). The book of Acts does not state whether Paul and Barnabas did any missionary work in the city of Perga or simply passed through the city on their way to Antioch of Pisidia. After visiting several cities in Asia Minor, including Antioch, Lystra, Derbe, and Iconium, Paul and Barnabas returned to Perga. This time they did preach to the people in Perga and shared the Christian message with them before heading south to Attalia (Antalya), from which they sailed back to Antioch in Syria (Acts 14:25–26).

Site Visit

One of the most impressive structures remaining at Perga is the **theater**, which is the first building encountered at the site, located immediately to the left of the road leading to ancient Perga. At the time of this writing, the theater was closed for further restoration and repair. Originally built in the Hellenistic era (or at least in the Hellenistic style), the theater was later modified by the Romans. The cavea, or seating area, which is built into the hillside, contained seating for 13,000–15,000 spectators. A roofed, colonnaded gallery ran along the top of the cavea, with an entrance from the hillside located in the middle of the gallery. (The gallery provides a great view of the site of Perga.) The orchestra (the area between the cavea and the stage building) was used during the late Roman period as an arena for gladiatorial contests and fights with wild animals. In order to

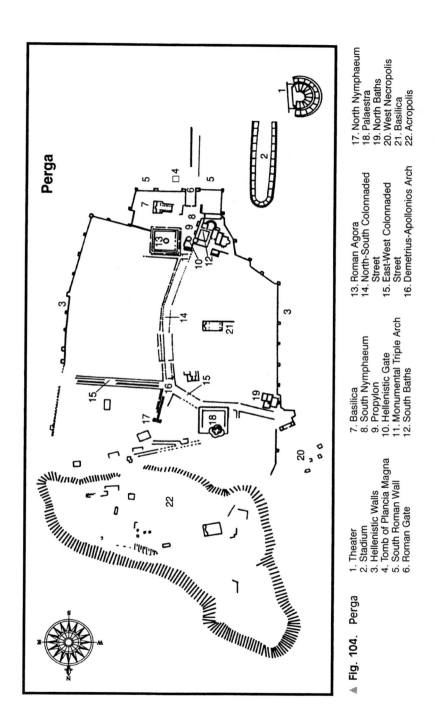

▲ **Fig. 104.** Perga

1. Theater
2. Stadium
3. Hellenistic Walls
4. Tomb of Plancia Magna
5. South Roman Wall
6. Roman Gate

7. Basilica
8. South Nymphaeum
9. Propylon
10. Hellenistic Gate
11. Monumental Triple Arch
12. South Baths

13. Roman Agora
14. North-South Colonnaded Street
15. East-West Colonnaded Street
16. Demetrius-Apollonios Arch

17. North Nymphaeum
18. Palaestra
19. North Baths
20. West Necropolis
21. Basilica
22. Acropolis

Perga

▲ **Fig. 105.** Stadium at Perga

contain the animals and protect the audience, a wall was constructed between the seats and the orchestra. The stage building, built during the 2nd century C.E., was two stories high and richly decorated with friezes, most of which depicted scenes from the life of Dionysus, the god of the theater. Several of the panels containing the friezes are still in place. At a later time a **nymphaeum** (fountain) was added to the outer façade of the stage building (facing the road). The nymphaeum consisted of five niches with fountains and pools.

Northeast of the theater (across the modern paved road) is the Roman **stadium**, one of the best-preserved in Turkey. Built in the 2nd century C.E., the stadium had a capacity of approximately 12,000 spectators. The stadium was horseshoe-shaped, with seating on the west, north, and east sides. The southern end of the arena, which is now open, probably contained an ornamental entrance to the stadium. Underneath the tiers of seats are vaulted chambers, all of which were interconnected. Every third chamber served as an entryway to a passage that led around the inside of the stadium at ground level, while the remaining chambers served as shops. At some time, a portion of the northern end of the stadium was walled off to form an arena for animal and gladiator contests. A protective wall was also added in front of the seats in this area.

The main part of Perga was surrounded by **city walls**, the earliest portions of which date to the 3rd century B.C.E. (The stadium and the theater are outside the walls.) Much of the walls and the defense towers that were part of the walls are still intact. The walls on the west and east are Hellenistic. (No wall was needed on the north because the acropolis provided protection from that direction.) The southern Hellenistic wall was torn down during the Roman period when the city expanded to the south. During the 4th century C.E. a new wall was built farther south to enclose a larger area for the city. The gate in the present southern wall is also from the 4th century C.E. (Roman period). The gate incorporates an earlier Roman monumental ceremonial gate. Outside and to the right of the Roman gate are the scant remains of the **tomb of Plancia Magna**, the wealthy benefactor of the city, priestess, and public official.

Inside the walls to the right are the remains of a **basilica** from the 6th century C.E. that was used as a church. Just beyond the Roman Gate on the left is a **nymphaeum** built during the reign of Septimius Severus as emperor (193–211 C.E.). The nymphaeum, which was dedicated to Artemis Pergaea, **Septimius Severus**, and his family, had a rectangular pool backed by a two-story façade wall. The wall was ornamented with columns, triangular pediments, friezes, and statues. The statues of Septimius Severus and his wife **Julia Domna**, now on display in the Antalya Museum, were located at the nymphaeum. In the front part of the pool were two semicircular basins, which can still be seen today, to make access to the water easier. Between the nymphaeum and the west Hellenistic tower was the **propylon**, a monumental entrance to the South Baths. As with the nymphaeum, the propylon was built during the reign of Septimius Severus. The propylon contained eight columns (two rows of four columns each) set on a marble platform with two steps. The columns, which supported a richly decorated roof, flanked the entryway. The three niches located between the propylon and the Hellenistic tower were covered with marble and contained statues, including two statues of Plancia Magna. This area in which the nymphaeum, the propylon, and the three niches were located, including the open space between the late Roman Gate and the Hellenistic Gate, is known as **Septimius Severus Square**.

As noted above, the propylon served as the grand entrance to one of the Roman baths at Perga, the **South Baths**. The entrance from the propylon led first into a palaestra, or exercise yard, and then into the other components of the bath complex. The palaestra was surrounded by a colonnaded porch. The room farthest west was the caldarium (hot room). At its south end was a pool, above which were three arched windows. A hypocaust, or heating system, ran underneath the floor of the caldarium. The room east of the caldarium was the tepidarium, or warm room. Like the caldarium, the tepidarium also contained a pool and a hypocaust system. The next room was the frigidarium, which housed a large pool that would have contained cold water. The long room that abutted the north

▲ **Fig. 106.** Towers of the Hellenistic Gate at Perga

end of the frigidarium originally contained over thirty different sculptures. The statues discovered here, as well as some from elsewhere in the baths, are displayed in the Antalya Museum. The bath complex contained at least four additional rooms, some of which also had pools or hypocaust systems.

The two round **towers** are part of the **Hellenistic Gate** of Perga, one of the most impressive remains of the city. The towers, built during the 3rd century B.C.E., were three stories tall and likely had wooden roofs. Originally this gate was a part of the southern wall of the city, but the wall was removed by the Romans and replaced with one farther south. On the north side of the gate was a horseshoe-shaped courtyard with walls that were 36 feet tall. Niches in both of the walls contained statues of gods and goddesses. During the 2nd century C.E., Plancia Magna altered the courtyard by covering the walls with slabs of marble, adding more niches to the walls for additional statues, and erecting a two-story Corinthian colonnade in front of the walls. She also erected a monumental **triple arch** at the north end of the courtyard.

East of the Hellenistic Gate is the **Roman agora**, thought to have been built during the 4th century C.E. The Hellenistic agora would not have been located here but farther north, perhaps near the intersection of the two main streets, since the southern wall of the city during Hellenistic times would have bisected the area covered by the Roman agora.

Covering an area measuring 246 feet on each side, the agora consisted of a large open area surrounded by a colonnaded stoa of Corinthian columns. Behind the stoa, on all four sides, were numerous shops, some with their entrances facing the stoa and the agora square and some with their entrances facing the streets. The beautiful mosaic floors in some of the shops are still visible. In the middle of the agora square was a **round building** encircled by sixteen marble columns. The purpose of this building is uncertain, although it was possibly a temple dedicated to Hermes, the patron deity of merchants, or to Tyche, the goddess of fortune. On the north side of the agora was a colonnaded street known as **Tacitus Avenue**.

The major **north-south street** of Perga, which was approximately 65 feet wide, was both functional and beautiful. Like many Hellenistic and Roman streets, this street was flanked on each side by colonnaded stoas. (Several of the columns have been put back in place.) These covered areas offered protection for the citizens from the rain in winter and the scorching summer sun and provided a place for the people to converse and socialize. Behind the stoas, on each side of the street, were various shops and businesses. The most impressive aspect of the street was the water channel that ran through the middle of the street. The water flowing through the city street added to the aesthetics of the ancient city and would have helped cool the area in the heat of summer. Four of the columns on the east side of the street are decorated with figures in relief. One of these columns contains a relief that is damaged. It likely depicts Apollo riding in his horse-drawn chariot. Another relief is that of Artemis, the goddess of the hunt. She has a torch in her right hand and a bow and arrow in her left. Another column contains a relief of a figure holding a libation bowl in front of an altar and is usually identified as Calchas, one of the legendary founders of the city. The fourth relief depicts Tyche, the goddess of fortune, wearing a crown and holding a cornucopia in her left hand.

Several side streets intersect the main colonnaded street at various points. The major **east-west street** is not at the midpoint of the city but is more to the north, with the northern area of the city smaller than the southern area. This major east-west street, which connected the east and west city gates, had covered colonnades along both sides and also had a water channel running in the middle of it. At the intersection of the main east-west and north-south streets is the reconstructed **Demetrios-Apollonios Arch** (or the **Domitian Arch**), erected in the late 1st century C.E. in honor of **Emperor Domitian** (r. 81–96 C.E.). The arch, dedicated to Artemis Pergaea and Apollo, was built by two brothers, **Demetrios** and **Apollonios**, who were leading citizens of Perga, each of whom served as priest of Artemis Pergaea and as *demiourgos* of the city, among their many other responsibilities and honors. After Domitian suffered official condemnation (*damnatio memoriae*) after his death in 96 C.E., the inscription to him was erased from the monument. Approximately 125 yards west of the intersection, on the north side of the east-west street, is a large **palaestra**, yet to be excavated. According to an inscription, the building was constructed by a citizen of Perga named **C. Julius Cornutus** and dedicated to the emperor **Claudius** (r. 41–54 C.E.). The palaestra, which covered an area measuring 250 feet by 250 feet, consisted of an open courtyard for exercises and athletic practices, surrounded by various rooms. The wall facing the street, which is relatively well preserved, contained several large windows. Farther west, near the west gate in the city wall, are the remains of another public **bath**, this one built during the 3rd century C.E. Outside the west gate is a **necropolis**. Several sarcophagi that were discovered here are on display in the Antalya Museum. Another **necropolis** is outside the east gate. Approximately 150 yards south of the palaestra are the ruins of a 5th-century **basilica church**, which had a nave and two side aisles. A large apse was on the east end of the building. This area, as indeed much of the area on both sides of the north-south colonnaded street, is heavily overgrown.

At the north end of the north-south street was the **north nymphaeum**. Built in the middle of the 2nd century C.E., this structure was the source for the water that flowed through the central colonnaded street. The

nymphaeum consisted of a two-story façade, with side walls projecting forward from the back wall. Corinthian columns and architectural ornamentation added to the impressive appearance of the structure. Several statues adorned the nymphaeum, including the statues of Zeus, Apollo, Artemis, and Hadrian that are now in the Antalya Museum. In the center of the nymphaeum was a statue of Cestrus, the river god (part of it is still in place). Beneath the statue, water from a tank behind the façade flowed into a pool in front and from there into the channel that ran through the colonnaded street. (Today, goats often recline along with Cestrus on the nymphaeum.)

Behind the nymphaeum is the **acropolis** of the city. (A path behind the nymphaeum leads to the acropolis, for those interested in climbing to the top.) This is the area in which

▲ **Fig. 107.** North nymphaeum and street with water channel at Perga the earliest inhabitants of the site settled, as early as the Bronze Age. During Byzantine times the people of Perga occupied the acropolis once again. There is not much to see on the acropolis today, other than a large vaulted **cistern** on the south side. The acropolis does provide a good view across the entire site of the ancient city of Perga, however.

Pergamum

Pergamum is unquestionably one of the most impressive archaeological sites in all of Turkey. Pergamum's attractions are hard to surpass—the breathtaking view from its theater carved out of the side of the acropolis, the magnificent restored Temple of Trajan, the foundations of the Great Altar of Zeus, the ancient healing center of Asclepius, the Temple of Serapis (the Red Hall), and the archaeological museum. A visit to Pergamum should not be rushed. There is much here to reward the patient visitor who will explore the riches of this ancient city.

Location and History

The site of ancient Pergamum is scattered in and around the modern town of Bergama, located in the western part of Turkey, approximately 65 miles north of Izmir. According to ancient mythology, Pergamum was founded by **Telephus**, king of Asia Minor and the son of Hercules (and thus the grandson of Zeus). Archaeological evidence indicates that Pergamum was settled as early as the 8th century B.C.E. **Xenophon**, the Greek historian who was involved in a mercenary expedition against the Persians, mentions that in 399 B.C.E. he and his soldiers spent some time at Pergamum. Little is known about Pergamum until the Hellenistic period, when Pergamum and all of Asia Minor came under the control of **Alexander the Great**. After the death of Alexander in 323 B.C.E., **Lysimachus**, one of Alexander's generals (the Diadochoi) involved in the struggle for Alexander's kingdom, eventually gained control of all of Asia Minor. He deposited a considerable amount of wealth in the treasury of Pergamum and placed one of his officers, **Philetaerus**, in charge. Philetaerus eventually turned against Lysimachus. After Lysimachus' death, Philetaerus (r. 281–263 B.C.E.) used the money to establish a principality, with Pergamum as its capital. Unmarried (and supposedly a eunuch due to an accident), Philetaerus adopted his nephew **Eumenes I** as his successor. Eumenes I (r. 263–241 B.C.E.) was successful in defeating the Seleucid king **Antiochus I** at Sardis and expanding the rule of Pergamum throughout the Caicus River valley and all the way to the Aegean Sea. Upon his death, he was succeeded by his adopted son **Attalus I Soter** (r. 241–197 B.C.E.). One of the early successes of Attalus was the defeat of the Gauls (or Celts), who had invaded Asia Minor. For this victory, he earned the name Soter (savior) and took the title of king. To safeguard his kingdom from other Hellenistic rulers, Attalus initiated an alliance between Pergamum and Rome. This alliance was continued by the next king, **Eumenes II** (r. 197–159 B.C.E.), the son of Attalus I. Due to this alliance, Eumenes joined forces with the Romans and defeated the Seleucid king, **Antiochus III**, at the battle of Magnesia in 189 B.C.E. As a reward for Eumenes' assistance, the Romans granted most of Asia Minor to his kingdom. The reign of Eumenes II was the zenith of the Pergamene kingdom; during this time, Pergamum became one of the most powerful kingdoms in the region. Renowned for its impressive library, its sculptors, its magnificent buildings, and its Great Altar of Zeus, Pergamum was also one of the leading cultural centers in the Mediterranean world.

At the death of Eumenes II in 159 B.C.E., his brother **Attalus II Philadelphia** (r. 159–138 B.C.E.) became king. He continued the support of art and culture fostered by Eumenes II. One of his most famous accomplishments was the construction of the Stoa of Attalus in the agora of Athens, a structure that has been faithfully reconstructed in modern times in the agora near the Acropolis. (Eumenes II, also, had built a stoa near the Athens Acropolis.) Attalus II was followed by his nephew, **Attalus III Philometor Euergetes** (r. 138–133 B.C.E.), a weak and ineffective ruler. He ruled for only five years before he died. His death ended the Attalid dynasty that had ruled Pergamum for nearly 150 years. In his will he had bequeathed his kingdom to the Romans. Although accepted by the Roman Senate, the bequest of Attalus III was not accepted by all the people of Pergamum. **Aristonicus**, who claimed to be an illegitimate son of Eumenes II (and thus a half brother of Attalus III), laid claim to the throne. He declared all slaves free and led a three-year war against the Romans before he was captured and taken to Rome, where he was executed. In 129 B.C.E., the western part of the former Pergamene kingdom became the Roman province of Asia, while the remaining sections were annexed to various other Roman provinces or territories.

Although declared a free city by Rome, Pergamum did not fare too well initially under Roman rule. The treasure of Attalus was taken to Rome and the people were subjected to heavy taxation. When **Mithradates VI**, the king of Pontus, waged war against Rome (89–84 B.C.E.) and succeeded in conquering all of Asia Minor and Greece, he established Pergamum as one of his capital cities. Pergamum complied with Mithradates' order to put to death all the Romans in the city. When Rome defeated Mithradates, however, the Roman general **Sulla** punished the city. Pergamum lost its independent status, becoming a Roman city, and experienced a period of decline. During the early period of Roman rule, Pergamum possibly served as the capital of the province of Asia, although it was often overshadowed by Ephesus as the leading city of the area. Pergamum, Ephesus, and Smyrna frequently vied vigorously (and bitterly) for honors and bragging rights during the Roman period.

During the 1st century B.C.E., Pergamum began to regain much of its former importance. In 29 B.C.E., the emperor **Augustus** granted permission for the construction in Pergamum of a temple to honor the goddess Roma and the deified Augustus. Although no archaeological evidence of this temple has yet been found, the temple does appear on several coins from ancient Pergamum. By the early 2nd century C.E., Pergamum was again a leading city of Asia Minor. The city experienced growth, both in new buildings and in the geographical boundaries of the city. Under **Trajan** and **Hadrian**, several new buildings were constructed, including the Trajaneum, the Red Hall, and many of the buildings at the Asclepeion. The city also expanded beyond the acropolis and spread out into the area of the modern city of Bergama. The population of Pergamum during the 2nd century has been estimated at 150,000 people.

The 3rd century C.E. saw a decline in Pergamum, although it was apparently still of some significance as a cultural center, as evidenced by the study of philosophy there in 351 by the soon-to-be-emperor **Julian** (r. 361–363). During the 7th and 8th centuries, the city was overrun by the Arabs and never recovered its former importance. In subsequent centuries, Byzantines, Crusaders, Seljuks, and Ottomans ruled the once proud and magnificent city.

Pergamum enjoyed a rich and varied religious history. Temples to Athena, Zeus, Hera, Dionysus, Demeter, and Asclepius were among the many temples situated in the city. In addition, the city was a major center of the imperial cult in Asia Minor. Pergamum was one of the first two cities in the province (the other was Nicomedia) granted the privilege of erecting a temple to Augustus (29 B.C.E.). During the second century, it was once more granted this distinction for the building of a temple to Trajan and Hadrian, becoming the first city in Asia Minor to be twice *neokoros* (temple warden). Even more, the renovation of the Temple of Dionysus and its rededication to the emperor Caracalla meant that Pergamum achieved the unusual honor of being thrice *neokoros*.

A Jewish presence apparently existed in Pergamum at least as early as the 1st century B.C.E., as evidenced by a passage in Cicero (*Pro Flacco* 68) that describes how in 62 B.C.E. the Roman governor **Flaccus** had been accused of confiscating some gold in Pergamum that the Jews had collected to be sent to Jerusalem. By the end of the 1st century C.E., Pergamum contained a Christian community, since the book of Revelation addresses a message to the church at Pergamum (1:11; 2:12–17).

During the second century, the city became the seat of a bishopric. A few remains of several churches have been found at Pergamum, including one in the lower agora, one at the Megalesion, one at the Sanctuary of Athena, and one in the Red Hall. According to Christian tradition, Pergamum was the site of the martyrdom of three faithful Christians: **Carpus, Paylus,** and **Agathonice.** The date for their deaths is uncertain, either during the time of **Marcus Aurelius** (r. 161–180) or the time of **Decius** (r. 249–251).

Biblical Significance

The only specific reference in the Bible to the city of Pergamum occurs in the book of Revelation, written by **John of Patmos**. In the book John sends messages to churches in seven cities of Asia Minor, including the church at Pergamum. The church at Pergamum is both praised and criticized. The church is commended for its Christian faithfulness, even in the face of persecution and martyrdom. John praises one of its members by name, **Antipas**, who died as a martyr for his faith. The church is criticized, however, because it tolerates a group called the Nicolaitans, who "eat food sacrificed to idols and practice fornication" (Rev 2:14). The Nicolaitans, who also were present in Ephesus (and possibly in Thyatira), are an otherwise unknown Christian group whom John considered heretical. Revelation describes Pergamum as the place "where Satan's throne is" (2:13). Readers of Revelation have suggested several possibilities for the identification of "Satan's throne," with the most likely suggestions being the Great Altar, the Asclepeion, or Pergamum as a major center of emperor worship.

Pergamum is mentioned indirectly in 1 Maccabees 8:8, in a passage that describes Roman conquests in the ancient world. After telling of the defeat of Antiochus III by the Romans, the passage states that the Romans took some of the former territories of Antiochus and gave them "to King Eumenes," a reference to Eumenes II of Pergamum and his acquisition of additional lands after the defeat of Antiochus III at Magnesia in 189 B.C.E.

Site Visit

A visit to Pergamum involves four different locations: the **Asclepeion,** the **Bergama Archaeological Museum**, the **Red Hall**, and the **Acropolis**. Each of these is in a different location in and around Bergama and requires payment of a separate entrance fee. Between the Acropolis and the Asclepeion are the remains of the Roman stadium, theater, and amphitheater, all of which are in poor condition and are seldom visited.

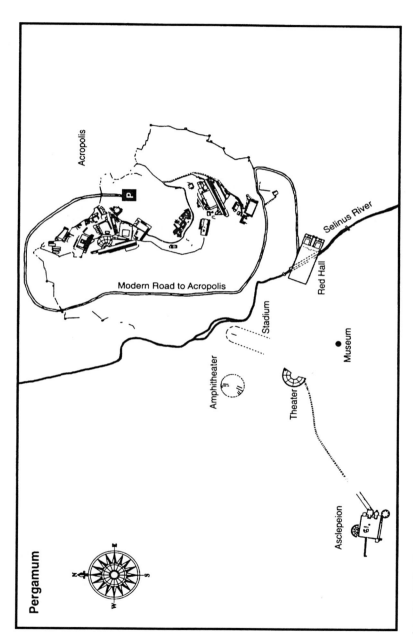

Pergamum

Acropolis

Modern Road to Acropolis

Selinus River

Red Hall

Stadium

Amphitheater

Theater

Museum

Asclepeion

Fig. 108. Pergamum

The Asclepeion

The most famous god of healing in the Greco-Roman world was Asclepius, whose major sanctuary was at Epidaurus in Greece. Other major sanctuaries were on the island of Cos and at Pergamum, with lesser sanctuaries located in numerous cities, including Athens, Corinth, and later in Rome. These sanctuaries usually contained a temple, a well or spring for purifications, and sleeping rooms. They also often included a theater, baths, a gymnasium, and library. Individuals who came for healing sometimes spent weeks at the sanctuary (similar to a modern spa), following prescribed regimens of treatment, rest, and exercise. Visitors to the sanctuaries brought offerings to Asclepius and normally made a thanksgiving gift or offering after being healed, in many cases a small replica of the body part that was healed. The museum in Bergama (as well as the Corinth museum) displays some of these body-part replicas.

The Asclepeion at Pergamum was a popular healing center. Begun during the 4th century B.C.E., the Pergamum Asclepeion reached the height of its popularity during the 2nd century C.E., during which time most of the buildings were built whose ruins are visible today. **Galen**, one of the most important physicians of antiquity, was born in Pergamum in 129 C.E. At the age of sixteen he began the study of medicine with the physicians at the Asclepeion in Pergamum. He continued his medical training at Smyrna, Corinth, and Alexandria. Returning to Pergamum when he was twenty-eight, he served for four years as a physician for a troop of gladiators. He then moved to Rome, where he eventually became the court physician to three of the Roman emperors. The 2nd-century-C.E. orator **Aelius Aristides**, a native of Smyrna who suffered from many ailments (or at least imagined that he did), spent two years at the sanctuary in Pergamum and wrote about his treatment there. In his *Sacred Tales,* he mentions several forms of treatment prescribed for him, either by the god Asclepius or by the physicians at the Asclepeion. Among the treatments he endured were baths in cold water, bloodlettings, fastings, exercises, various medications, and smearing himself with mud.

The entrance to the Pergamum Asclepeion is along the ancient **Sacred Way**, or Via Tecta, a colonnaded street leading to the center of the Asclepeion. The street, paved with large blocks of andesite stone, began in the Roman section of the city at the foot of the Acropolis near the Roman theater and ran about one-half mile to the Asclepeion. Approximately 150 yards of this street near the Asclepeion have been excavated, with some of the columns that once lined the street re-erected. These columns were a part of the stoas that lined both sides of the street. At the eastern end of this excavated section of the street, the visitor can have a good view of the Acropolis. On the northern side of the eastern end of this section are the remains of a **fountain**, built at a later time than the

Pergamum: Asclepeion

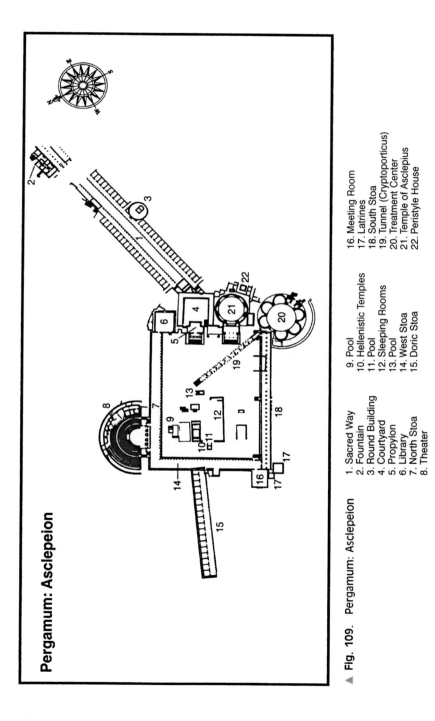

▲ **Fig. 109.** Pergamum: Asclepeion

1. Sacred Way
2. Fountain
3. Round Building
4. Courtyard
5. Propylon
6. Library
7. North Stoa
8. Theater

9. Pool
10. Hellenistic Temples
11. Pool
12. Sleeping Rooms
13. Pool
14. West Stoa
15. Doric Stoa

16. Meeting Room
17. Latrines
18. South Stoa
19. Tunnel (Cryptoporticus)
20. Treatment Center
21. Temple of Asclepius
22. Peristyle House

street. Approximately halfway to the Asclepeion, on the southern side of the street, are the remains of a **small, round building**, believed to be a circular tomb or monument (possibly a heroon) from the time of Augustus.

The Sacred Way ends at a **courtyard** in front of the propylon to the sanctuary. This courtyard was surrounded on three sides by colonnaded stoas whose columns were built in the Corinthian style. In the middle of the courtyard is an **altar to Asclepius** with reliefs of snakes, the symbol of Asclepius. (This altar was discovered outside the sanctuary. This one, or one similar, likely stood in the courtyard.) On the west side of the courtyard was the **propylon**, a large gate with four Corinthian-style columns that served as the entrance to the Asclepeion. This gate was built in the middle of the 2nd century C.E. by **Claudius Charax**, a consul and historian from Pergamum. The pediment over the entranceway contained an inscription stating that Charax had commissioned the construction of the propylon. This pediment now lies on the ground near the location of the propylon.

Stoas surrounded the sanctuary of Asclepius on its northern, southern, and western sides. At the eastern end of the north stoa, to the right of the propylon, is a square building that served both as a **library** and as a shrine to the emperors. (A statue of the naked emperor **Hadrian** was found in this room during excavations. The statue is now in the museum in Bergama.) The niches in the wall originally contained shelves for storing manuscripts. The large niche in the back wall was the location of the statue of Hadrian. The columns of the north stoa are still well preserved. Originally built in the Ionic style, ten of the columns nearest the library had to be replaced when they were destroyed in the earthquake of 175 C.E. The replacement columns, whose capitals combined elements of both Corinthian and Ionic styles, were shorter than the original columns and thus were placed on pedestals.

Behind the western end of the north stoa is the **Roman theater**, which had a seating capacity of 3,500 people. This theater was used for plays, orations, poetry readings, and musical performances for the enjoyment of the patients and visitors at the healing center. The theater had a three-story stage building, the earliest example of a three-tiered stage in Asia Minor. The first three rows in the middle section of the theater were reserved for dignitaries and important members of the audience.

Immediately south of the center of the theater was a **pool** (or **fountain**) used by the patients for bathing. Built during the Roman period and constructed of marble, this pool was not roofed. South of this pool are the traces of three small **Hellenistic temples** dedicated to Asclepius Soter, Apollo Kalliteknos, and Hygieia (daughter of Asclepius). A **shrine** dedicated to Telesphorus, the youthful god who was associated with Asclepius, was supposedly located here also. Further south and in front of the west stoa was another **pool**. Carved out of rock and originally roofed over, this pool was apparently used for mud bath treatments. A third **pool**, dated to the Hellenistic period, was located adjacent to the west side of the entrance to the tunnel. Water from the Sacred Spring flowed into this pool from a pipe. This pool, built of andesite and roofed, was used not for bathing, but only for drinking. The **Sacred Spring**, whose water was thought to have curative effects, was located nearby.

Southwest of the Hellenistic pool were the **sleeping rooms** (incubation rooms), which functioned as part of the medical treatment at the center. Here the patients would sleep in expectation of a visit from Asclepius in their dreams. The visit from Asclepius would cure the patient or would prescribe a treatment for the patient. Sometimes the message clearly stated the treatment; at other times, the message needed interpre-

▲ **Fig. 110.** Altar to Asclepius with reliefs of snakes at Pergamum

tation by the priests or physicians, who prescribed the necessary treatment. Treatment often consisted of baths in cold or hot water, exercises, mud baths, massages, special diets, colonic irrigation, and the use of herbs and ointments.

Behind the west stoa of the sanctuary was a colonnade built in the Doric style. The entrance to this **Doric stoa** was through a door located approximately at the midpoint of the west stoa. The Doric stoa, which ran from the west stoa in a southwesterly direction, was close to 400 feet long. Behind the columns along its northern side were several rooms, which were perhaps used as shops. Often missed by visitors to the site, the excavated ruins of the stoa/agora are worth a visit. Remains of a **Hellenistic gymnasium** have been uncovered south of the Doric stoa.

The **south stoa** of the sanctuary was built over a basement because the ground level was lower on this side. The stoa has not survived. Visible today are the remains of the basement with some of the pillars that supported the stoa. In addition to serving as a support for the south stoa, the basement was used also as an additional sleeping area for patients at the center, as indicated by the remains of a low stone bench running around the walls. At the corner of the south and west stoas are the remains of two **latrines**. The larger and more elaborate one (seating for forty people) was for the men. It had a marble floor and marble seats. In the center of the room were four Corinthian columns supporting the roof, which contained openings for light and ventilation. The smaller, plainer toilet (seating seventeen people) was for the women. Adjacent to the women's toilet on the north was a **room probably used for meetings**.

A 260-foot-long vaulted **tunnel** (or cryptoporticus) built during Roman times connects the central area of the sanctuary to a round building in the southeast corner of the sanctuary. The roof of the tunnel contains openings for sunlight and ventilation. In addition to serving as a passageway, the tunnel also would have provided a cool place to gather for relief from the summer heat. The round building, originally two stories, was built during the 2nd century C.E. and possibly served as a **treatment center**, although its exact usage is not known. The upper story is missing, but the lower part of the building is rather well preserved. The upper story consisted of a circular room surrounded by six apses. These apses were lower than the main part of the building, which had a wooden roof. The upper story, which was the main part of the building, was reached by two staircases (still visible) at the southern end of the edifice, one at the south and the other at the southeast end of the building. It has been suggested that the paved area, or terrace, in front of these stairs served as a place for the patients to enjoy sun and fresh air. The lower floor, or basement, which can be seen today, is divided into two concentric circles by a ring of stone pillars. At the base of some of these pillars are recessed water troughs used for drinking or bathing.

North of the treatment center (between the treatment center and the courtyard of the propylon) was the **Temple of Asclepius**, the most important temple of the sanctuary. Only the base of this temple remains today. The temple, built in 150 C.E. as a gift from the Roman consul **Lucius Rufinus**, was a circular building, smaller than, but modeled after, the Pantheon in Rome. The domed roof of the temple was 78 feet in diameter and contained a hole in the center for illumination. The colonnaded entrance to the temple was on the west, reached by a flight of steps from the central courtyard. Remains of the steps and column bases can still be seen. Inside, the floor and walls of the temple were decorated with marble mosaics. Around the interior wall were seven alternating round and rectangular niches containing statues of healing gods. The niche opposite the entrance contained a statue of Asclepius. Adjacent to the Temple of Asclepius on its southeast are the remains of a small **peristyle house** (that is, the house was built around a courtyard surrounded by columns).

Bergama Museum

Archaeological discoveries from ancient Pergamum and the surrounding area are housed in the Bergama Museum, which was founded in 1936.

▲ **Fig. 111.** Relief of Demeter from the Sanctuary of Demeter at Pergamum, now in the Bergama Museum

The museum is well maintained and the artifacts usually have good descriptions in Turkish and in English. Various stone architectural pieces (column sections, capitals, friezes), grave stelae, and sarcophagi are displayed in the garden courtyard at the entrance to the museum. Among the many noteworthy items on display inside the museum are the following: a **statue of Hadrian** from the library in the Pergamum Asclepeion; a **3rd-century-c.e. mosaic floor** depicting the head of Medusa from the lower city of Pergamum; a display case containing **medical instruments** and various **votive offerings** and **offerings of thanksgiving to Asclepius** in gratitude for healing, several of which are replicas of body parts; a display case with an assortment of Hellenistic and Roman jewelry; a 2nd-century-c.e. **statue of Nike** that was part of the ornaments of the propylon of the Asclepeion; a **model of the Great Altar of Zeus**; some excellent 1st-century-c.e. marble reliefs from the heroon of the gymnasium of the middle acropolis, including **reliefs of a helmet, one with a lance and sword**, and **one with a victorious rooster with a palm branch**; a **relief from the Sanctuary of Demeter** on the middle acropolis, depicting Demeter standing by the altar holding a torch in one hand with a tethered sacrificial animal at her side; a **stele from the Red Hall** with scenes of gladiators fighting wild animals; and a **Roman-period altar** with a relief of an eagle.

Red Hall

In the modern town of Bergama lie the remains of the **Red Hall**, or Red Court, so called because this building is built of red bricks. Originally the building was faced with marble, portions of which can still be seen on the upper part of the building. The **Red Hall** is flanked on each side by two circular buildings, which, like the Red Hall, were temples. These buildings, along with the large courtyard in front, formed a temple complex devoted to the worship of the Egyptian gods. Constructed during the first half of the 2nd century c.e., the Red Hall was dedicated to either Serapis or Isis. For this reason, the building is sometimes called the **Temple of Serapis** (or the Serapeion). Various suggestions have been made for the deities to whom the two towers may have been dedicated— Harpocrates, Isis, Osiris, Horus, or Anubis.

The main structure, the red-brick building, was a large hall, approximately 197 feet long by 85 feet wide. The inside of the hall was divided into two sections by a water channel that ran north to south. The western part of the hall contained five windows on each side of its upper story. This part of the building was open to the public. A shallow water basin, approximately 17 feet wide, ran parallel to the water channel at the eastern end of the western section. Inside the basin were three rectangular marble tubs. This water basin was probably used for purification rituals. Along the walls of the north and south walls of the western section were five niches each. A niche was also located on each side of the entrance door of the western wall. These twelve niches probably held statues of various gods.

The eastern part of the hall, which contained no windows (unless the now destroyed eastern wall contained windows), was restricted to the priests. The eastern part was filled by a large podium, 5 feet high and 29 feet wide. On the podium was a large statue, estimated to have been at least 33 feet tall. The base of the statue is still visible. In the center of the base is a hole about 5 feet square, indicating that the statue was hollow. Priests would enter the hollow statue from the base and deliver messages to the people as if the statue were speaking. Access to the interior of the statue was gained from a tunnel system that connected the main hall to the two side towers. A staircase located just north of the statue, as well as a staircase outside the south wall of the Red Hall, allowed entrance to the tunnels. A gallery ran along both the north and south walls, supported by four columns on each side. The eastern wall of the Red Hall was straight on the inside but was originally convex in shape on the outside, forming a large outside niche. When the Red Hall was converted into a Christian basilica dedicated to St. John the Apostle (likely during the 5th century), the eastern wall was destroyed and replaced with an apse. At the same time, the level of the floor was raised and two rows of columns were added to the interior of the Red Hall (the foundations of the columns are

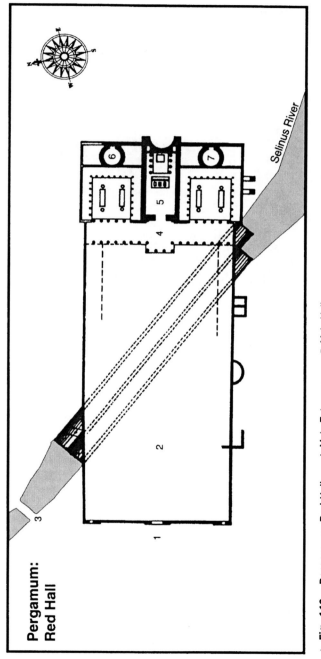

Pergamum:
Red Hall

▲ **Fig. 112.** Pergamum: Red Hall

1. Main Entrance
2. Courtyard
3. Roman Bridge
4. Portico

5. Main Hall
6. North Tower-Temple
7. South Tower-Temple

Selinus River

▲ **Fig. 113.** The Red Hall (Temple of Serapis) of Pergamum

still visible), creating a nave and two side aisles. Above the side aisles was a balcony around the interior of the building.

The **twin towers** on the north and south sides of the Red Hall were round temples. These buildings, rather well preserved, are built of brick and were originally covered with marble. The buildings are approximately 64 feet high, with an inner diameter of 39.5 feet. The towers were not freestanding but were connected to the Red Hall by walls and court-yards. The north tower is now used as a mosque, having earlier served as a church. The south tower is used today for storage, having also func-tioned as a church earlier. In front of each of the towers was a courtyard, surrounded by stoas. The supports for these stoas were *atlantes* (col-umns shaped like male figures) and caryatids (columns shaped like fe-male figures). Each column had two figures back to back. In some cases both figures were female; in other cases one was male and one was fe-male. In both of the side courtyards are two elongated water basins, ap-proximately 3 feet deep. Small circular basins are situated at the ends of each of the rectangular basins. Portions of these basins are still visible. At the western end of the courtyards, the stoas were connected to a **large portico** that ran the entire width of the sanctuary complex in front of the tower courtyards and the Red Hall. In the center of this large portico, which separated the temple buildings from the main courtyard, was the huge propylon of the Red Hall, whose four columns were 46 feet tall.

In front (to the west) of the entire complex of buildings and the large portico was a large **courtyard**, measuring approximately 650 feet long by 325 feet wide. The courtyard was surrounded by a wall at least 43 feet high. The main entrance to the sanctuary was through a large door in the center of the western wall of the courtyard, as well as through a smaller door on each side of the central one. Colonnades probably ran along the interior walls of the courtyard. In ancient times, as today, the Selinus River (today known as the Bergama Çayï) ran diagonally underneath the courtyard through two vaulted tunnels. Portions of the ancient courtyard are covered by modern houses and other buildings.

The Acropolis

Signs in the city of Bergama indicate the road that leads up the steep mountain to the **acropolis** of Pergamum. Atop this mountain is the site of the oldest part of Pergamum, the ancient Hellenistic city. With the exception of the temple to Trajan, as well as some additions or alterations of other structures, the buildings on the acropolis date to the Hellenistic period. The drive to the acropolis offers some splendid views of the Red Hall, the ancient aqueducts, and the area of the Roman stadium, theater, and amphitheater. The archaeological remains of the ancient city spill down the mountainside, grouped into three areas: the **upper acropolis**, the **middle acropolis**, and the **lower acropolis**. Most visitors to the acropolis make a tour of the upper acropolis only. If time allows, however, all three areas should be visited. The best way to see all three areas is to start at the upper acropolis, work one's way down the mountainside, and arrange to be picked up on the side of the road near the lower acropolis.

Upper Acropolis

Entrance to the upper acropolis is along a path that leads from the parking lot through the gate of the ancient city wall. On the left, prior to the entrance gate, is a **heroon** (a shrine honoring a deified hero) built to honor the Pergamene kings, especially **Attalus I** and **Eumenes II**. The heroon consisted of a peristyle courtyard (that is, surrounded by columns), an entrance hall northeast of the courtyard, and a cult room adjoining the hall on the northeast. Immediately west of the heroon was a row of **shops** or **storage rooms** from the Hellenistic period. In antiquity the main street to the upper acropolis ran between the heroon and the row of shops, leading to a large **gate**. Inside the gate, on each side were rooms for the guards stationed at the gate. To the left of this entryway stood the **propylon** that was the entrance to the **Sanctuary of Athena**.

Ahead and to the right are the remains of several **residential buildings** and other buildings from the Hellenistic period. Many of these buildings were built in the peristyle plan, that is, with various rooms constructed

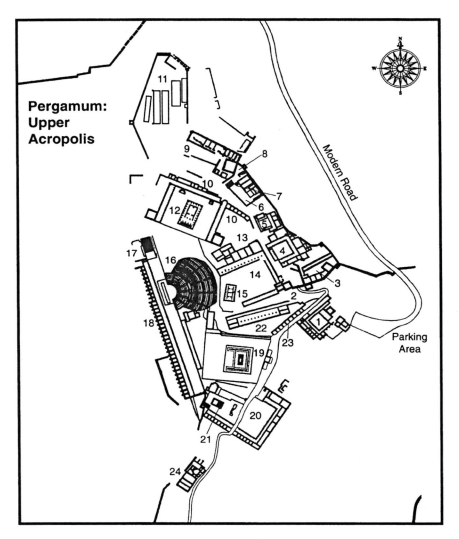

▲ Fig. 114. Pergamum: Upper Acropolis

1. Heroon
2. City Gate
3. Building Group VI
4. Palace V
5. Palace IV
6. Palace III
7. Cistern
8. Palace II
9. Palace I (Barracks)

10. Shops
11. Arsenals
12. Temple of Trajan
13. Library
14. Sanctuary of Athena
15. Temple of Athena
16. Theater
17. Temple of Dionysus

18. Stoa
19. Great Altar of Zeus
20. Upper Agora
21. Temple of Zeus
22. Late Hellenistic Stoa
23. Hellenistic Storage Rooms/Shops
24. Roman Bath

around a colonnaded courtyard. Identification of these buildings is uncertain, although some of them have often been considered to be **palaces** of the ancient Pergamene kings, specifically residences of Eumenes II, Attalus I, Attalus II, and Philetaerus. The dating of Palace V, a peristyle building at the southern end assigned to Eumenes II, is the most certain, based on a floor mosaic and some stone fragments related to the Great Altar of Zeus (built by Eumenes II), all of which were discovered in the palace. South of Palace V were the quarters for the guards at the gate and sleeping rooms for soldiers, as well as an arsenal. The northernmost of the residences/palaces (supposedly the palace of Philetaerus) was converted into a barracks during the Hellenistic age. Near the highest point of the citadel (today occupied by a fire lookout tower) is a **circular cistern**.

To the west of the residential buildings, along the backside of the Trajan Temple and down to the east end of the library, was a row of **shops** during the Hellenistic and Roman periods. On the eastern side of the citadel, behind the residences, can be seen the remains of the **Hellenistic city wall**. A path through the wall at its northern end (behind the barracks) leads down to the remains of five long, parallel buildings that served as **arsenals**. Found in the arsenals were a variety of round andesite stones weighing between 6 pounds and 166 pounds. These stones, now stored in the lower agora, were for launching from catapults. The arsenals were located at the northern edge of the acropolis. It is easy to see why the arsenals were located here, for this location provides a spectacular view over the region below. From this vantage point, it is possible to see the ruins of the Roman amphitheater, the Asclepeion, and part of the Roman aqueduct that brought water to Pergamum for a distance of 28 miles from Mt. Pindasos (Madra Dağ) in the north.

From the arsenals, proceed back to the citadel and explore the reconstructed remains of the **Temple of Trajan**, or **Trajaneum**. Whereas many of the Hellenistic buildings on the acropolis were renovated and used by the Romans, the Temple of Trajan is the only truly Roman building on the acropolis. Whatever buildings stood here earlier, the Romans removed them and made the area level by building a terrace partly supported by arches and vaults. The Temple of Trajan was begun during the reign of Trajan (r. 98–117) and completed during the reign of Hadrian (r. 117–138). Both of the emperors were worshiped in the temple, as is evidenced by remains (heads and fragments of other body parts) of colossal statues of the two emperors that excavators found in the ruins of the temple. The temple was also dedicated to Zeus and contained a large seated statue of Zeus. The terrace of the temple was a paved platform 189 feet by 217 feet. Stoas enclosed the terrace on the east, west, and north sides. The temple building itself stood in the middle of the terrace platform. It was a peristyle temple in the Corinthian order, measuring 105 feet by 65.5 feet. Nine columns lined the two longer sides, while six columns lined

▲ Fig. 115. Artist's rendering of the upper acropolis as seen from the west in the lower city (after Bohn and Koch. 1886)

each of the two shorter sides. The German archaeological team that excavated and reconstructed the Trajaneum has erected several helpful signs around the site with descriptions and sketches of the temple complex.

Exiting the Trajaneum at steps on the southeast, one enters the area where there are remains of some **houses** from Hellenistic times. East of these houses is the supposed site of the famous **library** at Pergamum, built during the time of Eumenes II. This library, the second largest in the ancient world (after the library at Alexandria), reportedly contained over 200,000 volumes. Pliny the Elder (*Natural History* 13.21) recounts the story from Marcus Varro that, due to rivalry between Ptolemy of Egypt and Eumenes II over the Alexandrian and Pergamene libraries, Ptolemy prohibited the export of papyrus to Pergamum. As a result, the people of Pergamum invented the use of parchment (animal skins) for a writing surface. Although often repeated, the story is apparently untrue, since parchment had been used for many years elsewhere in Asia Minor and in Egypt. Pergamum did, however, lend its name to this writing material, for the English word *parchment* is actually derived from the Greek word for Pergamum.

The library consisted of four rooms, the largest of which possibly served as the reading hall. This room, located on the eastern side, was approximately 44.5 feet by 52 feet. On the north and east walls of this room is a horizontal row of holes. The suggestion has been made that these holes were for brackets to support bookcases holding the library books. The cases were not attached directly to the walls, however. A space of approximately 20 inches separated the bookcases from the wall. About 20 inches out from the wall is a three-foot wide foundation upon which the bookcases rested, attached by supports to the walls. The purpose of this gap between the bookcases and the walls was to protect the books from damage from moisture. The books were made of papyrus or parchment, rolled into scrolls or folded flat, and stored on the shelves. These shelves would have held fewer than 20,000 volumes, not the reported 200,000 volumes. The remainder of the works must have been stored elsewhere.

In front of the north wall in the reading room was a large **statue of Athena** (10 feet tall), modeled after the colossal Athena statue that stood in the Parthenon in Athens. Discovered in the front of the reading room, the Pergamum Athena statue is now in the Staatliche Museum in Berlin. The entrance to the library was on the south, by way of the second floor of the north stoa of the Sanctuary of Athena.

The eventual fate of the Pergamum library is unknown. Plutarch (*Antony* 58.9–59.1) recounts the story that Mark Antony gave the entire Pergamum library collection to Cleopatra, but whether he actually did so is doubtful. Even Plutarch seems to be dubious of the story.

The **Sanctuary of Athena** was located on the broad terrace south of the library. At the west end of the sanctuary was the **Temple of Athena**. Built in the 3rd century B.C.E., the temple was a Doric temple with six columns at both ends and ten columns along both sides. Today only portions of the foundation of the temple remain. At the southeastern end of the terrace was the entrance to the sanctuary, a beautiful two-story **propylon** built by Eumenes II. All that remain at the site today of this gateway are portions of the foundation. The Greek inscription on the propylon read, "King Eumenes to Athena bearer of victory." The restored propylon is now in the Staatliche Museum in Berlin. Two-story stoas surrounded the sanctuary on the north, east, and south sides. The stoas, along with the propylon, were later additions to the sanctuary, having been added in the 2nd century B.C.E. Portions of some of the columns from the stoas can be seen at the site. In the interior of the sanctuary were displayed several bronze statues, the most famous being the so-called **Dying Gaul**, a marble copy of which is now in the Capitoline Museum in Rome. The circular marble base in the center of the sanctuary was the base for a statue. It is thought that a statue of Athena at one time stood on this base but was replaced in Roman times by a bronze statue of the emperor Augustus.

At the western end of the terrace are remains of a **Byzantine tower**. Beside it are steps leading down to the Pergamum **theater**. One of the most spectacular buildings at Pergamum, the theater was originally built during the 3rd century B.C.E., enhanced by Eumenes II, and modified again by the Romans. Situated on the steep hillside, the theater would

▲ **Fig. 116.** Theater on the upper acropolis of Pergamum

have provided its patrons with a spectacular view across the city and the plain while they watched the theater performances. Today, even without the impressive theater buildings, the view from the seats is still breathtaking. The theater has eighty rows of seats, divided into three sections, with a total seating capacity of approximately 10,000 persons. The marble seat for the king was located just above the center of the lower tier of seats. The stage building, or *skene,* was a portable structure built of wood. It was set up on the theater terrace (which was also the road to the Temple of Dionysus) for a production but taken down when not in use so as not to obstruct the view over the plain nor the front view of the **Temple of Dionysus**. This temple, located at the northern end of the terrace, was originally built of andesite during the 2nd century B.C.E. The Roman emperor **Caracalla** (r. 211–217 C.E.) rebuilt the structure in marble. (The building then was used for the worship of Caracalla, seen as the "new Dionysus.") The temple, with an elaborate entrance of twenty-five steps, was built in the Ionic style. In front of the temple was the altar. Much of the remains of the lower part of the temple, including the stepped entrance, can still be seen.

The terrace extended south from the temple for a distance of over 800 feet, passing in front of the theater and ending in a double-arched gateway. Running the length of the western side of the terrace was a **long stoa**. On the eastern side of the terrace a **short stoa** ran between the theater and the gateway. The building between the theater and the east stoa perhaps was used by the performers. This terrace with its stoas, the temple to Dionysus, and the theater not only was a spectacular sight, but also would have been a pleasant promenade on which to stroll and socialize.

▲ **Fig. 117.** Site of the Great Altar of Zeus at Pergamum

After exploring the terrace, climb back up the theater and exit the theater about midway on its southern side. A path leads to the **Great Altar of Zeus**, which is located on a terrace that is south of the Temple of Athena. (Between the Altar of Zeus and the Temple of Athena are the remains of a **stoa** from the Hellenistic period.) All that is left on the site of the Great Altar of Zeus is its five-stepped base. The altar, which was probably dedicated to both Zeus and Athena, was destroyed during the Byzantine period and parts of it used in the construction of a fortification wall and for the building of houses. In the late 1800s, German archaeologists excavating Pergamum recovered a large number of the pieces of the altar and transported them back to Germany, where the altar was reconstructed. Today it is on display in the Staatliche Museum in Berlin (formerly the Pergamum Museum). Dedicated to Zeus and Athena, the construction of the altar was begun by Eumenes II and completed by his successor, Attalus II, in the early 150s B.C.E. The base of the altar was approximately 120 feet by 112 feet. On top of this five-stepped base (or crepidoma) was a large platform that extended along the north, east, and south sides. On the west side was a broad flight of marble stairs that led to the upper part of the structure. Running around the midsection of this platform was a relief frieze that depicted the mythological battle between the giants and the Greek gods. This frieze contains more than one hundred larger-than-life-size figures. A colonnaded stoa ran along the top of the platform and across the top of the stairs, thus creating an open court in the middle of the structure. The altar for burnt offerings was in the middle of the court. Another frieze on a wall inside this court depicted the story of Telephus, the son of Hercules and the legendary founder of Pergamum.

Immediately south of the Great Altar was the city's **upper agora**, or market, which was partially surrounded by Doric stoas. In the western portion of the agora, which would have contained numerous shops and storerooms, stood a small **temple to Zeus**. Dated to the reign of Attalus I (241–197 B.C.E.), the temple's foundation is all that remains today. Immediately north of this temple are the remains of an **unidentified building** from the Roman period. The main street to Pergamum ran from the southeast to the northwest through the agora and eventually to the gate of the citadel, or upper acropolis. Visitors who do not wish to visit the middle or lower parts of the acropolis may follow the ancient street and return to the parking lot. The street, which is like a ramp, passes east of the Great Altar and runs between the heroon on the right and the remains of a row of **Hellenistic storage rooms** on the left. At the place where the street leaves the northern end of the agora is located the **grave of Carl Humann**, the German archaeologist who discovered and excavated the Great Altar. The grave, marked by a plain granite slab, is located on the east side of the street.

▲ **Fig. 118.** Model of the Great Altar of Zeus in the Bergama Museum

Middle Acropolis

To visit the **middle acropolis**, proceed south along the main street from the upper agora. The remains of a **Roman bath** are located on the west side of the street, approximately 100 yards south of the upper agora. Further along the street, on the left, is a **small gymnasium complex**, consisting of a **bath**, an **odeion**, and a **cult hall** (heroon). A side street coming down the hill from the north runs along the western side of the bath and connects to the main street. On the west side of the side street, a few yards north of the main street, are the ruins of a **latrine**, which was associated with the baths. The entrance to the **bath** was from the main street. A courtyard, whose columns have been re-erected, served as a **palaestra**, or exercise yard. The semicircular niche in the northern wall was the frigidarium (cold-water pool). The circular room south of the courtyard was the sudatorium, or sweat room. Between the bath and the odeion are three small rooms, which may have served as a pantry and a kitchen for meals for the heroon.

The odeion and the heroon have been partially restored under a modern shelter by archaeologists. The **odeion**, with its concentric rows of seats, was likely used for performances and meetings. The **heroon** was a cult hall in honor of **Diodorus Pasparos**, an early-1st-century-B.C.E. citizen and benefactor of Pergamum who was deified during his lifetime. (The heroon is sometimes called the "marble room" because the walls

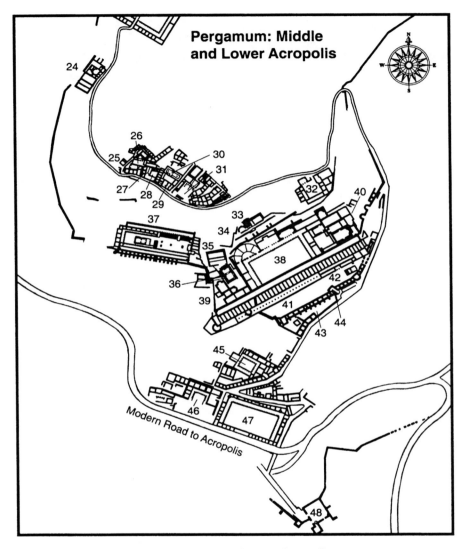

▲ **Fig. 119.** Pergamum: Middle and Lower Acropolis

24. Roman Bath
25. Latrine
26. Bath
27. Odeion
28. Heroon
29. Restaurants/Shops
30. Podium Hall
31. Peristyle House
32. Peristyle Structure
   (Megalesion ?)

33. Sanctuary of Hera
34. Prytaneion
35. Meeting House
36. Temple of Asclepius
37. Sanctuary of
   Demeter
38. Upper Gymnasium
39. West Bath
40. East Bath

41. Middle Gymnasium
42. Temple and Altar
43. Lower Gymnasium
44. Vaulted Staircase
45. House of Attalus
46. Peristyle House
47. Lower Agora
48. Gate of Eumenes

and floor were covered with marble.) During the excavations of the heroon, archaeologists found the marble portrait head of Diodorus and several marble relief wall decorations. Replicas of the portrait head and reliefs are located at the site; the originals are in the Bergama Museum. The reliefs include a lance and sword, a victorious rooster with a palm branch, a helmet and star, and a phallus (symbol of fertility and abundance). The latter, carved on a stone block, has been incorporated into one of the walls of the modern shelter.

To the right of the heroon was a **small dining hall or restaurant**, containing the remains of an oven and a grill. Adjacent to the dining hall was another **restaurant** or a **shop**. Next was a **wine or oil shop**. Holes in the floor (and probably in counters) held pithoi (clay jars) for the storage of wine or oil. A narrow staircase along the eastern wall of the wine or oil shop leads to an upper terrace, where a large hall stood that was used for the worship of Dionysus. This hall is called the **Podium Hall** because of the podium (8 feet wide, 3 feet tall) that lined the interior walls. Worshipers of Dionysus reclined on the podium, sharing sacred meals. The niche in the northern wall, opposite the entrance to the hall, was for a statue of Dionysus. In use from the 2nd to the 4th centuries c.e., the hall would have been used for banquets and other festivities related to the cult of Dionysus. East of the Podium Hall are the partial remains of a **peristyle house** with a bath. Portions of some of the re-erected columns of the house are in place. Ruins of various shops, workrooms, and residential buildings are on both sides of the main street. The restored arch on the left belonged to a **fountain or public water house**.

Farther along on the main street, on the right, are the ruins of a large peristyle structure that is possibly the **Megalesion** where the goddess Cybele, the Great Mother, was worshiped. (During the Byzantine period, the temple was destroyed and replaced with a Christian church.) Just beyond this structure, the path leaves the main street and turns back west, following a small street that leads to the **Sanctuary of Hera** (wife of Zeus), located on a narrow terrace. The **Temple of Hera**, built during the 2nd century B.C.E., faced south. The wide flight of twelve steps, flanked on the left by an exedra (semicircular recess) and on the right by a stoa, led to the temple. (The marble **altar** in the exedra is an altar to the Anatolian god Men. It does not belong in this location, but was moved here after being excavated elsewhere on the site.) The altar to Hera was situated on a lower terrace. This area provides a great view over the Demeter sanctuary and the upper gymnasium.

Immediately to the left of the Hera sanctuary are the scant remains of a building that may have been the **prytaneion**, or city hall, of Pergamum. Southwest of these ruins stood a building that possibly functioned as a **meeting hall**, perhaps connected with the cult of Dionysus. South of this building are the remains of a structure believed to have been a **temple to Asclepius,** although scholars disagree over the identification of this building. From here, continue to the west to the temenos of the **Sanctuary of Demeter,** passing through the **propylon** and down a flight of steps. Two of the columns of this entrance to the temenos have been re-erected. At the western end of the temenos, which was surrounded on three sides by stoas, was situated the **Temple of Demeter,** whose foundation can still be seen. In front of the eastern portion of the north stoa were ten rows of seats used by the worshipers during festivals and other ceremonies at the sanctuary. The temenos contained five **altars,** the largest of which has been partially restored. Only the foundations of the other four altars still exist. One of the major Demeter festivals was the Thesmophoria, an agrarian festival celebrating fertility, nurturing, and growth. This festival, as with much of the Demeter cult, was for women; men were not allowed to participate in the festival. The festival involved a reenactment (through sacrifices, ritual washings, and feastings) of the story of the abduction by Hades (the god of the underworld) of Demeter's daughter Kore (or Persephone), her being carried off to the underworld, and her eventual return.

One of the largest structures in the middle city was the **gymnasium complex,** located on three different terraces. The three parts of the complex—the **upper, middle, and lower gymnasiums**—were built during Hellenistic times and altered during Roman times, with the upper gymnasium experiencing the most renovation. The upper gymnasium was reserved for young men, the middle for adolescent boys, and the lower for children. The upper gymnasium was the largest, containing a large courtyard (used for exercises and games) surrounded by stoas. On each end of the courtyard was a **bath complex.** In the northwestern corner was a **small theater,** or **odeion,** with a seating capacity of one thousand persons, likely used for lectures and musical concerts. In the middle of the north stoa was a room called the *ephebeion,* where important ceremonies related to the gymnasium were held. The room to the northeast of the *ephebeion,* according to inscriptions found here, was reserved for the Roman emperor whenever he would visit the city. Originally decorated with marble, the room has an apse at each end. The south stoa of the upper gymnasium has not survived. Underneath it was a long track, sometimes called the Basement Stadium, used for races and athletic events.

Below the upper gymnasium is the **middle gymnasium,** built on a separate, smaller terrace. The middle gymnasium consisted of a courtyard used for races, exercising, and other athletic events, as well as a Corinthian-style stoa along the length of its northern side. At the east end of the courtyard are the remains of a **small temple and altar,** which were dedicated to Hermes and Hercules. A **vaulted staircase** at the east end of the courtyard leads from the middle gymnasium down to the next terrace, on which the even smaller **lower gymnasium** was located. This architecturally interesting staircase, like the gymnasium complex, was built during the Hellenistic period. (The adjacent stone tower is from the Byzantine period.) East of the staircase was a rectangular **public fountain**. The lower terrace, approximately 262 feet long, is irregularly shaped. Portions of the north wall of the lower gymnasium are still present. This wall was constructed as a retaining wall to buttress the middle terrace.

Lower Acropolis

The ancient street leading from the lower gymnasium (approximately 16 feet wide) is paved with large andesite blocks, in many of which can be seen grooves worn into them from ancient chariot and wagon wheels. On the right, at the point where the street, running southwest down the mountain, makes a more westward turn, are the ruins of several **shops**. Behind these stood the **house of the consul Attalus**. This peristyle house, with two stories and a central courtyard, was built during the Hellenistic period and altered during the Roman period. The house contained murals on the walls and mosaic floors, some of which can still be seen. A roof has been constructed to protect wall paintings and mosaics. The street continues through an area with several **shops** and **houses**, including another **peristyle house**. The modern buildings located here are used as offices and storerooms for the German archaeologists working at the site.

East of this area is the **lower agora**, which was surrounded on all sides by two-story stoas. (The south stoa had three stories. A lower story was necessary due to the slope of the terrain.) Shops were situated behind the columns of the stoas. The central area of the agora was paved and contained a fountain whose water was supplied by pipes from the large cistern in the courtyard of the house of Attalus. Inscribed tablets found in the agora, which were originally displayed there, contained rules and regulations related to the construction of roads, fountains, drains, and houses of Pergamum. An excellent marble head of Alexander the Great, dating to the 3rd or 2nd century B.C.E., was found in the northwest part of the courtyard of the agora. It is now on display in the Istanbul Archaeological Museum. Today the lower agora is used to store the collection of stone missiles (intended to be shot from catapults) that were found in the arsenals on the upper acropolis. A small church was built in the courtyard of the agora during Byzantine times. The ancient road continued around the north and east of the agora and led southeast to the **Gate of Eumenes**, part of the city wall built by Eumenes II. The gate is down the hill and across the modern highway from the agora.

Philadelphia

The ancient city of Philadelphia is primarily remembered as one of the seven cities mentioned in the book of Revelation. Because the city was in an earthquake-prone area, not much remains to be seen of ancient Philadelphia. What might still exist lies buried, for the most part, under the modern city.

Location and History

Situated approximately 30 miles southeast of the site of ancient Sardis on highway 585, Alaşehir is the name of the modern city located on the site of ancient Philadelphia. Philadelphia was on a plateau in the Cogamus River valley (today the Alaşehir Çayï), a tributary of the Hermus River. In antiquity, the Persian Royal Road from Sardis to Susa (in modern Iran) ran through Philadelphia. Prior to the Hellenistic founding of the city of Philadelphia, an earlier settlement here was known as Calletebus, dating back several centuries. The city was named for **Attalus II Philadelphus**, the Attalid king of Pergamum from 159 to 138 B.C.E., whose loyalty to his brother **Eumenes II Soter**, who preceded him as king (r. 197–159 B.C.E.), earned him the nickname "Philadelphus," meaning "brotherly love." Either Eumenes or Attalus founded the city, which was in the Lydian region of ancient Anatolia. After **Attalus III** (r. 138–133 B.C.E.) bequeathed the Pergamene kingdom to the Romans in 133 B.C.E., Philadelphia came under Roman control.

The area around Philadelphia was a fertile agricultural area, especially good for growing grapes. Unfortunately, the area was also susceptible to frequent earthquakes. A particularly devastating earthquake struck the area in 17 C.E., destroying the city of Sardis and doing extensive damage to Philadelphia. To help the city recover from this disaster, **Emperor Tiberius** remitted the tribute owed to Rome for a period of five years. In gratitude, Philadelphia took the name Neocaesarea and dedicated a temple to Tiberius. Although the city was slow to recover from the devastation caused by the earthquake and its aftershocks, it eventually prospered under Roman rule. By the 5th century it was sometimes referred to as "little Athens" because of its many temples and religious festivals. Evidence of the city's continued existence during Byzantine times is seen in the remains of the city wall and church from this period. In 1391 the Ottoman Turks conquered Philadelphia, the last Byzantine city in Asia Minor to fall to the Turks.

Because of the importance of grapes and wine production in Philadelphia, the principal god worshiped at Philadelphia was Dionysus. Christianity took root there before the end of the 1st century, as evidenced by the church in the city being one of the churches addressed in the book of Revelation. Early in the 2nd century, **Ignatius**, bishop of Antioch in Syria, passed through Philadelphia as a prisoner on his way to his martyrdom in Rome. Farther along on his journey, while at Troas, he wrote a letter to the church at Philadelphia encouraging the people to remain united and to support their bishop and other church leaders. Later (ca. 155 C.E.), when **Polycarp** of Smyrna was martyred, some members of the church at Philadelphia were martyred at the same time. Although no direct evidence exists of Jewish inhabitants of Philadelphia in Hellenistic and Roman times, the book of Revelation gives indirect evidence. The Christians at Philadelphia had apparently been suffering in some way from the hands of the Jewish community in Philadelphia, a group that John describes pejoratively as "those of the synagogue of Satan who say that they are Jews and are not" (3:9).

Biblical Significance

One of the seven churches addressed in the book of Revelation, the church in Philadelphia was one of only two churches to receive praise and not condemnation. (The other church was in Smyrna.) The church was praised for its faithfulness to Christ. **John** reported the words of Christ to the church: "I know that you have but little power, and yet you have kept my word and have not denied my name. . . . Because you have kept my word of patient endurance, I will keep you from the hour of trial that is coming on the whole world to test the inhabitants of the earth" (3:8, 10). Christ promised the faithful Christians at Philadelphia that he would "make them a pillar in the temple of my God" (3:12). Being a pillar in the temple of God is a metaphor for a place of honor and security in the presence of God. As a pillar represents a firm support for a building, John assured the faithful that their presence among God's people was firm and secure. These words of assurance have sometimes been interpreted in light of the history of earthquakes in Philadelphia. For people who had experienced firsthand the instability and impermanence of buildings during a severe earthquake and who at times had to flee their homes and city to keep from being injured or killed by tumbling buildings, the promise that they would be a pillar (of strength) and would never have to go out of the temple would indeed be good news.

Site Visit

In the city of Alaşehir the ruins of a Byzantine church are about all that remain of the Christian past of Philadelphia. A rectangular building of

⚠ **Fig. 120.** Church of St. John the Theologian in Philadelphia (Alaşehir)

six pillars, the church is known as the **Church of St. John the Theologian**. Three of the church's pillars are still standing, with their lower portion made of stone and their upper portion made of bricks. Some 11th-century frescoes in very poor condition are barely discernible on some of the pillars. Some marble sarcophagi and tombstones, along with column capitals and other architectural pieces, can be seen near the church. A portion of the **Byzantine wall** around the city still exists on the north side of Alaşehir. Most of the Roman and Hellenistic ruins of ancient Philadelphia apparently lie buried underneath the modern city, although some remains have been uncovered on the ancient acropolis of the city. In 1986 archaeologists excavated the ruins of an ancient **theater** and a **temple** on the acropolis, both thought to date to the Roman period, possibly the 2nd century C.E. A large part of the stage building and a small portion of the cavea (seating area) of the theater were uncovered. From the temple, the foundation and some marble architectural blocks were discovered. The **museum at Manisa** contains some archaeological finds from Philadelphia.

Sardis

A city with a strong and vibrant Jewish community during the Roman period, as well as a center for the worship of Artemis and home to a significant Christian community, Sardis is an intriguing place to visit for anyone interested in biblical studies or ancient religious history. The partially restored 3rd-century-C.E. synagogue in the city is the largest known synagogue outside Palestine from ancient times. Ancient shops, a bath-gymnasium complex, and the Temple of Artemis provide glimpses of the life of this ancient city.

Location and History

Once the capital of the ancient Lydian Kingdom, Sardis (Sart) lies approximately 60 miles east of Izmir along the modern highway (E96/300) connecting Izmir to Ankara in the Hermus River valley (today called the Gediz River). Portions of the ruins of Sardis are situated adjacent to the highway and are easily accessible. The ancient city was built along the Pactolus River, a tributary of the Hermus, and at the foothills of the Tmolus Mountains. The city's acropolis was strategically located atop a spur of the Tmolus Mountains. The Tmolus Mountains (or Mt. Tmolus) were, according to some ancient traditions, the birthplace of the gods Dionysus and Zeus. Sardis first came to prominence during the 1st millennium B.C.E. when it served as the center of the powerful Lydian kingdom, which encompassed most of the western half of Asia Minor. The Lydians supposedly were the first to develop a technique to dye wool and also to invent dice games, knucklebones, and other games. (Interestingly, archaeologists found a terra-cotta die in the ruins at Sardis.) Legend says that **Midas**, the mythical Phrygian king, was able to rid himself of his golden touch by bathing in the Pactolus River. As a result, the sands of the river turned to gold. Though legendary, this account points nonetheless to the enormous wealth enjoyed by the Lydian kingdom.

The earliest Lydian rulers belonged to the Heraclid dynasty, which according to Herodotus (5th-century-B.C.E. Greek historian) lasted 505 years. They were succeeded by the Mermnad dynasty, of which the first king was **Gyges** (r. ca. 680–ca. 652 B.C.E.). Herodotus credits the Mermnad rulers with the invention of coinage. Many scholars consider Gyges, known to the Assyrians as Gugu, to be the model for the mythical ruler Gog in Ezekiel 38 and Revelation 20:8, who serves in those scriptures as a representative figure of evil. Herodotus records a famous story that describes how Gyges became king: The last king of the Heraclid dynasty was **Candaules**, who was much in love with his wife, whom he considered the most beautiful of all women. In order to convince Gyges, his favorite bodyguard, of the beauty of his wife, Candaules invited Gyges to hide in his wife's room and observe her naked when she undressed. Shocked by this suggestion, Gyges initially declined. Candaules convinced Gyges that he could observe her without being detected. Unable to overcome the king's insistence, Gyges consented. Seen by the queen as he fled the bedroom, Gyges was given a choice by the queen—kill Candaules and marry her, or be killed himself. Gyges chose the first option (hardly surprising) and became the new king. (Several variations of this story exist among ancient writers, including one recounted by Plato in which Gyges becomes invisible, seduces the queen, and takes over the kingdom.)

The most famous of the Lydian kings was **Croesus** (r. 561–547 B.C.E.), according to ancient legend the richest person in the world. Archaeological finds at Sardis include an area devoted to the refining of gold, lending support to the tradition of Lydian wealth. During the reign of Croesus, supposedly both the ancient storyteller **Aesop**, a Phrygian by birth, and **Solon**, the great lawgiver of Athens, spent time at Sardis (although the time period of Solon is apparently too early for this account to be true).

The Lydian kingdom came to an end when the Persian king **Cyrus** captured Sardis and defeated Croesus in 547 B.C.E. Herodotus reports that Croesus consulted the Greek oracle at Delphi and was told that if he crossed the Halys River (the eastern boundary of his kingdom), he would destroy a great empire. Misunderstanding this oracle as a prediction of the downfall of the Persians—his own kingdom would be the one destroyed—Croesus crossed the river and captured the city of Pteria. After an indecisive battle with the Persians, Croesus withdrew to Sardis for the winter, not expecting Cyrus to continue the engagement during the winter months. Cyrus marched against Sardis, however, and sought means to conquer the nearly impregnable city on its steep acropolis. Initially frustrated, Cyrus offered a reward to any of his soldiers who could find a way to scale the mountain and capture the city. One day one of his soldiers observed a Lydian soldier who accidentally dropped his helmet over the city wall. Not aware that he was being observed, the Lydian climbed over the wall and made his way down the precipice to retrieve his helmet. Under the cover of night, the Persian soldier led a group of his comrades up the same route the Lydian soldier had taken. Since the soldiers in Sardis thought this part of the wall was inaccessible, it was left unguarded. The Persians successfully entered the city, and Cyrus was able to bring the Lydian kingdom of Croesus to an end.

Under Persian rule, Sardis became the capital of a satrapy (province) and was the most important Persian city in Asia Minor. Sardis became the western terminus of the Royal Road connecting Asia Minor to the capital city of Susa in Persia. The city was partially destroyed in 499 B.C.E. by Athenian soldiers who were assisting the Ionians (Ionia was a region along the western coast of Asia Minor) in a revolt against their Persian rulers. In 490 and 480 B.C.E. the Persian kings **Darius I** and **Xerxes I** used Sardis as a staging area from which to invade Greece during the Greek and Persian wars.

The Persian period of Sardis ended when the city surrendered without resistance to **Alexander the Great** in 334 B.C.E. After Alexander's death, the city eventually came under the control of the Seleucid kings from 281 to 190 B.C.E. and became one of three governmental centers for Seleucid rule. During the reign of the Seleucid king **Antiochus III**, a rival captured the city for a brief period. Antiochus regained the city by secretly entering an unguarded section, similar to the earlier conquest of Sardis by Cyrus. In 188 B.C.E. the treaty of Apamea, following the Roman defeat of Antiochus III, gave Sardis to **Eumenes II**, king of Pergamum, who had assisted the Romans in the conquest of Sardis. The city came back under Roman rule in 133 B.C.E. when the last Pergamene king, **Attalus III**, left the city to the Romans in his will.

Under the control of the Romans, Sardis became an administrative center and enjoyed a time of great prosperity due to trade and industry. After a major earthquake struck the region in 17 C.E., devastating Sardis, the Roman emperor **Tiberius** provided funds to rebuild the city. During the 1st and 2nd centuries C.E., the city had a large population that may have reached 100,000. Sardis continued to be a vital center during the early Byzantine period (ca. 350–600 C.E.), when renovation and construction of several buildings occurred. From the 7th century onward the city declined. The 7th century saw destruction of the lower city by the Sassanid Persians and heavy damage to the remaining buildings by earthquakes. During the 8th century, Arabs attacked the city, and beginning in the 11th century, the city was intermittently under the control of Seljuk Turks. Occupation of Sardis came to an end in 1402, when the Mongol Turk **Tamerlane** (or Timur) sacked the city.

The patron deities of Sardis were Cybele and Artemis. Remains of the temple to Artemis are still standing. Both Judaism and Christianity also flourished at Sardis. According to the Jewish historian Josephus (37 C.E.– 100 C.E.), Antiochus III transported 2,000 loyal Jewish families from Mesopotamia and settled them in Phrygia and Lydia (*Jewish Antiquities* 12.147–153). Around 49 B.C.E., **Lucius Antonius**, the proconsul of the province of Asia, issued an edict guaranteeing the Jews in Sardis the right to form their own associations, to have a meeting place (perhaps a synagogue), and to have jurisdiction over their own civil matters (Josephus, *Jewish Antiquities* 14.235). Josephus reports also that the Roman emperor **Augustus** gave orders that the Jews of Sardis were not to be prevented from collecting funds (apparently the half-shekel temple tax) to be sent to Jerusalem (*Jewish Antiquities* 16.171). The presence of a prominent, large synagogue, in use as early as the 3rd century C.E., gives solid testimony to the sizeable population of Jews in Sardis and their social importance. Christianity had taken root in the city by the end of the first century, as evidenced by its mention in the book of Revelation (1:11; 3:1–6). During the 2nd century the bishop of Sardis, **Melito**, was an outspoken church leader who was involved in the Quartodeciman controversy (concerning the correct date on which to celebrate Easter). Sardis continued to be the seat of an important bishopric until the 14th century. During this time several churches were built at Sardis; some of their remains are still visible.

Biblical Significance

The earliest biblical reference to Sardis may occur in Obadiah 20. This text, written in the 6th or 5th century B.C.E., proclaims the eventual return of Judah's exiles to the promised land. The verse claims that "the exiles of Jerusalem who are in Sepharad shall possess the towns of the Negeb." The identity of Sepharad is unknown, but because of linguistic similarities between *Sepharad* and *Sfard* (the Lydian and Persian word for Sardis), the possibility that Sepharad is ancient Sardis is strong. If this identification is correct, a sizeable population of Jews existed in Sardis as early as the 6th century B.C.E.

The only other mention of Sardis in the Bible is in the book of Revelation, where the church at Sardis was one of the seven churches to which **John** sent a written message (1:11; 3:1–6). The warning given to the Sardis Christians that they should be awake or alert lest Christ come in judgment upon them "like a thief" is likely an allusion to the two occasions in the city's history when the city was taken by surprise by its conquerors.

Site Visit

The first part of the ancient site of Sardis to catch the visitor's eye is the area immediately north of the modern highway. This area contains a large **bath-gymnasium complex** and a large **synagogue**. The bath-gymnasium complex, a common feature in Roman cities, covered approximately 5.5 acres and was situated in the heart of the city. The majority of this complex was completed around the middle of the 2nd century C.E.; the Marble Court was added in 211. Various repairs and modifications of the complex were carried out in the succeeding centuries until the abandonment of the structure in the 7th century, when the Sassanids invaded Sardis.

The primary entrance to the complex was on the east side through a large courtyard (the palaestra, or exercise area), where visitors to the gymnasium engaged in games and exercises after first undressing in rooms

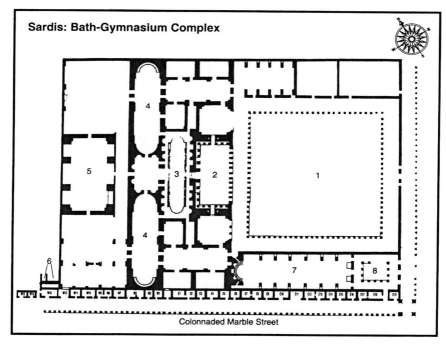

Sardis: Bath-Gymnasium Complex

Fig. 121. Sardis: Bath-Gymnasium Complex

1. Palaestra
2. Marble Court
3. Frigidarium (Cold Bath)
4. Tepidaria (Warm Baths)
5. Caldarium (Hot Bath)
6. Byzantine Latrines

7. Synagogue
8. Synagogue Forecourt

E1–E19 and W1–W15—
Byzantine Shops

inside the complex. After exercising they proceeded through the fabulous colonnaded **Marble Court** (partially restored; the brick walls seen today were all covered with marble in the 2nd century, and the floors were patterned marble) to the warm baths (tepidaria) and eventually to the hot bath (caldarium) in the western section of the complex. After the hot bath, visitors entered the cold bath (frigidarium), which included a large swimming pool and small basins and pools located in the central hall immediately west of the Marble Court. A massage often served as the finishing touch for a visit to the baths.

On the south side of the palaestra is a large **basilica-style building** that underwent three major renovations during its history. Originally built to be used as three dressing rooms or lecture halls, the building was redesigned in the 2nd century C.E. as a large hall, perhaps intended to be used for a Roman civil court. Late in the 2nd century, or perhaps during the 3rd century, this basilica-style hall was turned over to the Jewish community at Sardis and renovated as a **synagogue**. At that time the benches (perhaps for the elders) in the apse at the western end and some of the marble facings on the walls were added. The third renovation occurred in the middle or latter half of the 4th century, when the colonnaded forecourt, the fountain, the shrines, the bema (rostrum, or elevated platform), the eagle table, and most of the mosaic floor were installed.

The Sardis synagogue, the largest of any Diaspora (non-Palestinian) synagogue ever found, has several interesting features. Of particular interest is its location. Situated in the heart of the Roman city and an integral part of the bath-gymnasium complex, the synagogue is evidence of the social prominence of the Jewish inhabitants of Sardis and their integration into the society of Sardis. The synagogue had a capacity of at least a thousand people. Also of interest is the incorporation into the synagogue of non-Jewish items. The **eagle table** and the **two lion statues** (each with a pair of lions back to back), prominently situated in the synagogue, were reclaimed from other buildings or shrines and reused in the synagogue, indicating that the Jews in Sardis were heavily acculturated to Roman life. The supports of the eagle table were from an earlier Roman monument (the eagle was a symbol for Rome). The lions have been identified as 6th-century-B.C.E. sculptures representing the lions that often accompany depictions of the goddess Cybele; reused, they could have been understood as the lion of Judah (cf. Gen 49:9–10). The eagle table and the lions that are present in the synagogue today are reproductions; the originals are in the museum at Manisa.

The entrance to the synagogue was at the eastern end and led into a forecourt containing a large fountain in the center. Three doors led from the forecourt into the main hall. Between the three doors were two large shrines; the southern shrine likely housed the Torah scrolls. Contrary to the usual pattern for synagogues, the one at Sardis did not contain benches along the wall. Furthermore, the Sardis synagogue gives no evidence of a balcony or any other area that would have segregated women. Women either were not permitted to attend synagogue services or, more likely among Jews of the Diaspora, worshiped along with the men. The interior of the synagogue (not including the forecourt) was approximately 197 feet long and 59 feet wide. Mosaics of elaborate geometric patterns covered the floor. The lower portions of the walls were covered with decorative marble inlays, portions of which have been restored. Inscriptions found in the synagogue reveal the social and political status of the Jewish community in Sardis; at least eight of the donors to the synagogue who are mentioned in the inscriptions were city councilors, a position open only to the wealthy. Also mentioned are a former procurator and an imperial financial administrator.

▲ **Fig. 122.** Bath-gymnasium complex at Sardis

Immediately south of the synagogue and the bath-gymnasium com-plex was a row of **shops** built in the 4th century C.E. and in use until the 7th century. These shops were two-story structures, with the top floor sometimes in use as a residence. (The bottom floor of some these struc-tures also seems to have served as a residence.) Inscriptions and artifacts in the shops have suggested the religious background and occupation of many of the shopkeepers. The structures labeled E6, E7, E8, E12, E13, and E14 have been identified as Jewish shops or residences. W1, W2, W8, W9, E1, E2, E3, E4, E5, and E18 have been identified as Christian shops or residences. W1 and W2 formed a restaurant, as did also E1 and E2. The structures E3, E4, and E5 were probably residences. E6, E7, and E8, whose owner was Jacob, according to inscribed amphorae found in-side, were part of an establishment for dyeing cloth. The shop in E10 was a hardware store. E12 and E13 apparently served together as a shop for glassware. E14 was a paint and dye shop. An amphora with the name "Jacob the elder" was found in this shop, perhaps the same Jacob who owned E6, E7, and E8.

These shops opened onto a **colonnaded street**, paved with marble. This street, a portion of which is visible in front of the shops, was origi-nally lined with columns and shops on both sides. The columns and shops on the south side now lie buried under the modern highway. This street is

▲ **Fig. 123.** Shops and colonnaded street adjacent to the synagogue at Sardis

likely near the location of the ancient **Persian Royal Road,** which ran
for 1,600 miles from Sardis to Susa, the winter residence and main capital of the Persian Empire. At the southwestern end of this entire bath-
gymnasium complex were the **public latrines.**

On the south side of the modern highway archaeologists have uncovered numerous ruins from the late Roman period (4th–7th centuries C.E.)
and from the Lydian period (7th–6th centuries B.C.E.). (Because this is currently an active archaeological site, parts of this area are not accessible to
visitors.) A **residential complex** from the Roman period contains rooms
with frescoed walls and tiled floors and a courtyard surrounded by columns. Also in this area are the remains of a house from the 6th century C.E.
that has been labeled the **House of Bronzes** due to the many bronze objects found in the basement, which appear to have been for use in worship.
What appears to be an altar was also uncovered in the basement. The presence of the bronze liturgical objects and the altar has led to the suggestion
that this was the house of an important religious official, perhaps a Christian bishop. Portions of a Roman **colonnaded street** have also been found.
From the Lydian period, remains of the Lydian **defensive wall,** the **marketplace, workshops,** and a **residential quarter** have been uncovered.

A small road leads south from the main highway along the Pactolus
River. On the right side of the road, in an area called Pactolus North by the

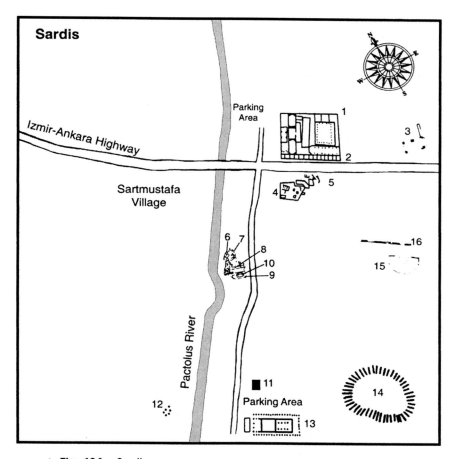

▲ **Fig. 124.** Sardis

1. Bath-Gymnasium Complex
2. Synagogue
3. Byzantine Church
4. Lydian Market
5. House of Bronzes
6. Lydian Gold Refinery
7. Altar of Cybele
8. Roman Villa

9. Early Christian Basilica
10. Byzantine Church
11. Excavation Headquarters
12. Necropolis
13. Temple of Artemis
14. Acropolis
15. Theater
16. Stadium

excavators, are ruins of structures from several periods. The earliest ruins come from the early 6th century B.C.E., when mud-brick buildings, some with decorative tile roofs, occupied the site. The remains of an **altar to Cybele**, the supreme Lydian goddess, are located here as part of a larger sacred precinct. Archaeologists have reconstructed the crouching lions that sit at the corners of the altar. The altar to Cybele sat in the middle of an area that contained several **gold refineries** in operation during the time of Croesus. During the 4th century C.E. a **Roman villa** was constructed south of the Lydian area. Farther south are the remains of a **Byzantine church** (ca. 13th century) that had five domes, built over the site of a 4th-century basilica-style church that was in use until the 7th century.

Farther south down the road, on the left, are the ruins of the **Temple of Artemis**, the fourth largest Ionic temple in the world and one of the seven largest of all Greek temples. The temple is approximately 300 feet long and 160 feet wide. Most of the ruins that remain are from the Roman period. Even with only two complete columns still standing (other, partial columns are erect), the temple is still an impressive sight, particularly when viewed with the acropolis in the background. When this temple was begun, around 300 B.C.E., it was likely designed as a dipteros (a temple with two rows of columns around an inner, enclosed section). This phase of its construction was perhaps partially funded by the Seleucid kings. The original plan was not completed, however (perhaps from lack of funding), so the columns around the exterior of the temple were never added. At some point both Artemis and Zeus were likely worshiped in this temple. A large head of Zeus was found in the temple, and an early inscription indicates that both Artemis and Zeus were honored in the same sacred precinct, perhaps in the same temple.

Heavily damaged by the earthquake of 17 C.E. that destroyed much of Sardis, the temple underwent a major renovation in the 2nd century, at which time the columns visible today were added. The renovated design was for a pseudodipteros ("false dipteros"), a dipteros with the inner row of exterior columns omitted. As planned, the temple would have contained seventy-eight columns in all, including those inside the temple and those surrounding it. The Roman plan was not completely executed, however; and many of the columns were never erected. The temple was also likely altered at this time to serve as a temple for the imperial cult as well. This alteration involved erecting a wall that divided the inner part of the temple into two sections, thus creating in effect a double temple. In both sections against this dividing wall stood a base for a cult statue. One side of the temple was likely dedicated to Artemis and **Faustina** (wife of Antoninus Pius, Roman emperor from 138 to 161 C.E.); the other side was dedicated to Zeus and **Antoninus Pius**. Colossal heads of Faustina and Antoninus Pius were recovered from the interior of the temple. The temple was abandoned in the 4th century, at which time a small **Christian chapel** was built against its southeast corner. On the

⚏ **Fig. 125.**   Temple of Artemis at Sardis with acropolis in the background

western side of the temple is an **altar** that dates to the 6th or 5th century B.C.E. Originally this was a freestanding altar to Artemis.

Immediately to the north of the temple is the compound used by the excavators of Sardis. Archaeologists have reconstructed some of the terracotta and tile walls and roofs of ancient **Lydian houses**. These reconstructions can be viewed from outside the south wall of the compound.

The **acropolis**, which lies to the east of the Temple of Artemis, is a difficult climb (allow at least forty-five minutes for the ascent) but provides an impressive view of the countryside. The few remains visible there belong mainly to the Byzantine period. North of the acropolis are the scant remains of a **Roman theater** (seating capacity approximately 20,000) and a **stadium**. To the north beyond these ruins, across the highway, are the remains of a **Byzantine church**.

Ancient **tombs**, dating from the 6th century B.C.E. Lydian period to the Roman period, are scattered in the hills and cliffs on both sides of the Pactolus River, including along the slopes of the acropolis. These range in type from cavities dug in the ground to limestone chambers covered with dirt and chamber tombs carved into the cliffs. Many of these have deteriorated badly. The area directly west of the Temple of Artemis on the western side of the Pactolus River seems to have been one of the main burial grounds at Sardis.

Other Sites of Interest

Approximately 6 miles north of Sardis is **Bin Tepe** ("thousand hills"), the site of the ancient Lydian royal burial ground. The large burial mounds, or tumuli, are quite conspicuous. The mounds are clearly visible from the highway; entrance to the interior of the tombs is not permitted. Based on statements of ancient writers, two of these burial places have traditionally been identified as the graves of the Lydian king **Alyattes** (father of Croesus) and **King Gyges**. The so-called **Tomb of Gyges** is misnamed, however, since the tumulus dates to about a century after the time of Gyges. The identity of the individual buried in the **Tomb of Alyattes** is also uncertain. Herodotus claimed that the merchants, craftsmen, and prostitutes of Lydia built the tomb of Alyattes and that inscriptions at the tomb still visible during his day said that the prostitutes contributed the bulk of the work on the tomb. (In an additional interesting note, Herodotus stated that all the young women of Lydia served as prostitutes in order to raise money for their dowries.)

The **Archaeological and Ethnographical Museum** in the city of **Manisa**, approximately 35 miles northwest of Sardis, contains many artifacts found at Sardis. (The ancient name of Manisa was Magnesia ad Sipylum. It was here in 189 B.C.E. that the Romans defeated **Antiochus III** and ended Seleucid rule in Asia Minor.) Note particularly the beautiful **mosaics**, including mosaics from the Sardis synagogue. Also of interest are the **fountain, lions,** and **eagle table** from the synagogue, a **helmet** from the mid-6th century B.C.E., **drinking vessels** from the Lydian period, bronze items, pottery, and inscriptions.

Seleucia Pieria

Seleucia Pieria, the ancient seaport for Antioch of Syria, once played a central role in the travels of the 1st-century Christian missionaries. Little remains of the city or its port. Nevertheless, one outstanding attraction still remains, and it alone is worth a visit to the site: the spectacular tunnel of Vespasian and Titus.

Location and History

To reach Seleucia Pieria, travel 18 miles south of Antakya (ancient Antioch) to the village of Samandağ, then proceed north along the beach road approximately 2 miles to the little settlement of Çevlik. Portions of the ancient breakwater are clearly visible from the refreshment stand above the beach. (Do not plan to swim—not that anyone would be tempted after viewing the polluted condition of the water.)

The city and port of Seleucia Pieria were founded at the beginning of the 3rd century B.C.E. by one of the generals of Alexander the Great, **Seleucus Nicator**, who also founded Antioch. (The name *Pieria* was derived from Mt. Pieria, the mountain above the city.) His descendants, known as the Seleucids, battled for many years with the Ptolemies for control of Syria, Palestine, and Egypt, eventually losing out entirely. Originally Seleucia Pieria served as the capital of the new kingdom of **Seleucus I**. After Seleucus was assassinated (281 B.C.E.), however, his son, **Antiochus I**, moved the capital to Antioch, and Seleucia Pieria served as its strongly fortified port. During the Roman era the port was captured by **Pompey**, who granted it the status of a free city. Later, it became the location of a Roman fleet. At its zenith the city had a population of some 30,000 inhabitants.

Many famous persons passed through the ancient port during its history. Besides the Christian missionaries **Paul** and **Barnabas** and several of the Roman emperors, other notables included the renowned wonder-worker **Apollonius of Tyana**, in his own way a missionary of Pythagorean reform. According to Philostratus, Apollonius, too, set sail from Seleucia Pieria to go to Cyprus at virtually the same time as the Christian missionaries (*Life of Apollonius* 3).

Biblical Significance

Seleucia Pieria is mentioned in the New Testament only in connection with the first missionary voyage of **Paul** and **Barnabas** (Acts 13:4): "So, being sent out by the Holy Spirit, they went down to Seleucia; and from there they sailed to Cyprus." Without question, however, other references to missionary journeys departing from Antioch imply setting sail from the port of Seleucia Pieria. It was common for vessels to sail the short distance from Antioch down the Orontes River to Seleucia, and then out to sea. That should be inferred from other biblical references such as Acts 14:26 and 15:39. Seleucia Pieria, therefore, was well known to the early apostles and missionaries.

Site Visit

Unfortunately, little exists of the ancient port city. Two fragments of the **ancient breakwater**, known locally as **Paul** and **Barnabas**, still remain in the murky waters. The city itself was divided into two parts. The lower city surrounded the harbor; the upper city lay on a sloping plain above the cliff that rises behind the harbor. A **wall**, over 7 miles long, enclosed both parts of the city. Portions of this wall remain in both sections.

In the **lower city**, the Roman **Market Gate** can be reached by walking inland approximately 200 yards from the road at the location of a small gray house (a water installation) on the eastern side of the harbor, prior to the area of the jetties. In this location **two large towers** and sections of the wall remain that comprised the Market Gate. Inside the market area, excavations revealed the previous existence of a **square** and a **stoa** that contained a row of shops. To the north of the square, the hypocaust (hot room) of a **bath** was discovered with its pipes and water conduits intact.

If the wall is followed to the west of the Market Gate toward the village of Çevlik, a small **triangular tower** and a large **rectangular tower** may be seen, as well as a **section of wall** with enormous stone blocks. Some other remains lie in this area, but likely most visitors will prefer at this point to proceed to the parking lot to view the spectacular **tunnel of Vespasian and Titus.**

▲ **Fig. 126.** Entrance to the Tunnel of Vespasian and Titus at Seleucia Pieria

Because of catastrophic flash floods that were common in the area (known locally in ancient times as "donkey drowners"), the emperors Vespasian and Titus sought to divert such floodwaters away from the lower city and its port. So they constructed an enormous **channel**, nearly a mile long, which at one point passes through 400 yards of solid rock. This tunnel, some 20 feet wide and 20 feet high, is one of the most remarkable accomplishments of ancient engineering. It was built by Roman soldiers and conscripted labor consisting of Jewish prisoners from Judea. (Other captives from Judea were used to dig the attempted canal at Corinth during the reign of Nero.)

From the parking lot, the tunnel may be reached by climbing the steps that lead up the hill to a ticket booth (there may or may not be an attendant). The terrain is remote and fascinating, but visitors must wear sturdy shoes with non-skid soles and be especially careful. The floor of the tunnel is wet and extremely slippery. Also carry a flashlight, since part of the tunnel is dark.

At the upper end of the tunnel, an **inscription** on the rock face states that the tunnel was constructed by Vespasian (r. 69–79 C.E.) and Titus (r. 79–81 C.E.), although the project actually was not completed until the Antonine rulers of the 2nd century C.E. Beyond the tunnel is what appears to be a rock bridge that spans the ravine at that point, but actually it is a portion of a Roman **aqueduct**.

Farther along the gorge, where the rock sides attain a height of 40–50 feet, there is a **bridge** made of uncut rock that spans the gorge. This is the best access point to view an elaborate, decorated **multiple tomb** in the cliff face to the east, above the rock bridge, between the lower and upper cities. Follow the path from the rock bridge for approximately 200 yards to reach the **tomb**, known as **Beşikli Magara**. The tomb is accessed by a sloping ramp that passes other tombs to arrive at the arched entrance. Two columns flank the entrance to the **first tomb chamber**, known as the Tomb of the Cradles because of the canopy-shaped rocks above two sarcophagi. Other tombs line the walls. The **second chamber**, to the right of the first, has a low roof supported by four piers in the center and other piers on two sides of the wall. Tomb niches to receive sarcophagi line the walls.

The **upper city** has a few remains. Those interested can reach the area by driving from Magarcik to Kapisuyu, a small village within the area of the ancient upper town. **Polygonal sections** of the wall, **towers**, and the remains of a **Hellenistic temple** (it may be even earlier) have been located. It is best to have the services of a knowledgeable guide to explore this area thoroughly.

Smyrna

Izmir, the modern name for the city that once was known as Smyrna, is the third largest city in Turkey, with a population of around 3 million. Situated on the Aegean coast, it is Turkey's second busiest port. Not only is Izmir an interesting place itself to visit, but the city also serves as a good base from which to visit several important sites in the area, such as the ancient cities of Ephesus, Sardis, Miletus, Didyma, and Priene.

Location and History

The ancient city of Smyrna, which according to some reports was the birthplace of **Homer**, was commercially successful due to its harbor and its location (approximately 35 miles north of Ephesus) at the end of a major route through Asia Minor. The earliest settlement at this location was in the first half of the 3rd millennium B.C.E. on a hill known as Tepekule in the Bayraklï suburb of the city. In the 10th century B.C.E., the first Greek colonists from Aeolia settled at Tepekule. They remained there until the end of the 8th century, when Ionian Greeks took over. Excavations at the site have uncovered houses from the 9th to the 7th centuries B.C.E. In the 7th century a temple to Athena was built. This temple was destroyed around 600 B.C.E. by **King Alyattes** of Lydia when he captured the city. The people of Smyrna rebuilt and enlarged the temple, but it was destroyed again around 545 B.C.E., this time by the Persians. An insignificant settlement in the 5th and 4th centuries B.C.E., the site was finally abandoned.

According to a story related by Pausanias (*Description of Greece* 7.5.1– 3), the city was refounded by **Alexander the Great**, who was instructed in a dream to establish a new city on Mt. Pagus (now the site of the Kadifekale, or "Velvet Fortress"). The new city was actually not started until the beginning of the 3rd century by the Hellenistic ruler **Lysimachus**. During the subsequent centuries Smyrna, situated around the harbor, grew and prospered. By the 1st century B.C.E., Strabo was able to describe Smyrna as "the most beautiful of all" cities (*Geography* 14.646). Ancient sources describe the city as having straight, paved streets, a temple to the Mother Goddess, a gymnasium, and a Homerion with a statue of Homer and a shrine dedicated to his worship. The city came under Seleucid control in 281 B.C.E., but it gained the status of a free city after Rome defeated the Seleucid king **Antiochus III** in 189. The city's loyalty to Rome was evidenced by its construction of a temple to the goddess Roma in 195 B.C.E., the first city in Asia Minor to do so. Soon after the beginning of the 1st century B.C.E., Smyrna came under the control of the Roman province of Asia.

Smyrna was a major center for the imperial cult. In 23 B.C.E. the city was granted the privilege of building a temple to the emperor **Tiberius**. Later, it added temples to **Hadrian** and **Caracalla**. Various other buildings from the Roman period are mentioned: a theater and a stadium on the slopes of Mt. Pagus, a silo built by Hadrian near the harbor, a commercial agora near the harbor, and a state agora. Nothing remains today of these structures except the state agora. After a major earthquake extensively damaged the city in 178 C.E., Smyrna was able to rebuild due to help from the emperor **Marcus Aurelius**. During the Arab raids of the 7th century, the city was damaged but not destroyed. Subsequent centuries saw Smyrna under the control of Seljuk Turks, Byzantine rulers, Crusaders, and Ottoman Turks.

Evidence from Christian writers (the book of Revelation and the *Martyrdom of Polycarp*) indicates the presence of a Jewish community in Smyrna as early as the 1st and 2nd centuries C.E. The origins of Christianity in the city are unknown. The city earned a spot in Christian history, however, when **Ignatius**, bishop of Antioch in Syria, stopped at Smyrna while being transported to Rome for execution around 107 C.E. While there, Ignatius met with Christian leaders from Asia Minor and wrote letters to several congregations. Four of his letters were written while at Smyrna. Later during his journey, he sent a letter back to the church at Smyrna, as well as one to their bishop, **Polycarp**. Polycarp, like Ignatius, suffered a martyr's fate, being burned at the stake in the stadium in Smyrna around 156 C.E.

⚎ **Fig. 127.** Columns in the agora at Smyrna (Izmir)

Biblical Significance

In the New Testament book of Revelation, **John of Patmos** sent messages to churches in seven cities in Asia Minor; the message to the church at Smyrna is the shortest. The church at Smyrna was one of only two churches that received only praise and no criticism from John (the other was Philadelphia). Two traits characterized this congregation: it had suffered affliction, and it was poor. Although the city of Smyrna was commercially prosperous, its Christian inhabitants apparently did not share in its prosperity. The cause of their poverty is not mentioned. The church at Smyrna may have drawn its adherents from the lower socioeconomic groups of the city, or their poverty may have resulted from some type of economic discrimination against the Christians by the citizens of Smyrna. In spite of this material poverty, however, John told them that they were "rich," meaning spiritually rich (2:9).

The Jews and the Christians of Smyrna were apparently in conflict, as evidenced by the statement in Revelation 2:9: "I know the slander on the part of those who say that they are Jews and are not, but are a synagogue of Satan." This harsh verbal attack on the Jews possibly reflects a local situation in which the Jews were denouncing the Christians. In the eyes of the government officials, as well as most of the populace at large, Jews and Christians belonged to the same group. Since Judaism was a legally protected religion, Christians, as long as they were thought to be a part of Judaism, would have enjoyed the same privileges and protections given to the Jews. If the Christians had been denounced to the authorities as being non-Jews, they would have been vulnerable to arrest or punishment (for such offenses as illegal assemblies). John thus accused the Jews of not truly being the people of God (Jews) but instead belonging to "a synagogue of Satan." John warned the church at Smyrna that such persecution would soon intensify and encouraged them to be faithful.

Site Visit

Not much exists from the Roman period of Smyrna. The best remains are the ruins of the **state agora** (or forum, to use the Roman term), which is located in the Namazgah quarter of Izmir near the intersection of Eşref Paşa Caddesi and Anafartalar Caddesi. This agora was rebuilt with assistance from **Marcus Aurelius** after the devastating earthquake of 178 C.E. The central courtyard of the agora measured nearly 400 feet by at least 260 feet. On the west side and the east side of the agora were two-story porticoes, each divided by two rows of columns. Several of the columns on the west side have been re-erected. Over one of the arches of the west portico is a portrait carving of **Faustina II**, wife of Marcus

Aurelius. This portrait was likely placed here by the residents of the city in gratitude for the emperor's assistance after the earthquake destruction. In the basement area at the north end of the west portico are the remains of a **fountain**. The north stoa also had two stories, but in addition contained a large basement area with vaulted supports. Part of this basement area contained several shops. A gate in the northern basement area opened onto the main road behind the agora during Roman times. The south side of the agora has yet to be excavated, but it, too, likely was a two-story portico. Literary evidence indicates that an altar to Zeus was located in the center of the agora. Various artifacts from Roman, Byzantine, and Ottoman times are gathered in the courtyard.

Approximately a thousand yards south of the agora, along Eşref Paşa Caddesi, is a portion of the ancient **Golden Road**. A section of the road with its large stone paving blocks is still visible. This road, built during Roman times, was one of the two main thoroughfares of the city and was an important part of the Roman road network.

One of the oldest parts of the city is the area now known as **Kadifekale**, or "Velvet Fortress," which is the ancient Mt. Pagus, the site where **Lysimachus** founded the city. The walls and towers on the top of the mountain today are the well-preserved walls of a medieval fortress, although it is built over the foundations of earlier structures. The major

▲ **Fig. 128.** Portrait carving of Faustina II on an arch in the agora at Smyrna (Izmir)

reason to visit Kadifekale is for the spectacular view over Izmir. From the walls of the fortress there is an excellent view of the ancient agora and of the harbor.

The **Archaeological Museum** contains artifacts found in ancient Smyrna, Ephesus, Pergamum, and other locations in the area. The upper floor contains a collection of jewelry, coins, glassware, bronze objects, lamps, tools, and pottery. The first floor and the basement contain an assortment of statues, busts, reliefs, and sarcophagi. Particularly note-worthy are the Roman-period **head of Hermes** found at Pergamum, the **statue of a priest** found at Halicarnassus from the Roman period, the **statue of a priest** from the 2nd century C.E. from Ephesus, the large **high reliefs of the god Poseidon and the goddess Demeter** from the 2nd century C.E. found in the agora of ancient Smyrna, the **head of Athena** from the 2nd century B.C.E. from ancient Smyrna, and a **statue of Kaistros** (or Cayster, the river god) from the 2nd century C.E. from Ephesus. Adjacent to the Archaeological Museum is the Ethnographical Museum.

The site of the earliest Aeolian and Ionian settlement in Izmir is in the Bayrakli area, north of the main part of the city, on a hill called **Tepekule**. Much of the site (sometimes called **Old Smyrna**) is overgrown. Archae-ologists have uncovered the remains here of **houses** dating from the 9th to the 7th centuries B.C.E. The most impressive discovery here is the **Temple to Athena**. First built around the end of the 7th century B.C.E., the temple was destroyed around 600 B.C.E., rebuilt and enlarged, and then destroyed again in 545 B.C.E. Archaeologists have reconstructed part of this temple, considered one of the earliest and finest temples in the eastern part of the Greek world.

On the road between Izmir and Ephesus are the **Sirinyer and Yesildere aqueducts**, which span the Meles River. These Roman aqueducts deliv-ered water to the city.

Tarsus

Tarsus, best known as the home of the Apostle Paul, was the principal city of the eastern Cilician plain. A city renowned in antiquity as a center of culture and learning, Tarsus was visited by such figures as Julius Cae-sar, Mark Antony, and Cleopatra. Recent excavations have uncovered more remains of the city from Hellenistic and Roman times, including a paved, colonnaded street.

Location and History

Tarsus, the capital of the ancient province of Cilicia, is located near the eastern Mediterranean coast of Turkey. Situated today 10 miles inland from the sea, Tarsus served as a port city because the Cydnus River (today the Tarsus Çayï) passed through Tarsus on its way to the sea. The river was navigable by ships from the Mediterranean coast to Tarsus. Lake Rhegma, a lagoon near the Mediterranean coast into which the river flowed, served as the harbor for Tarsus. During the 6th century c.e., **Emperor Justinian** moved the course of the Cydnus River to the east of Tarsus, while leaving several minor branches of the river to flow through the city.

The city of Tarsus belonged to the region of Asia Minor known as Cilicia. Ancient Cilicia was composed of two parts, Cilicia Pedias ("flat" or "smooth" Cilicia) and Cilicia Trachaei ("rough" Cilicia). Cilicia Pedias was a fertile plain in the eastern part of the region, whereas Cilicia Trachaei was a rugged, heavily forested mountainous region in the western part, dominated by the Taurus Mountains. Tarsus, the major city of Cilicia Pedias, was located just south of the Cilician Gates, the main pass through the Taurus Mountains. Through this pass ran the major road connecting Syria to Asia Minor, thus providing Tarsus access to trade and travel over land as well as over the Mediterranean.

The earliest settlement at Tarsus was likely at Gözlü Kule, a tumulus on the southeast side of modern Tarsus. Excavations under the direction of Hetty Goldman of Princeton University before and immediately after World War II at the tumulus discovered evidence that the site was occupied from Neolithic to Islamic times. At least as early as the 3rd millennium b.c.e., a fortified town existed at the site of Tarsus. According to Hittite records, during the 2nd millennium Tarsus (known then as Tarša) was one of the important cities, and possibly even capital, of the country of Kizzuwatna (ancient Cilicia). The Sea Peoples, during their invasion and conquest of the region, destroyed Tarsus around 1200 b.c.e., but the city was subsequently refounded by Greek settlers. During the 9th century, all of Cilicia came under the control of the Assyrians. Later the Persians controlled the region, including Tarsus. In 333 b.c.e. **Alexander the Great** conquered Cilicia and defeated the Persians. His visit to Tarsus almost ended disastrously for him when he became seriously ill as a result of bathing in the cold waters of the Cydnus. After the death of Alexander in 323 b.c.e., Tarsus came under the rule of the Seleucids, who gave the city a new name—Antioch on the Cydnus. By 67 b.c.e., Rome had taken control of the area and made Tarsus the capital of the province of Cilicia.

Cicero lived in the city from 51 to 50 b.c.e., when he served as proconsul (governor) of Cilicia. In 47 b.c.e. **Julius Caesar** visited the city, which changed its name to Iuliopolis in his honor. A few years later, in 41 B.C.E., the city was the site for the famous rendezvous between **Mark Antony** and **Cleopatra**. Cleopatra, dressed like Aphrodite, sailed up the Cydnus on a barge to meet Antony, who was visiting the city. Shakespeare, borrowing from Plutarch's account of her visit, described the scene as follows:

> The barge she sat in, like a burnish'd throne,
> Burn'd on the water: the poop was beaten gold;
> Purple the sails, and so perfumed that
> The winds were love-sick with them; the oars were silver,
> Which to the tune of flutes kept stroke, and made
> The water which they beat to follow faster,
> As amorous of their strokes. For her own person,
> It beggar'd all description: she did lie
> In her pavilion—cloth-of-gold of tissue—
> O'er-picturing that Venus where we see
> The fancy outwork nature: on each side her
> Stood pretty dimpled boys, like smiling Cupids,
> With divers-colour'd fans. (*Antony and Cleopatra,* Act 2, Scene 2)

Under the Romans, Tarsus prospered and was a city of culture and learning. **Paul the Apostle**, the most famous citizen of the city, reportedly described Tarsus as "no unimportant city" (Acts 21:39; author's translation), a modest description of the city that **Strabo** described as having "surpassed Athens, Alexandria, or any other place that can be named where there have been schools and lectures of philosophers" (*Geography* 14.5.13). During the 2nd and 3rd centuries, several Roman emperors visited Tarsus and bestowed various honors on the city. After the Romans, the city was controlled by Byzantine, Arab, Seljuk, and Ottoman rulers.

Biblical Significance

In none of **Paul**'s letters contained in the New Testament does he ever mention Tarsus as the place of his birth. That information comes from the book of Acts, which several times names Tarsus as Paul's hometown (9:11, 30;

▲ **Fig. 129.** Painting of Paul near "St. Paul's Well" in Tarsus

11:25; 21:39; 22:3). According to Acts, Paul left Tarsus and was educated in Jerusalem, studying under the famous Jewish teacher Gamaliel (22:3). After his conversion to Christianity, he returned to Tarsus for a brief period prior to becoming the important missionary of the Christian church. While the accuracy of the information in Acts about Paul's stay in Jerusalem has been seriously questioned by scholars, there is no reason to doubt the tradition of Tarsus as his birthplace and possibly the place where he spent all his formative years.

The only other reference to Tarsus in biblical literature is in 2 Maccabees 4:30, which tells that the citizens of Tarsus, along with the citizens of Mallus (east of Tarsus), revolted against the Seleucid king **Antiochus IV** "because their cities had been given as a present to Antiochis, the king's concubine." Some readers have tried to identify Tarsus with the city of Tarshish, mentioned several times in the Bible (e.g., Jonah 1:3; Jer 10:9; Ezek 27:12). The location of Tarshish is uncertain. The most likely suggestion is that it refers to a port city in Spain and not to Tarsus.

In addition to several references to the region of Cilicia in the book of Acts, another reference to this region occurs in 1 Kings 10:28, which states that King Solomon imported horses "from Egypt and Kue," the latter term being a name for Cilicia.

Site Visit

Because the modern city of Tarsus is built over the location of the earlier phases of the city, little can be seen today of the ancient Hellenistic and Roman structures. Whatever ancient ruins may still exist lie mostly unexcavated under the modern city. (For example, the foundation of a 1st-century-C.E. Roman hippodrome lies under part of the grounds of the Tarsus American College, whose campus, not far from the town center, is located on the periphery of the slopes of Gözlü Kule; across the street, some exposed portions of a Roman theater are visible.) The tumulus of Gözlü Kule, where the earliest archaeological work at Tarsus was performed, has now been planted with trees and is used as a park.

In the middle of a traffic circle in Tarsus on the road to Mersin is a Roman gate called, variously, **Kancık Kapïsï** ("Gate of the Bitch"), **Cleopatra's Gate**, and **St. Paul's Gate**. The gate actually has no historical connection to either Cleopatra or Paul. Rather, it is likely a 4th-century-C.E. gate set in the ancient city walls to provide access to the harbor. North of the gate, in the Camii Cedid district of the city, is the so-called **St. Paul's Well**. Tradition claims that Paul used this well frequently and that it has special curative powers. The well, which is claimed to be over

▲ **Fig. 130.** "Cleopatra's Gate" in Tarsus

100 feet deep, is supposedly built where Paul's house once stood. Although there is no historical basis for these claims, the well apparently dates back at least to Roman times, since about three feet underground it is surrounded by Roman paving.

A little further north in the city, on the opposite side of the road to Mersin, is the **Makam Cami**. Islamic legend claims that near this mosque is buried the body of **Daniel**, the main character in the book of Daniel, who was carried away into Babylon as one of the exiles. A funerary monument on the east side of the mosque is supposedly the tomb of Daniel. The **Tarsus Museum**, which opened in 1971, is located nearby in the Kubat Paşa Medresesi, built during the 16th century. The museum contains both an archaeological section and an ethnographical section. The archaeological section has an interesting collection of coins, jewelry, architectural pieces, sarcophagi, and other archaeological artifacts from various time periods discovered in Tarsus and the surrounding area.

Near the museum is the **Ulu Cami**, the major mosque in Tarsus. Built in the 16th century on the site of a Christian church, the mosque contains three sacred **tombs**—supposedly the tombs of the 9th-century caliph **Mamun**, the famous Muslim physician **Lokman Hekim**, and **Seth**, the son of Adam and Eve. According to Islamic legend, Seth was the founder of Tarsus. Back near the Makam Cami is another mosque, the **Eski Cami** (or **Kilise Cami**). Adjacent to this mosque is a large arched wall segment, built of bricks, that is thought to be part of a **Roman bath**.

The most recent archaeological discovery in the city, and the place not to be missed, is the **ancient street**. Located in Republic (Cumhuriyet) Square, approximately 500 feet southwest of St. Paul's Well, this ancient street is in an area that was discovered in 1993 when excavation was under way for an underground parking garage. Work on the parking garage was stopped, and an archaeological investigation was begun under the supervision of Professor Leven Zoroğlu of Selçuk University. Excavations are continuing in the area. The initial excavation uncovered an east-west street approximately 23 feet wide, built of black basalt blocks, some of which are over 6 feet wide. The street is slightly convex to drain water into the limestone gutters on each side. A sewer system ran underneath the street. In several places, ruts worn into the street from wagon and chariot wheels can be seen. The street was likely built during the middle of the 2nd century B.C.E. during the Seleucid period. The colonnaded portico that flanked the street was built at a later time, during the 2nd–4th centuries C.E. In the southwestern part of the excavation area, excavators have uncovered the remains of a **mosaic courtyard house**. This single-story structure is thought to date from the 2nd century C.E. In addition to the mosaic courtyard, excavators have found the floor of a single room in the house, a corridor, and a pool. As the excavation in this area continues, more houses, shops, and other structures are being uncovered.

Donuktaş, or the "Frozen Stones," is the name given to the ruins of a 2nd-century-C.E. **Roman temple**, although local tradition identifies it as the tomb of the 7th-century-B.C.E. Assyrian king **Sardanapalus**, who died during the siege of Nineveh. Since the ruins, located in the Tekke Quarter off small streets on the east side of town on the right bank of the Tarsus Çayï, are rather difficult to find, the visitor would be well advised to seek the assistance of a local guide or taxi driver.

Located near the entrance to Tarsus on the Ankara-Adana road is an **ancient bridge** built in the 6th century by the Byzantine emperor **Justinian** (r. 527–565 C.E.). This triple-arched bridge, no longer in use, was restored in 1978. It was known as the Bac ("tax") Bridge because a tollgate stood at the end of the bridge in ancient times to collect taxes on goods transported across the bridge.

Other Sites of Interest

Near the village of Sağlïlï, which is about 10 miles north of Tarsus, is a 1.5-mile section of the paved **Roman road** that led from the city to the Cilician Gates. On the left-hand side of the highway from Tarsus is a sign that reads "Roman Yolu" (Roman Road), indicating the way to the ancient road. An **arch**, dated to the time of **Septimius Severus** (193–211 C.E.), spans the nearly 10-foot-wide road.

Approximately 30 miles north of Tarsus is the main pass through the Taurus Mountains, called the **Cilician Gates** (Gülek Boğazï, or Gülek Pass). Through this pass traveled many important figures of history, including **Xerxes**, **Darius**, **Cyrus the Persian**, **Alexander the Great**, and the Crusaders. **Paul** also likely traveled through this pass on his journeys through Cilicia, although the Bible never mentions the Cilician Gates.

Thyatira

The ancient city of Thyatira, known for being one of the cities named in the book of Revelation, continues today as the modern city of Akhisar. A wealthy commercial city in antiquity, the city today is a modern one with a population of more than 80,000. Agriculture is a large part of the economy of the area, with major crops of olives, olive oil, wheat, cotton, grapes, melons, and raisins. The region is especially famous for its tobacco production.

Location and History

Akhisar is located in western Turkey, approximately 30 miles from the Aegean coast and 50 miles northeast of Izmir on highway 565. Situated on the broad Akhisar Plain, the city was in the northern part of the ancient kingdom of Lydia. Because of its location in the center of the large level plain, the city had few natural defenses. Archaeological evidence demonstrates that a settlement existed here as early as 3000 B.C.E. During the 5th century B.C.E., the Persians gained control of the area, followed by **Alexander the Great** toward the end of the 4th century. At the beginning of the 3rd century, the Seleucid ruler **Seleucus I Nicator** refounded the city and apparently settled Macedonian soldiers in the city. Serving as a military outpost, Thyatira became a part of the Pergamene kingdom under the Attalid rulers by 189 B.C.E. (if not earlier). After **Attalus III** bequeathed his Pergamene kingdom to the Romans in 133 B.C.E., the Romans established the province of Asia in 129 B.C.E., and Thyatira came under Roman rule. Located at the crossroads of the major routes leading northwest to Pergamum, southeast to Sardis, and southwest to Magnesia and Smyrna, Thyatira became an important trade, industrial, and commercial center. Inscriptional evidence indicates that the city was host to numerous trade guilds, which functioned as social, civic, and religious clubs or organizations. Among the guilds represented at Thyatira were the guilds of coppersmiths, tanners, leatherworkers, dyers, wool workers, and linen workers. The wool and textile industries were particularly strong in Thyatira, as was also the production of purple dye. During the Roman era the city prospered. Inscriptions discovered in the city mention the existence of three gymnasiums, a colonnaded portico of one hundred columns, stoas, shops, and shrines to the sun god Apollo Tyrimnaeus and to Artemis Boreitene. The emperor **Hadrian** apparently visited the city around 124 C.E., and **Caracalla** visited in 214. Emperor Caracalla made the city the center of a judicial district. The city responded by bestowing on the emperor the titles of founder and savior of the city.

Biblical Significance

The city of Thyatira is first mentioned in the Bible in the book of Acts. According to Acts 16, when **Paul** and **Silas** (and apparently also **Timothy**) traveled to Philippi, they met there a woman named **Lydia**, who is described as "from the city of Thyatira and a dealer in purple cloth"

▲ **Fig. 131.** Portions of the arches and columns from a monumental entrance to a colonnaded street in Thyatira

(16:14). Lydia became a convert to Christianity and, along with her household, was baptized. Lydia then insisted that Paul and Silas stay at her home during their visit to Philippi. Nothing more is known of this first Christian convert on European soil.

In Revelation 2:18–29, the risen Christ sends a message to the church in Thyatira, a church that received strong praise for its "love, faith, service, and patient endurance" (2:19). The major problem at Thyatira was the church's toleration of a woman symbolically called Jezebel. This woman, considered a false prophet and teacher, was a seducer who led the people astray, causing them to "eat food sacrificed to idols" and to "commit adultery with her" (2:20, 22). (Jezebel, an infamous character from the Hebrew Bible, was the wife of King Ahab of Israel. She was a promoter of Baal worship and a persecutor of the prophets of the God of Israel.) The accusation that the Jezebel of Thyatira caused people to "commit adultery with her" is a metaphor for her leading them to be unfaithful to God. The specific way she led them astray was her acceptance and perhaps even encouragement of Christians eating meat that had been ritually offered to other gods, as much of the meat sold in the markets of the ancient world had been. Eating meat that was ritually offered to gods and goddesses was particularly a problem for Christians who were members of trade guilds, which were numerous in Thyatira. Such trade guilds usually had a patron god or goddess. **John**, the author of Revelation, saw such accommodation to the practices and customs of the larger society as a dangerous compromise of one's faith.

Site Visit

Because the modern city of Akhisar occupies the site of ancient Thyatira, few archaeological remains of the ancient city have been uncovered. In the center of the city, on what are now the grounds of the State Hospital, archaeologists discovered a **tomb** and some **Hellenistic ruins**. Other artifacts found on the site indicate that the area was inhabited as early as 3000 B.C.E. The small hill on which the hospital is located is assumed to be the site of the ancient acropolis of the city. A **Hellenistic sarcophagus** can be seen in the garden of the hospital. The building that houses the oldest mosque in the city, the **Ulu Cami** (or the Great Mosque), was transformed into a mosque in the 1400s. Prior to that, the building seems to have been a **Byzantine church**, and before that a **civic building**, and earlier a **Roman temple**.

The main ruins of the ancient city that can be viewed today are in the Tepemezari section of downtown Akhisar. Excavations have uncovered the remains of a large building complex consisting of a **basilica-style building** with an apse and another **rectangular building** adjacent to it.

This building complex, likely from the 5th or 6th century C.E., was probably a civic building rather than a church. Nearby are portions of the arches and columns from a **monumental entrance** to a colonnaded street, as well as portions of the columns that lined the street, from the 2nd and 4th centuries C.E. Recently this area has been improved, fenced, and made into more of a tourist site (complete with a small entrance fee).

Many artifacts discovered in Thyatira can be seen in the archaeological museum in the city of Manisa, located about 30 miles southeast of Akhisar toward Izmir.

Troas

Called Alexandria Troas to distinguish it from other cities named Alexandria, the city is often referred to simply as Troas. ("The Troad" is the name used for the area around the ancient city of Troy.) What was once a large and important city on the western coast of Asia Minor has today been reduced to a few ruins overgrown by trees and shrubs, receiving only a cursory visit from a small number of sightseers.

Location and History

Troas was an important city in antiquity because of its location. Situated on the Aegean coast almost directly opposite the island of Tenedos (modern Bozcaada), the city became a major trading center. To reach the site of ancient Troas, take highway E87/550 to Ezine. In Ezine turn west onto the road marked for Geyikli and Odunluk Iskelesi. In Geyikli turn south toward Odunluk Iskelesi. The ruins of Alexandria Troas are by the highway that continues south to Gülpinar.

Troas was founded circa 310 B.C.E. by **Antigonus I Monopthalmus** ("the One-Eyed"), one of the successors of Alexander the Great. Antigonus created the new city by forcing the residents of several smaller neighboring towns and communities to move to the new location. Antigonus named the new settlement after himself, giving it the name Antigonia. When Antigonus was killed in 301 by the Macedonian king **Lysimachus** at the battle of Ipsus in Phrygia, Lysimachus took control of the city and renamed it Alexandria in honor of **Alexander the Great**. Because of its proximity to Troy, the city became known as Alexandria Troas. With its artificial harbor, the city grew as a commercial and transportation center, becoming the leading city of the Troad during Hellenistic times. Eventually Troas developed into one of the most important cities in the Greco-Roman world due to its command of the western entrance to the Hellespont. Claims were made in the ancient world that **Julius Caesar** considered moving the capital of the empire to Troas, as also reportedly did Augustus (and, even later, **Constantine**). Whether true or not, that such ideas circulated in the Roman era and were believed by some people indicates the importance of the city. **Augustus** made the city a Roman colony, with its official name being Colonia Augusta Troadendisum. During the 2nd century C.E., under the reign of **Hadrian**, Troas prospered, owing to a great extent to the beneficence of Hadrian himself and to the work of **Herodes Atticus**, who completed several major building projects in the city, including an aqueduct to bring water from Mt. Ida and a large bath-gymnasium complex.

Christianity came early to Troas, with **Paul** traveling to the city on at least two or three occasions. Early in the 2nd century, **Ignatius of Antioch**, who had been arrested for his Christian faith and was being sent to Rome for execution, sailed from Troas to Neapolis (the port of Philippi). While in the city, he wrote three of his letters—to Polycarp, to the church at Smyrna, and to the church at Philadelphia. Later, during the Byzantine period, the city was the seat of a bishop. The city declined during the Byzantine era, apparently due to the growth and prominence of Constantinople. Eventually Troas, like the rest of the area surrounding it, came under Ottoman control. Some of the marble and other stone materials used for building the Blue Mosque (Sultan Ahmet Camii) in Istanbul in the 17th century were plundered from the buildings of Troas.

Biblical Significance

When the **Apostle Paul** was on his second missionary journey, as described in the book of Acts, he traveled "through the region of Phrygia and Galatia, having been forbidden by the Holy Spirit to speak the word" in the Roman province of Asia (western Asia Minor) and went to Troas (Acts 16:6–8). One night while at Troas, Paul had a vision of a man of Macedonia imploring him, "Come over to Macedonia and help us" (Acts 16:9). In response to the vision, Paul and his companions set sail from Troas to travel to Macedonia. At the end of his third journey while returning from Greece, Paul again visited Troas, where he stayed for seven days (Acts 20:5–12). The Acts account tells of Paul engaging in a lengthy discussion in an upstairs room while at Troas. On that occasion Paul was a rather long-winded speaker, continuing his talk until midnight. One young man, **Eutychus**, who was sitting in a window, dozed off and fell out of the window. Having fallen to the ground three floors below, the young man was believed to be dead. Paul, however, picked him up, noting that he was still alive. Returning upstairs, Paul continued his discussion until dawn, at which time he left Troas for Assos.

In 2 Corinthians 2:12–13, Paul himself mentions a visit to Troas. Paul had sent a letter to the troubled church at Corinth by way of his assistant, **Titus**. Later, Paul went to Troas to preach the Christian message and to meet Titus there on his return from Corinth and receive a report about the situation in Corinth. Even though in Troas "a door was opened" for his preaching, Paul was too anxious to hear from Titus to remain in the city. So, since Titus was not there, Paul left and went on to Macedonia, where he met Titus. It is difficult to coordinate the Acts itineraries of Paul's travels with information in Paul's own letters about his missionary activities. It is possible that this visit described in 2 Corinthians was a part of the third journey described in Acts 18–21. During the trip, Paul traveled from Ephesus to Macedonia, likely going through Troas on the way.

The only other mention of Troas in the New Testament occurs in 2 Timothy 4:13. In this passage, Paul (or the pseudonymous author writing as Paul), writing from prison in Rome (2 Tim 1:16–17), asks **Timothy** to bring to him his cloak, the books, and the parchments that he had left with **Carpus** in Troas.

Site Visit

The site of ancient Troas, which supposedly covers more than 1,000 acres, is today overgrown with weeds, trees, and shrubs and partially covered by sand dunes and fields. Most of the site is unexcavated, although recently excavations have begun at the site under the direction of Turkish and German archaeologists, with plans for further excavations as well. Portions of the ruins are visible. Specifically, sections of the **city walls** and the **bath-gymnasium complex of Herodes Atticus** can be seen. The walls were originally over 5 miles long. The baths may be easily visited, since they are close to the highway. Herodes Atticus, wealthy benefactor and citizen of Athens, erected the baths in 135 C.E. and also constructed an aqueduct for the city. He was a friend of the emperor Hadrian, who appointed him to an administrative post in Asia Minor. While fulfilling the duties of this office, Atticus lived in Troas. (This is the same Herodes Atticus who built the odeion on the south slope of the Acropolis in Athens.)

To visit much of the rest of the ruins is somewhat challenging because of the trees and shrubs. The site is large and basically unmarked, making identification of the occasional ruins difficult. Recent excavations have uncovered the foundation of a **temple** (identified by archaeologists as a temple to Apollo Smintheus) apparently built during the end of the 1st

▲ **Fig. 132.** Bath-gymnasium complex of Herodes Atticus at Troas

century B.C.E., during the time of Augustus. Adjacent to the temple on the east is a still unexcavated **theater** or **odeion**. Also nearby are the ruins of a **basilica** and a recently uncovered **podium**. Near the small village of Dalyan is the **harbor** area of ancient Troas. The harbor itself has silted up and is no longer usable. Nearby on the beach, parts of a few **columns** can be seen protruding from the water. These columns are presumably ones that were brought here for transport to Istanbul to be reused for building materials there in the 17th century. They were apparently damaged during transport to the harbor or during loading and thus, being no longer suitable for building materials, were left behind.

Other Sites of Interest

One of the best-known stories from antiquity is the episode of the Trojan Horse, which takes place in the city of **Troy**. Many people are surprised to learn that ancient Troy is not in Greece but near the Aegean coast in modern Turkey. The site of ancient Troy (Truva, in Turkish) is north of Troas, approximately 18 miles south of Çanakkale off highway E87/550. According to the ancient story (the best-known version of which is in Homer's *Iliad*), Paris of Troy abducted Helen, the wife of Menelaus of Sparta. Agamemnon, the brother of Menelaus, led an army of Greeks (including Odysseus and Achilles) to Troy to get Helen back but was initially unsuccessful. Finally, some of the Greeks hid inside a large wooden horse they had built and left outside the gates of Troy, while the remainder of the Greek expedition pretended to sail away. Curious about the wooden horse, the Trojans brought it inside the city walls. During the night the soldiers climbed out of the horse and opened the gates for the rest of the Greek soldiers, who entered and destroyed the city of Troy.

Although this story of the Trojan War likely is not historical, it perhaps is based on an actual conquest of Troy by the Greeks (or Mycenaeans) in the 13th or early 12th century B.C.E. (Many historians, however, dispute the claim that the Greeks or Mycenaeans ever fought a war against Troy.) The site of ancient Troy has been occupied from around 3000 B.C.E. to 400 C.E., with nine different cities being built at this location. Remains of these different cities can be seen at the site. Troy VI and Troy VIIa are claimed by different scholars as the city of the Trojan War. A large display at the site and several informative markers help visitors make sense of the archaeological remains from the various periods of Troy's history (which can be very confusing). A large wooden horse at the entrance serves as a reminder of the legend of the ancient city.

Part III

Sites in Cyprus

In ancient times Cyprus suffered invasions from virtually all of its more powerful neighbors. Like Palestine, its location made it valuable as a strategic military outpost. Only 40 miles from the Turkish coast, 60 miles from the coast of Syria, and 250 miles from Egypt, the island was seen as an important military naval base and stepping-stone to other nations. Furthermore, its rich stores of copper made it doubly valuable. This turbulent history of Cyprus continued into the 20th century. Disputes between its Greek-speaking Christian inhabitants and Turkish Muslim population led to sometimes violent conflicts and the eventual invasion of the island in 1974 by 40,000 Turkish troops. The ultimate settlement of the conflict left the island partitioned into a Turkish north and a Greek south, while Nicosia/Lefkoşa, cut in two by the infamous "Green Line" maintained by U.N. troops, continues as the only remaining divided city in the world.

In recent times the island has returned to a more peaceful existence, and tourists are treated with unfailing courtesy on either end of the island. But since only Turkey recognizes northern Cyprus as an independent country and the major international airlines will not fly into the north, it has been necessary to make two separate trips to spend any length of time visiting both ends of the island. This situation, however, may be changing, as unification efforts are underway. At this writing, it is not possible to predict the eventual outcome, since these hopes have been continually frustrated in the past. Travelers to Cyprus should check carefully on the current situation before planning a trip to the island. It is to be hoped that this situation eventually will be resolved to the mutual benefit of both northern and southern Cyprus.

Northern Cyprus

When the island of Cyprus was divided and the Turkish Republic of Northern Cyprus was formed, the majority of the finest tourist facilities and beaches were in the north, as was much of the best farming land. Today Northern Cyprus is a beautiful and hospitable country not visited enough by Western tourists, but highly rewarding to those who do visit there.

Salamis

Ancient Salamis is the most impressive and extensive site in Northern Cyprus, and the most visited. More than any of the other archaeological sites on Cyprus, north or south, Salamis reveals the nature of Roman life on the island.

Location and History

Salamis is only 6 miles north of Gazimagusa/Famagusta, some 40 miles east of Girne, and 30 miles east of the Ercan airport. Follow the signs to Gazimagusa, then to ancient Salamis. A small road turns off to the right toward the sea; the entrance to the site is behind a small restaurant overlooking the fine beach and beautiful water beyond, a delightful place for a cooling drink after touring the ruins. In the summer it is likely to be quite hot at the site (and dehydrating), so it is best to arrive early. Perhaps plan on viewing the St. Barnabas monastery and church during the heat of the day.

Salamis took its name and its Mycenaean culture from the Greek island of the same name (close to the Athenian port of Piraeus). By the 8th century B.C.E. it was already the leading city-state of the ten others on Cyprus. The city led in the rebellion against the Persians at the battle of Salamis (5th century B.C.E.), which was lost largely because of the defection of the city-state of Kourion. Salamis later supported **Alexander the Great** in his wars with the Persians, and it subsequently prospered for a brief time. But when **Ptolemy I**, one of the successors to Alexander, besieged the city, its last king, **Nicocreon**, committed suicide rather than surrender. His remaining relatives did the same, burning down the palace in the process.

During the Roman period Salamis remained an important trading center, though Paphos was the new capital and developed a large Jewish population. In fact, the Romans had to put down a Jewish revolt there in 116 C.E., and thereafter Jews were banned from the island. The **Apostle Barnabas**, who traveled with **Paul** and played a major role in his acceptance by the Jerusalem Church, was a native of Cyprus. (The local tradition that he was killed on the island is not substantiated by history, though according to Acts he and **John Mark** returned to the island, whereupon nothing further was heard of them.)

Under the Byzantines, Salamis was renamed Constantia and once again made the capital of the island, as well as an archbishopric. A series of earthquakes in the 4th century c.e. destroyed much of the city, and the Arab raids of the 7th century led to the city's eventual abandonment.

Biblical Significance

Salamis holds the distinction of being the first port of call for the **Apostle Paul** and his traveling companions, **Barnabas**, a native of Cyprus, and the youthful **John Mark**. In truth, at this stage of their endeavors it might be more appropriate to refer to the missionaries as "Barnabas and his traveling companions," since until this time Paul's connection with Christianity had been largely dependent upon the good graces of Barnabas (see Acts 9:26–28; 11:19–26). Paul—who at that time was called by his Jewish name, Saul—and Barnabas were in Antioch (Syria) when they were set aside by the church for mission work in other countries.

The book of Acts then reports their journey to Cyprus in a few words: "So, being sent out by the Holy Spirit, they went down to Seleucia; and from there they sailed to Cyprus. When they arrived at Salamis, they proclaimed the word of God in the synagogues of the Jews. And they had John also to assist them" (Acts 13:4–5). Their choice of Cyprus was a logical one for several reasons. Besides the fact that it was the home of Barnabas and already must have contained a Christian contingent, Cyprus had been a part of the administrative province of Cilicia, whose capital was Tarsus, Paul's hometown, before it became a senatorial province of its own. So both of the missionaries had some identification with the island.

Seleucia was the port city for Antioch, approximately 16 miles to the west. It was a significant ancient port until its harbor silted up and it dwindled in importance. Transport for individuals could be arranged by purchasing passage on the merchant sailing vessels that plied the waters of the Mediterranean, which the early Christian missionaries would do many times in their lives. All travel was dangerous in ancient times, and travel by boat across open water was especially dangerous. Sailing vessels preferred to hug the shoreline whenever possible, but, of course, travel to the islands made that impossible. Salamis was the nearest port of Cyprus to Seleucia, and so the missionary group logically landed there.

In Salamis Paul established a pattern he would repeat throughout his journeys, that of using synagogues as his pulpit for attempting to gain converts to Christianity. Nothing is said in Acts about the reception given him, or whether a Christian church was established there. From Salamis, Paul, Barnabas, and John apparently went overland to Paphos, since Acts says, "When they had gone through the whole island as far as Paphos" (Acts 13:6). Much less is known about the means by which Paul traveled

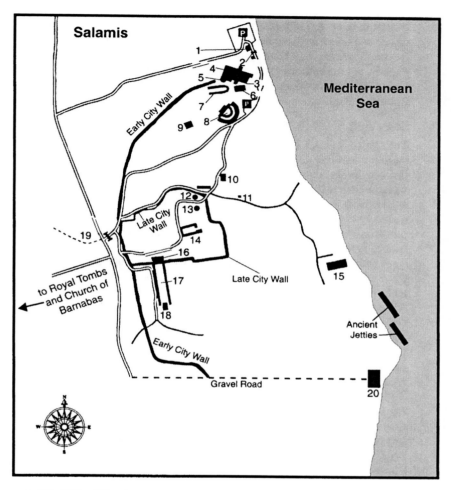

▲ **Fig. 133.** Salamis

1. Restaurant	11. Byzantine Cistern
2. Ticket Booth	12. Granite Forum
3. Baths	13. Water Clock
4. Gymnasium	14. St. Epiphanius Basilica
5. Latrines	15. Kambanopetra Basilica
6. Odeion	16. Byzantine Cistern
7. Stadium	17. Stone Forum
8. Amphitheater	18. Temple of Zeus
9. Roman Baths	19. Aqueduct Ruins
10. Roman Villa	20. Campground

overland, but much of it likely was done by walking. Occasionally, wagons or donkeys may have been used (horses generally were used only by the wealthy). He may have spoken in synagogues elsewhere in route to Paphos, but the author of Acts seems only to have known the tradition of his encounter with the magician **Elymas** and the Roman governor **Sergius Paulus** at Paphos.

Site Visit

The site of Salamis is quite large. Allow one to two hours for viewing, though a half day easily could be spent roaming about the extensive ruins. The largest remains nearest to the entrance gate can be seen on foot with no difficulty. However, to view the remaining locations of interest it is advisable to go by automobile. More than 4 miles of walking are required to cover the entire area of the site, and it is easy to become confused on the dirt roads. Like many of the archaeological sites on the island, few markers identify routes or objects.

A pathway from the parking area by the ticket booth leads to the eastern portico of the **gymnasium** with its **marble pool** surrounded by **headless figures**. One of these statues, in black marble, represents Persephone. All were defaced by early Christians as relics of pagan religion. The Greek gymnasium was an educational facility that combined intellectual and athletic training for youth. It is believed that Salamis originally had three such facilities, two for boys and one for girls. To the right beyond the pool, the **colonnaded courtyard** served as the palaestra, or exercise area for the gymnasium.

To the left are the massive walls of the **Byzantine bath** with its various facilities: first, the **frigidarium**, or cold room (there are two of these); then the **caldarium**, or hot room; and behind both of these, the **sweating rooms** or steam rooms. At the far end of the walk, opposite the east pool, **two other pools** completed the symmetry of the arrangement. The western hall between the pools is thought to have been the **tepidarium**, or warm room, of the bath complex.

Turn to the right at the end of the baths. On the left are the remains of a **stoa**, or covered porch. At the end of this area, on the left, are the **latrines** for the facility, with seating for forty-four persons. The Romans had no modesty about such things; the early Christians did, and had the place walled up.

Return past the stoa and exit the gymnasium and bath complex. On the left, the rows of elevated stone benches probably belonged to an **odeion**. To the right, the partially excavated location of a **stadium** is visible. Continue ahead to the reconstructed **theater**, which once seated approximately 15,000 spectators. The size of this theater, the largest on Cyprus, gives an indication of the population of Salamis at the time of its construction. Since the population of a city was usually ten times that of

Salamis: Main Area

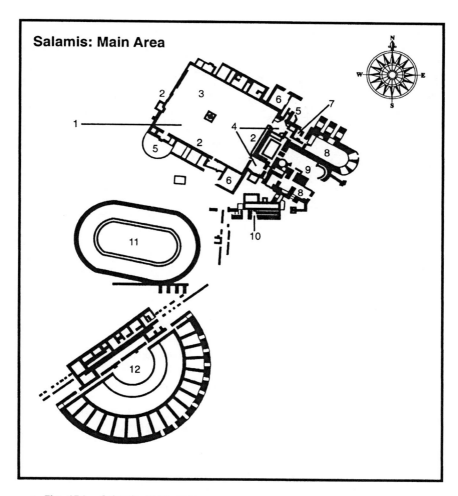

▲ **Fig. 134.** Salamis: Main Area

1. Gymnasium
2. Stoa
3. Columned Courtyard
4. Cold Rooms (Frigidaria)
5. Latrines
6. Swimming Pools
7. Stoking Rooms (Praefurnia)
8. Sweating Room (Sudatoria)
9. Hot Water Baths (Caldaria)
10. Aqueduct
11. Amphitheater
12. Theater

▲ **Fig. 135.** The theater at Salamis

its theater, the population of Salamis may have been as much as 150,000. Only eighteen of the original fifty rows of seats have been restored; the first eight rows are original. The top of the theater provides a fine view of the area.

To see the remaining sites, it is best to take a car beyond the theater. These sites are only partly excavated and most are in poor condition, but the tour is interesting nonetheless. (It is easy to become confused in the loop of roads, but have no fear—all the roads are connected within the enclosed site.) From the theater, take the left-hand fork in the road. The fragmentary remains of a **Roman villa** are on the left.

Next, take the dirt road to the left, past a **Byzantine cistern**, and go approximately a quarter of a mile to a basilica that overlooks the sea. Built in the 4th century, the **Kambanopetra basilica** is fascinating in its lonely setting. The central apse of the church contained seats for church dignitaries, and the floors throughout were provided with fine **geometric mosaics**. Several marble columns and **sarcophagi** have been restored at the site. The columns to the east mark the location of another **bath complex** featuring the most elaborate mosaic at Salamis, an outstanding example of an **opus sectile floor**.

Return to the main road. On the right are remains of a **late city wall**. Also on the right is the **Granite Forum**, distinguished by its remaining columns of pink Aswan granite brought to this location from hundreds of miles up the Nile River in Egypt. On the other side of the road a circular hole marks the location of an ancient **water clock**, which apparently told time at night by reflecting the stars in its pool.

The road next passes on the left the fragmentary ruins of the **Basilica of St. Epiphanius**, once the largest basilica on Cyprus. Also on the left are the remains of a large **reservoir**; behind it lies the **Stone Forum**, one of the largest forums in the ancient world, measuring 700 feet by 170 feet. At the far end of the forum, along a dirt road, nothing remains of the **Temple of Zeus** except a set of marble steps and a single column among scattered fragments.

For those interested in viewing the **ancient harbor** where Paul and his companions landed, ignore the advice of some guidebooks that recommend walking from the seaside basilica to the beach—unless fighting through heavy brush and deep sand is appealing. The better part of valor is to return by automobile to the highway to Gazimagusa/Famagusta, then take a sharp turn to the left at a gravel road running along the outside of the wire fence that encloses the Salamis site. This road ends at a camping site with a small restaurant (a generous title) and some nondescript buildings at the beachside. Pass beside them on foot and turn left, then walk a few hundred feet down the beach. In the water just offshore, the curving lines of the **breakwaters** for the ancient port of Salamis are plainly visible. Some large **foundation stones** for the port structures are still present at the water's edge. It was at this spot that Paul, Barnabas, and John Mark first set foot on Cyprus.

Other Sites of Interest

The road back to Gazimagusa/Famagusta passes four sites of interest, all virtually in sight of one another: the **Royal Tombs** and **ancient Enkomi** on the left, the **Church of St. Barnabas** and the **Tomb of St. Barnabas** on the right.

From Salamis, the first of these sites is the area of the so-called **Royal Tombs**. Because of their extravagant structure and elaborate contents, initially these tombs were believed to have been the burial places of royalty, but now they are known to have been the tombs of wealthy nobility from the Salamis area (7th century B.C.E.). At the entrance to the site there is a small **museum** connected with the ticket office. Its displays are largely replicas of items now in the Cyprus Museum, but they give some idea of the objects that were recovered from the tombs.

There are six major tombs on the site. **Tombs 47** and **79**, the most interesting of the group, had not been looted before the archaeologists did their work. They yielded a large number of objects for the use of the dead in the afterlife. Perhaps the most famous of these finds were an **ivory inlaid throne** and **bed**. The **skeletons** of the unfortunate **horses** that pulled the hearses to the tombs and were ritually slaughtered are displayed under glass plates in grotesque fashion. **Servants** were also sacrificed (unwillingly, as evidenced by their bound hands and feet) to serve their masters in the afterlife. (Unfairly, their masters are not also displayed under glass.)

The large dome-shaped tomb close by the highway is known as **St. Catherine's Prison (Tomb 50)**, based on a strictly legendary account that the Alexandrian saint once was imprisoned there. A **Byzantine chapel** later was built on top of it. **Tomb 3**, across the road from the ticket office, closely resembles the "beehive" tombs of Mycenae in Greece. Commoners from Salamis were buried in a separate area. Follow the blacktop road past the ticket office to view the site of these **underground tombs**.

Continue ahead a short distance to the **Church of St. Barnabas**. The church is largely unremarkable. The many **icons** are mostly late and of questionable quality; "**Herod's Banquet**" (1858) is an exception. (A much finer collection of icons mysteriously disappeared twenty years ago.) However, the only significant **archaeological museum** of a general nature in Northern Cyprus is housed around the courtyard of the church in rooms of the former monastery (8th century; the original 5th-century building was destroyed in the Arab raids). The museum collection,

almost exclusively pottery, is exhibited in three sections arranged as Neolithic, Bronze Age, Archaic, Classical, Hellenistic, Roman, and Ottoman displays. A few pieces of sculpture are included in the later time periods. **Refreshments** are sold from another of the former monastery's rooms. There is also small **gift shop**.

After exiting the church, the **Tomb of St. Barnabas** lies at the opposite end of the small path that crosses the parking area. This structure was erected in the 1950s over the site of an ancient **underground tomb** much older than the Christian era. The building is in sad condition. Steps lead down to two rock chambers with typical ledges (six) for the bodies of the dead. A number of guidebooks

▲ **Fig. 136.** The Tomb of St. Barnabas near Salamis

to the contrary notwithstanding, there is no evidence that Barnabas was martyred by the Jews on Cyprus (or, for that matter, that he died in any manner on Cyprus), or even that he lived the remainder of his life in Cyprus (though he well may have done so) or became the bishop of Cyprus. Likewise, the tradition that his body was found clasping the original copy of the Gospel of St. Matthew is certainly legendary. (No original copies of any of the books of the Bible have ever been found.) Such stories were commonplace in the Middle Ages to attract pilgrims/tourists to churches all over the Christian world (persuasive then, and still effective today).

Across the road a short distance are the rather unpromising-looking ruins of **Enkomi**. Yet this area yielded some of the finest treasures found on Cyprus, including the famous **"Horned God" of Enkomi**, many fine bronzes (in the Cyprus Museum), Mycenaean pottery (now in the British Museum), and many other important objects. The city was originally known as **Alasia**, and that name first appears on Egyptian tablets from 1600 B.C.E., when it was the preeminent city on Cyprus. Alasia became wealthy as a trading hub between Egypt, Syria, and the Hittite Empire, principally exporting copper from the area. By the 12th century B.C.E. the city had a population of some 12,000, but a century later it was abandoned due to an earthquake and Salamis became the principal city of the island.

Unfortunately, after the original French and British excavators left the site virtually no attention has been given to it. No signs mark any of the ruins. Nevertheless, Enkomi is a rare example of a **Bronze Age city**, one of the very few extant sites in the world that show the streets and houses from that ancient time. The layout of Enkomi is much more visible from the far end of the site, and it is well worth the half hour or so it takes to examine it.

Since most tourists prefer to stay around the beautiful harbor area of **Girne** rather than in Lefkoşa/Nicosia, one site in Girne should not be missed. **Girne Castle** is largely regarded by tourists as the Northern Cyprus version of a Disney attraction, complete with dungeons and tacky wax figures of prisoners (nude, unlike Disney, and all too anatomically correct) in various forms of torture. But the finest archaeological exhibit in Northern Cyprus is housed there in the **Shipwreck Museum**: a magnificently displayed **Hellenistic sailing vessel** more than 2,300 years old. It is the oldest ship ever recovered anywhere from the sea. Raised from the floor of the sea about a mile from the harbor of Girne in 1967 by a team of underwater archaeologists from the University of Pennsylvania, it took another six years to reconstruct the small vessel. Like the famous Wasa warship in Stockholm, Sweden, it is now kept in a temperature- and moisture-controlled room. Several other rooms contain the many artifacts found with the ship, each clearly labeled, and numerous photographs and drawings illustrate every facet of the find. Do not miss this magnificent exhibit.

Southern Cyprus

In Southern Cyprus the principal site of interest is Paphos, where the Apostle Paul encountered the Roman governor of Cyprus, Sergius Paulus. But other fine sites of interest range from Paphos to Larnaca, a distance of approximately 80 miles. Since there are airports in both locations and ferries arrive at Limassol, a visit might begin at any one of these places. In any case, with an early start it is possible to make a round trip between Paphos and Larnaca in one day and see the principal sites. A much easier itinerary, however, involves seeing the sites in the Paphos area on one day and the sites in Larnaca on another day, along with those between Paphos and Larnaca. The two sites in the south referred to in the Bible are Paphos and Kition (Kittim), which is mentioned in the Hebrew scriptures. Related sites include St. Paul's Pillar, the Catacombs of Agia Solomoni, the Tombs of the Kings, Paleopaphos, the Temple of Aphrodite, Kourion, the Temple of Apollo, and the Church of St. Lazarus, as well as several museums. The route below begins at Larnaca and proceeds toward Paphos, since that is the direction Paul and his companions traveled.

Larnaca: Kition/Kittim

At one time, Kition was one of the greatest naval powers in the Mediterranean, and its mercenaries even served in the deserts of southern Judea. Today its ruins still suggest the might of this ancient city.

Location and History

The site of ancient Kition, known in the Bible as Kittim, is located in the modern city of Larnaca. In the construction of Larnaca, whose name likely came from the Greek word for sarcophagus (*larnax*), or coffin, many sarcophagi were unearthed from ancient Kition. Larnaca was the location of a settlement of Mycenaeans as early as the 13th century B.C.E. Later abandoned, the site was rebuilt around 1200 B.C.E. by Achaean refugees following the destruction of the great Mycenaean centers of mainland Greece. A second wave of immigrants arrived about 1150 B.C.E. The original mud-brick city walls were rebuilt in the 12th century B.C.E. with cyclopean stones, huge rectangular ashlar blocks. After an earthquake in 1075 B.C.E., the city was resettled closer to the sea.

Beginning in the 9th century B.C.E., Phoenician merchants from Tyre settled at Kition and gradually formed a strong community. Around 850 B.C.E. an impressive temple was built to Astarte, the Phoenician goddess, over part of the abandoned earlier city. Kition later fell to the Assyrians under **King Sargon II** (r. 721–705 B.C.E.), as did all of the other city-states of Cyprus. After Persia defeated the Babylonians, successors to the Assyrians, Cyprus became a part of its empire. But in 499 B.C.E. some of the Cypriot city-states revolted against Persia, and the Persians supported the Phoenicians of Kition in seizing dominance over the area. After 479 B.C.E., a Phoenician dynasty ruled from Kition. During these years Kition conducted extensive trading relations with Athens.

Ever flexible in their loyalties, in 332 B.C.E. the Cypriot kings transferred their allegiance to **Alexander the Great** during his siege of Tyre and gained their freedom from Persia. After Alexander's death, the **Ptolemies**, his successors in Egypt, destroyed the city walls and temple of Kition (312 B.C.E.) and subsequently abolished its kingdom, along with all the other Cypriot kingdoms. During the period of Ptolemaic rule, however, philosophy and the arts flourished at Kition; the Stoic philosopher **Zeno** came from Kition. In 58 C.E. the Romans gained control of Cyprus, and over the following centuries the city of Kition gradually declined. After repeated invasions by first one world power and then another, the city eventually collapsed—literally—not from war, but from a great earthquake and subsequent fire in 280 B.C.E.

Biblical Significance

The Jewish historian Josephus identifies the biblical Kittim (Num 24:24; Dan 11:30; Jer 2:10; Ezek 27:6) as Kition in Cyprus. Several passages speak of a connection between Kittim and Assyria (Num 24:24), and Kittim also is identified as a naval power (Dan 11:30). Later the word was used to refer to any of the distant islands of the Mediterranean, and occasionally even to mainland Greece itself. Ezekiel's oracle against Tyre connects Kittim with Tyre as the supplier of pine for the decks of its ships (Ezek 27:6). Various biblical references allude to the far distance to Kittim, and it seems to have become proverbial as a distant place (Jer 2:10; Isa 23:12). Recent finds of inscribed pottery shards at Arad, to the west of the Dead Sea, indicate that mercenaries from Kition formed part of the military force of Judea in the 7th century B.C.E. (The "Kittim" are also mentioned in some of the Dead Sea Scrolls such as the War Scroll, the Habakkuk commentary, and the Isaiah commentary, but there it is a symbolic name for the Romans.)

Site Visit

Ancient Kition was much closer to the sea than it is today, and its maritime power was legendary. Recent excavations have revealed the foundations of long **boathouses** (5th century B.C.E.) that housed the royal fleet of Kition, originally located near the dock of the presently silted-up harbor. These facilities sheltered powerful triremes (galleys with three banks of oars), 120 feet long, which slid directly into the water on skids.

▲ **Fig. 137.** Temple 2 at Kition in Larnaca, Cyprus

This area, directly behind the **District Archaeological Museum of Larnaca**, is known as Bamboula and was once the **acropolis** of the city. It is not open to the public because of continuing excavations, though it can be viewed beyond a wire fence.

Two other sections of Kition were likely **residential areas**. The first, known as **Area I**, is located on Kimonos Street, some 20 feet below street level. It is visible through a wire fence. The other, **Area III**, is directly behind it on Chrisopolitissa Street. Neither is particularly impressive, though some restoration work is continuing.

The principal excavated area of ancient Kition, **Area II**, is not easy to locate. Go north from the District Archaeological Museum on Kilkis Street; turn left onto Leontiou Street, left again at Ioanni Paskirati Street, and the site entrance is at the end of the road.

The ruins can be viewed from a wooden catwalk that crosses the area. Unfortunately, the remains below lack labeling, making identification of objects difficult. However, the principal structures on the site are adjoining temples, **Temple I** on the right side of the catwalk, **Temple II** on the left. The wall that separated the two temples runs directly beneath the catwalk. In the 12th century B.C.E., Temple II was rebuilt with rectangular ashlar blocks. **New temples (I, IV, V)** were also constructed of stone with **altars and horns of consecration** in their courtyards. The most impressive of these temples, Temple I, is 105 feet long by 90 feet wide.

The scant remains of smaller temples lie beyond Temple II, as does a **workshop area** where smelting was conducted. For centuries copper was the principal export of Cyprus, and the close connection of the temples to a workshop for smelting copper provides some evidence that the metal played a prominent role in revered cultic objects of this period. Twin temples (I and II) associated with copper workshops may suggest worship of a male and female deity, as patron divinities of metalworking.

The **District Archaeological Museum** of Larnaca contains an outstanding collection from Kition and elsewhere. Principal objects include: a copy of a 7-foot **stele** (inscribed) **of Sargon II** of Assyria (724–705 B.C.E.), original now in the Staatliche Museum, Berlin; a fine **clay chariot** being pulled by three horses, jewelry, and pottery.

A local tradition (highly improbable) claims that **Lazarus**, who was raised from the dead by Jesus (John 11), moved to Cyprus and was later ordained as a bishop by **Barnabas**. After serving as bishop for thirty years, he died and was buried in Larnaca. His supposed **tomb**, which can be visited, is under the altar of the **Church of St. Lazarus**, located on Agiou Lazarou Square. Supposedly his remains were taken to Constantinople in 890 C.E. In the courtyard of the church is a small Byzantine museum.

The **Pierides Museum** (at Zinonos Kitieos 4), housed in a fine old home, contains a large collection of terra-cotta figures, clay lamps, and glassware from every ancient period. There is an unusual **statue of Baal** (Phoenician: Hamman, the sun god) from Kition as a human figure (400–300 B.C.E.). The museum's most famous object however, and without doubt the strangest, is the so-called **Howling Man** from the Chalcolithic period (3000 B.C.E.). Water poured into his hollow head emerges from the appropriate member below. Unless it was constructed strictly for amusement, no one has the slightest clue what it was for. The museum also displays a number of folk costumes and has a small **museum shop**.

Other Sites of Interest

Kourion is likely the best known and most popular of the ancient sites in Cyprus. Sitting atop a sheer bluff overlooking the sea, it certainly has the most dramatic location. It was established as a city by the Mycenaeans sometime between the 14th and 12th centuries B.C.E. During the Cypriot rebellion against the Persians, Kourion defected to the Persians, ensuring the defeat of the rebellion. It supported **Alexander the Great**, however, against the Persians and reached its glory days during the Hellenistic and Roman eras. Kourion remained a significant city into the Byzantine period, but it was totally destroyed in the earthquake of 365 C.E. After the Arab raids of the 7th century C.E., it was abandoned.

To reach Kourion from Larnaca, take highway A1 to Erimi (approximately 50 miles); this route bypasses Limassol. Then take the road to Episcopi and follow the signs to Kourion.

To the right of the site entrance is the **theater**, originally built in the Hellenistic period and refurbished in the 2nd century C.E. It is still used for performances, the most prominent being the Shakespeare plays in June. A 4th-century-C.E. **villa** and **baths** under a roof shelter can be viewed from wooden catwalks that cross them. Several outstanding mosaics are also located there, including the **5th-century inscription** identifying the villa as belonging to a Christian: "In place of rock and iron, or gleaming bronze and diamonds, this house is girded with the much venerated signs of Christ." The **atrium floor** holds mosaics of fish and birds, popular early Christian symbols.

A path leads westward to the remnants of an extensive 5th-century **basilica** with its deep **hexagonal cistern** that supplied water for the adjacent **baptistery**. On the south side of the nave, the **marble font** appears to have been modified for infant baptism. The arches beyond the basilica are thought to have been part of a **bishop's palace**. North of the baptistery are the remains of a house from the late Roman period, known as the **House of the Gladiators** from one of its mosaics. The Roman **agora** and **nymphaeum** are still undergoing excavation.

A little over a mile to the west, just off highway B6, is the **Sanctuary of Apollo Hylates**, god of the woodland, the sacred precinct of Kourion. Originally built in the 8th century B.C.E., the remaining structures date from the Roman period. The buildings here were destroyed in the earthquake of 365 C.E. On the right of the path from the ticket office is the area of the **palaestra**, or exercise area for athletes. The large jar resting there held cooling water. The ruins of the **baths** for the sanctuary area are under the metal roof to the north; just before it is the **priests' house**. Between the bath and palaestra, and below the priests' house, is the **Treasury**. The processional way begins at the **dormitory**, or **inn** for pilgrims (*xenon*), and continues up to the symbolically restored **Temple of Apollo** with its two columns and angular corner wall. The **Roman stadium**, 1,500 feet to the east, that once seated 6,000 now consists of only a few rows of seats in poor condition. Farther to the east are the remains of a **late Byzantine basilica** (6th century C.E.).

Paphos

The most popular of tourist destinations on Cyprus, picturesque Paphos is delightful for its modern holiday atmosphere, its world-famous ancient mosaics, and its abundance and variety of historical sites of interest.

Location and History

Paphos is easily reached from Larnaca along highway A1, one of the best motorways in Cyprus. It is important, however, to distinguish Palea

Paphos (Ancient Paphos; more below), now called Kouklia and 9 miles to the east, from Paphos or Nea Paphos (New Paphos). Furthermore, the entrance to Paphos displays signs to Kato Paphos and Kitima; both are sections of Paphos. For the major archaeological site, go toward Kato Paphos and the harbor. Parking is available in a large lot to the right of the harbor and just before the entrance to the archaeological site. Kitima is the upper town and the center of the city, as well as the location of the fine archaeological museum.

Nea Paphos seems to have been little more than a small settlement before the Hellenistic period when the Ptolemies, Hellenistic rulers of Egypt, developed it into a significant administrative center. The Ptolemies saw Paphos as a vital location for two principal reasons. First, its good port was the closest to Alexandria, their capital (later it would serve as their largest military outpost outside of Egypt). Second, its supply of timber was important for their shipbuilding operations. In the 2nd century B.C.E., the Ptolemies made Paphos the capital of all Cyprus.

When the Romans took over Cyprus in 58 B.C.E., Paphos remained the capital and the seat of the Roman proconsul. **Cicero** served as its proconsul for two years. **Sergius Paulus**, who had an encounter with the **Apostle Paul**, was another of its proconsuls. The town reached its zenith in the early 3rd century C.E., as attested by the wealth of the tombs and the notable buildings that have been discovered from that period. But at the end of the early 4th century C.E., a series of earthquakes rocked the island, severely damaging Paphos. Rebuilding followed, but the city was never the same, and Salamis soon became the capital of the island. After the 7th century C.E., Paphos went into a long decline, its harbor silted up, and its prominence was ended. At the First Ecumenical Council at Nicaea in 325 C.E., however, one of the bishops at the council was from Paphos, indicating a strong Christian tradition in the area.

Biblical Significance

After **Paul, Barnabas,** and **John Mark** left Salamis, Acts 13 records no other visits to places on Cyprus until they reached Paphos. For this reason, some scholars believe that they sailed around the island to Paphos. On the other hand, the text says that they went "through the whole island," which would imply an overland journey. At Paphos they were summoned to an interview with **Sergius Paulus**, proconsul of the island. Crete had been made a Roman senatorial province shortly before this time (22 C.E.), and a proconsul was assigned to the capital, Paphos, as its governor. Apparently the apostles had been preaching in the area when Sergius Paulus heard of them and became curious about their purpose and message. A Jewish magician attached to the court of the governor, however, attempted to dispute the testimony of the apostles and to persuade the governor to ignore their words. Paul angrily denounced him as a "son of the devil" and "full of all deceit and villainy," whereupon the magician, **Elymas**, was blinded "for a while, unable to see the sun." When he saw what had happened, Sergius Paulus then believed, "for he was astonished at the teaching about the Lord." Since there is no mention of Sergius Paulus being baptized, some commentators have questioned whether he was actually converted to the Christian faith. However, that seems to be the intention of the text in Acts.

Subsequently, the apostles left Cyprus, setting sail from Paphos and journeying to Perga in Pamphylia (a province on the southern coast of Asia Minor, modern Turkey). This was Paul's only visit to Cyprus. According to Acts, however, Barnabas and John Mark did return, and a tradition developed that Barnabas became the first bishop of the island.

Elymas is otherwise unknown, but it was not unusual for such persons to be consulted by the Romans for insight into future events. No doubt he was attempting to protect his place at court when he disputed the words of Paul. As for Sergius Paulus, three different Roman officials with the name have been identified historically. One of these is connected with a family of wealthy landowners in Pisidia, and some have suggested that the governor provided Paul with introductions to the aristocracy in Pisidian Antioch. Sufficient evidence does not currently exist to make positive identification possible. A stone was discovered, however, in a town near Paphos with the inscription "Sergius Paulus, proconsul," and another memorial stone with the same name was found in Rome, to which Sergius Paulus returned after his service in Cyprus. If these inscriptions in fact refer to the governor of Cyprus at the time of Paul, then they record one of the very few names of people mentioned in the New Testament yet unearthed by archaeology.

Site Visit

Paphos contains a variety of sites, all well worth a visit. This suggested route begins with the Central Archaeological Park, across from the harbor.

Main Site

The site of Nea Paphos is pleasant to visit, with its well laid-out walks and covered mosaics. As in most locations in Cyprus, more identifying signs would be helpful. Located on the point of the peninsula, with a commanding view of the sea, this largest excavated area of ruins belongs to a building known as the **House of Theseus**, or the **Governor's Palace**. It is generally regarded to have been the palace of the Roman governor, or proconsul, of the island. Discovered in 1966 by the Polish Archaeological Mission of the University of Warsaw, the House of Theseus (named for its finest mosaic) is the largest residential structure on Cyprus and one of the largest in the entire Mediterranean, measuring over 360 feet east to west and over 250 feet north to south. Because of its

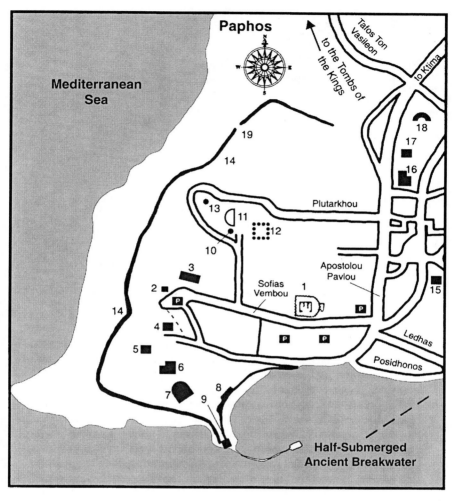

▲ **Fig. 138.** Paphos

1. Saranda Kolones
2. Ticket Office
3. House of Dionysus
4. House of Aion
5. House of Orpheus
6. House of Theseus
7. Ancient Greek Theater
8. Old Customs House
9. Castle
10. Asclepeion
11. Odeion
12. Agora
13. Lighthouse
14. Roman Walls
15. Agia Kyriaki/St. Paul's Pillar/Early
    Basilica
16. Agia Solomoni
17. Rock-cut Burial Chambers
18. Hellenistic Theater
19. Northwest Gate

▲ **Fig. 139.** The House of Theseus at Paphos

extensive size, the villa seems to have served some sort of administrative function. Likewise, the building is divided into separate public and private areas, further indication that it served as an official residence. Finally, the presence of an inscription in Latin, used only for official matters in the Greek-speaking portions of the Roman Empire, suggests the presence of Romans in the history of the structure.

The palace was constructed with four wings around a central courtyard. Most of it can be viewed from the wooden walkway that crosses a good portion of the villa. At the front of the **east wing**, to the right of the steps to the catwalk, is a long room that may have served the function of a **reception hall** to the building. The waiting area is lined with benches and decorated with a geometric mosaic on the floor. Originally the walls were covered with a white lime plaster. On the back wall, three doorways lead into the palace. The center doorway opens into the atrium beyond; the two doors on either side lead to the household areas. A rectangular pool stood in the center of the **atrium**, which was built in the familiar style of those at Pompeii. The floor of the atrium was covered with another geometric mosaic, typical of all but a few of the mosaics in the building. The large open courtyard beyond the atrium had no flooring. It was surrounded by three **porticoes** with geometric mosaics on their floors. The best-preserved of these mosaics lies directly behind the reception hall and is oriented from north to south.

To the right of the courtyard, the **north wing** is in poor condition, having been stripped of its stone in later times. The ruins visible today date from before the construction of the palace. This wing likely contained rooms for servants, and the presence of large cisterns and waterproof cement floors suggests that originally the palace **laundry** also was in this wing. Bordering the wing on the north was a street approximately 10 feet wide with a water drain in the center. Its outline is still visible.

To the left of the entrance to the palace is the **south wing**, the oldest portion of the palace. Nearest to the front of the building, in the southeast corner, a group of rooms constitute an extensive **bath complex**. Two small rooms at the juncture of the south and east walls contained the **furnace** and an **elevated water tank**. Behind these rooms are **dressing rooms** and a **latrine** for several people at a time. The long room in the center of the complex is the **frigidarium**, or cold room; the basin for foot washing was added at a later period. Across from the frigidarium, along the south wall, are the **tepidarium** (the warm bath), the **caldarium** (the hot bath), and the **sudatorium** (the steam room) between them. To the right of the frigidarium is a room with the mosaic that gave the building its name. There a circular mosaic portrays the duel between Theseus, son of Poseidon, and the legendary Minotaur of Crete.

Prominent beyond the bath complex on the left is a large **double room** consisting of a rectangular hall and a horseshoe-shaped apse that is slightly elevated. Two steps lead up to it. The Roman governor likely held audiences in this room, seated within the elevated apse. The encounter between the **Apostle Paul** and the proconsul **Sergius Paulus** must have occurred in a hall such as this. The entire floor of the rectangular portion of the room was originally covered in mosaics; the large panel that remains shows the first bath of Achilles, during which his heel was not immersed in water, thereby leaving him vulnerable.

A large number of statues now in the Paphos District Museum were found in the **west wing**, which seems to have functioned as **living quarters** for the palace. A room in the southwest corner of the villa contains a mosaic of Poseidon. Unfortunately, it is in poor condition. The **watchtower** at the rear of the wing was added in a later period.

In 1983 the Polish Archaeological Mission began excavations on a building now known as the **House of Aion**, named for the central figure in the **exceptional mosaic** found in its reception hall. Only three of the rooms of the house have been excavated thus far. The mosaic consists of five panels of exceptionally high quality. The top left panel portrays the myth of the seduction of Leda, queen of Sparta, by a swan, actually Zeus in disguise. The top right panel shows Dionysus in the lap of Hermes being handed to Tropheus, his future tutor. The large central panel contains two scenes, one on land and one on sea, portraying a beauty contest between Cassiopeia, wife of the king of Tyre, and the Nereids, daughters of the god of the waters, Nereus. Cassiopeia has won (left side of the panel), and she is being crowned by Krisis (Judgment). The judge of the contest is Aion, the personification of eternal time. Aion is the figure holding a staff with a nimbus surrounding his head. Three of the most beautiful of Nereus' daughters are shown on the right side of the panel as they ride away on the back of Bythos, a sea centaur and personification of the depths of the sea. Zeus and Athena watch from above. The bottom left panel shows Dionysus (mostly obliterated in the panel) in a procession as he rides in a cart pulled by a pair of centaurs. He is followed by his tutor Tropheus, riding upon a mule. The bottom right panel depicts the moment at which Marsyas is led away to his death for daring to challenge Apollo to a musical contest. The double flute of Marsyas lies at the feet of Apollo, who has his lyre by his side. The executioners are Scythians; they wear Phrygian caps. The woman on Apollo's right is Plane, who personifies the "errant mind" that led Marsyas into such folly.

Beyond the Villa of Theseus lies the **House of Orpheus**, only partially excavated. The nature and plan of the building are not completely understood. Systematic excavation of the House of Orpheus began in 1982 and is continuing. **Three outstanding mosaics**, however, have been uncovered. The first is **Hercules and the Lion of Nemea**. Hercules is shown as he is about to strangle the mythical, invulnerable lion of Nemea with his bare hands. His club, which already has proved useless in the struggle, lies on the ground. This scene depicts the first of the labors of Hercules. The second is **the Amazon**. Amazons were the warrior daughters of Mars and Venus who lived in a mythical country in Asia Minor inhabited only by women. They fought on horseback and carried double axes such as the one in the mosaic. The Amazon portrayed wears the Phrygian cap and typical laced-up boots. Her right breast is uncovered; according to legend, Amazons cut off one of their breasts so that it would not interfere with shooting the bow. The last is **Orpheus and the Beasts**. This large mosaic gave the house its name. It depicts Orpheus, the legendary musician from Thrace, surrounded by creatures enchanted by his music. He, too, wears the Phrygian cap. At the top left of the panel is the **inscription** "Titus (or Gaius) Pinnius Restitutus made it," which could denote either the artist who made the mosaic or, perhaps more likely, the person who had it made, that is, the owner of the house. Interestingly, the inscription is in Greek characters while the name is Roman.

At the time of this writing, the **House of the Four Seasons** was not yet open to the public. From the fine mosaics discovered in it, however, the structure was obviously another large mansion of a wealthy owner. It was given its name because of a mosaic panel representing autumn, which led the excavators to believe that at one time all four seasons must have been portrayed. Most of the mosaics discovered thus far are representations of various animals, including a hunting scene showing an encounter between a hunter and a lion. The house was located in 1992, and excavations are continuing.

The most famous of the mansions located here, if for no other reason than the sheer number of its mosaics, is the **House of Dionysus**. This large and elaborate residence covers more than 6,000 square feet and contains 1,700 square feet of remarkably well-preserved mosaic floors. Dionysus, or Bacchus, the god of wine, is featured in several of the mosaics. Originally thought to be the residence of the governor, the house is now regarded as simply an example of the extravagant and luxurious living at Paphos during the Roman period. The earliest structure on the site, cut into the bedrock, seems to have been a **sanctuary to the god Harpocrates** (Egyptian, Horus). This conclusion is based upon a bone knife handle with a carving of the god that was found on the site. Stone robbers and other misfortunes have destroyed most of the structure of the building over the centuries, but it is nevertheless apparent that the house surrounded a central atrium. Built at the end of the 2nd century C.E., it was likely destroyed during the great earthquakes in the first half of the 4th century C.E. The present shed over the structure provides a look not unlike the original configuration.

The following list includes some of the most noteworthy mosaics of the house. (Room numbers correspond to the diagram at the site.)

Room 1: To the left of the entry, this room contains the only pre-Roman mosaic in the house. The **Scylla Mosaic** is a Hellenistic work dating from the late 4th or early 3rd century B.C.E., the earliest mosaic yet found on Cyprus. It was discovered 3 feet below floor level at the southwest corner of the atrium and relaid in this location for viewing. Unlike the Roman mosaics, the Scylla Mosaic is composed of pebbles rather than specially cut stones. Scylla was a legendary sea monster in Greek legends, part woman, part fish, and part dog. Here she holds in her left hand the mast of a sunken ship; her left hand seems to hold a stylized trident.

Room 2: Narcissus is shown as admiring his reflection in a pool of water. Much of the geometric decoration has been added.

Room 3: This room seems to have been the antechamber of the original house since it contains the **inscription** XAIPEI ("rejoice") and CY ("you as well"), familiar greetings. In its four corners the mosaic depicts the Four Seasons; the figure in the center is unknown.

Room 4: The largest room in the house, Room 4 likely served as a **dining room** (triclinium). This function is suggested by the arrangement of floor mosaics, which would have permitted all the guests who reclined at dinner to enjoy equally good views of the mosaic art. The major panels depict the famous legend of the triumphant return of the god Dionysus from an expedition to India, where he obtained the slaves and the panthers shown in the mosaic. Dionysus sits in a two-wheeled chariot, holding a spear; among the other figures are Pan holding a shepherd's crook; bacchantes, female followers of Dionysus; and others.

Room 6: The two figures in the mosaic are Phaedra and Hippolytus, her stepson. He is shown holding a note in which she has just confessed her forbidden love for him. In typical Greek fashion, both of them later die tragic deaths. In the course of renovating this mosaic, more than 10,000 important seal impressions in clay were found under the mosaic; they had been put there as filler to level the floor of the mosaic. These seals, depicting emperors, gods, and Ptolemaic kings, were brought there from the ruins of the archive building in Nea Paphos after it had burned down.

Room 8: The elaborate mosaic in Room 8 depicts the rape of Ganymede. Ganymede, a Trojan shepherd, was so admired for his beauty that Zeus, disguised as an eagle, carried him away to Olympus to serve as cupbearer to the gods.

Room 16: The mosaic in this room consists of four rectangular panels. The first panel on the left depicts the story of Pyramos and Thisbe, two more star-crossed lovers, whose story is like that of Romeo and Juliet. Frustrated by their rival parents, the young lovers eventually commit suicide, Pyramos because he thinks Thisbe has been killed by a lion; Thisbe when she discovers Pyramos' body. To the right, the large panel represents the legend of Icarios, the human who was taught to make wine by Dionysus. The following panel depicts the story of Neptune and Amymone. In exchange for her love, the god revealed to her the source of a spring of water in a time of terrible drought. The last panel illustrates the legend of Apollo and Daphne. Daphne, daughter of the river god Peneus, had pledged herself to eternal chastity. Nevertheless, Apollo attempts to take her by force, whereupon Daphne prays to her father for help and is turned into a laurel (in Greek, *daphne*) tree.

Room 18: This elaborate **bedroom** of the house contains a pool in its center lined with pink waterproof plaster, much of which has been preserved. The fish that were kept in the pond could find cooling shade within the small alcoves built into its walls.

Beyond the House of Dionysus to the north, a path leads to the **Asclepeion** and the **odeion**. The odeion is clearly recognizable on the left-hand side of the path; the Asclepeion is the rather unremarkable group of ruins, also on the left, just before it. Named for the healing god Asclepius, these structures were created throughout the Greco-Roman world. They featured small rooms where priests of Asclepius ministered to the sick. Frequently narcotics were used to induce dreamlike states, during which the priests suggested the presence of Asclepius. Subsequent cures were attributed to the god.

An odeion in the ancient world was a place of musical, oratorical, and sometimes theatrical performances. (Interestingly, these places, just as today, never seated as many people as the places where athletic competitions were held.) This amphitheater was first restored in the 1970s. In 2001, additional renovation was performed. It is still used today for various performances. Directly across from these structures, the large field is the location of the **Roman agora**. It remains to be systematically excavated.

Agia Kyriakis (Chrisopolitissa) and St. Paul's Pillar

Other sites of interest in the vicinity can be easily reached by walking from the parking lot across from the harbor. Return to Apostolou Pavlou Street; turn left. Go to Leda (behind Woolworth) and take the small lane to the left. **Agia Kyriakis**, a Byzantine church of the 12th century, is not particularly significant, but it is surrounded by the foundations of a **large basilica** and **bishop's palace** of the 4th century. Numerous geometric mosaics have been uncovered, as well as the representation of a wine krater and grape clusters with the inscription "I am the True Vine" (John

▲ **Fig. 140.** St. Paul's Pillar at Agia Kyriakis Basilica (Chrisopolitissa) in Paphos

15:1). On the far left-hand side of the front courtyard of the basilica, inside the wall, there is a column with a rounded top known as **St. Paul's Pillar**. According to local legend, the apostle was tied to this pillar and scourged. (There is no historical evidence, however, for such an event.)

The Catacombs of Agia Solomoni

Continue up Apostolou Pavlou a short distance to the **Catacombs of Agia Solomoni**, which are on the right (east) of the road. Tradition says that these underground chambers once served as the **synagogue** of Roman Paphos. The place takes its name from the seven Jewish martyrs and their mother (Solomoni), who were tortured and killed during the reign of terror of **Antiochus Epiphanes**, one of the Seleucid rulers of Palestine. (The story is told in both 2 Maccabees and 4 Maccabees.) That tradition likely began because there are eight burial places within the chambers, and because at one time the Seleucids ruled Cyprus.

The Tombs of the Kings

The **Tombs of the Kings** lie approximately 1 mile to the northwest of the catacombs on the left-hand side of Leophoros Tafon ton Vasileon. These underground burial places, some of which are dated as early as the 3rd century B.C.E., belonged not to kings at all but to wealthy families from the area. Archaeological work on the site began in 1917 and continued with lengthy interruptions until 1951, but it was not until 1977 that systematic excavation was begun by the Cyprus Department of Antiquities. The tombs have been recognized by UNESCO as a World Heritage Site.

Beyond the ticket office, the first tomb immediately to the left (no. 1) is a **rock-cut chamber tomb** with burial places for two children and five adults. A number of tombs occupy the area on the left-hand side of the walk, but the **most interesting tombs** (nos. 3, 4, and 8) are peristyle in design (Doric columns encircling an open court). These impressive structures were carved out of the native rock; some were given elaborate decoration. The style of these tombs has much in common with those in Macedonia, whose influence was passed to Cyprus from the Seleucid culture of its onetime rulers following the time of Alexander the Great. A brochure available at the gate gives extensive descriptions of each of the major tombs.

Paphos District Archaeological Museum in Kitima

Leaving the Tombs of the Kings, return to Apostolou Pavlou Avenue, continue north, and follow the signs to the right to the **museum** on Griva Digeni Avenue. The collection contains pottery, bronze, and glass objects from various ancient time periods as well as some items from the House of Theseus and the House of Dionysus. By far the most unique items are a strange collection of **clay hot-water bottles**, shaped to fit various body parts, from the Hellenistic period.

Other Sites of Interest

Palea (old) **Paphos** (modern Kouklia), approximately 9 miles to the east of **Nea** (new) **Paphos**, once was the capital of an empire that extended over much of the island. (Nearby, **Petra tou Rumiou**, often photographed by tourists, is the spot where Aphrodite was said to have been born from the sea.) Most noted for its **Temple of Aphrodite**, where temple prostitution was practiced, Palea Paphos was visited by pilgrims from all over the ancient world. Even though it was destroyed by the Persians in 498 B.C.E., Palea Paphos was rebuilt, and its last king founded Nea Paphos as the new capital (321 B.C.E.). Roman emperors, such as **Titus**, who visited Palea Paphos in 69 C.E. on his way to Syria (and the destruction of Jerusalem), patronized the site until its eventual decline in the 4th century C.E.

Today there is little to be seen on the ancient site except the scant remains of two sanctuaries: the **Late Bronze Age Sanctuary I**, nearest to the museum, and the **Roman Sanctuary II** beyond it. The wall of Sanctuary I contains large limestone building blocks with many deep holes in the side, the purpose of which is not known. The shallow depression in the stone before the tall pier served as a **basin for lustrations** (washings) by worshipers at the sanctuary. This pier stands on the edge of the **South Stoa** of Sanctuary II; across the adjoining courtyard was the **North Stoa**. To the northwest of these sanctuaries, the remains of a large Roman **peristyle house** were found.

The **museum**, housed in a Turkish building, contains a number of interesting items, including an 11th-century-B.C.E. **tomb**; a **conical stone**, representing Aphrodite; a fine **limestone head** found in the Persian siege ramp (600–475 B.C.E.); a fascinating and unique **copy of the oath of the Cypriots to Augustus** upon his ascension to the throne (14 C.E.); and a considerable collection of bronzes and pottery.

The **Cyprus Museum in Nicosia** contains the largest and best assembly of archaeological objects on the island. Located between the municipal gardens and the Tripoli bastion, two hours are required to view this extensive collection. Outstanding pieces include objects from the Early Bronze Age illustrating an early cult of bull worship (**priests wearing bull masks**, and a **model sanctuary** with bull heads); from the Late Bronze Age, extensive Mycenaean objects, including a **gold inlaid bowl** from Enkomi; a **statue of Zeus** from Kition; a Roman **statuette of Aphrodite** (1st century C.E.); a bronze life-size nude **statue of Emperor Septimius Severus** (2nd century C.E.); the famous **bronze statue of the "Horned God" of Enkomi**; the equally famous **bronze cauldron** from the "Royal Tombs" of Salamis, in one of the **underground tomb rooms** that illustrate types of burials on Crete; the original **mosaic of Leda and the Swan** from Palea Paphos; and numerous terracotta figurines, including one of **three people and a dog in a boat**.

Area Maps and Charts

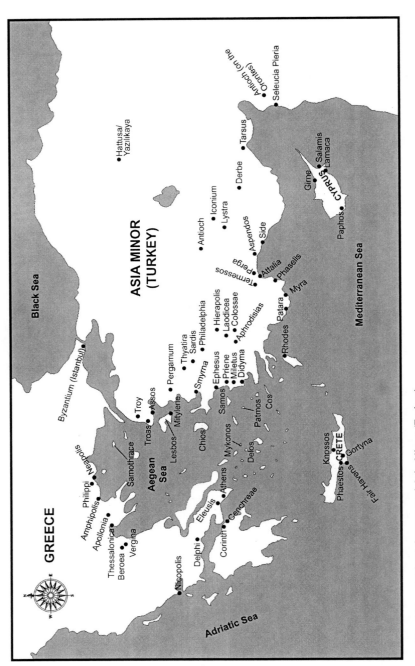

▲ Fig. 141. Ancient Greece and Asia Minor (Turkey)

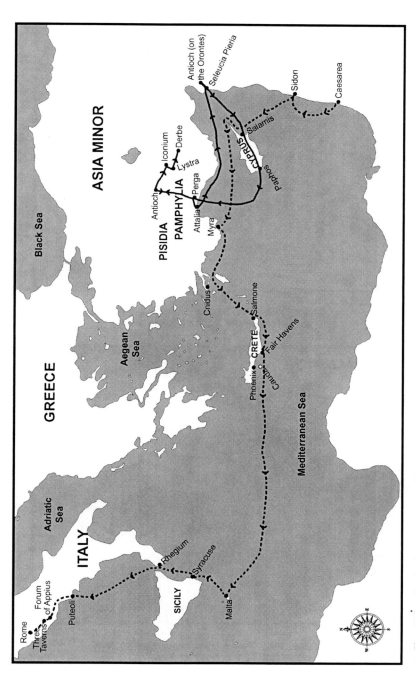

▲ Fig. 142. Paul's first missionary journey (——) and his journey to Rome (----) according to the book of Acts

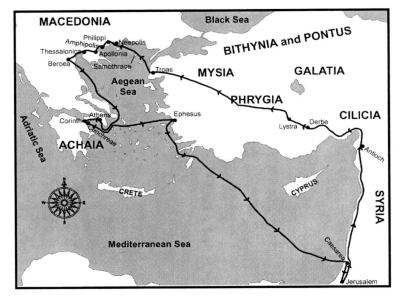

▲ **Fig. 143.** Paul's second missionary journey according to the book of Acts

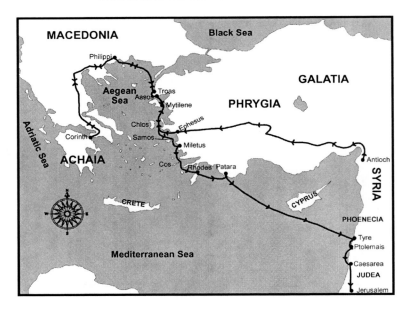

▲ **Fig. 144.** Paul's third missionary journey according to the book of Acts

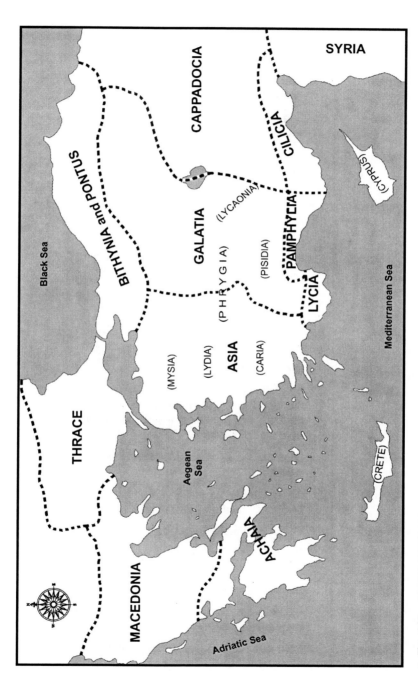

▲ Fig. 145. Roman provinces

▼ **Fig. 146.** Gods of Greece, Rome, and Asia Minor (with their chief attributes and symbols indicated in parentheses; gods described are Greek unless otherwise noted)

Aphrodite	Goddess of beauty and erotic love; mother of Eros (seashell, swan, pomegranate, dove)
Apollo	God of music, oracles, health, perpetual youth (lyre, bow and arrows)
Ares	Son of Hera and Zeus; fierce Thracian god of violence and warfare; never popular in Greece (plumed helmet)
Artemis	In Greece, goddess of the hunt and of children; in Asia Minor, nurturing goddess (many-breasted goddess, deer, bee)
Asclepius	Physician-god, son of Apollo (staff with coiled snake)
Athena	Martial goddess of military strategy, virgin goddess of wisdom (owl, helmet, shield, spear)
Attis	Consort of Cybele; renewed life in nature (youth wearing a Phrygian cap)
Bacchus	(Roman; *see* Dionysus)
Cabeiri	Mysterious, volcanic gods of the underworld; among the "great gods" of Samothrace; often confused with the Dioscuri; protectors against storms (hammers over their shoulders)
Ceres	(Roman; *see* Demeter) Goddess of grain (sheaf of wheat)
Cybele	Anatolian mother goddess, first known as the Great Mother (seated on a throne between two lions)
Demeter	Goddess of agriculture (scepter, ears of wheat)
Diana	Roman goddess of the hunt, identified with Artemis (deer, bow and arrows)
Dike	Implacable goddess of justice (scales)
Dionysus	God of wine, fertility, and vegetation (drinking cup, ivy wreath, panther)
Dioscuri	Sons of Zeus; twin gods, Castor and Pollux, "the Heavenly Twins"; patrons of sailors (helmets)

Eros	God of physical desire; son of Aphrodite (winged child)
Great Mother	Earliest name for the Anatolian mother goddess, later known in Rome as Magna Mater and identified with Artemis (in Anatolia, seated nude woman giving birth)
Hadad	Syrian god of the storm, fertility (lightning bolt)
Hades	God of the underworld; brother of Zeus and Poseidon
Hecate	Goddess of magic; keeper of the underworld (keys and cords)
Hephaestus/ Hephaistos	God of fire and the forge; patron of skilled craftsman (hammer, tongs)
Hera	Wife of Zeus, patroness of marriage; respected by the Olympian deities as if a queen (crown, peacock)
Heracles	Mythical hero of supernatural strength (club)
Hercules	(Roman; *see* Heracles)
Hermes	Messenger of the gods; protector of travelers (staff, winged sandals)
Hestia	Most ancient goddess; goddess of the altar and the hearth (hearth and altar fires)
Hygieia	Daughter of Asclepius; goddess of the preservation of health
Isis	Originally Egyptian; later, fusion of all goddesses; popular with women (knot at the breast of her gown)
Juno	(Roman; *see* Hera)
Jupiter	(Roman; *see* Zeus)
Kore	(*see* Persephone; the word *kore* means "girl/daughter")
Mars	Roman god of war, protector of youth (*see* Ares)
Muses	Nine goddesses of the arts (lyre, nightingale)
Mercury	(Roman; *see* Hermes)
Minerva	(Roman; *see* Athena)
Mithras	Cosmic warrior god who controlled the universe; protector of oaths (Persian garb and peaked cap, slaying a bull)

Nemesis	Goddess of divine justice, punished hubris/arrogance toward the gods (griffin)
Neptune	(Roman; *see* Poseidon)
Orpheus	Mythical Thracian hero, skilled in music and epic poetry (lyre)
Osiris	Egyptian lord of the underworld, husband-brother of Isis; funerary god (flail and crook)
Pan	Pastoral god, son of Hermes; could cause "panic" with his wild cries (pan flute; goats)
Persephone (*also* Kore)	Daughter of Demeter; her return from the underworld each year brought springtime and crops (torch and sheaf of wheat)
Pluton (*also* Pluto)	God of the underworld, brother of Zeus (*see* Hades)
Poseidon	God of the sea; also caused earthquakes, which were believed to come from underground rivers (trident)
Roma	Patron goddess of Rome, modeled on Minerva (breastplate)
Serapis	Hellenistic fusion of Greek and Egyptian gods; god of healing, life after death, and fertility
Sirens	Evil sea spirits, lured sailors onto rocks by their singing (heads of beautiful women, bodies of birds)
Themis	Goddess of moral order and institutions (scroll of laws)
Tyche	Goddess of fate, good fortune; patron of city-states (Horn of Plenty, crown of city walls)
Venus	(Roman; *see* Aphrodite)
Vesta	(Roman; *see* Hestia)
Vulcan	(Roman; *see* Hephaestus)
Zeus	Chief of the Olympian gods; controlled the phenomena of the heavens (thunderbolt, eagle)

▼ **Fig. 147.** Roman emperors during the biblical period

Augustus	27 B.C.E.–14 C.E.	Vitellius	69
Tiberius	14–37 C.E.	Vespasian	69–79
Gaius Caligula	37–41	Titus	79–81
Claudius	41–54	Domitian	81–96
Nero	54–68	Nerva	96–98
Galba	68–69	Trajan	98–117
Otho	69	Hadrian	117–138

▼ **Fig. 148.** Historical periods in Turkey

The dates given for the various periods are approximations. In many cases a particular period began or ended at different times in different parts of Anatolia, with various periods overlapping one another. Furthermore, there is often no precise moment when one period ended and a subsequent one began. For example, some scholars date the beginning of the Byzantine Empire to 330 C.E., when Constantine moved the capital of the Roman Empire to Byzantium (Constantinople). Other historians date the start of the empire to 395, when, after the death of Theodosius I, the Roman Empire was divided into the Eastern Empire and the Western Empire.

The Paleolithic Age	Prior to 8000 B.C.E.
The Neolithic Age	8000–5000
The Chalcolithic Age	5000–3000
The Bronze Age	3000–1200
The Hittite Period	2000–1180
The Period of Anatolian Kingdoms and Greek City-States	1200–547
The Persian Period	547–334
The Hellenistic Period	334–133
The Roman Period	133 B.C.E.–395 C.E.
The Byzantine Empire	395–1453 C.E.
The Seljuk Empire	1071–1242
The Ottoman Empire	1299–1923
The Republic of Turkey	1923–present

▼ **Fig. 149.** The Attalid rulers of Pergamum

Philetaerus	282–263 B.C.E.	Eumenes II Soter	197–159
Eumenes I	263–241	Attalus II	159–138
Attalus I Soter	241–197	Attalus III	138–133

▼ **Fig. 150.** The Seleucid rulers of Syria and Asia Minor

Seleucus I Nicator	321–280 B.C.E.
Antiochus I Soter	280–261
Antiochus II Theos	261–246
Seleucus II Callinicus	246–226
Seleucus III Soter	226–223
Antiochus III the Great	223–187
Seleucus IV Philopator	187–175
Antiochus IV Epiphanes	175–164
Antiochus V Eupator	164–162
Demetrius I Soter	162–150
Alexander Balas	150–146
Demetrius II Nicator	146–140, 129–125
Antiochus VI Epiphanes	145–142
Tryphon	142–139
Antiochus VII Sidetes	139–129
Seleucus V	125
Antiochus VIII Grypus	121–96
Antiochus IX Cyzicenus	115–95

▼ **Fig. 151.** A chronology of the life of the Apostle Paul

Activity	Approximate Date (C.E.)
Paul is called (conversion experience)	32–33
Preaching in Arabia and Damascus	33–36
First visit to Jerusalem	36
Mission to Syria, Cilicia, and Galatia; return to Antioch	36–49
Second visit to Jerusalem; Jerusalem Council	49
Mission to Asia Minor, Macedonia, and Achaia (including Corinth)	49–52
Paul in Corinth	50–52
Writes 1 Thessalonians	50
Returns to Antioch	52
Mission to Galatia, Ephesus, Macedonia, and Corinth	53–56
Paul in Ephesus	53–55
Writes Galatians	53
Writes 1 Corinthians and portions of 2 Corinthians	54–55
Perhaps writes Philippians and Philemon	55
Travels to Macedonia	56
Writes remainder of 2 Corinthians	56
Travels to Corinth	56
Writes Romans	56
Third visit to Jerusalem; arrested and sent to Caesarea as a prisoner	57
Travel to Rome for trial before Caesar	59
Imprisonment in Rome (house arrest)	60–62
Perhaps writes Philippians and Philemon	60–62

▼ **Fig. 152.** Biblical references to places in Greece, Turkey, and Cyprus

This list includes islands, cities, provinces, and regions that are mentioned in the Hebrew Bible, the New Testament, and the Apocrypha. Some places mentioned do not have an entry in the book. A few obscure or uncertain places or references are omitted.

Greece

Greece	Dan 8:21; 10:20; 11:2; Zech 9:13; 1 Macc 1:1; Acts 20:2; see also Joel 3:6
Achaia	Acts 18:12, 27; 19:21; Rom 15:26; 1 Cor 16:15; 2 Cor 1:1; 9:2; 11:10; 1 Thess 1:7, 8
Amphipolis	Acts 17:1
Apollonia	Acts 17:1
Athens	2 Macc 9:15; Acts 17:15, 16; 18:1; 1 Thess 3:1; see also Acts 17:22; 2 Macc 6:1
Beroea	Acts 17:10, 13; 20:4
Cauda	Acts 27:16
Cenchreae	Acts 18:18; Rom 16:1
Chios	Acts 20:15
Corinth	Acts 18:1; 19:1; 1 Cor 1:2; 2 Cor 1:1, 23; 2 Tim 4:20; see also Acts 18:8; 2 Cor 6:11
Cos	1 Macc 15:23; Acts 21:1
Crete	1 Macc 10:67; Acts 27:7, 12, 13, 21; Titus 1:5; see also Acts 2:11; Titus 1:12; possibly the meaning of "Caphtorim" in Gen 10:14; Deut 2:23; 1 Chr 1:12; and "Caphtor" in Jer 47:4; Amos 9:7
Fair Havens	Acts 27:8
Gortyna	1 Macc 15:23
Lasea	Acts 27:8
Phoenix	Acts 27:12
Salmone	Acts 27:7
Delos	1 Macc 15:23

Macedonia	Acts 16:9, 10, 12; 18:5; 19:21, 22; 20:1, 3; Rom 15:26; 1 Cor 16:5; 2 Cor 1:16; 2:13; 7:5; 8:1; 11:9; Phil 4:15; 1 Thess 1:7, 8; 4:10; 1 Tim 1:3; see also 1 Macc 1:1; 6:2; 8:5; 2 Macc 8:20; Add Esth 9:24; 16:10, 14; Acts 19:29; 27:2; 2 Cor 9:2, 4
Mitylene	Acts 20:14
Neapolis	Acts 16:11
Nicopolis	Titus 3:12
Patmos	Rev 1:9
Philippi	Acts 16:12; 20:6; Phil 1:1; 1 Thess 2:2; see also Phil 4:15
Rhodes	1 Macc 15:23; Acts 21:1; likely the meaning of "Rodanim" in Gen 10:4 and 1 Chr 1:7
Samos	Acts 20:15; 1 Macc 15:23
Samothrace	Acts 16:11
Sicyon	1 Macc 15:23
Sparta	1 Macc 14:16; see also 1 Macc 12:2, 5, 6, 20, 21; 14:20, 23; 15:23
Thessalonica	Acts 17:1, 11, 13; Phil 4:16; 2 Tim 4:10; see also Acts 20:4; 27:2; 1 Thess 1:1; 2 Thess 1:1

Turkey

Adramyttium	Acts 27:2
Antioch of Pisidia	Acts 13:14; 14:19, 21; 2 Tim 3:11
Antioch on the Orontes	1 Macc 3:37; 4:35; 6:63; 10:68; 11:13, 44, 56; 2 Macc 4:9, 33; 5:21; 8:35; 11:36; 13:23, 26; 14:27; Acts 6:5; 11:19, 20, 22, 26, 27; 13:1; 14:26; 15:22, 23, 30, 35; 18:22; Gal 2:11; see also 2 Macc 4:19
Ararat	Gen 8:4; 2 Kgs 19:37; Isa 37:38; Jer 51:27; Tob 1:21
Asia (province)	1 Macc 8:6; 11:13; 12:39; 13:32; 2 Macc 3:3; 10:24; 3 Macc 3:14; 2 Esd 15:46; 16:1; 4 Macc 3:20; Acts 2:9; 6:9; 16:6; 19:10, 22, 26, 27; 20:16, 18; 21:27; 24:19; 27:2; Rom 16:5; 1 Cor 16:19; 2 Cor 1:8; 2 Tim 1:15; 1 Pet 1:1; Rev 1:4, 11; see also Acts 20:4

Assos	Acts 20:13, 14
Attalia	Acts 14:25
Bithynia	Acts 16:7; 1 Pet 1:1
Cappadocia	Acts 2:9; 1 Pet 1:1
Carchemish	2 Chr 35:20; Isa 10:9; Jer 46:2; 1 Esd 1:25
Caria	1 Macc 15:23
Cilicia	1 Kgs 10:28 (called Kue); Jdt 1:7, 12; 2:21, 25; 1 Macc 11:14; 2 Macc 4:36; 4 Macc 4:2; Acts 6:9; 15:23, 41; 21:39; 22:3; 23:34; 27:5; Gal 1:21
Cnidus	1 Macc 15:23; Acts 27:7
Colossae	Col 1:2
Daphne	2 Macc 4:33
Derbe	Acts 14:6, 20; 16:1; 20:4
Ephesus	Acts 18:19, 21, 24; 19:1, 17, 26, 35; 20:16, 17; 1 Cor 15:32; 16:8; 1 Tim 1:3; 2 Tim 1:18; 4:12; Rev 1:11; 2:1; mentioned in some ancient manuscripts of Eph 1:1; see also Acts 19:28
Galatia	Acts 16:6; 18:23; 1 Cor 16:1; Gal 1:2; 2 Tim 4:10; 1 Pet 1:1; see also 2 Macc 8:20; Gal 3:1
Halicarnassus	1 Macc 15:23
Haran	Gen 11:31, 32; 12:4, 5; 27:43; 28:10; 29:4; 2 Kgs 19:12; Isa 37:12; Ezek 27:23; Acts 7:2, 4
Hierapolis	Col 4:13
Iconium	Acts 13:51; 14:1, 19, 21; 16:2; 2 Tim 3:11
Laodicea	Col 2:1; 4:13, 15, 16; Rev 1:11; 3:14
Lycaonia	Acts 14:6; see also Acts 14:11
Lycia	1 Macc 15:23; Acts 27:5
Lydia	1 Macc 8:8; possibly identified with some or all references to "Lud" or "Ludim" in Gen 10:13, 22; 1 Chr 1:11, 17; Isa 66:19; Ezek 27:10; 30:5; Jdt 2:23
Lystra	Acts 14:6, 8, 21; 16:1, 2; 2 Tim 3:11
Miletus	Acts 20:15, 17; 2 Tim 4:20

Myndos	1 Macc 15:23
Myra	Acts 27:5; mentioned in some ancient manuscripts of Acts 21:1
Mysia	Acts 16:7, 8; see also 2 Macc 5:24
Pamphylia	1 Macc 15:23; Acts 2:10; 13:13; 14:24; 15:38; 27:5
Patara	Acts 21:1
Perga	Acts 13:13, 14; 14:25
Pergamum	Rev 1:11; 2:12
Phaselis	1 Macc 15:23
Philadelphia	Rev 1:11; 3:7
Phrygia	Acts 2:10; 16:6; 18:23; see also 2 Macc 5:22
Pisidia	Acts 13:14; 14:24
Pontus	Acts 2:9; 18:2; 1 Pet 1:1
Sardis	Rev 1:11; 3:1, 4; in Obad 20, "Sepharad" may be a reference to Sardis
Seleucia Pieria	1 Macc 11:8; Acts 13:4
Side	1 Macc 15:23
Smyrna	Rev 1:11; 2:8
Tarsus	2 Macc 3:5; 4:30; Acts 9:11, 30; 11:25; 21:39; 22:3
Thyatira	Acts 16:14; Rev 1:11; 2:18, 24
Troas	Acts 16:8, 11; 20:5, 6; 2 Cor 2:12; 2 Tim 4:13
Trogyllium	Mentioned in some ancient manuscripts of Acts 20:15

In addition to these specific references, additional biblical terms have frequently been identified as possible references to regions or peoples in ancient Turkey. These would include Magog (Gen 10:2; 1 Chr 1:5; Ezek 38:2; 39:6), Gomer (Gen 10:2, 3; 1 Chr 1:5, 6; Ezek 38:6), Riphath (Gen 10:3; 1 Chr 1:6), Tubal (Gen 10:2; 1 Chr 1:5; Isa 66:19; Ezek 27:13; 32:26; 38:2, 3; 39:1), Meschech (Gen 10:2; 1 Chr 1:5; Ezek 27:13; 32:26; 38:2, 3; 39:1), Togarmah (Gen 10:3; 1 Chr 1:6; Ezek 27:14; 38:6), and Javan (Gen 10:2, 4; 1 Chr 1:5, 7; Isa 66:19; Ezek 27:13, 19). Javan seems to have referred initially to the southwest area of Asia Minor known as

Ionia, which was settled by Greeks. Later the term was used to mean Greece as well. For the latter usage, see listings above for "Greece."

The biblical references to "Hittites" are not references to the Hittite kingdom of the 2nd millennium B.C.E., located in what is now modern Turkey. The biblical Hittites are likely people from the area of Syria (or their descendants), where a neo-Hittite culture developed during the first half of the 1st millennium B.C.E. Among the many references to "Hittites" in the Hebrew Bible are 1 Kgs 10:29; 2 Kgs 7:6; 2 Chr 1:17; 1 Esd 8:69.

Cyprus

Cyprus	1 Macc 15:23; 2 Macc 12:2; Acts 4:36; 11:19, 20; 13:4; 15:39; 21:3, 16; 27:4; likely the meaning of "Kittim" in Gen 10:4 and 1 Chr 1:7; possibly the meaning of Elishah in Gen 10:4; 1 Chr 1:7; and Ezek 27:7
Paphos	Acts 13:6, 13
Salamis	Acts 13:5

Glossary

Unless otherwise indicated, a word in parentheses is the form of the Turkish word when it is immediately preceded by a noun.

Abaton, Adyton   The innermost sanctuary of a temple

Acanthus   A spiny-leaved plant used in the decoration of Corinthian capitals

Acropolis   Ancient fortified hilltop

Acroterion   A figure or ornament on a roof ridge or the top of a pediment

Agora   Market area and gathering place of an ancient Greek city

Amphora   A two-handled jar for oil or wine

Anta (pl. antae)   The projecting pilaster of a cella wall

Archaic art   Art of the 7th and 6th centuries B.C.E. in Greece

Architrave   The "top beam," a horizontal stone lintel resting on the columns of a temple

Ashlar   Dressed, squared stone blocks

Atrium   Central open courtyard of a building

Agios/Agia   Saint or holy; also spelled ayios or ayia

Basilica   In Roman architecture, a large covered hall; later, a style of Christian church developed in the 4th century with three or five aisles

Bouleuterion	Council chamber of a Greek city
Byzantine Empire	Greek-speaking Christian state, ruled from Constantinople (modern Istanbul), after the eastern Roman Empire divided from the west (4th century C.E.)
Byzantium	Original name for Constantinople
Cadde (caddesi)	Avenue, street
Caldarium	Hot room of a Roman bath
Cami	Mosque
Çarşi (çarşisi)	Market
Cathedra	Bishop's throne
Cavea	Auditorium seating of a Greek theater
Cella	Inner chamber of a temple where the cult statue was kept
Çeşme (çeşmesi)	Fountain
Chancel	The part of a church reserved for the clergy
Chiton	A pleated linen garment worn with a belt
Chlamys	A short cloak
Choregos	Leader of the chorus in a Greek tragedy; the patron of a chorus
Cist grave	A stone chest for burial
Citadel	Fortress
Classical	Art of the 5th to the 4th century B.C.E. in Greece
Corinthian column	A column with an ornate capital decorated with scrolls and acanthus leaves
Cyclopean masonry	Masonry of large irregular blocks of stone in the Archaic period, attributed to giants, or the Cyclopes
Dağ (dağï)	Mountain
Deme	People; popular assembly; also *demos*
Dervish	In the Islamic tradition, a person of the spiritual life, a mystic; from the Persian *darwish* (poor man)
Dipteros	Temple surrounded by a double row of columns

Dipylon	A double gateway
Doric column	A column with no ornamental base, developed by the Dorian Greeks
Dromos	Ramp leading to the entrance of a Bronze Age tomb; a passage
Drum	One of the cylindrical sections of a column
Entablature	The superstructure carried by a colonnade (architrave, frieze, and cornice)
Entasis	A bulge in the lower part of a column
Eski	Old
Exedra (*pl.* **exedrae**)	A semicircular seat, such as stone or marble benches
Exonarthex	Outer vestibule of a church
Forum	Market area of a Roman-era city
Frieze	A decorative band above the architrave of a temple
Frigidarium	Cold-pool room of a Roman bath
Geometric style	Archaeological era (1050–700 B.C.E.) named for the abstract designs of its pottery
Göl (gölü)	Lake
Gymnasium (*pl.* **gymnasia**)	School and athletic center in an ancient Greek city
Hamam	Turkish bath
Hellenism	Spread of Greek culture
Heraion	A temple or sanctuary of Hera
Herm	A square pillar with a head of Hermes or another god; later with a portrait head and a phallus on one side
Heroon	Shrine of a deified hero
Hieron	A sacred place; sanctuary
Hexastyle	Temple front with six columns
Hippodrome	Course for chariot races
Höyük (höyügü)	Mound

Hypocaust	A series of small chambers beneath the floor of a bath through which heat is distributed
Icon	(Greek: *eikon*, "image, likeness"); a sacred picture, usually on a panel
Imam	The prayer leader at a mosque
Impluvium	A shallow pool in the floor of the atrium of a house, designed to receive the rain falling through the opening in the roof
In antis	Between the antae
In situ	In its original place
Ionic column	A column of uniform thickness, with ornamental base and volute capital
Isodomic	Regular horizontal courses of masonry
Kale (kalesi)	Castle or fortress
Kantharos	A Greek drinking cup with two handles
Kapï (kapïsï)	Door or gate
Kato	"Lower"; common part of a town name
Konak	Mansion (Ottoman)
Kore	Girl, maiden; votive statue
Kouros	Statue of a naked youth; votive statue
Krater	A two-handled jar for mixing water and wine
Lintel	Horizontal beam above a door or window opening, or between two columns or piers
Lusignan Dynasty	French Catholic nobility who ruled Cyprus (1191–1489 C.E.)
Macellum	Meat/fish market of a Greco-Roman city
Meander	A continuous fret or key pattern, from the winding river by the same name; also, the name of a river god
Martyrion	Shrine of a Christian martyr
Medrese (medresesi)	Islamic school of learning
Megaron	A large hall, esp. the main room of a Mycenaean palace

Metope	A panel of stone or marble, often sculptured in relief, in a Doric frieze
Minare	Minaret (Turkish)
Minoan culture	Culture on the island of Crete from 2600 to 1100 B.C.E.
Monopteros	Temple without a naos, usually circular
Muezzin	Man who delivers the call to prayer from the minaret of a mosque
Mycenaean culture	Greek culture from 1580 to 1150 B.C.E., named after Mycenae, where it developed
Naos	Interior room of a temple
Narthex	Vestibule of a church
Nave	Central lengthwise aisle of a church
Necropolis	Cemetery (literally, "city of the dead")
Neos, Nea, Neo	"New"; common part of a town name
Nymphaeum	Monumental fountain
Odeion	Small theater for music and oratory, usually roofed
Opisthodomos	Rear porch of a temple
Opus sectile	Ornamental paving or wall covering made from tiles, usually geometric
Orthostat	A large, vertical block of stone in the lower part of a wall
Palaestra	Exercise area of a Greco-Roman gymnasium
Paleos, Palea, Paleo	"Old"; common part of a town name
Panhellenic	"All Greece," games or festivals
Pantokrator	Christ (literally, "the Almighty One")
Pediment	The triangular termination of a ridge roof
Peripteral	A temple whose cella is surrounded by a colonnade
Peristyle	A covered colonnade surrounding a building; or an inner court with a colonnade
Pithos	A large storage jar

Plateia	Square, plaza
Portico	A colonnaded porch, with a roof supported on at least one side by columns
Pronaos	Vestibule at the entrance to a temple
Propylaea	A monumental, columned entrance-complex ("before the gate"); more than one door
Propylon	A columned gateway, of moderate size; one door
Proskenion	The stage between the orchestra and the stage building (skene)
Prostyle	Temple with columned portico in front
Pseudo-dipteral	A dipteral temple with the inner row of columns omitted
Quadriga	Four-horse chariot
Rhyton	A drinking vessel, often in the form of an animal's head
Stadium	A measure of length, 600 feet, or a running track of the same length; also *stadion*
Stele (*pl.* **stelae**)	Upright stone slab, usually inscribed or decorated
Stoa	A covered walkway with columns in front, often with shops or offices behind
Stylobate	The top step of the base of a column
Su (suyu)	Water or stream
Sufi	An adherent of Sufism, one of the mystical branches of Islam
Tekke	Dervish lodge or monastery
Temenos	The sacred enclosure or precinct of a temple
Templum-in-antis	A temple whose only external columns are between its antae
Tepidarium	Warm pool of a Roman bath
Tesserae	Cubes used to compose a mosaic, made either of naturally colored rock or of painted glass
Tetrastyle	Temple front with four columns

Tholos	A circular building
Transept	The side rooms of a church, perpendicular to the nave.
Triglyph	Stone or marble divisions between the metopes
Trireme	A 150-oared Greek war galley, with the oars grouped in threes
Tympaneum	Greek drum, struck with the hand
Volute	The spiral scroll of an Ionic capital

Index

9 780195 139181